Environmental Communication

and the Public Sphere

Third Edition

For Michelle, Harrison, Daniel, Keenan, and Cam.
May the work of those reported here leave a more sustainable and just world for you.

Environmental Communication
and the Public Sphere
Third Edition

Robert Cox
The University of North Carolina at Chapel Hill

Los Angeles | London | New Delhi
Singapore | Washington DC

Los Angeles | London | New Delhi
Singapore | Washington DC

FOR INFORMATION:

SAGE Publications, Inc.
2455 Teller Road
Thousand Oaks, California 91320
E-mail: order@sagepub.com

SAGE Publications Ltd.
1 Oliver's Yard
55 City Road
London EC1Y 1SP
United Kingdom

SAGE Publications India Pvt. Ltd.
B 1/I 1 Mohan Cooperative Industrial Area
Mathura Road, New Delhi 110 044
India

SAGE Publications Asia-Pacific Pte. Ltd.
3 Church Street
#10-04 Samsung Hub
Singapore 049483

Acquisitions Editor: Matthew Byrnie
Associate Editor: Nathan Davidson
Editorial Assistant: Stephanie Palermini
Production Editor: Astrid Virding
Copy Editor: Pam Schroeder
Typesetter: C&M Digitals (P) Ltd.
Proofreader: Ellen Brink
Indexer: Molly Hall
Cover Designer: Candice Harman
Marketing Manager: Liz Thornton
Permissions Editor: Karen Ehrmann

Printed in the United States of America

Library of Congress Cataloging-in-Publication Data

Cox, Robert.

Environmental communication and the public sphere/Robert Cox.—3rd ed.

p. cm.
Includes bibliographical references and index.

ISBN 978-1-4129-9209-1 (pbk.)

1. Communication in the environmental sciences—Textbooks. 2. Mass media and the environment—Textbooks. I. Title.

GE25.C69 2013
333.7201′4—dc23   2011052586

This book is printed on acid-free paper.

Certified Sourcing
www.sfiprogram.org
SFI-00453

12 13 14 15 16 10 9 8 7 6 5 4 3 2 1

Brief Contents

Detailed Contents

Preface for Third Edition

Much has changed since the earlier editions of this book: New media, forums, and communication practices about the environment are appearing almost daily. Even as "legacy" media—newspapers and broadcast TV—decline, environmental news continues to migrate online. Social media and Web 2.0 applications are enabling users (formerly known as the *audience*) to report, tag, and distribute environmental content widely: Farmworkers in California are documenting abandoned waste dumps and shoddy migrant housing online; cleanup volunteers during the BP oil spill in the Gulf of Mexico took advantage of location-based apps (like Gowalla) on their smartphones to identify oil disaster sites; and activists are mobilizing citizens globally through social networking sites like 350.org to call attention to climate change.

Our knowledge of the many forms of environmental communication also continues to grow. The third edition of *Environmental Communication and the Public Sphere* gives me the opportunity to share some of this new research occurring across all areas of the field—climate communication, social media, message construction, collaboration and conflict management, climate justice, *green jobs* movements, and more. This edition also explores recent controversies—conflicts over *hydro-fracking* for natural gas, the Fukushima Daiichi nuclear plant crisis in Japan, the BP *Deepwater Horizon* oil spill, and *mountaintop removal* coal mining in Appalachia—to illustrate principles of environmental communication.

A book attempting to introduce such a range of communication practices about the environment could not have been conceived initially or revised for this third edition without the help of many of colleagues, students, and friends in academe and the U.S. environmental movement nor without the many helpful suggestions from colleagues on the Environmental Communication Network's LISTSERV. I particularly want to thank Chris Warshaw, Natalie Foster, Dave Karpf, and participants at the 2011 digital strategies summit in Washington, DC, for their knowledgeable insights. And, always, I thank my students at the University of North Carolina at Chapel Hill who inspired me every day with their intelligence, dedication, and passion for a better world.

The following reviewers are gratefully acknowledged:

Third edition:

Jennifer Adams, *DePauw University*

Lisa Heller Boragine, *Cape Cod Community College*

Chin-Chung Chao, *University of Nebraska at Omaha*

Kim Diana Connolly, *State University of New York at Buffalo Law School*

Jeff Courtright, *Illinois State University*

Patricia O. Covarrubias, *University of New Mexico*

Katie M. Cruger, *University of Colorado at Boulder*

Steve Schwarze, *University of Montana*

At Sage, my thanks go to my editors Matt Byrnie and Nathan Davidson for their astute suggestions for this edition, to Astrid Virding for her skillful work as project director, and also to Pam Schroeder for her careful eye in saving me from many embarrassing errors in the text itself. Although I have benefited from the suggestions and help of many, I am clearly responsible for any mistakes that have found their way into the text.

Finally, none of this would be possible without my life partner and colleague, Julia Wood. Her encouragement, smart counsel, support, and amazing patience sustain me daily.

Is the natural world silent? Who speaks for (or about) nature, or about what constitutes an *environmental problem?*

Introduction: Speaking for and About the Environment

Communication about the environment continues to increase at a faster pace—from reports of a warming climate to an accelerating rate of extinction of plants and animals. Interest cuts across all media—cable TV news, social media, films, YouTube, newspapers, public rallies, and in classrooms. Popular blogs like *Treehugger* (treehugger.com) and *HuffPost Green* (huffingtonpost.com/green) showcase breaking environmental news daily. *The Discovery Channel, Planet Green,* and the *National Geographic Channel,* as well as documentary series like *Planet Earth* portray threats to the natural world as well as its wonders. And, social networking sites like 350.org link us globally with news about climate change, actions to take, and videos from across the world.

The ways we learn and talk about the environment are also changing. Social media and online sites provide seemingly unlimited access to and information about the problems affecting us and our world. And, while individuals still speak at public hearings about pollution in their communities, others are organizing globally to address the harmful consequences of climate change. There is also a palpable sense of urgency in our communications about the environment. The online news service Climatewire .com, for example, is reporting that the North Atlantic current that carries water into the Arctic Ocean is the warmest in 2,000 years and is likely a major factor in the Arctic becoming ice free in the future (Morello, 2011, paras. 1, 4).

The importance and sense of urgency about many environmental problems has also invited interest in the field of environmental communication, the subject of this book. But, why communication? As I'll explain in the following pages, our understanding of the environment, our efforts to alert, educate, or persuade others, and our ability to work together can't be separated from the need to communicate with others. Indeed, our language, visual images, and modes of interacting with others influence our most basic perceptions of the world and what we understand to be a problem itself.

But, we do not speak alone. As we'll see throughout this book, many different voices claim to speak for or about the environment. The public sphere is filled with competing visions, agendas, and modes of speaking. It is these different voices, media, and forums that influence our understanding of and relationships with the environment that I'll explore in this book.

Communication and Nature's Meaning

Not everyone sees herself or himself as an environmental advocate or envisions being an environmental communication professional such as a journalist, science educator, or filmmaker. Some of you may be reading this book simply to learn more about environmental issues. Yet, it is impossible to separate our knowledge about environmental issues from the ways we communicate about these issues. As environmental communication scholars James Cantrill and Christine Oravec (1996) once observed, the "environment we experience and affect is largely a product *of* how we come to talk about the world" (p. 2). That is, the way we communicate with one another about the environment powerfully affects how we perceive both it and ourselves and, therefore, how we define our relationship with the natural world. For example, Harvard University scientist and author E. O. Wilson (2002) drew upon the language of biology to describe the environment as he experienced it, as "a membrane of organisms wrapped around Earth so thin it cannot be seen edgewise from a space shuttle, yet so internally complex that most species composing it remain undiscovered" (p. 3).

Furthermore, the images of the planet and the information we receive from friends, blogs, the news media, teachers, or popular films play a powerful role in influencing not only how we perceive the environment but also what actions we take. Can the United States meet its energy needs through renewable sources like wind and solar power, or must it drill for oil in deep water offshore? Is it safe for the U.S. Army to burn stores of chemical weapons near schools and residential neighborhoods? In engaging such questions, particularly in public forums, we rely on news reports, photographs, films, and public debates to imagine, describe, debate, and celebrate our multiple relations with the natural world.

That's one reason I wrote this book: I believe that communication about the environment matters. It matters in the ways we interact with our friends, at work, and in naming certain conditions in our environment as problems. And, it matters ultimately in the choices we make in response to these problems. This book, therefore, focuses on the role of communication in helping us negotiate the relationship between ourselves and the thin "membrane of organisms" that makes up our natural and human environments.

The purpose of *Environmental Communication and the Public Sphere* is threefold: (1) to increase your insight into how communication shapes our perceptions of environmental issues; (2) to acquaint you with some of the media and public forums that are used for environmental communication, along with the communication practices of scientists, corporate lobbyists, ordinary citizens, and others who seek to influence

The images of the planet and information we receive from friends, blogs, the news media, or popular films play a powerful role in influencing not only how we perceive the environment but also in naming certain conditions as problems.

decisions about nature and the human environment; and (3) to enable you to join in conversations and debates that are already taking place locally and globally that may affect the environments where you yourself live, study, work, and play.

Why Do We Need to Speak for the Environment?

At first glance, there appears to be little need for persuasion or debate about environmental issues. Who supports dirty air or polluted water? Although public opinion about environmental issues varies—depending on worries about the economy or war—the U.S. public has generally shown strong support for environmental values. And, in a recent poll of U.S. college students, 78.2% agreed with the statement, "The federal government is not doing enough to control environmental pollution," while 63.1% agreed that global warming should be a priority for the United States (A profile of this year's freshmen, 2011).

Although the public's support for environmental values is strong, differences exist over how society should solve specific environmental problems. A good example is the controversy over deepwater drilling for oil off the U.S. coast. After the disastrous 2010 oil spill in the Gulf of Mexico, debate has flared over safety measures and the need for stronger government oversight of deepwater drilling. President Obama's National Oil Commission on the BP *Deepwater Horizon* Oil Spill and Offshore Drilling recommended a series of safety reforms before allowing such drilling to resume. "If the recommendations are not carried out," the commission's cochair warned, "the probability of another failure will be dramatically greater" (Associated Press, 2011, para. 15). Still, some officials along the Gulf Coast have balked at this. The president of Jefferson Parish in Louisiana, for example, cautioned, "I don't want the federal government to overreact and now put additional regulations that cripple the oil industry" (para. 6).

The complexity of issues such as deepwater oil drilling makes a public consensus difficult. And, as the different voices of marine scientists, the oil industry, and environmental groups enter the public debate, widely divergent viewpoints compete for our support.

There exists, therefore, a dilemma. Although in a sense, nature is silent, others—politicians, business leaders, environmentalists, the media—claim the right to speak for nature or for their own interests in the use of natural resources. Hence, here's the dilemma: If nature cannot speak (at least not in public forums), who has the right to speak on nature's behalf? Who should define the interests of society in relation to the natural world? Is it appropriate, for example, to drill for oil along fragile coastlines? Who should bear the cost of cleaning up abandoned toxic waste sites—the businesses responsible for the contamination or taxpayers? These questions illustrate the inevitable communication dimensions of environmental controversies. Only in a society that allows debate can the public mediate among the differing voices and ways of understanding the environment–society relationship. That is one of my purposes in writing this book: I believe that you, I, and everyone in a democratic society have pivotal roles in speaking about these larger environmental issues.

Background and Perspective of the Author

After inviting you to join in conversations about the environment, perhaps it's time I described my own involvement in this challenging field. For a number of years, I have been a professor of Communication Studies and the Curriculum in the Environment and Ecology at the University of North Carolina at Chapel Hill, where I've engaged in environmental and climate communication research and teaching. I have also held leadership roles in the U.S. environmental movement, serving as president of the Sierra Club, based in San Francisco, CA. I continue to serve on its board of directors, as well as on the board of Earth Echo International in Washington, DC. And, I continue to advise a number of environmental organizations about their communication programs.

However, my interest in the environment arose long before I had heard of the Sierra Club. As a boy growing up in the Appalachian region of southern West Virginia, I fell in love with the wild beauty of the mountains near my home and the graceful flow of the Greenbrier River. However, as I grew older, I saw coal mining's devastating effects on the natural landscape and on the streams and water supplies of local communities. In graduate school, I saw the health effects of air pollution from steel mills in the North and later from chemical plants in poor neighborhoods in Mississippi. I began to realize how intimately people and their environments are bound together. Human beings and nature do not stand apart from each other.

While teaching at the University of North Carolina, I also began volunteering with environmental groups. Although I was motivated initially by my personal experiences, I soon became aware of the essential role of communication in the work of these groups as they sought to educate public audiences and policy makers. I also spent my time as president of the Sierra Club communicating with the public in some form: briefing newspaper editorial boards, speaking at public rallies, testifying before Congress, organizing in communities, talking with reporters, and helping to design advocacy campaigns.

As a result of these experiences and also from my own research and teaching in environmental communication, I've become more firmly persuaded of several things:

1. Individuals and communities have stronger chances to safeguard the environmental health and quality of their local environments if they understand some of the dynamics and opportunities for communication about their concerns.

2. Environmental issues and public agencies do not need to remain remote, mysterious, or impenetrable. The environmental movement, legal action, and the media have helped to demystify governmental procedures and open the doors and computer files of government bureaucracies to greater public access and participation in environmental decisions.

3. As a consequence, individuals have many opportunities to participate in meaningful ways in public debates about our environment, and indeed, there is more urgency than ever in doing so. That is why I wrote *Environmental Communication and the Public Sphere.*

Let me mention one other thing: Largely because of my work in the U.S. environmental movement, I cannot avoid personal perspectives on some of the issues discussed in this book, nor do I wish to. In this sense, I am biased in certain values and approaches to environmental protection. I do three things, however, to balance this as I develop the topics in this book. First, when I introduce views or positions, I try to acknowledge any bias or personal experience that I might have. Second, I explain how I arrived at my perspective based on my experience and my knowledge or research.

Finally, I include "Another Viewpoint" and "FYI" units in each chapter to alert you to important disagreements as well as "Suggested Resources" at the ends of chapters to provide additional information. For example, because I believe that government has an important role to play in protecting the environment, I also refer you to sources that favor private-sector or market approaches. My aim is not to set up false dichotomies but to introduce a multiplicity of perspectives. I also refer you to sources and URLs that challenge my own stance to allow you to learn about other views.

Distinctive Features of the Book

As its title suggests, the framework for *Environmental Communication and the Public Sphere* is organized around two core concepts:

1. The importance of human communication in influencing our perceptions of the natural world and our relationships with the environment

2. The role of the public sphere in mediating or negotiating among the different voices seeking to influence decisions about the environment

I use the idea of the **public sphere** throughout this book to refer to the sphere of influence created when different individuals engage each other in communication—through conversation, argument, debate, and questions—about subjects of shared concern or that affect a wider community. (I describe the idea of the public sphere more in Chapter 1.) Nor is communication limited to words: Visual images and nonverbal symbolic actions such as photographs, videos, marches, Greenpeace banners, and documentary films have prompted discussion, debate, and questioning of environmental policy as readily as editorials, speeches, and TV newscasts.

Visual images and nonverbal actions such as documentary films, protests, or sit-ins have prompted discussion, debate, and questioning of environmental policy in the public sphere as readily as editorials, speeches, and TV newscasts.

AP Photo/J. Scott Applewhite

Along with the focus on human communication and the public sphere, this third edition includes a number of distinctive features:

1. A comprehensive introduction to the field of environmental communication—social and symbolic constructions of environment, public participation in environmental decisions (right to know, public comment, and legal standing), conflict resolution, environmental journalism, social media, environmental advocacy campaigns, science communication, environmental justice and climate justice movements, risk communication, green marketing, and corporate advocacy campaigns.

2. A new chapter on social media and communication about the environment, including uses of Twitter, Facebook, and mobile applications in environmental campaigns.

3. Updated emphasis on communicating about climate science, the movement for climate justice, and challenges to the credibility of climate scientists.

4. Discussion of the resources of language—including new sections on framing and visual images.

5. Use of cases studies and personal experiences to illustrate key points; also a "Suggested Resources" section in each chapter.

6. New illustrations and research throughout all chapters and a comprehensive "Glossary of Key Terms" at the end of the book.

7. Opportunities to apply the principles of environmental communication through "Act Locally!" exercises as well as practical ways in many chapters showing how you can influence decisions about the environment, including your right to know about potential impacts to the environment.

The study and applications of environmental communication are growing in many regions of the world. Although this book highlights the U.S. context, the third edition attempts to do two things: (1) increase the potential for application of many concepts more globally, and (2) provide case studies and recognize recent developments in environmental communication in selected nations. For example, European nations are making great strides in implementing the **Aarhus Convention**—an agreement ensuring access to environmental information and public participation in environmental decisions in Europe (see Chapter 4).

New Terrain and New Questions

I recognize that you probably bring a range of views to the subject of the environment and study of environmental communication. Some of you may be a little suspicious of environmentalists, perhaps thinking they're somewhat strange (as in the popular image of *tree huggers*). Others of you may hope to work in the environmental field in the future or already are environmental activists. Many of you—perhaps the majority—may not label yourself environmentalists at all but nevertheless support recycling, clean air, and preserving more green space on your campus. And, I suspect that some of you may have questions about your ability to affect any of the big problems, such as climate change, loss of rainforests, or the safety of offshore oil drilling.

In this book, I start at the beginning. I do not assume any special knowledge on your part about environmental science or politics. Nor do I assume that you know about particular theories of communication. For example, I use **boldface** type when I introduce an important communication or environmental term. I also include a list of these "Key Terms" at the end of each chapter and the book. In some cases, an "FYI" feature provides background information to help you become familiar with theories or issues raised in a chapter.

In turn, I hope you'll be open to exploring the distinct perspective of this book— the ways in which language, symbols, discourse, and ideology shape our perceptions of nature and our own relationships with the environment. If you are, then I believe you'll find new possibilities for voicing your own concerns. By becoming aware of some of the dynamics of human communication in constructing our response to environmental problems, I hope you're able to join in public conversations about not only the fate of the Earth in the abstract but urgent debates over the fate of the places where you live, work, and enjoy everyday life.

KEY TERMS

Aarhus Convention   7

Public sphere   6

REFERENCES

Associated Press. (2011, January 11). Spill report rekindles Democratic push for reform. Retrieved January 29, 2011, from http://www.npr.org/

Cantrill, J. G., & Oravec, C. L. (1996). Introduction. In J. G. Cantrill & C. L. Oravec (Eds.), *The symbolic earth: Discourse and our creation of the environment* (pp. 1–8). Lexington: University of Kentucky Press.

Morello, L. (2011, January 28). Warmest current in 2,000 years found to be thawing the Arctic. Retrieved January 28, 2011, from: http://www.eenews.net

A profile of this year's freshmen. (2011, February 4). *The Chronicle of Higher Education, LVII*(22), p. A22.

Wilson, E. O. (2002). *The future of life.* New York. Knopf.

PART I

Conceptual and Historical Contexts

The natural world affects us, but our language and other symbolic action also have the capacity to affect or construct our perceptions of nature itself.

CHAPTER 1

Study and Practice of Environmental Communication

Stories about the environment surround us daily—on CNN or the *Daily Show* or the award-winning blog *Dot Earth* (http://dotearth.blogs.nytimes.com). We find in-depth environmental news in the *Los Angeles Times* and *New York Times* as well as at online sites or RSS feeds from the *Environment News Network* (www.enn .com) or *Real Climate* (www.realclimate.org). Our ideas about nature are influenced when we watch popular movies such as *Avatar*, and the list goes on.

This chapter describes environmental communication as a multidisciplinary field of study and a practice or mode of influence in daily life in the media, in business and government affairs, and in civic life. Environmental communication describes the many ways and the forums in which citizens, corporations, public officials, journalists, and environmental groups raise concerns and attempt to influence the important decisions that affect our planet. They and others realize that our understanding of nature and our actions toward the environment depend not only on science but on public debate, media, the Internet, and even ordinary conversations.

Chapter Preview

- The first section of this chapter describes the field of environmental communication, defines the term, and identifies seven principal areas of study and practice in this field.
- The second section introduces three themes that constitute the framework for this book:

  (1) human communication is a form of symbolic action, that is, our language and other ways of conveying purpose and meaning affect our consciousness itself, shaping our perceptions and motivating actions;

(Continued)

(Continued)

    (2) as a result, our beliefs and behaviors about nature and environmental problems are mediated or influenced by such communication; and finally,

    (3) the public sphere (or spheres) emerge as a discursive space in which competing voices engage us about environmental concerns.

- The final section describes some of these diverse voices, whose communication practices we'll study in this book: local citizens, scientists, public officials, journalists, online news services, environmental groups, corporations, and others.

After reading this chapter, you should have an understanding of environmental communication as an area of study and an important practice in public life. You should also be able to recognize the range of voices and practices through which environmental groups, ordinary citizens, businesses, and others discuss important environmental problems—from management of public lands to global climate change. As a result, I hope that you'll not only become a more critical consumer of such communication but also discover opportunities to add your own voice to the vibrant conversations about the environment that are already in progress.

The Field of Environmental Communication

Along with the growth of environmental studies, educational and professional opportunities that stress the role of human communication in environmental affairs also have emerged. On many college campuses, environmental communication courses study a range of related topics: environmental news media, methods of public participation in environmental decisions, environmental rhetoric, risk communication, environmental conflict resolution, advocacy campaigns, "green" marketing, and images of nature in popular culture. And, a growing number of scholars in communication, journalism, literature, science communication, and the social sciences are pioneering research in the role and influence of environmental communication in the public sphere.

Finally, on a practical level, the study of environmental communication helps to prepare you to enter many professions in which communication is central to an entity's involvement in environmental affairs. Indeed, some predict that, like the Internet, "the green economy will create a massive new set of opportunities" for professionals in new technologies as well as businesses (Martini & Reed, 2010, p. 74). For example, businesses, government agencies, law firms, public relations (PR) firms, and nonprofit environmental groups employ consultants or staff in environmental communication. As one firm noted, "Environmental communications professionals are working in every sector of the economy. . . . The field is becoming more and more important as the stakes have become greater . . . and the tools for communicating become more diverse" (EnviroEducation.com, 2004, para. 2).

Growth of the Field

Communication scholar Susan Senecah (2007) has observed, "Fields of inquiry do not simply happen by wishing them into existence. The field of [environmental communication] is no different" (p. 22). In the United States, the field grew out of the work of a diverse group of communication scholars, many of whom used the tools of rhetorical criticism to study conflicts over wilderness, forests, farmlands, and endangered species as well as the rhetoric of environmental groups (Cox, 1982; Lange, 1990, 1993; Moore, 1993; Oravec, 1981, 1984; Peterson, 1986; Short, 1991). Christine Oravec's 1981 study of the "sublime" in John Muir's appeals to preserve Yosemite Valley in the 19th century is considered by many to be the start of scholarship in what would become the field of environmental communication.

At the same time, the subjects that such scholars studied widened to include the roles of science, media, and industry in responding to threats to human health and environmental quality. Early studies investigated issues such as industry's use of PR and mass-circulation magazines to construct "ecological" images (Brown & Crable, 1973; Greenberg, Sandman, Sachsman, & Salamone, 1989; Grunig, 1989); the nuclear power industry's response to dramatic accidents at Three Mile Island and Chernobyl (Farrell & Goodnight, 1981; Luke, 1987); and risk communication in conveying the dangers of recombinant DNA experiments (Waddell, 1990). Scholars in the fields of journalism and mass communication began a systematic study of the influence of media depictions of the environment on public attitudes (Anderson, 1997; Shanahan & McComas, 1999, pp. 26–27). In fact, the study of environmental media has grown so rapidly that many now consider it a distinct subfield, and journalists practicing in this area formed the Society of Environmental Journalists (SEJ, sej.org).

By the 1990s, a biennial Conference on Communication and Environment began to attract scholars from a range of academic disciplines in the United States and other nations. Also, a new Environmental Communication Network and website were launched to provide online resources for scholars, teachers, students, and practitioners. And, new journals in communication and environmental topics have begun to appear, including *Environmental Communication: A Journal of Nature and Culture*.

In 2011, scholars and practitioners established the International Environmental Communication Association (http://environmentalcomm.org) to coordinate research and activities worldwide. Interest has grown not only in the United States, but Europe, particularly, has seen "ample signs that environmental communication has grown substantially as a field" (Carvalho, 2009, para. 1). Professional associations linking communication or media with environmental topics now exist in China, Southeast Asia, India, Russia, and Latin America. The Environmental Communication Network of Latin America and the Caribbean, for example, offers support for environmental reporters in fifteen countries in the regions. (For a list of some of these associations and journals, see "FYI: Professional Associations and Journals in Environmental Communication.")

FYI | **Professional Associations and Journals in Environmental Communication**

Journals:

- Environmental Communication: A Journal of Nature and Culture: www.tandf.co.uk/journals/titles/17524032.asp
- SEJ Journal: www.sej.org/publications/sejournal/overview
- Applied Environmental Education and Communication: http://www.aeec.org/
- Science Communication: http://scx.sagepub.com
- Journal of Environmental Education: http://www.tandf.co.uk/journals/titles/00958964.asp

Associations and Institutes:

- International Environmental Communication Association: http://environmentalcomm.org
- North American Association for Environmental Education: www.naaee.org
- Public Relations Society of America, Environment Section: www.prsa.org/Network/Communities/Environmental
- Society of Environmental Journalists (SEJ): www.sej.org
- International Institute for Environmental Communication: www.envcomm.org
- Science and Environment Communication Section of the European Communication Research and Education Association: www.ecrea.eu/divisions/section/id/16
- Environmental Communication Network of Latin America and the Caribbean: http://www.redcalc.org
- International Federation of Environmental Journalists: www.ifej.org

The sheer range of subjects makes defining the field of environmental communication somewhat difficult. For example, environmental communication scholar Steve Depoe (1997) earlier defined the field as the study of the "relationships between our talk and our experiences of our natural surroundings" (p. 368). Yet, Depoe cautioned that the field is more than simply "talk" about the environment. Let's look at some of the areas that such scholars study.

Areas of Study

Although the study of environmental communication covers a wide range of topics, most research and the practice of communication fall into one of seven areas. I explore many of these areas more in later chapters. For now, I'll briefly identify the kinds of concerns that environmental communication scholars currently are studying.

1. *Environmental rhetoric and the social–symbolic "construction" of nature.* Studies of the rhetoric of environmental organizations and campaigns emerged as an early focus of the new field. Along with the related interest in how our language helps to construct or represent nature to us, this is one of the broadest areas of study.

Studies of the persuasion of groups and individuals have given us rich insights into a wide range of practices aimed at influencing the public's views about the environment. For example, Marafiote (2008) has described the ways in which environmental groups reshaped the idea of *wilderness* to win passage of the 1964 Wilderness Act; and Brian Cozen (2010) has examined the images of food in advertising by corporations such as Shell and Chevron, concluding that food images help to "naturalize" the energy industry's "essential role in supplying substance to bodies" (p. 355).

Relatedly, studies of language and other symbolic forms have allowed scholars to probe the constitutive power of communication to shape our ideas and the meanings of nature and the environment that it invites. For example, scholars have studied Earth First! activists' questioning of the ideology of progress (Cooper, 1996) and, more recently, challenged the assumptions behind popular documentary films. DeLuca (2010), for example, questions Ken Burns' film *The National Parks: America's Best Idea* for its treatment of wilderness "as an historic relic and vacation spot . . . [sapping] it of its vital relevance and political power" (p. 484). (I'll explore this area more in Chapters 2–3.)

2. *Public participation in environmental decision making.* The National Research Council has found that, "when done well, public participation improves the quality and legitimacy of a decision and . . . can lead to better results in terms of environmental quality" (Dietz & Stern, 2008). Still, in many cases, barriers prevent the meaningful involvement of citizens in decisions affecting their communities or the natural environment. As a result, a number of scholars have scrutinized government agencies in the United States and other nations to identify both the opportunities for—and barriers to—the participation of ordinary citizens, as well as environmentalists and scientists, in an agency's decision making.

Environmental communication scholars' work in this area has ranged from the study of citizens' comments on national forest management plans (Walker, 2004), public access to information about pollution in local communities (Beierle & Cayford, 2002), obstacles to meaningful public dialogue with the Department of Energy over the cleanup of nuclear weapons waste (Hamilton, 2008), and ways that public involvement in a hydropower (dam) project in India was compromised by communication practices that denied citizens access to information and privileged technical discourse (Martin, 2007). (We take up the study of public participation in Chapter 4.)

3. *Environmental collaboration and conflict resolution.* Dissatisfaction with some of the adversarial forms of public participation has led practitioners and scholars to explore alternative models of resolving environmental conflicts. They draw inspiration from the successes of local communities that have discovered ways to bring disputing parties together. For instance, groups that had been in conflict for years over logging in Canada's coastal Great Bear Rainforest reached agreement recently to protect 5 million forest acres (Armstrong, 2009).

At the center of these modes of conflict resolution is the ideal of **collaboration,** a mode of communication that invites stakeholders to engage in problem-solving discussion rather than advocacy and debate. Collaboration is characterized as "constructive, open, civil communication, generally as dialogue; a focus on the future; an emphasis on learning; and some degree of power sharing and levelling of the playing field" (Walker, 2004, p. 123). (I describe collaboration further in Chapter 5.)

4. *Media and environmental journalism.* In many ways, the study of environmental media has become its own subfield. The diverse research in this area focuses on ways in which the news, advertising, and commercial programs portray nature and environmental problems as well as the effects of different media on public attitudes. Subjects include the agenda-setting role of news media, that is, its ability to influence which issues audiences think about; journalist values of objectivity and balance in reporting; and media framing or the way that the packaging of news influences readers' or viewers' sense-making and evokes certain perceptions and values.

| Figure 1.1 | How do news, advertising, and other media affect our perceptions and attitudes toward the natural world or our understanding of environmental issues? |

Studies in environmental media are also beginning to explore online news and the role of social media in engaging environmental concerns. These range widely, from an analysis of Facebook profiles created by environmental advocacy groups (Bortree & Seltzer, 2009) to studies of postnetwork television such as TreeHugger.com, a "collection of online videos that explores how to create, consume, and live in environmentally friendly ways" (Slawter, 2008). (I will describe both environmental journalism and social media in more detail in Chapters 6 and 7.)

5. *Representations of nature in corporate advertising and popular culture.* The use of nature images in film, television, photography, music, and commercial advertising is hardly new or surprising. What is new is the growing number of studies of how such popular culture images influence our attitudes or perceptions of nature and the environment. Scholars explore such questions by examining a range of cultural products—film (Retzinger, 2002, 2008); green advertising (Henry, 2010); Hallmark greeting cards, SUV ads, and supermarket tabloids (Meister & Japp, 2002); and wildlife films and nature documentaries (Hansen, 2010). For example, Brereton (2005) has traced the evolution of images of nature in science fiction, Westerns, nature, and road movies from the 1950s to the present, including films like *Emerald Forest, Jurassic Park, Easy Rider, Thelma and Louise, Invasion of the Body Snatchers,* and *Blade Runner.*

Scholars in cultural studies also are mapping some of the ways in which images in popular media sustain attitudes of dominance and exploitation of the natural world. For example, a special issue of *Environmental Communication: A Journal of Nature and Culture* examined the idea of food in modern society, where food is "the thin end of environmental awareness—a site where fundamental questions can . . . be asked, questions that . . . lead to challenging re-conceptions of our environments, our societies, and ourselves" (Opel, Johnston, & Wilk, 2010, p. 251). (I look at the role of green advertising in Chapter 10.)

6. *Advocacy campaigns and message construction.* A growing area of study is the use of public education and advocacy campaigns by environmental groups, corporations, and by climate scientists concerned about global warming. Sometimes called social marketing, these campaigns attempt to educate, change attitudes, and mobilize support for a specific course of action. They range from mobilizing the public to protect a wilderness area, convincing the U.S. Congress to raise the fuel efficiency of cars and SUVs, and influencing public attitudes about coal (e.g., "clean coal" TV ads) to corporate accountability campaigns to persuade businesses to abide by strict environmental standards, for example, convincing building supply stores to buy lumber that comes only from sustainable forests.

Scholars have used a range of approaches in the study of advocacy campaigns. For example, a growing number of communication scholars, scientists, and others are now studying the challenge of communicating the risks from climate change to the public as well as barriers to the public's sense of urgency (Moser & Dilling, 2007). A pivot concern in such studies is the effectiveness of different messages or basic framings in conveying the urgency of climate change (Brulle, 2010; Cox, 2010; Lakoff, 2010). (I look more closely at campaigns and messaging in Chapters 8, 9, and 10.)

7. *Science and risk communication.* Do signs announcing a beach is closed and warning that the water is unsafe adequately inform the public of the risk of water pollution? Did federal regulators ignore warnings about the risks from deepwater oil drilling in the Gulf of Mexico? How can science educators communicate the risks of climate change more clearly to a public worried about the economy or jobs? These questions illustrate a growing interest in public health and science communication—the study of environmental risks and communication about them to affected audiences.

Risk communication encompasses a range of practices—public education campaigns about the risks from eating fish with high levels of mercury; risk communication plans for use after a potential biological attack that unleashes the plague (Casman & Fischhoff, 2008); or guides for scientists, journalists, and educators for communicating about climate change created by the Center for Research on Environmental Decisions at Columbia University (2009) are just a few examples.

Since the late 1980s, scholars also have begun to look at the impact of cultural understandings of risk and the public's judgment of the acceptability of a risk (Plough & Krimsky, 1987). For example, risk communication scholar Jennifer Hamilton (2003) found that sensitivity to cultural—as opposed to technical— understandings of risk influenced whether the residents living near the polluted Fernald nuclear weapons facility in Ohio accepted or rejected certain methods of cleanup at the site. (I will describe more of the practices of science and risk communication in Chapters 11 and 12.)

Defining Environmental Communication

With such a diverse range of topics, the field can appear at first glance to be confusing. If we define *environmental communication* as simply *talk* or the transmission of information about the wide universe of environmental topics—whether it's global warming or grizzly bear habitat—our definitions will be as varied as the topics for discussion.

A clearer definition takes into account the distinctive roles of language, art, photographs, street protests, and even scientific reports as different forms of *symbolic action.* This term comes from Kenneth Burke (1966), a rhetorical theorist. In his book *Language as Symbolic Action,* Burke stated that even the most unemotional language is necessarily persuasive. This is so because our language and other symbolic acts do something as well as say something.

The view of communication as a form of symbolic action might be clearer if we contrast it with an earlier view, the **Shannon–Weaver model of communication.** Shortly after World War II, Claude Shannon and Warren Weaver (1949) proposed a model that defined human communication as simply the transmission of information from a source to a receiver. There was little effort in this model to account for meaning or for the ways in which communication acts on, or shapes, our awareness. Unlike the Shannon–Weaver model, symbolic action assumes that language and symbols do more than transmit information: They actively shape our understanding, create meaning, and orient us to a wider world. Burke (1966) went so far as to claim that "much that we take as observations about 'reality' may be but the spinning out of possibilities implicit in our particular choice of terms" (p. 46).

If we focus on symbolic action, then we can offer a richer definition. In this book, I use the phrase **environmental communication** to mean the pragmatic and constitutive vehicle for our understanding of the environment as well as our relationships to the natural world; it is the symbolic medium that we use in constructing environmental problems and in negotiating society's different responses to them. Defined this way, environmental communication serves two different functions:

1. *Environmental communication is **pragmatic.*** It educates, alerts, persuades, and helps us to solve environmental problems. It is this instrumental sense of communication that probably occurs to us initially. It is the vehicle or means which we use in problem solving and is often part of public education campaigns. For example, a pragmatic function of communication occurs when an environmental group educates its supporters and rallies support for protecting a wilderness area or when the electric utility industry attempts to change public perceptions of coal by buying TV ads promoting "clean coal" as an energy source.

2. *Environmental communication is **constitutive.*** Embedded within the pragmatic role of language and other forms of symbolic action is a subtler level. By constitutive, I mean that our communication about nature also helps us construct or compose representations of nature and environmental problems as subjects for our understanding. Such communication invites a particular perspective, evokes certain values (and not others), and thus creates conscious referents for our attention and understanding. For example, different images or constructions of nature may invite us to perceive forests and rivers as natural resources for use or exploitation, or as vital life support systems (something to protect). While a campaign to protect a wilderness area uses pragmatic communication for planning a press conference, at the same time, it may invoke language that taps into cultural constructions of a pristine or unspoiled nature.

Communication as constitutive also assists us in defining certain subjects as problems. For example, when climate scientists call our attention to tipping points, they are naming thresholds beyond which warming "could trigger a runaway thaw of Greenland's ice sheet and other abrupt shifts such as a dieback of the Amazon rainforest" (Doyle, 2008). Such communication orients our consciousness of the possibility of an abrupt shift in climate and its effects; it therefore constitutes, or raises, this possibility as a subject for our understanding. Finally, in seeing something as a problem, such communication also associates particular values with these problems—health and well-being, caring, economic prosperity, and so forth. (In Chapter 3, we look closely at this constitutive role of communication in shaping perceptions of a pristine American West in 19th-century art, photographs, and literature.)

Act Locally!

**Pragmatic and Constitutive
Communication in Messages About Climate Change**

Examples of communication about climate change occur daily in news media, websites, blogs, TV ads, and other sources. Select one of these messages about climate change that particularly interests you. It might be, for example, news reports about a new scientific study of rising sea levels or acidification of oceans, a YouTube video about the impacts of global warming on the Arctic, or a TV ad about coal as a form of "clean energy."

The message or image you've chosen undoubtedly uses both pragmatic and constitutive functions of communication; that is, it may educate, alert, or persuade while also subtly creating meaning and orienting your consciousness to a wider world. After reflecting on this message, answer these questions:

1. What pragmatic function does this communication serve? Who is its intended audience? What is it trying to persuade this audience to think or do? How?

2. Does this message draw on constitutive functions, as well, in its use of certain words or images? How do these words or images create referents for our attention and understanding, invite a particular perspective, evoke values, or orient us to the external world? And, how do these representations of nature or the environment affect our response to this ad?

Environmental communication as a pragmatic and constitutive vehicle serves as the framework for the chapters in this book and builds on the three core principles:

1. Human communication is a form of symbolic action.

2. Our beliefs, attitudes, and behaviors relating to nature and environmental problems are mediated or influenced by communication.

3. The public sphere emerges as a discursive space in which diverse voices engage the attention of others about environmental concerns.

These principles obviously overlap (see Figure 1.2). As I've noted, our communication (as symbolic action) actively shapes our perceptions when we see the natural world through myriad symbols, words, images, or narratives. And, when we communicate publicly with others, we share these understandings and invite reactions to our views.

Nature, Communication, and the Public Sphere

Let's explore the three principles that organize the chapters in this book. I'll introduce and illustrate these briefly here and then draw on them in each of the remaining chapters.

Human Communication as Symbolic Action

Earlier, I defined environmental communication as a form of **symbolic action.** Our language and other symbolic acts do something. They actively shape our understanding,

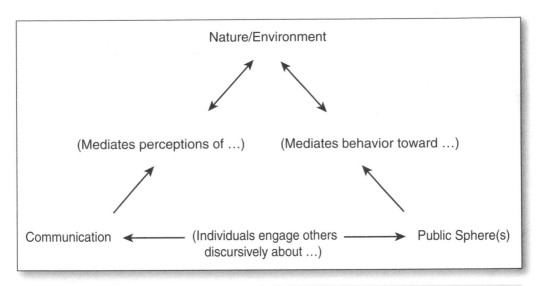

Nature/Environment

(Mediates perceptions of ...) (Mediates behavior toward ...)

Communication ← (Individuals engage others → Public Sphere(s)
discursively about ...)

Figure 1.2 Nature, communication, and the public sphere.

create meaning, and orient us to a wider world. Films, online sites and social media, photographs, popular magazines, and other forms of human symbolic behavior act upon us. They invite us to view the world this way rather than that way to affirm these values and not those. Our stories and words warn us, but they also invite us to celebrate.

And, language that invites us to celebrate also leads to real-world outcomes. Consider the American gray wolf. In late 2008, a federal judge restored protection to wolves in the Northern Rocky Mountains under the nation's Endangered Species Act (ESA) (Brown, 2008). But, it was not always this way. Wolves had become almost extinct until the federal government initiated a restoration plan in the mid-1990s.

In 1995, former Secretary of Interior Bruce Babbitt delivered a speech celebrating the return of wolves to Yellowstone National Park. Earlier that year, he had carried the first American gray wolf into the transition area in the national park where she would mate with other wolves also being returned. After setting her down, Babbitt recalled, "I looked ... into the green eyes of this magnificent creature, within this spectacular landscape, and was profoundly moved by the elevating nature of America's conservation laws: laws with the power to make creation whole" (para. 3).

Babbitt's purpose in speaking that day was to support the beleaguered ESA, under attack in the Congress at the time. In recalling the biblical story of the flood, Babbitt evoked a powerful narrative for revaluing wolves and other endangered species. In retelling this ancient story to his listeners at Yellowstone, he invited them to embrace a similar ethic in the present day:

> And when the waters receded, and the dove flew off to dry land, God set all the creatures free, commanding them to multiply upon the earth.
>
> Then, in the words of the covenant with Noah, "when the rainbow appears in the clouds, I will see it and remember the everlasting covenant between me and all living things on earth."

Thus we are instructed that this everlasting covenant was made to protect the whole of creation. . . . We are living between the flood and the rainbow: between the threats to creation on the one side and God's covenant to protect life on the other. (Babbitt, 1995, paras. 34–36, 56)

Because communication provides us with a means of sense making about the world, it orients us toward events, people, wildlife, and choices that we encounter. And, because different individuals (and generations) value nature in different ways, we find our voices to be part of a conversation about which meaning of nature is the best or the most useful. Secretary Babbitt invoked an ancient story of survival to invite the American public to appreciate anew the ESA. So, too, our own communication mediates or helps us to make sense of the different narratives, ideologies, and appeals that people use to define what they believe is right, feasible, ethical, or just common sense.

Human communication therefore is symbolic action because we draw upon language and other symbols to construct a framework for understanding and valuing and to bring the wider world to others' attention. I explore this aspect of communication more closely in Chapters 2 and 3.

| Figure 1.3 | Secretary of Interior Bruce Babbitt, releasing the first American gray wolf into Yellowstone National Park in 1995. |

U.S. National Park Service

Mediating "Nature"

It may seem odd to place "nature" in quotation marks. The natural world definitely exists: Forests are logged or left standing; streams may be polluted or clean; and large glaciers in Antarctica are calving into the Southern ocean. So, what's going on? As one of my students asked me, "What does communication have to do with nature or the study of environmental problems?" My answer to her question takes us into the heart of this book.

Simply put, whatever else nature and the environment may be, they are entangled with our very human ways of interacting with, and knowing, the natural world. At a very basic level, our beliefs, attitudes, and behaviors toward nature are mediated by human modes of representation—by our language, television, film, photos, art, and contemplation (Cox, 2007, p. 12). *Mediating* is another way of saying that the acts of pointing to and naming something in the world are our means for recognizing and understanding it. As Tema Milstein (2011) explains, "Pointing and naming generate certain kinds of ecocultural knowledge that constitute aspects of nature as considered, unique, sorted, or marked" (p. 4).

When we name the natural world, we also orient ourselves in this world. We become located or interested in it; we have a view onto this world. As Christine Oravec (2004) observed in her essay on Utah's Cedar Breaks National Monument, this act of naming is not only a mode by which we socially construct and know the natural world, but it orients us and thus "influences our interaction with it" (p. 3). For instance, is *wilderness* a place of primeval beauty, or is it a territory that is dark, dangerous, and alien to humans? Early settlers in New England viewed North American forests as forbidding and dangerous. The Puritan writer Michael Wigglesworth named or described the region as

A waste and howling wilderness,

Where none inhabited

But hellish fiends, and brutish men

That Devils worshiped. (quoted in Nash, 2001, p. 36)

As a result of these different orientations to the natural world, writers, scientists, business leaders, citizens, poets, and conservationists have fought for centuries over whether forests should be logged, rivers dammed, air quality regulated, and endangered species protected.

Consider the weather (and climate): The last two winters in the United States and Europe have been harsh, with record cold temperatures and blizzards. As I write, in winter 2011, another snowstorm is pounding the Midwest in the United States. As you might image, the search for the cause of such cold weather invites caustic remarks, such as "Where's that global warming?" as well as competing narratives about climate change from skeptics and climate scientists. Conservative FOX TV commentator Glenn Beck (2011), for example, quipped, "Um . . . if the globe is warming why is my car buried under all this snow?" (para. 1). On the other hand, National Oceanic and Atmospheric Administration (NOAA) scientists offered this interpretation: The winds that normally circle the North Pole (the Polar Vortex) act as a fence keeping cold air in; however, when "this circle of winds . . . breaks down, cold air spills south," while warmer air rushes in (Schoop, 2011). (I suspect many of you also encounter very different views about weather and its relation to global warming!)

For those enduring frigid winters, Glenn Beck's sarcasm makes "common sense." For some, it is counterintuitive to believe the Earth is warming when they can see and experience cold weather personally. Yet, climate scientists insist such localized weather does not contradict research that, globally, the Earth is continuing to warm. While parts of the United States and Europe were shivering, for example, northeastern Canada and Greenland were experiencing 15 F° to 20 F° warmer temperatures than normal (Gillis, 2011). And, National Aeronautics and Space Administration (NASA) scientists concluded that 2010 tied 2005 as the warmest year, and 2001–2010 as the warmest decade since measurements began in 1880 (National Aeronautics and Space Administration, 2011).

In their own way, commentators like Beck and climate scientists are offering their construction or view of complex, atmospheric systems, that is, the weather and what it means. And, depending on which view we adopt in our own sense-making about climate change, we will have differing beliefs and will be likely to act in different ways. This is what I meant earlier in saying that our beliefs, attitudes, and behaviors relating to nature are mediated by communication.

My point is that, although nature invites different responses from us, it is, in itself, politically silent. Ultimately, it is we—through our symbolic actions—who invest its seasons and species with meaning and value. Similarly, some problems become problems only when someone identifies a threat to important values we hold. Decisions to preserve habitat for endangered species or impose regulations on greenhouse gases seldom result from scientific study alone. Instead, our decisions to take action arise from a crucible of debate and (often) controversy in the wider public sphere.

Public Sphere as Discursive Space

A third theme central to this book is the idea of the **public sphere** or, more accurately, public spheres. Earlier, I defined the public sphere as the realm of influence that is created when individuals engage others in communication—through conversation, argument, debate, or questioning—about subjects of shared concern or topics that affect a wider community. The public comes into being in our everyday conversations as well as in more formal interactions when we talk about the environment. And, the public sphere is not just words: Visual and nonverbal symbolic actions, such as marches, banners, YouTube videos, photographs, and Earth First! tree sits, also have prompted debate and questioning of environmental policy as readily as editorials, speeches, and TV newscasts.

The German social theorist Jürgen Habermas (1974) offered a similar definition when he observed that "a portion of the public sphere comes into being in every conversation in which private individuals assemble to form a public body" (p. 49). As we engage others in conversation, questioning, or debate, we translate our private concerns into public matters and thus create spheres of influence that affect how we and others view the environment and our relation to it. Such translations of private concerns into public matters occur in a range of forums and practices that give rise to something akin to an environmental public sphere—from a talk at a local ecology club to a scientist's testimony before a congressional committee. In public hearings, newspaper editorials, online alerts, speeches at rallies, street festivals, and countless other occasions in which we engage others in conversation, debate, or other forms of symbolic actions, the public sphere emerges as a potential sphere of influence.

But, private concerns are not always translated into public action, and technical information about the environment may remain in scientific journals, proprietary files of corporations, or other private sources. Therefore, it is important to note that two other spheres of influence exist parallel to the public sphere. Communication scholar Thomas Goodnight (1982) named these areas of influence the *personal* and *technical* spheres. For example, two strangers arguing at an airport bar is a relatively private affair, whereas the technical findings of biology that influenced Rachael Carson's (1962) discussion of dichlorodiphenyltrichloroethane (DDT) in *Silent Spring* were originally limited to technical journals. Yet Carson's book presented this scientific information in a context that engaged the attention—and debate—of millions of readers and scores of public officials. In doing this, *Silent Spring* gave rise to a sphere of influence as she translated technical matters into subjects of public interest.

Goodnight cautioned that, in contemporary society, information needed for judgments about the environment and other technical subjects may cause both private and public conversations to defer to scientific or technical authority. The danger in such situations obviously is that the public sphere can decline. It can lose its relevance as a sphere of influence that exists in a democracy to mediate among differing viewpoints and interests. Goodnight (1982) himself feared that "the public sphere is being steadily eroded by the elevation of the personal and technical groundings of argument" (p. 223).

The idea of the public sphere itself is often misunderstood. Three common misconceptions occur about it. These are the beliefs that the public sphere is (a) only an official site or forum for government decision making, (b) a monolithic or ideal collection of all citizens, and (c) a form of "rational" or technical communication. Each of these ideas is a misunderstanding of the public sphere.

First, the public sphere is not only, or even primarily, an official space. Although there are forums and state-sponsored spaces such as public hearings that invite citizens to communicate about the environment, these official sites do not exhaust the public sphere. In fact, discussion and debate about environmental concerns more often occur outside of government meeting rooms and courts. The early fifth-century (BCE) Greeks called these meeting spaces of everyday life *agoras,* the public squares or marketplaces where citizens gathered to exchange ideas about the life of their community. At the dawn of one of the first experiments in democracy, Greek citizens believed they needed certain skills to voice their concerns publicly and influence the judgment of others, skills they called the art of rhetoric. (I return to this background in Chapter 3.)

Second, the public sphere is neither monolithic nor a uniform assemblage of all citizens in the abstract. As the realm of influence that is created when individuals engage others discursively, a public sphere assumes concrete and local forms: They include calls to talk radio programs, blogs, letters to the editor of newspapers, or local meetings where citizens question public officials, for example, about risks to their health from contaminated well water. As Habermas (1974) might remind us, the public sphere comes into existence whenever individuals share, question, argue, mourn, or celebrate with others about their shared concerns.

Third, far from elite conversation or "rational" forms of communication, the public sphere is most often the arena in which popular, passionate, and democratic communication occurs, as well as reasoned or technical discourse. Such a view of the public sphere acknowledges the diverse voices and styles that characterize a robust, participatory democracy. In fact, in this book, I introduce the voices of ordinary citizens and the special challenges they face in gaining a hearing about matters of environmental and personal survival in their communities.

Diverse Voices in a "Green" Public Sphere

The landscape of environmental politics and public affairs can be as diverse, controversial, colorful, and complex as an Amazonian rainforest or the Galapagos Islands' ecology. Whether at press conferences, in local community centers, on blogs, or in corporate-sponsored TV ads, individuals and groups speaking about the environment appear today in diverse sites and public spaces.

In this final section, I'll describe some of the major sources, or voices, communicating about environmental issues in the public sphere. I use Myerson and Rydin's (1991) concept of *voices* to stress the different concerns (for example, the "anxious citizen voice" or "expert voice") that place certain "voices in relation to other voices" (pp. 5, 6). These include the voices of:

1. Citizens and community groups

2. Environmental groups

3. Scientists and scientific discourse

4. Corporations and lobbyists

5. Anti-environmentalist and climate change critics

6. News media and environmental journalists

7. Public officials

These seven voices also include multiple, specific roles or professional tasks—writers, press officers, group spokespersons, information technology specialists, communication directors, marketing and campaign consultants, and other communication roles.

Citizens and Community Groups

Local residents who complain to public officials about pollution or other environmental problems and who organize their neighbors to take action are the most common and effective sources of environmental change. Some are motivated by urban sprawl or development projects that destroy their homes as well as green spaces in their cities. Others, who may live near an oil refinery or chemical plant, may be motivated by noxious fumes to organize resistance to the industry's lax air-quality permit.

In 1978, Lois Gibbs and her neighbors in the working-class community of Love Canal in upstate New York became concerned when, after they noticed odors and oily substances surfacing in the school's playground, their children developed headaches and became sick. Gibbs also had read a newspaper report that Hooker Chemical Company, a subsidiary of Occidental Petroleum, had buried dangerous chemicals on land it later sold to the local school board (Center for Health, Environment, and Justice, 2003).

Despite an initial denial of the problem by state officials, Gibbs and her neighbors sought media coverage, carried symbolic coffins to the state capital, marched on Mother's Day, and pressed health officials to take their concerns seriously. Finally, in 1982, the residents succeeded in persuading the federal government to relocate those who wanted to leave Love Canal. The U.S. Justice Department also prosecuted Hooker Chemical Company, imposing large fines (Shabecoff, 2003, pp. 227–229). As a result, Love Canal became a symbol of toxic waste sites and fueled a citizens' anti-toxics movement in the United States.

Lois Gibbs's story is not unique. In rural towns in Louisiana, in inner-city neighborhoods in Detroit and Los Angeles, on Native American reservations in New Mexico, and in communities throughout the country, citizens and community groups have launched campaigns to clean up polluting plants and halt mining operations on sacred tribal lands. As they do, activists and residents face the challenges of finding their voices and the resources to express their concerns and persuade others to join them in demanding accountability of public officials.

Environmental Groups

Environmental and allied concerns such as health and social justice groups are frequent sources of communication about the environment. This diverse movement comprises a wide array of groups and networks, both online and on the ground. And, each has its own focus and mode of communication. They range from thousands of grassroots groups to regional and national environmental organizations such as the Natural Resources Defense Council, Sierra Club, Audubon Society, and National Wildlife Federation to international groups such as Conservation International, Greenpeace, World Wildlife Fund, and groups across the planet fighting unsustainable development in their communities. Online networks have proliferated by the tens of thousands, included global networks like 350.org, linking other groups in the fight against climate change.

These groups address a diversity of issues and often differ in their modes of advocacy. For example, the Sierra Club and Natural Resources Defense Council focus on climate change through their advocacy campaigns and lobbying of the U.S. Congress on energy policy. On the other hand, the Nature Conservancy and local conservancy groups protect endangered habitat on private lands by purchasing the properties themselves. Other groups such as Greenpeace and Rainforest Action Network use "image events" (DeLuca, 1999) to shine the spotlight of media attention on concerns as diverse as global warming, illegal whaling, and the destruction of tropical rainforests.

Scientists and Scientific Discourse

The warming of the Earth's atmosphere first came to the public's attention when climate scientists testified before the U.S. Congress in 1988. Since then, scientific reports, such as the periodic assessments of Intergovernmental Panel on Climate Change (IPCC), have prompted spirited public debate over appropriate steps that national governments should take to prevent a "dangerous anthropogenic interference" with the global climate (Mann, 2009, para. 1). As we shall see in succeeding chapters, the work of climate scientists has become a fiercely contested site in today's public sphere, as environmentalists, public health officials, ideological skeptics, political adversaries, and others question, dispute, or urge action by Congress to adopt clean energy policies. (The IPCC's next report is scheduled for release by 2014.)

As in the case of climate change, scientific reports have led to other important investigations of—and debate about—problems affecting human health and Earth's biodiversity. From asthma in children caused by air pollution and mercury poisoning in fish to the accelerating loss of species of plants and animals, scientific research and the alerts of scientists have contributed substantially to public awareness and to debate about environmental policy.

As we'll see in Chapter 11, research by environmental scientists is sometimes disputed or ignored, the findings distorted by radio talk show hosts, ideological skeptics, and affected businesses. For example, the respected journal *Science* described a campaign by partisans to discredit the work of atmospheric scientists on ozone depletion in the 1990s (Taubes, 1993). In this and other chapters, I'll describe the importance of science communication as well as the ways in which environmental sciences themselves have become a site of controversy in recent years.

| Figure 1.4 | Warnings of environmental dangers constitute an important area of study called *risk communication* (Chapter 12). |

© istockphoto.com/andipantz

Corporations and Lobbyists

Environmental historian Samuel Hays (2000) reports that, as new environmental sciences began to document the environmental and health risks from industrial products, the affected businesses challenged the science "at every step, questioning both the methods and research designs that were used and the conclusions that were drawn" (p. 222). As part of this opposition, industries organized trade associations to defend their practices and to lobby against environmental regulations.

Organized corporate opposition to environmental measures appears to be based on two factors: (1) restrictions on the traditional uses of land (for example, mining, logging, or oil and gas drilling) and (2) threats to the economic interests of newer industries such as petrochemicals, energy production, computers, and transportation. Worried by the threat of tighter limits on air and water discharges from factories and refineries, many corporations have formed trade associations such as the Business Round Table and the Chemical Manufacturers Association to conduct PR campaigns or lobby Congress on behalf of their industries. For example, the

American Coalition for Clean Coal Electricity, a coal and electricity-generating industry group, has been active online and on TV, airing extensive ads promoting coal as a "clean energy" source.

Finally, some large corporations recently have begun to go green—improving their operations and committing to standards for sustainability (lower energy use and lower impact on natural resources) in their operations. Others, however, have skillfully adopted practices of "green marketing" that give false appearances of environmental values.

Anti-Environmentalists and Climate Change Critics

Although it may be difficult to conceive of groups that are opposed to protection of the environment (clean air, healthy forests, safe drinking water, and so on), a backlash against government regulations and even environmental science has arisen periodically in U.S. politics. This is often fueled by the perception that environmental regulations harm economic growth and jobs.

One early expression of this opposition was the **Sagebrush Rebellion** in the 1970s and 1980s, fueled by traditional users of public lands and natural resources in the West. Environmental journalist Philip Shabecoff (2003) reported that "the [cattle] stockmen, miners, and other range users, long accustomed to treating the public lands as a private fiefdom, reacted angrily to what they perceived as a threat to their rights and their livelihood" (p. 155). In response, sagebrush rebels "evoked states' rights, the free market, and . . . attacked, sometimes physically, and vilified federal land managers and sought to discredit conservationists as un-American left-wingers" (p. 155).

By the 1990s, offshoots of the Sagebrush Rebellion became **Wise Use groups,** or *property rights* groups. These groups objected to restrictions on the use of their property for such purposes as protection of wetlands or habitat for endangered species. They include groups like Ron Arnold's Center for the Defense of Free Enterprise (which is opposed to environmental regulations generally). Arnold, a controversial figure in the anti-environmentalist movement, once told a reporter, "Our goal is to destroy environmentalism once and for all" (Rawe & Field, 1992, in Helvarg, 2004, p. 7).

More recently, climate change skeptics have opposed the science, and many of the policies being proposed to reduce greenhouse gases or enable communities to adapt to climate change. Using online sites, conservative think tanks (Jacques, Dunlap, & Freeman, 2008), and films like *The Great Global Warming Swindle,* such skeptics have fueled debate and sometimes stalled government action on climate change in the United States.

News Media and Environmental Journalists

It would be difficult to overstate the impact of news media on the public's understanding of environmental concerns. Media not only report events but act as conduits for other voices seeking to influence public attitudes. These voices include scientists, corporate spokespersons, environmentalists, and citizen groups. News media also exert influence through their **agenda-setting** role or their effect on the public's perception of the salience or importance of issues. As journalism scholar Bernard Cohen (1963) first explained, the news media filter or select issues for attention and therefore set the public's agenda, telling people not what to think but what to think about. For example, the public's concern about pollution and harm to Gulf Coast economies soared after extensive news coverage of the millions of gallons of oil that spilled from the BP *Deepwater Horizon* well in 2010.

Although the BP *Deepwater Horizon* oil spill story focused on a single, dramatic event that fulfilled criteria for newsworthiness, most environmental topics, even quite serious ones, are less dramatic. As a result, media often have discretion in choosing what events or information to cover and also how to frame or package a news story. Indeed, the many voices and platforms that distribute news and information—from newspapers to blogs and Internet news sites—illustrate a wide range of approaches to environmental concerns. They range from a business story about how "Climate Change May Cause 'Massive' Food Disruptions" to a story in the *New York Times* about Congress's plans to "slash EPA's budget by $3 billion and defund the agency's climate program" (Nelson & Chemnick, 2011, para. 2).

Public Officials

At the heart of debates over the environment are public officials at every level of government—both elected and appointed persons—whose roles are to shape or enforce local ordinances, enact state and national laws, and develop and enforce environmental regulations. Such individuals are at the heart of the political and legislative process because it is they who must reconcile the arguments and interests of the diverse voices speaking for or against specific measures. For legislators, particularly, this is "characteristically, a balancing act," as they must "reconcile a variety of contending forces [who are] affected in various ways" by a proposed law (Miller, 2009, p. 41).

As we shall see throughout this book, public officials are, therefore, the audience for a range of environmental communication practices—for example, citizens testifying before state regulators about permits for a coal-fired power plant or industries' advocacy campaigns to mobilize public opinion in hopes of persuading members of Congress to preserve tax breaks for oil companies or extend tax credits for wind and solar energy groups.

Less visible to the public, but arguably as important as legislators, are *environmental regulators*. These are the professional staff whose role is to ensure that laws are actually implemented and enforced. As political scientist Norman Miller (2009) explains, public officials "must turn to engineers, scientists, land use planners, lawyers, economists, and other specialists . . . to set protocols, standards," and so forth to ensure that a law can be carried out (p. 38). The wordings of these regulations frequently have powerful implications for industry, local communities, or the public's health. As a result, interested parties often attempt to persuade regulators to adopt a certain definition, interpreting the intent of a statute favorably to their interests.

SUMMARY

This chapter described the emerging field of environmental communication, its major areas of study, and the principal concepts around which the chapters of this book will be organized:

- The field of environmental communication consists of several major areas of study, including: environmental rhetoric and the social–symbolic "construction" of nature, public participation in environmental decision making, environmental collaboration and conflict resolution, media and environmental journalism, representations of nature in corporate advertising and popular culture, advocacy campaigns and message construction, and science and risk communication.
- The term *environmental communication* itself was defined as the pragmatic and constitutive vehicle for our understanding of the environment as well as our relationships to the natural world; it is the symbolic medium that we use in constructing environmental problems and in negotiating society's different responses to them.
- Using this definition, the framework for the chapters in this book builds on three core principles:

  (1) Human communication is a form of symbolic action.

  (2) Our beliefs, attitudes, and behaviors relating to nature and environmental problems are mediated or influenced by communication.

  (3) The public sphere emerges as a discursive space for communication about the environment.

Now that you have learned something about environmental communication and its practices, I hope you'll feel inspired to join the public conversations about the environment that are already in progress. Along the way, I hope you'll discover your own voice in speaking on behalf of the natural world and your own communities.

SUGGESTED RESOURCES

- Anders Hansen, *Environment, Media and Communication.* London and New York: Routledge, 2010.
- Judith Henry, *Communication and the Natural World.* State College, PA: Starta, 2010.

- Richard R. Jurin, Donny Roush, and K. Jeffrey Dantor, *Environmental Communication. Second Edition: Skills and Principles for Natural Resource Managers, Scientists, and Engineers.* 2nd ed. New York: Springer, 2010.
- Libby Lester, *Media and Environment.* Cambridge, UK: Polity Press, 2010.
- Julia Corbett, *Communicating Nature: How We Create and Understand Environmental Messages,* Washington, Covelo, London: Island Press, 2006.
- Visit the website for the International Environmental Communication Association (http://environmentalcomm.org) for information about programs, research, conferences, and courses.

KEY TERMS

Agenda setting   31

Collaboration   15

Constitutive   19

Environmental
   communication   19

Pragmatic   19

Public sphere   24

Shannon–Weaver model of
   communication   18

Symbolic action   20

Sagebrush Rebellion   30

Wise Use groups   30

DISCUSSION QUESTIONS

1. Is nature ethically and politically silent? What does this mean? If nature is politically silent, does this mean it has no value apart from human meaning?

2. The rhetorical theorist Kenneth Burke (1966) claims that, "Much that we take as observations about 'reality' may be but the spinning out of possibilities implicit in our particular choice of terms." Does this mean we cannot know "reality" outside of the words we use to describe it? What did Burke mean by this?

3. In our society, whose voices are heard most often about environmental issues? What influence do corporations, TV personalities, and partisan blogs have in the political process? Are there still openings for ordinary citizens, scientists, or environmental groups to be heard?

REFERENCES

Armstrong, P. (2009, July 30). Conflict resolution and British Columbia's Great Bear Rainforest: Lessons learned 1995–2009. Retrieved November 2, 2010, from www.coastforestconservationinitiative.com/

Anderson, A. (1997). *Media, culture, and the environment.* New Brunswick, NJ: Rutgers University Press.

Babbitt, B. (1995, December 13). Between the flood and the rainbow. [Speech].

Retrieved April 20, 2001, from www
.fs.fed.us/eco/eco-watch

Beck, G. (2011, February 1). Al Gore blames
blizzards on . . . global warming? Retrieved February 10, 2011, from www
.glennbeck.com

Beierle, T. C., & Cayford, J. (2002). *Democracy
in practice: Public participation in environmental decisions.* Washington, DC:
Resources for the Future.

Bortree, D. S., & Seltzer, T. (2009). Dialogic
strategies and outcomes: An analysis of
environmental advocacy groups' Facebook profiles. *Public Relations Review,
35,* 317–319.

Brereton, P. (2005). *Hollywood utopia:
Ecology in contemporary American cin-
ema.* Bristol, UK: Intellect Books.

Brown, M. (2008, October 5). Molloy
restores ESA protection for wolves. *The
Missoulian.* Retrieved October 5, 2008,
from http://www.missoulian.com.

Brown, W. R., & Crable, R. E. (1973).
Industry, mass magazines, and the ecology issue. *Quarterly Journal of Speech,
59,* 259–272.

Brulle, R. J. (2010). From environmental campaigns to advancing the public dialog:
Environmental communication for civic
engagement. *Environmental Communication: A Journal of Nature and Culture, 4,*
82–98.

Burke, K. (1966). *Language as symbolic action.*
Berkeley: University of California Press.

Carson, R. (1962). *Silent spring.* Boston:
Houghton Mifflin.

Carvalho, A. (2009, September 16). Environmental communication in Europe. *Indi-
cations.* [Blog]. Retrieved February 13,
2011, from http://indications.wordpress
.com/

Casman, E. A., & Fischhoff, B. (2008).
Risk communication planning for the
aftermath of a plague bioattack. *Risk
Analysis: An International Journal, 28,*
1327–1342.

Center for Health, Environment, and Justice.
(2003). *Love Canal: The journey continues.*

Retrieved October 5, 2008, from http://
www.chej.org/

Center for Research on Environmental
Decisions at Columbia University.
(2009). *The psychology of climate change
communication.* Retrieved February 10,
2011, from http://www.cred.columbia
.edu/

Cohen, B. C. (1963). *The press and foreign
policy.* Princeton, NJ: Princeton
University Press.

Cooper, M. M. (1996). Environmental rhetoric
in an age of hegemony: Earth First! and
the Nature Conservancy. In C. G. Herndl
& S. C. Brown (Eds.), *Green culture: Environmental rhetoric in contemporary
America* (pp. 236–260). Madison: University of Wisconsin Press.

Corbett, J. B. (2006). *Communicating nature:
How we create and understand environ-
mental messages.* Washington, DC:
Island Press.

Cox, J. R. (1982). The die is cast: Topical and
ontological dimensions of the *locus* of
the irreparable. *Quarterly Journal of
Speech, 6,* 227–239.

Cox, J. R. (2010). Beyond frames: Recovering
the strategic in climate communication.
*Environmental Communication: A Journal
of Nature and Culture, 4,* 122–133.

Cox, R. (2007, May). Nature's "crisis disciplines": Does environmental communication have an ethical duty? *Environmental
Communication: A Journal of Nature and
Culture, 1*(1), 5–20.

Cozen, B. (2010). This pear is a rhetorical
tool: Food imagery in energy company
advertising. *Environmental Communication: A Journal of Nature and Culture,
4,* 355–370.

DeLuca, K. M. (1999). *Image politics: The
new rhetoric of environmental activism.*
New York: Guilford.

DeLuca, K. M. (2010). Salvaging wilderness
from the tomb of history: A response to
*The national parks: America's best idea.
Environmental Communication: A Journal
of Nature and Culture, 4,* 484–493.

Depoe, S. (1997). Environmental studies in mass communication. *Critical Studies in Mass Communication, 14,* 368–372.

Dietz, T., & Stern, P. C. (2008). *Public participation in environmental assessment and decision making.* National Research Council. Washington, DC: National Academies Press.

Doyle, A. (2008, February 4). "Tipping point" on horizon for Greenland ice. Reuters. Retrieved October 4, 2008, from http://www.reuters.com.

EnviroEducation.com. (2004, May 24). Environmental communications/Journalism: Education and career outlook. Retrieved February 3, 2011, from www.enviroeducation.com/

Farrell, T. B., & Goodnight, G. T. (1981). Accidental rhetoric: The root metaphors of Three Mile Island. *Quarterly Journal of Speech, 48,* 271–300.

Gillis, J. (2011, January 25). Cold jumps Arctic "fence," stocking winter's fury. *The New York Times,* pp. A1, 3.

Goodnight, T. G. (1982). The personal, technical, and public spheres of argument: A speculative inquiry into the art of public deliberation. *Journal of the American Forensic Association, 18,* 214–227.

Greenberg, M. R., Sandman, P. M., Sachsman, D. B., & Salamone, K. L. (1989). Network television news coverage of environmental risk. *Risk Analysis, 9,* 119–126.

Grunig, L. (Ed.). (1989). *Environmental activism revisited: The changing nature of communication through organizational public relations, special interest groups, and the mass media.* Troy, OH: North American Association for Environmental Education.

Habermas, J. (1974). The public sphere: An encyclopedia article (1964). *New German Critique, 1*(3), 49–55.

Hamilton, J. D. (2003). Exploring technical and cultural appeals in strategic risk communication: The Fernald radium case. *Risk Analysis, 23,* 291–302.

Hamilton, J. D. (2008). Convergence and divergence in the public dialogue on nuclear weapons cleanup. In B. Taylor, W. Kinsella, S. Depoe, & M. Metzler (Eds.), *Nuclear legacies: Communication, controversy, and the U.S. nuclear weapons complex* (pp. 41–72). Lanham, MD: Lexington Books.

Hansen, A. (2010). *Environment, media, and communication.* New York, NY: Routledge.

Hays, S. P. (2000). *A history of environmental politics since 1945.* Pittsburgh, PA: University of Pittsburgh Press.

Helvarg, D. (2004). *The war against the greens: The "wise-use" movement, the new right, and the browning of America.* Boulder, CO: Johnson Books.

Henry, J. (2010). *Communication and the natural world.* State College, PA: Strata.

Jacques, P. J., Dunlap, R. E., & Freeman, M. (2008). The organization of denial: Conservative think tanks and environmental skepticism, *Environmental Politics, 17,* 349–385.

Lakoff, G. (2010). Why it matters how we frame the environment. *Environmental Communication: A Journal of Nature and Culture, 4,* 70–81.

Lange, J. (1990). Refusal to compromise: The case of Earth First! *Western Journal of Speech Communication, 54,* 473–494.

Lange, J. I. (1993). The logic of competing information campaigns: Conflict over old growth and the spotted owl. *Communication Monographs, 60,* 239–257.

Lester, L. (2010). *Media and environment: Conflict, politics, and the news.* Cambridge, UK: Polity Press.

Luke, T. W. (1987). Chernobyl: The packaging of transnational ecological disaster. *Critical Studies in Mass Communication, 4,* 351–375.

Mann, M. (2009, March 17). Defining dangerous anthropogenic interference. *Proceedings of the National Academy of Sciences, 106* (11), 4065–4066.

Marafiote, T. (2008). The American dream: Technology, tourism, and the transformation of wilderness. *Environmental*

Communication: A Journal of Nature and Culture, 2, 154–172.

Martin, T. (2007). Muting the voice of the local in the age of the global: How communication practices compromised public participation in India's Allain Dunhangan environmental impact assessment. *Environmental Communication: A Journal of Nature and Culture, 1,* 171–193.

Martini, K., & Reed, C. (2010). *Thank you for firing me! How to catch the next wave of success after you lose your job.* New York: Sterling.

Meister M., & Japp, P. M. (Eds.). (2002). *Enviropop: Studies in environmental rhetoric and popular culture.* Westport, CT: Praeger.

Miller, N. (2009). *Environmental politics: Stakeholders, interests, and policymaking* (2nd ed.). New York: Routledge.

Milstein, T. (2011, March). Nature identification: The power of pointing and naming. *Environmental Communication: A Journal of Nature and Culture, 5*(1), 3–24.

Moore, M. P. (1993). Constructing irreconcilable conflict: The function of synecdoche in the spotted owl controversy. *Communication Monographs, 60,* 258–274.

Moser, S. C., & Dilling, L. (2007). *Creating a climate for change: Communicating climate change and facilitating social change.* Cambridge, UK: Cambridge University Press.

Myerson, G., & Rydin, Y. (1991). *The language of environment: A new rhetoric.* London: University College London Press.

Nash, R. (2001). *Wilderness and the American mind* (4th ed.). New Haven, CT: Yale University Press.

National Aeronautics and Space Administration. (2011, January 12). NASA research finds 2010 tied for warmest year on record. Goddard Institute for Space Studies. Retrieved February 17, 2012, from www.giss.nasa.gov/research/news/20110112.

Nelson, G., & Chemnick, J. (2011, February 14). EPA budget proposal focuses on air and climate rules, cuts water grants. *The New York Times.* Retrieved February 15, 2011, from www.nytimes.com/

Opel, A., Johnston, J., & Wilk, R. (2010). Food, culture and the environment: Communicating about what we eat. *Environmental Communication: A Journal of Nature and Culture, 4,* 251–254.

Oravec, C. (1981). John Muir, Yosemite, and the sublime response: A study of the rhetoric of preservationism. *Quarterly Journal of Speech, 67,* 245–258.

Oravec, C. (1984). Conservationism vs. preservationism: The "public interest" in the Hetch Hetchy controversy. *Quarterly Journal of Speech, 70,* 339–361.

Oravec, C. L. (2004). Naming, interpretation, policy, and poetry. In S. L. Senecah (Ed.), *Environmental communication yearbook* (Vol. 1, pp. 1–14). Mahwah, NJ: Lawrence Erlbaum.

Peterson, T. R. (1986). The will to conservation: A Burkeian analysis of Dust Bowl rhetoric and American farming motives. *Southern Speech Communication Journal, 52,* 1–21.

Plough, A., & Krimsky, S. (1987). The emergence of risk communication studies: Social and political context. *Science, Technology, & Human Values, 12,* 4–10.

Rawe, A. L., & Field, R. (1992, Fall). Interview with a "wise" guy. *Common Ground of Puget Sound,* 1.

Retzinger, J. P. (2002). Cultivating the agrarian myth in Hollywood films. In M. Meister & P. M. Japp (Eds.), *Enviropop: Studies in environmental rhetoric and popular culture* (pp. 45–62). Westport, CT: Praeger.

Retzinger, J. P. (2008). Speculative visions and imaginary meals. *Cultural Studies, 22,* 369–390.

Schoop, R. (2011, January 30). Winter storms don't contradict global warming science, experts say. *The News & Observer,* p. 7A.

Senecah, S. L. (2007). Impetus, mission, and future of the environmental communication/division: Are we still on track? Were we ever? *Environmental Communication: A Journal of Nature and Culture, 1*(1), 21–33.

Shabecoff, P. (2003). *A fierce green fire: The American environmental movement* (Rev. ed.). Washington, DC: Island Press.

Shanahan, J., & McComas, K. (1999). *Nature stories: Depictions of the environment and their effects.* Cresskill, NJ: Hampton Press.

Shannon, C., & Weaver, W. (1949). *The mathematical theory of communication.* Urbana: University of Illinois Press.

Short, B. (1991). Earth First! and the rhetoric of moral confrontation. *Communication Studies, 42,* 172–188.

Slawter, L. D. (2008). TreeHuggerTV: Re-visualizing environmental activism in the post-network era. *Environmental Communication: A Journal of Nature and Culture, 2,* 212–228.

Taubes, G. (1993). The ozone backlash. *Science, 260,* 1580–1583.

Waddell, C. (1990). The role of pathos in the decision-making process: A study in the rhetoric of science policy. *Quarterly Journal of Speech, 76,* 381–401.

Walker, G. B. (2004). The roadless area initiative as national policy: Is public participation an oxymoron? In S. P. Depoe, J. W. Delicath, & M-F. A. Elsenbeer (Eds.), *Communication and public participation in environmental decision making* (pp. 113–135). Albany: State University of New York Press.

"Wilderness . . . is so heavily freighted with meaning of a personal, symbolic, and changing kind as to resist easy definition" (Nash, 2001, p. 1).

CHAPTER 2

Contested Meanings of *Environment*

What could they see but a hideous and desolate wilderness, full of wild beasts & wild men?

—William Bradford, *Of Plymouth Plantation*, 1620–1647 (1898/1952)

Forests provide shelter to people and habitat to biodiversity; are a source of food, medicine and clean water; and play a vital role in maintaining a stable global climate. . . . Forests are vital to the survival and well-being of people everywhere, all 7 billion of us.

—United Nations International Year of Forests (2011)

Writing of settlers' hardships at Plymouth in 1620, William Bradford described the landscape as a "hideous and desolate wilderness." With that phrase, he began what environmental historian Roderick Nash (2001) called a "tradition of repugnance" for nature (p. 24). His account of the New England forests also would be the start of a long-running controversy over how to define and shape the meaning of the relationship between human society and the environment.

Before we look at the different areas of environmental communication, it is important to realize that our views about the environment are highly *contingent;* that is, different voices and interests have "battled mightily and often" over the best ways to define humans' relationships to the natural world (Warren, 2003, p. 1). This chapter, therefore, traces this history and the contested meanings of *environment* in the United States and, to a lesser extent, globally.

Chapter Preview

In this chapter, I'll describe four pivotal antagonisms, or times when individuals and new movements contested the dominant attitudes about nature and what society accepted as an environmental problem.

- The first section describes two early movements in the United States that challenged dominant views about the exploitation of nature—a 19th-century preservationist movement and an early 20th-century ethic of conservation of nature.
- The second section describes the rise in the 20th century of a challenge to urban pollution and a movement to protect human health.
- In the third section, I describe the discourse of environmental justice, which contests a view of nature as a place apart from the places where people live and work.
- Finally, the last section identifies the related movements for sustainability and climate justice, addressing global climate change.

Important to contesting the prevailing ideas about nature are **antagonisms.** In everyday language, the term *antagonism* means a *conflict* or *disagreement*. Here, I am using the term more specifically to signal the recognition of the *limit* of an idea, a widely shared viewpoint, or ideology (Laclau & Mouffe, 2001). A limit is recognized when questioning or criticism reveals a prevailing view to be inadequate or unresponsive to new demands. Recognizing this inadequacy creates an opening for alternative voices and ideas to redefine what is appropriate, wise, or ethical—in this case, the relationship between society and the environment. In the history of the U.S. environmental movement, particularly, four major antagonisms define such recognition of limits, where new voices challenged the prevailing views of society:

- Preservation or conservation of nature versus human exploitation of nature
- Human health versus unregulated business and pollution of the *commons* (air, water, and soil)
- Environmental justice versus a view of nature as a place apart from the places where people live and work
- Sustainability or climate justice versus unsustainable social and economic systems

One important note about histories of the U.S. environmental movement is this: Traditional accounts describe the 19th century as an era that focused on protection of wilderness and the post-1960s as a period of awakening to concerns about human health. As Gottlieb (1993b) observed, the problem with this historical divide in recounting the movement is "who is left out and what it fails to explain" (p. 1). Although I follow this standard account to some extent, I also try to bring in who is left out—figures such as Dr. Alice Hamilton (1925), who urged a concern for the "dangerous trades" of urban environments as early as the 1920s. Also, in describing the post-1960s period, I highlight low-income citizens' demands for *environmental justice* as well as new concerns for climate justice in the face of global warming.

Challenging the Exploitation of Nature

By the 21st century, respect for the environment had emerged as a first-tier concern in the United States. Yet, the roots of this achievement lay in centuries-old efforts to transform society's views by challenging its **discourses** about human dominion and the conquest of nature.

Serious questioning of the dominant tradition of loathing wilderness and exploitation of wild nature did not begin until the late 18th century. Puritans such as Michael Wigglesworth (1662), for example, described the dark forests of his era as "a waste and howling wilderness" (p. 83, quoted in Nash, 2001, p. 36). Nevertheless, voices in art, literature, and on the lecture circuits had begun to challenge the view of nature as alien or exploitable. In his classic study, *Wilderness and the American Mind*, Roderick Nash identifies three major sources of these challenges:

(1) *Romantic and primitivist aesthetics in art and literature*—In the 18th and early 19th centuries, English nature poets and aestheticians such as William Gilpin "inspired a rhetorical style for articulating [an] appreciation of uncivilized nature" (Nash, 2001, p. 46). These poets fostered in American art and literature an ideal of sublimity in wild nature. The **sublime** was an aesthetic category that associated God's influence with the feelings of awe and exultation that some experienced in the presence of wilderness. "Combined with the primitivistic idealization of a life closer to nature, these ideas fed the Romantic movement which had far-reaching implications for wilderness" (p. 44).

(2) *A search for U.S. national identity*—Believing that America could not match Europe's history and soaring cathedrals, advocates of a uniquely American identity championed the distinctive characteristics of its landscape. "Nationalists argued that far from being a liability, wilderness was actually an American asset" (p. 67). Writers and artists of the Hudson River school, such as Thomas Cole, celebrated the wonders of the American wilderness by defining a national style in fiction, poetry, and painting. In his 1835 "Essay on American Scenery," for example, Cole argued, "American scenery . . . has features, and glorious ones, unknown to Europe. The most distinctive, and perhaps the most impressive, characteristic of American scenery is its wildness" (quoted in Nash, 2001, pp. 80–81).

(3) *Transcendentalist ideals*—The 19th-century philosophy of **transcendentalism** also proved an important impetus for revaluing wild nature. Transcendentalists held that "natural objects assumed importance because, if rightly seen, they reflected universal spiritual truth" (Nash, 2001, p. 85). Among those who drew upon such beliefs to challenge older discourses about wilderness was the writer and philosopher Henry David Thoreau (1893). Thoreau argued that "in Wildness is the preservation of the World;" and that there exists "a subtle magnetism in Nature, which, if we unconsciously yield to it, will direct us aright" (pp. 251, 265).

By the late 19th century, Thoreau's writings had influenced others, including the Scottish immigrant John Muir, to preserve remnants of the vanishing American wilderness.

John Muir and the Wilderness Preservation Movement

By the 1880s, key figures in California and elsewhere had begun to argue explicitly for the preservation of wilderness areas.[1] Arising out of these efforts were campaigns to protect spectacular regions of natural scenery such as Yosemite Valley in the Sierra Nevada Mountains. **Preservationism** sought to ban commercial use of these areas, instead preserving them for appreciation, study, and outdoor recreation.

One of the leaders of the preservation movement was John Muir, whose literary essays in the 1870s and 1880s did much to arouse national sentiment for preserving Yosemite Valley. Communication scholar Christine Oravec (1981) has observed that Muir's essays evoked a **sublime response** from his readers through his description of the rugged mountains and valleys of the Sierra Nevada. This response on the part of readers was characterized by (a) an immediate awareness of a sublime object (such as Yosemite Valley), (b) a sense of overwhelming personal insignificance and awe in the object's presence, and (c) ultimately a feeling of spiritual exaltation (p. 248).

Muir's influence and the support of others led to a national campaign to preserve Yosemite Valley. By 1890, these efforts had resulted in the U.S. Congress's

| Figure 2.1 | In 1903, John Muir led President Theodore Roosevelt into Yosemite Valley (posing on Overhanging Rock at the top of Glacier Point) as part of his continuing efforts to preserve wilderness areas. |

creation of Yosemite National Park, "the first successful proposal for preservation of natural scenery to gain widespread national attention and support" from the public (Oravec, 1981, p. 256).

Logging of giant redwood trees along California's coast in the 1880s also fueled interest in the preservation movement. Laura White and the California Federation of Women's Clubs were among those who led successful campaigns to protect redwood groves in the late 19th century (Merchant, 2005). As a result of these early campaigns, groups dedicated to wilderness and wildlife preservation began to appear: John Muir's Sierra Club (1892), Audubon Society (1905), Save the Redwoods League (1918), National Parks and Conservation Association (1919), Wilderness Society (1935), and National Wildlife Federation (1936). In the 20th century, these groups launched other preservation campaigns that challenged exploitation of these wild lands. (For a history of this period, see Merchant, 2005, and Warren, 2003.)

Another Viewpoint: The Trouble With Wilderness

The idea of wilderness has been challenged in recent years and appears to conflict with Muir's reverential attitude of the sublime. Historian William Cronon (1996) has argued that wilderness "is quite profoundly a human creation" (p. 69) that diverts attention from the places nearby, where people live and work. Cronon argued:

> The trouble with wilderness is . . . the illusion that we can somehow wipe clean the slate of our past and return to the tabula rasa that supposedly existed before we began to leave our marks on the world. . . . This, then, is the central paradox: Wilderness embodies a dualistic vision in which the human is entirely outside the natural. If we allow ourselves to believe that nature, to be true, must also be wild, then our very presence in nature represents its fall. The place where we are is the place where nature is not. (pp. 80–81)

Interestingly, Cronon is arguing not for the elimination of wild areas but for a questioning of the idea embraced in some understandings of the term *wilderness* as a place beyond human presence. Such a view, he argues, devalues the places where humans are.

Conservation: Wise Use of Natural Resources

Muir's ethic of preservation clashed with a competing vision that sought to manage America's forests for efficient and sustainable use. Influenced by the philosophy of **utilitarianism,** the idea of the greatest good for the greatest number, some in the early 20th century began to promote a new conservation ethic. Associated principally with Gifford Pinchot, President Theodore Roosevelt's chief of the Division of Forestry (now the U.S. Forest Service), the term *conservation* meant "the wise and efficient use of natural resources" (Merchant, 2005, p. 128). For example, in managing public forest lands as a source of timber, Pinchot instituted a sustained yield policy, according to which logged timberlands were to be reforested after cutting, to ensure future timber supplies (Hays, 1989; Merchant, 2005.)

The tension between Muir's ethic of preservation and Pinchot's conservation approach came to a head in the fierce controversy over the building of a dam in Hetch Hetchy Valley in Yosemite National Park. In 1901, the City of San Francisco's proposal to dam the river running through this valley as a source for its water sparked a multiyear dispute over the purpose of the new park. This conflict between aesthetic and practical values of wild areas would continue long after the Hetch Hetchy dam was approved in 1913.

In the following decades, Pinchot's conservation approach strongly influenced the management of natural resources by agencies such as the Forest Service and the Bureau of Land Management (BLM). Preservationists, however, also won significant victories. One major accomplishment was the National Parks Act of 1916, which established a national system of parks that continues to expand today. Other designations of parks, wildlife refuges, and wild and scenic rivers would follow into the 21st century. Preservationists' most significant victory was the 1964 Wilderness Act. It authorizes Congress to set aside wild areas in national forests and other public lands to preserve their "primeval character and influence" (Warren, 2003, p. 243). (For another viewpoint, see "The Trouble With Wilderness.")

The tension between the discourses of wilderness preservation and conservation continues to be a feature in some current debates. As early as the 1980s, a split had developed in the U.S. movement as a result of the perceived failure of mainstream green groups to preserve more wild lands. Disillusioned wilderness activists formed the radical group Earth First! to engage in **direct action,** or physical acts of protests, such as road blockades, sit-ins, and **tree spiking**[2] to prevent logging in old growth forests. Other groups, such as the Earth Liberation Front, turned for a while to arson and property damage in a controversial effort to protect the shrinking habitat of endangered species.

Today, both regional and national environmental groups in the United States continue to press for measures of protection for the nation's remaining wild areas, while different economic interests—logging and mining companies, real estate developers, and others—also seek access to many of these same areas. Still other groups have continued to voice a more critical rhetoric, contesting many core values of contemporary society from a biocentric perspective, sometimes called Deep Ecology (deepecology .org), and from a feminist or ecofeminist perspective. *Ecofeminism* is a diverse cultural and political movement that sees parallels between the oppression of women and the degradation of nature. (For an introduction, see www.ecofem.org.) (I'll return to this idea of *critical rhetoric* in Chapter 8.)

Internationally, environmental, indigenous, and climate justice groups have also campaigned for the protection of remaining large areas of forests, both for their importance for habitat and the homes of indigenous peoples and also for their importance in mitigating or slowing climate change. For example, scientists, environmental activists, and advocates for indigenous peoples like the Coalition of Rainforest Nations have succeeded in gaining some measure of protection through the United Nation's program, Reducing Emissions from Deforestation and Forest Degradation (REDD). Using financial incentives, REDD encourages developing nations not to cut their forests. Although a major goal is to reduce carbon dioxide (CO_2) emissions from deforestation, the protection of these areas also preserves biodiversity, natural resources, and communal areas for forest communities. Overall, the contemporary movement to protect wild nature consists of a broad and diverse range of both voices and strategies for the protection of wild nature.

Public Health and Pollution of the Commons

By the 1960s, a second antagonism had arisen in the United States that contested an accepted view of nature as a space in which an industrialized society could simply dispose of its air or water pollutants. At a time when environmental protections for the *commons* (air, water, and the soil) were weak or nonexistent, citizens began to question the effects of urban pollution, nuclear fallout, and chemical pesticides on human health. Their concerns included the air and water emissions from factories and refineries, abandoned toxic waste sites, exposure to pesticides used on agricultural crops, and the radioactive fallout from aboveground nuclear testing.

Traditional accounts of the U.S. environmental movement credit biologist and writer Rachel Carson for voicing the first public challenge to business practices that affect the natural environment and human health. In her book *Silent Spring*, Carson (1962) wrote, "We are adding a . . . new kind of havoc—the direct killing of birds, mammals, fishes, and indeed, practically every form of wildlife by chemical insecticides indiscriminately sprayed on the land" (p. 83). Fearful of the consequences for human health from insecticides like DDT, she warned that modern agribusiness had "armed itself with the most modern and terrible weapons, and that in turning them against the insects it has also turned them against the earth" (p. 262).

With her prescient writings, Rachel Carson is widely considered the founder of the modern environmental movement. Although *Silent Spring* did prefigure a popular movement, earlier voices from the 1880s through the 1920s had warned of dangers to human health from poor sanitation and occupational exposures to lead and other chemicals. Trade unions, *sanitarians*, or reformers from Jane Addams's Hull House in Chicago, and public health advocates had warned of hazards to both workplace and urban life: "contaminated water supplies, inadequate waste and sewage collection disposal, poor ventilation and polluted and smoke-filled air, [and] overcrowded neighborhoods and tenements" (Gottlieb, 1993a, p. 55).

Urban environmental historian Robert Gottlieb (1993a) has called attention particularly to the influence of Dr. Alice Hamilton, "a powerful environmental advocate in an era when the term had yet to be invented" (p. 51), who worked in the 1920s to reform the "dangerous trades" of urban workplaces. With the publication of *Industrial Poisons in the United States* and her work with the Women's Health Bureau, Hamilton (1925) became "the country's most powerful and effective voice for exploring the environmental consequences of industrial activity," including the impacts of occupational hazards on women and minorities in the workplace (p. 51).

Still, until *Silent Spring* in 1962, there was no such thing as an environmental movement in the United States in the sense of a "concerted, populous, vocal, influential, active" force (Sale, 1993, p. 6). However, by the late 1960s, news coverage of air pollution, nuclear fallout, fires on the Cuyahoga River near Cleveland when its polluted surface ignited, and oil spills off the coast of Santa Barbara, California, fueled a public outcry for greater protection of the environment. By the first **Earth Day** on April 22, 1970, students, public health workers, activist groups, and urban workers had coalesced into a movement to champion environmental controls on industrial pollution. Some 20 million people took part in protests, teach-ins, and festivals throughout the country in one of the largest demonstrations in American history.

At the same time, new groups arose to address the relationship between human health and the environment. Among the earliest were the Environmental Defense Fund (1967), Environmental Action (1970), and the Natural Resources Defense Council (1970). Finally, the popularity of the *ecology movement*—the term used in the 1970s—led lawmakers to enact new legislation to strengthen protections for air and water quality and to regulate production and disposal of toxic chemicals.

By the end of the 1970s, concerns about health also arose at the local level. Communities became increasingly worried by the chemical contamination of their air, drinking water, soil, and school grounds. For example, the small New York community of Love Canal became a symbol of the nation's widening consciousness of the hazards of chemicals. (See the brief description of the Love Canal case in Chapter 1.) Ordinary citizens felt themselves surrounded by what Hays (1989) termed the "toxic 'sea around us' " (p. 171) and began to organize in community-based groups to demand cleanup of their neighborhoods and stricter accountability of corporate polluters.

Prompted by the toxic waste scandals at Love Canal and other places, such as Times Beach, Missouri, the U.S. Congress passed the **Superfund** law of 1980, which authorized the Environmental Protection Agency (EPA) to clean up toxic sites and take action against the polluting parties. Local citizens also took advantage of new federal laws such as the Clean Water Act to participate in agencies' issuance of air and water permits for businesses. (I describe these guarantees for public participation in Chapter 3.)

Environmental Justice: Challenging Nature as a Place Apart

Even as the environmental movement widened its concerns in the 1960s to include public health along with wilderness preservation, there remained a language of the environment that provided contradictory accounts of humans' place in nature and assumed a "long-standing separation of the social from the ecological" (Gottlieb, 2002, p. 5). By the 1980s, however, new activists from low-income groups and communities of color had begun to challenge the view of nature as a place apart from where people lived and worked, disclosing a third antagonism in prevailing views of the environment.

Figure 2.2 By the late 1960s, news coverage of urban air and water pollution and other problems fueled a public outcry for greater protection of the environment.

© iStockphoto.com/Victor Melniciuc

Redefining the Meaning of *Environment*

Despite earlier efforts to bring environmentalist, labor, civil rights, and religious leaders together in the 1960s and 1970s[3], environmental groups largely failed to recognize the problems of urban residents and minority communities. Sociologist Giovanna Di Chiro (1996) reported, for example, that in the mid-1980s, residents in south central Los Angeles who were trying to stop a solid waste incinerator from being located in their neighborhood discovered that "these issues were not deemed adequately 'environmental' by local environmental groups" (p. 299). Activists in communities of color were particularly vocal in criticizing mainstream environmental groups for being "reluctant to address issues of equity and social justice, within the context of the environment" (Alston, 1990, p. 23).

By the 1980s, activists in some low-income neighborhoods and communities of color had started to take matters into their own hands. In a historically significant move, many proposed to rearticulate or redefine the word *environment* to mean the places "where we live, where we work, where we play, and where we learn" (Lee, 1996, p. 6).

A key moment in the launching of this new movement occurred in 1982 with the protests by residents of the largely African-American community of Warren County, North Carolina. Local residents and leaders of national civil rights groups tried to halt the state's plans to locate a toxic waste landfill in this rural community by sitting in roads to block 6,000 trucks carrying polychlorinated biphenol (PCB)-contaminated soil.[4] More than 500 protesters were arrested in what sociologists Robert Bullard and Beverly Hendrix Wright (1987) called "the first national attempt by blacks to link environmental issues (hazardous waste and pollution) to the mainstream civil rights agenda" (p. 32). (For more on the significance of this event as a *story of origin* in the movement, see Pezzullo, 2001.)

With similar struggles in other parts of the nation and reports of the heavy concentration of hazardous facilities in minority neighborhoods, some charged that these communities suffered from a form of **environmental racism** (Sandler & Pezzullo, 2007, p. 4) or more broadly as **environmental injustice** (Roberts, 2007, p. 289). Residents and critics alike began to speak of being poisoned and "dumped upon" and of certain communities targeted as "sacrifice zones" (Schueler, 1992, p. 45). Importantly for these critics, the term *environmental racism* meant not only threats to their health from hazardous waste landfills, incinerators, agricultural pesticides, sweatshops, and polluting factories but also the disproportionate burden that these practices placed on people of color and the workers and residents of low-income communities.

Envisioning Environmental Justice

Emerging from these struggles was a robust vision of **environmental justice.** For most activists, this term connected the safety and quality of the environments where people lived and worked with concerns for social and economic justice. Residents and movement activists insisted that environmental justice referred to the basic right of all people to be free of poisons and other hazards. At its core, environmental justice also was a vision of the democratic inclusion of people and communities in the decisions that affect their health and well-being. Many people criticized decision-making processes that failed to provide meaningful participation "for those most burdened by environmental decisions" and called for at-risk communities to share more fully in those decisions that adversely impact their communities (Cole & Foster, 2001, p. 16; Gerrard & Foster, 2008).

The demand for environmental justice received significant publicity in 1991, when delegates from local communities, along with national leaders of civil rights, religious, and environmental groups, convened in Washington, DC, for the first People of Color Environmental Leadership Summit. For the first time, different strands of the emerging movement for environmental justice came together to challenge mainstream definitions of environmentalism. The delegates also adopted a powerful set of **Principles**

| Figure 2.3 | Environmental justice is a vision of the democratic inclusion of people and communities in the decisions that affect their health and well-being. Activists demand decision-makers "listen to the people" during a protest as experts hold UN climate talks, on December 3, 2011, in Durban, South Africa. |

AFP/Getty Images

of Environmental Justice that enumerated a series of rights, including "the fundamental right to political, economic, cultural, and environmental self-determination of all peoples" (*Proceedings*, 1991, p. viii).

☞ **FYI** **Principles of Environmental Justice (1991)**

The following are excerpts from the 1991 text adopted by delegates to the First People of Color Environmental Leadership Summit, Washington, DC.

WE, THE PEOPLE OF COLOR, gathered together at this multinational People of Color Environmental Leadership Summit, to begin to build a national and international movement of all peoples of color to fight the destruction and taking of our lands and communities . . . do affirm and adopt these Principles of Environmental Justice:

1) Environmental Justice affirms the sacredness of Mother Earth, ecological unity and the interdependence of all species, and the right to be free from ecological destruction.

(Continued)

(Continued)

2) Environmental Justice demands that public policy be based on mutual respect and justice for all peoples, free from any form of discrimination or bias. . . .

3) Environmental Justice demands the right to participate as equal partners at every level of decision-making, including needs assessment, planning, implementation, enforcement and evaluation.

4) Environmental Justice affirms the right of all workers to a safe and healthy work environment without being forced to choose between an unsafe livelihood and unemployment. It also affirms the right of those who work at home to be free from environmental hazards.

5) Environmental Justice protects the right of victims of environmental injustice to receive full compensation and reparations for damages as well as quality health care. . . .

6) Environmental Justice affirms the need for urban and rural ecological policies to clean up and rebuild our cities and rural areas in balance with nature, honoring the cultural integrity of all our communities, and provides fair access for all to the full range of resources. . . .

SOURCE: "Principles of Environmental Justice" at: www.ejnet.org/ej/principles.html.

In 1994, the movement achieved an important goal when President Clinton issued an executive order directing each federal agency to "make achieving environmental justice part of its mission by identifying and addressing . . . disproportionately high and adverse human health or environmental effects of its programs, policies, and activities on minority populations and low-income populations in the United States" (Clinton, 1994, p. 7629). Nevertheless, the movement continues to face real-world, on-the-ground challenges to building sustainable and healthy communities. (I describe the movement for environmental justice in more detail in Chapter 9.)

Movements for Sustainability and Climate Justice

Over the past two decades, a diverse movement has grown in many countries. Throughout Europe, Asia, North and South America, Africa, Australia, and the Pacific Islands, countless numbers of local and regional groups have challenged unsustainable and inequitable practices in their societies. These challenges often are similar to the antagonisms described earlier—efforts to protect natural systems, safeguard human health, and secure social justice. In his remarkable account, *Blessed Unrest*, Paul Hawken (2007) describes these diverse efforts:

> It is composed of families in India, students in Australia, farmers in France, the landless in Brazil, the Bananeras of Honduras, the "poors" of Durban, villagers in Irían Jaya, indigenous tribes of Bolivia, and housewives in Japan. . . . These groups defend against corrupt politics and climate change, corporate predation and the death of oceans, governmental indifference and pandemic poverty, industrial forestry and farming, and depletion of soil and water. (pp. 11, 164–165)

These and thousands of other efforts reflect diverse agendas and methods of communication. Yet, running through all is the growing recognition of a "limit" or the unsustainability of "the currently disruptive relationship between earth's two most complex systems—human culture and the living world" (Hawken, 2007, p. 172).

A fourth antagonism has, therefore, begun to emerge—the challenge of building a more sustainable world in the face of disruptive or unsustainable social and economic systems. ***Sustainability*** is admittedly an elusive term. For some, the sustainability movement "is nothing less than a rethinking and remaking of our role in the natural world. It is a recalibration of human intentions to coincide with the way the biophysical world works" (Edwards, 2005, p. xiv). For many, the movement encompasses three goals or aspirations—environmental protection, economic health, and equity or social justice—often called the Three Es (Edwards, 2005, p. 17).

For climate scientists, sustainability refers to the relationship between sources of global energy and biological systems, including human societies. As a consequence, they and environmental activists are critical of the unrestrained growth of carbon-based economies, often called a **business as usual (BAU)** scenario of the future. Carbon is the energy source—primarily fossil fuels such as oil, coal, and natural gas—used by human societies to produce electricity, fuel transportation, and sustain other dimensions of life. Questioning these energy sources has been important because scientists believe there is an increased warming of the Earth due principally to the emissions (CO_2) caused by combustion of fossil fuels as well as other so-called greenhouse gases.

That the Earth is warming is no longer in doubt. The United Nations Intergovernmental Panel on Climate Change (2007) determined that warming of the Earth's climate is now "unequivocal" (p. 30). Furthermore, it has warned that such anthropogenic (human-caused) emissions are "very likely" the cause of the increase in global average temperatures since the mid-20th century (p. 39).

As a result, growing numbers of scientists, health officials, and students and many grassroots groups are questioning the BAU or unsustainable approach to economic growth. This is because the impacts of a rapidly warming climate are already occurring in many regions. These include:

- Melting of glaciers, Arctic sea ice, and permafrost
- Decline in snow-fed rivers and water sources in North and South America, Asia, and Africa
- Decline of coral reefs and increased acidity of oceans
- Sustained droughts and heat waves in parts of the United States, Africa, and other areas
- Migration (and increased extinction) of plant and animal species

And, with greater warming, severe consequences for human health and well-being are appearing: spreading disease, failures of crops, flooding of populated regions, heat-related deaths, and regional conflicts over scarce resources. (For further information, see the Intergovernmental Panel on Climate Change's *Climate Change 2007: Synthesis Report* at www.ipcc.ch/ipccreports.)

| Figure 2.4 | Students, concerned citizens, local groups, and other activists are connecting globally through social networking sites and organizing locally to demand climate justice and action on climate change. |

AP Photo/Pat Roque

In response, a movement for climate justice has emerged, urging local and global leaders to take immediate action. (For more details on the climate justice movement, see Chapter 9.) In the United States, student activism, TV ads, and campaigns by environmental organizations have raised the alarm and set off a public debate over U.S. energy policy. Both in the United States and globally, tens of thousands of activists and local groups are connecting through social networking sites such as 350.0rg, http://itsgettinghotinhere.org, and the Climate Action Network (climatenetwork .org). And scientists, concerned about the slowness of governmental response, have spoken publicly. In a series of reports, the U.S. National Research Council advised the U.S. Congress that, "climate change . . . poses significant risks for a broad range of human and natural systems" (Top U.S. scientists, 2010, para. 2).

Act Locally!

Local Resources and the Four Antagonisms

There are undoubtedly many resources on your campus or in your community—faculty, community leaders, activists, and other professionals—who are knowledgeable about one or more of the four antagonisms described in this chapter—wilderness and natural resource protection, public health and environmental pollution, environmental justice, and climate change.

Invite someone with knowledge about or personal experience in one of these areas to visit your class or campus organization. Ask them to speak about the specific antagonism you've chosen, that is, speak about the efforts by individuals, groups, or movements to contest prevailing views and raise awareness among wider publics about the protection of natural areas, the effects of air or water pollution on public health, the persistence of environmental racism in society, and so forth. Among the questions you might ask these individuals, consider these:

- How did you come to study (or be engaged with) this issue? What do you find most interesting, troublesome, or significant?
- What progress has been made in addressing this problem, and what are the most difficult challenges remaining?
- What role has communication, specially, played in either perpetuating the problem or in helping to raise awareness or bring about change?
- What resources exist locally, and how can you become more involved with this issue?

As we've seen in the development of these four antagonisms, the concepts of nature and the environment are highly contingent. That is, they are subject to redefinition as new voices and interests contest prevailing understandings of the natural world and our human environments. The core of these challenges is a distinctly rhetorical process of human influence, questioning, and persuasion, and it is this social–symbolic construction of nature and the environment that I'll explore in the following chapter.

SUMMARY

In this chapter, I've described four historical periods in which individuals and groups contested the dominant ideas of society about nature or the environment.

- The questioning of society's prevailing views creates an antagonism or the recognition of the limit of this idea, viewpoint, or ideology. A limit is recognized when questioning or contesting a prevailing view reveals it to be inadequate or unresponsive to new demand, and, therefore, creates an opening for alternative voices and ideas.
- In U.S. history, there have been four major antagonisms in response to society's prevailing views about nature or the environment:
  1. The late 19th- and early 20th-century questioning of nature as repugnant by advocates wishing to preserve the wilderness and by others who articulated an ethic of conservation or efficient use of natural resources.
  2. The appearance of a movement in the early and later 20th century that criticized a system of poorly regulated industrial behavior, which contributed to human health problems from chemical contamination and other forms of air and water pollution.

3. A community-based movement for environmental justice, arising in the 1980s that challenged mainstream views of nature as a place apart from the places where people work, live, learn, and play.

4. A demand for sustainability and climate justice to alter society's business as usual (BAU) model of unsustainable economic growth in the face of global climate change and degradation of natural systems.

These four antagonisms reveal the highly contingent nature of our understanding and viewpoints about nature and the environment. Pivotal to these different views and our ability to contest them is a powerful process of social–symbolic construction of nature and what we consider to be an environmental problem. I'll describe this social construction of the environment in the next chapter.

SUGGESTED RESOURCES

- Paul Hawken, *Blessed Unrest: How the Largest Social Movement in History Is Restoring Grace, Justice, and Beauty to the World.* New York: Penguin Books, 2007.
- Philip Shabecoff, *A Fierce Green Fire: The American Environmental Movement.* (Rev. ed.). Washing, DC: Island Press, 2003.
- Luke W. Cole and Sheila R. Foster, *From the Ground Up: Environmental Racism and the Rise of the Environmental Justice Movement.* New York: New York University Press, 2001.
- Roderick Frazier Nash, *Wilderness and the American mind* (4th ed.). New Haven, CT: Yale University Press, 2001.
- Rachel Carson website at Rachelcarson.org, and the DVD, *American Experience: Rachel Carson's Silent Spring.*

KEY TERMS

Antagonism   40

Business as
   usual (BAU)   51

Conservation   43

Direct action   44

Discourse   41

Earth Day   46

Environmental justice   48

Environmental
   racism (and more
   broadly, environmental
   injustice)   48

Preservationism   42

Principles of Environmental
   Justice   49

Sublime   41

Sublime response   42

Superfund   46

Sustainability   51

Transcendentalism   41

Tree spiking   44

Utilitarianism   43

DISCUSSION QUESTIONS

1. Is wilderness merely a symbolic construction? Does this matter?

2. Attempts to set standards or regulate businesses to protect the environment periodically face opposition in the U.S. Congress. Where do you stand on government environmental regulations such as restrictions on CO_2 and other pollutants
from coal-burning power plants?

3. Do you believe the concentration of polluting industries such as oil refineries
and chemical manufacturing plants in low-income areas or communities of
color is a form of environmental racism? If so, where should they be located?

4. The prospect of global climate change seems unstoppable; indeed, the impacts of
climate disruptions are already being experienced. How likely is it that a successful antagonism can be created by a movement for climate justice? Can alternative
voices and views ever make an impact on global economies sufficient to change
the forms of energy societies use for modern life?

NOTES

1. In 1872, President Ulysses S. Grant signed a law designating 2 million acres for Yellowstone
National Park, the nation's first national park. And, 13 years later, the state of New York set aside
715,000 acres in its Adirondack Mountains. Still, these first acts were less motivated by an aesthetic
or spiritual appreciation of wilderness than by a desire to protect against land speculation and a
need to protect forest watersheds for New York City's drinking water (Nash, 2001, p. 108).

2. Tree spiking is the practice of driving spikes or long nails into some trees in an area that is
scheduled to be logged. The metal or, sometimes, plastic—spikes do not actually hurt the trees.
Tree spiking can discourage loggers from cutting the trees because of possible damage to their
chain saws or, later, to the machinery in timber mills when saw blades strike the hidden spikes.

3. The 1971 Urban Environment Conference (UEC) was one of the first successful efforts to
link environmental and social justice concerns. The UEC sought "to help broaden the way the public defined environmental issues and to focus on the particular environmental problems of urban
minorities" (Gottlieb, 1993a, pp. 262–263; Kazis & Grossman, 1991, p. 247).

4. Although the State of North Carolina completed the landfill in Warren County in 1982, local
activists persisted in calling for its detoxification. Two decades later, in 2004, their efforts finally paid
off when the state cleaned up the landfill.

REFERENCES

Alston, D. (1990). *We speak for ourselves: Social justice, race, and environment.* Washington, DC: Panos Institute.

Bradford, W. (1952). *Of Plymouth plantation, 1620–1647.* (S. E. Morison, Ed.). New York: Knopf. (Originally published 1898)

Bullard, R., & Wright, B. H. (1987). Environmentalism and the politics of equity: Emergent trends in the black community. *Midwestern Review of Sociology, 12,* 21–37.

Carson, R. (1962). *Silent spring.* Boston: Houghton Mifflin.

Clinton, W. J. (1994, February 16). Federal actions to address environmental justice in minority populations and low-income communities. Executive Order 12898 *printed in the Federal Register, 59,* 7629.

Cole, L. W., & Foster, S. R. (2001). *From the ground up: Environmental racism and the rise of the environmental justice movement.* New York: New York University Press.

Cronon, W. (1996). The trouble with wilderness, or, getting back to the wrong nature. In W. Cronon (Ed.), *Uncommon ground: Rethinking the human place in nature* (pp. 69–90). New York: Norton.

Di Chiro, G. (1996). Nature as community: The convergence of environment and social justice. In W. Cronon (Ed.), *Uncommon ground: Rethinking the human place in nature* (pp. 298–320). New York: Norton.

Edwards, A. R. (2005). *The sustainability revolution: Portrait of a paradigm shift.* Gabriola Island, BC, Canada: New Society.

Gerrad, M. B., & Foster, S. R. (Eds.). (2008). *The law of environmental justice* (2nd ed.). Chicago: American Bar Association.

Gottlieb, R. (1993a). *Forcing the spring: The transformation of the American environmental movement.* Washington, DC: Island Press.

Gottlieb, R. (1993b). Reconstructing environmentalism: Complex movements, diverse roots. *Environmental History Review, 17*(4), 1–19.

Gottlieb, R. (2002). *Environmentalism unbound: Exploring new pathways for change.* Cambridge, MA: MIT Press.

Hamilton, A. (1925). *Industrial poisons in the United States.* New York: Macmillan.

Hawken, P. (2007). *Blessed unrest: How the largest social movement in history is restoring grace, justice, and beauty to the world.* New York: Penguin Books.

Hays, S. P. (1989). *Beauty, health, and permanence: Environmental politics in the United States, 1955–1985.* Cambridge, UK: Cambridge University Press.

Intergovernmental Panel on Climate Change. (2007). *Climate change 2007: Synthesis report.* United Nations Environment Program. Retrieved November 2, 2008, from www. ipcc.ch/ipccreports

Kazis, R., & Grossman, R. L. (1991). *Fear at work: Job blackmail, labor and the environment* (New ed.). Philadelphia: New Society.

Laclau, E., & Mouffe, C. (2001). *Hegemony and socialist strategy: Toward a radical democracy* (2nd ed.). London: Verso.

Lee, C. (1996). Environment: Where we live, work, play, and learn. *Race, Poverty, and the Environment, 6,* 6.

Merchant, C. (2005). *The Columbia guide to American environmental history.* New York: Columbia University Press.

Nash, R. F. (2001). *Wilderness and the American mind* (4th ed.). New Haven, CT: Yale University Press.

Oravec, C. (1981). John Muir, Yosemite, and the sublime response: A study in the rhetoric of preservationism. *Quarterly Journal of Speech, 67,* 245–258.

Pezzullo, P. C. (2001). Performing critical interruptions: Rhetorical invention and narratives of the environmental justice movement. *Western Journal of Communication, 64,* 1–25.

Proceedings: The first national people of color environmental leadership summit. (1991, October 24–27). Washington, DC: United Church of Christ Commission for Racial Justice.

Roberts, J. T. (2007). Globalizing environmental justice. In R. Sandler & P. C. Pezzullo (Eds.), *Environmental justice and environmentalism: The social justice challenge to the environmental movement* (pp. 285–307). Cambridge, MA: MIT Press.

Sale, K. (1993). *The green revolution: The American environmental movement 1962–1992.* New York: Hill & Wang.

Sandler, R., & Pezzullo, P. C. (Eds.). (2007). *Environmental justice and environmentalism: The social justice challenge to the environmental movement.* Cambridge, MA: MIT Press.

Schueler, D. (1992). Southern exposure. *Sierra, 77,* 45–47.

Thoreau, H. D. (1893). Walking. In *Excursions: The writings of Henry David Thoreau* (Riverside ed., Vol. 9, pp. 251–304). Boston: Houghton Mifflin. (Original work published 1862)

Top U.S. scientists warn Congress on the dangers of climate change. (2010, May 20). *PhysicsWorld.com.* Retrieved September 17, 2010, from http://physicsworld.com/

United Nations. (2011). International year of forests—2011. Retrieved October 29, 2011, from http://www.un.org/en

Warren, L. S. (Ed.). (2003). *American environmental history.* Oxford, UK: Basil Blackwell.

Wigglesworth, M. (1662). God's controversy with New England. In *Proceedings of the Massachusetts Historical Society, 12* (1871), 83, in Nash (2001, p. 36).

Our language (terministic screens) powerfully shapes or mediates our experiences—what is selected for notice, what is deflected from notice, and therefore how we perceive the environment.

CHAPTER 3

Social–Symbolic Constructions of Environment

Symbolic and natural systems are mutually constituted. . .

—DePoe (2006, p. vii)

I think people have this insatiable desire to point at and name things. "Oh, that's a . . ." or "What is that?"

—Whale tour boat captain
(quoted in Milstein, 2011, p. 4)

As we saw in the in the last chapter, society's perceptions of nature are highly contingent. That is, our views about the environment may change as new voices and interests arise to contest or challenge prevailing understandings. The core of these challenges is a distinctly human process of construction, questioning, and persuasion, and it is this social–symbolic perspective that I explore in this chapter. This perspective builds on our definition of environmental communication in Chapter 1 as both a pragmatic and constitutive vehicle for our understanding of the environment as well as our relationships to the natural world.

Chapter Preview

- In the first section, I introduce a social constructionist understanding of nature and introduce two perspectives:

    (1) Use of terministic screens and naming

    (2) The construction of environmental issues as problems

(Continued)

(Continued)

- In the second section, I describe a rhetorical perspective on environmental communication and three dimensions of this approach:

  (1) Rhetorical tropes and genres

  (2) Communication frames

  (3) Dominant and critical discourses

- The final part of this chapter, "Visual Rhetoric," describes the ways in which photographs, art, and film can affect attitudes and behavior toward nature; I describe two aspects of visual rhetoric:

  (1) The ways in which visual images (re)present nature

  (2) Visualizing environmental problems

These different meanings of "environment" also illustrate the constitutive function of language, as well as the social and symbolic resources available to those who have challenged the dominant ideas of society about the natural world. In the following section, I'll explore this constitutive role and then introduce a "rhetorical" perspective on environmental communication.

The Social–Symbolic Construction of Nature

By late 20th century, scholars such as Donna Haraway (1991), Andrew Ross (1994), Klaus Eder (1996a), Bruno Latour (2004), and Neil Evernden (1992) had begun to describe the discursive constructions that shape our views of nature. This **social–symbolic perspective** focuses on the sources that constitute or construct our perceptions of what we consider to be natural or an environmental problem. For example, Herndl and Brown (1996) argue that "environment" is "a concept and an associated set of cultural values that we have constructed through the way we use language. In a very real sense, there is no objective environment in the phenomenal world, no environment separate from the words we use to represent it" (p. 3).

This is not to suggest that there is no material world out there. Of course, there is. But, it is through different social and symbolic modes that we understand and engage this world, infuse it with significance, and act toward it. As Depoe (2006), editor of the journal *Environmental Communication: A Journal of Nature and Culture* put it, "Symbolic and natural systems are mutually constituted" (p. vii). The natural world affects us, but our language and other symbolic action also have the capacity to affect or construct our perceptions of nature itself.

Terministic Screens and Naming

A similar recognition of this constitutive function appears within the field of rhetorical studies. For example, Kenneth Burke (1966) used the metaphor of **terministic screens** to describe the way our language orients us to see certain things, some aspects of the world, and not others: "If any given terminology is a reflection of reality, by its very nature as a terminology it must be a selection of reality; and to this extent it must function also as a deflection of reality" (p. 45). That is, our language (terministic screens) powerfully shapes or mediates our experiences—what is selected for notice, what is deflected from notice, and therefore how we perceive our world. As a result, whenever we speak or write, we actively participate in constituting our world.

One important dimension of this function of language is **naming**—the means by which we socially represent objects or people and therefore know the world, including the natural world. The act of pointing and naming something out there in the world, as Milstein (2011) reminds us, is "a foundational act"; pointing and naming are "the basic entry to socially discerning and categorizing parts of nature" (p. 4). And, in doing so, naming also indicates "an orientation" to the world and thus "influences our interaction with it" (Oravec, 2004, p. 3).

A striking example of the use of naming was the successful campaign by the Water Environment Federation (WEF) to rename sewage sludge as *biosolids*. (The WEF is a trade association that works with sewage treatment plants and other water facilities.) In the process of treating sewage, a sludge-like material is typically left over. This substance (which sometimes contains toxic chemicals such as dioxin) is often used as fertilizer on agricultural fields. As a result, many environmental and health groups have raised concerns about the risk from the chemicals found in sewage sludge.

Industry critic Seldon Rampton described the efforts of WEF in the 1990s to coin another term for sludge "in hope of escaping its negative connation" and, in the words of a WEF spokesperson, "to win public acceptance for the beneficial use of biosolids" (quoted in Rampton, 2002, p. 348). The campaign also succeeded in having biosolids placed in the *Merriam-Webster Dictionary*. A WEF official reported at the time that he was "pleased that the term 'sludge' will not appear in the definition of biosolids" (quoted in Rampton, 2002, p. 349). Today, WEF's website (www.wef.org/) describes biosolids as "the nutrient-rich organic materials resulting from the treatment of domestic waste at a wastewater treatment facility."

Constructing an Environmental Problem

As we've just seen, we may be alarmed (toxic sludge) or reassured (biosolids) as a result of the selective naming that constructs the issue or problem at hand. German sociologist Klaus Eder (1996b) explains that often it is "the methods of communicating environmental conditions and ideas, and not the state of deterioration itself, which explain . . . the emergence of a public discourse on the environment" (p. 209). This is

| **Figure 3.1** | Are biosolids good for fertilizing fields? How about sewage sludge? Here biosolids are spread on an agricultural field in the Mississippi Delta. |

Tinkerbrad/Flickr

particularly important in communication that names an environmental problem. Political scientist Deborah Stone (2002) observed that problems "are not given, out there in the world waiting for smart analysts to come along and define them correctly. They are created in the minds of citizens by other citizens, leaders, organizations, and government agencies" (p. 156).

The social–symbolic construction of nature arises from this ability to characterize certain facts or conditions one way rather than another and, therefore, to name it as a problem or not a problem. It is for precisely this reason that questions of "how and why certain environmental issues become identified as 'problems'" are such an important part of environmental communication (Tindall, 1995, p. 49). For example, climate skeptics who don't believe humans play any influence on global warming deny it is a problem; instead, they attribute any warming to natural causes: "Climate is always changing. We have had ice ages and warmer periods when alligators were found in Spitzbergen" (Lindzen, 2009, para. 1).

The environment, then, is something that we know, at least partly, through language and other symbols. The history we reviewed in Chapter 2 also made clear that different choices are possible and that these choices construct diverse meanings for the worlds we know. As a result, some scholars adopt a more specifically rhetorical perspective to study the different language choices by which journalists, scientists, corporations, environmentalists, and citizens attempt to influence our perceptions and behaviors toward the environment.

In the following section, I introduce the concept of rhetoric and also describe some of the rhetorical resources used by the environmental movement and its opponents, including rhetorical genres of melodrama and apocalypse. Finally, in the last section, I'll explore *visual rhetorics*—art, photos, film, and other image-based communications.

A Rhetorical Perspective

The study of rhetoric traces its origins to classical Greek philosopher–teachers such as Isocrates (436–338 BCE) and Aristotle (384–322 BCE), who taught the arts of citizenship to political leaders in democratic city–states such as Athens. The practice in these city–states was for citizens to speak publicly in law courts and the political assembly, where each citizen represented his own interests. (In Athens and other cities, civic speech was limited principally to native-born, property-owning, male citizens.) As a result, competency in public speaking, debate, and persuasion was vital for conducting civic business—war and peace, taxes, construction of public monuments, property claims, and so forth.

It was during this period that Aristotle summarized the teachings in the art of civic speaking when he defined **rhetoric** as the ability of discovering "in any given case the available means of persuasion" (Herrick, 2009, p. 77). This art of rhetoric rested not simply on skillful delivery but on the ability to discover the resources for persuasion that were available in a specific situation. This draws our attention to rhetoric as a purposeful choice among the available means of persuasion useful in accomplishing some effect or outcome. As a result, we can say that a **rhetorical perspective** focuses on purposeful and consequential efforts to influence society's attitudes and behavior through communication, including public debate, protests, advertising, and other modes of symbolic action (Campbell & Huxman, 2008).

Although rhetoric traditionally has been viewed as an instrumental or pragmatic activity—persuading others—its use clearly has a second function: The purposeful use of language also helps to shape (or constitute) our perception of the world itself. A rhetorical perspective, then, invites us to be sensitive to this deeper meaning, even as we identify the more pragmatic, available means used in communication about the environment. Let's look at a few of these rhetorical resources.

Rhetorical Tropes and Genres

The efforts of citizens, environmental groups, and others to educate, persuade, and mobilize draw on the resources of language itself. Rhetorical scholars explore a range of such resources—argumentation, narrative accounts, emotional appeals, tropes, and rhetorical genres—in websites, films, campaign materials, ads, and other communication in environmental controversies. Let's look briefly at two of these resources: tropes and rhetorical genres.

Among the most ubiquitous resources of language are **tropes.** Rhetorical tropes refer to the use of words that turn a meaning from its original sense in a new direction for a persuasive purpose. Tropes draw on a basic function of language itself. There is "no un-rhetorical 'naturalness' of language," 19th-century philosopher Friedrich Nietzsche observed. "All words in themselves and from the start are, in terms of their meaning, tropes" (quoted in Mayer, 2009, p. 37). Over time, specific tropes have acquired familiar names such as metaphor, irony, and synecdoche, or the part standing for the whole, as in references simply to melting glaciers to signal the wider impacts caused by global warming.

Metaphor, one of the major tropes, abounds in the landscape of environmental communication: Mother Nature, "population bomb, Spaceship Earth, and carbon footprint are just a few examples. Metaphor's role is to invite a comparison by "talking about one thing in terms of another" (Jasinski, 2001, p. 550). For example, some

| **Figure 3.2** | What does the metaphor Spaceship Earth signify? This is the first photo of Earth from space (taken by the Apollo 8 crew). |

NASA

compare the life-sustaining nature of planet Earth to our mother, while others call our personal contribution to global warming a footprint.

Newer metaphors have arisen as scientists, environmentalists, and others bring attention to new problems. Chris Russill (2008) identified climate scientists' use of tipping points as a metaphor to forewarn the public about irreversible and catastrophic occurrences if global warming continues. And, oil companies routinely use the metaphor of a footprint to influence news stories about the opening of the Arctic National Wildlife Refuge to oil drilling. In 2001, as a vote neared in the U.S. Congress, oil company officials evoked this image to suggest that the drilling would have little impact on the environment. Touting advances in technology, industry spokespeople insisted, "With sideways drilling and other advances, the oil beneath the 1.5 million-acre coastal plain can be tapped with a 'footprint' on the surface no larger than 2,000 acres" (Spiess & Ruskin, 2001, para. 1). The *Anchorage Daily News* reported that the oil industry's footprint metaphor "proved to be a potent piece of rhetoric," implying that drilling would affect less than 1 percent of the coastal plain" (para. 18).

☞ FYI Metaphor of Spaceship Earth

The practice of speaking of the Earth as a spaceship became widespread after astronauts took the first photos of it from space in the 1960s. The photos of the blue-green Earth against a dark universe invited a concern for the precarious existence of this small planet. U.S. Ambassador Adlai Stevenson famously evoked the metaphor of Spaceship Earth when he addressed the United Nations on July 9, 1965. He spoke about UN delegates traveling as passengers on "a little space ship, dependent on its vulnerable reserves of air and soil" (quoted in Park, 2001, p. 99). The metaphor was further popularized in the late 1960s by architect Buckminster Fuller (1963) in his *Operating Manual for Spaceship Earth.*

Economist Kenneth Boulding (1965) invoked the most prescient use of the Spaceship Earth metaphor in a 1965 address: "Once we begin to look at earth as a space ship, the appalling extent of our ignorance about it is almost frightening. This is true of the level of every science. We know practically nothing, for instance, about the long-run dynamics even of the physical system of the earth.... We do not even know whether the activities of man *[sic]* are going to make the earth warm up or cool off" (para. 7).

Second, environmental sources often rely on different rhetorical genres to influence perceptions of an issue or problem. **Rhetorical genres** are generally defined as distinct forms or types of speech that "share characteristics distinguishing them" from other types of speech (Jamieson & Stromer-Galley, 2001, p. 361). In the last chapter, for example, we observed John Muir's use of the genre of the **sublime** in his nature writing in the 19th century to evoke feelings of spiritual exaltation. Current examples of genres include *apocalyptic* rhetoric, the *jeremiad,* and what Schwarze (2006) has termed *environmental melodrama.* For example, Paul Ehrlich (1968) and Rachel Carson (1962), in their classic books *The Population Bomb* and *Silent Spring,* appropriated **apocalyptic narrative** literary styles to warn of impending and severe ecological crises. Literary critics Jimmie Killingsworth and Jacqueline Palmer (1996) explained that "in depicting the end of the world as a result of the overweening desire to control nature, [these authors] have discovered a rhetorical means of contesting their opponents' claims for the idea of progress with its ascendant narratives of human victory over nature" (p. 21).

More recently, scientists such as James Lovelock have evoked apocalyptic images to warn of the potentially catastrophic effects of global warming on civilization. For example, Lovelock (2006) cautioned that, "before this century is over billions of us will die and the few breeding pairs of people that survive will be in the Arctic where the climate remains tolerable" (para. 7). Yet, reliance on apocalyptic rhetoric may generate skepticism or charges that its claims are exaggerated. Scientists therefore face a dilemma: How do you raise awareness of future, serious effects from climate changes—rising sea levels, regional conflicts, and so on—without relying on visions of apocalypse?

Less familiar genres used in environmental controversies include the jeremiad and melodrama. For example, Wolfe (2008) draws on the genre of the jeremiad to sound an environmental alarm in Dr. Seuss's *The Lorax*. The genre of the **jeremiad,** originally named for the lamentations of the Hebrew prophet Jeremiah, has been a recurring genre of American public address (Bercovitch, 1978). It refers to speech or writing that laments or denounces the behavior of a people or society and warns of future consequences if society does not change its ways. *The Lorax*, of course, is a fable but one that is also a jeremiad in which the Lorax speaks for the trees, whose fate is imperiled by the Once-ler, a symbol of industrial society.

Other rhetorical critics such as Steven Schwarze (2006) and William Kinsella (2008) have used the genre of an **environmental melodrama** to clarify issues of power and the ways advocates moralize an environmental conflict. As a genre, melodrama "generates stark, polarizing distinctions between social actors and infuses those distinctions with moral gravity and pathos" and is therefore "a powerful resource for rhetorical invention" (Schwarze, 2006, p. 239). Schwarze says that melodrama, by identifying key social actors and where the "public interest" lies, can "remoralize situations" that have been obscured by inaccuracies and "the reassuring rhetoric of technical reason" (p. 250). He offers the example of Bill Moyers's PBS documentary *Trade Secrets* (2001) about the health dangers of the vinyl chloride chemical industry:

> *Trade Secrets* shuttles between images of confidential company memos describing toxic workplace exposure in scientific language, and episodes of workers on hospital beds or widows tearily recalling their spouse's suffering. These melodramatic juxtapositions offer a clear moral framework for interpreting the actions of company decision-makers. They characterize officials as being knowledgeable about toxic hazards in scientific terms, but utterly indifferent to the human suffering that resulted from those hazards. . . . Melodrama puts the inaccuracy of scientific language on display and highlights its potential blindspots. (p. 251)

As this example makes clear, melodrama can serve pragmatic purposes: public education and criticism of the chemical industry, for example. But, it also illustrates rhetoric's constitutive function, a reordering of public consciousness and specifically the restoration of a moral frame in judging the actions of this industry. This reference to a moral frame brings up another rhetorical resource—the use of communication frames that mediates or affects our understanding of environmental concerns.

Communication Frames

The term *frame* was first popularized by sociologist Erving Goffman (1974) in his book *Frame Analysis*. He defined **frames** as the cognitive maps or patterns of interpretation that people use to organize their understanding of reality. A frame, then, helps to construct a particular view or orientation to some aspect of reality. For example, the U.S. Food and Drug Administration (FDA) recently considered a ban on the use of antibiotics in industrial farms to spur growth and weight gain in cattle, pigs, and chickens. In an editorial, the *New York Times* argued this practice is "surely bad for the public's health; the overuse of antibiotics in farm animals is . . . thought to be stimulating the emergence of resistant bacterial strains that can infect humans" (Antibiotics and agriculture, 2010, p. A24). By invoking a public health frame, the *Times* highlighted the possible danger to the public while downplaying the economic benefits of growth antibiotics to the agricultural industry. Framing the issue in this way enabled the newspaper to add its support for the FDA's proposed ban on these antibiotics.

The example of a public health frame also illustrates the role of framing in the construction of a problem or recommendation of a solution. As communication scholar Robert Entman (1993) explained, "To frame is to select some aspects of a perceived reality and make them more salient . . . in such a way as to promote a particular problem definition, causal interpretation, moral evaluation, and/or treatment recommendation for the item described" (p. 56). As a result, different interests in a controversy may use competing frames in their attempts to influence news coverage or gain public support. For example, President Obama has argued that clean energy initiatives in the United States will help to grow the economy and create jobs. The president used this job creation frame in his weekly address to the nation, speaking from a hybrid bus plant in Indianapolis:

> The clean energy jobs at this plant are the jobs of the future—jobs that pay well right here in America. And, in the years ahead, it's clean energy companies like this one that will keep our economy growing, create new jobs, and make sure America remains the most prosperous nation in the world. (Headapohl, 2011, para. 3)

On the other hand, the Institute for Energy Research (2010), a free markets research group, invoked a classic jobs-versus-environment frame in the debate over U.S. energy policy. In a report on its website, the institute claimed a cap on greenhouse gas emissions from oil or coal-burning plants "would reduce U.S. employment by roughly 522,000 jobs in 2015, rising to over 5.1 million jobs by 2050" (para. 4). In each case, the competing uses of a jobs frame by President Obama and the institute construct different meanings for the public in the debate over energy policy.

Dominant and Critical Discourses

The rhetorical claims about a loss of jobs draw on a broader discourse in U.S. politics that asserts there is a trade-off of jobs versus the environment. This concept of *discourse* reminds us that rhetorical resources are broader than any single metaphor, frame, or utterance. Instead, a **discourse** is a recurring pattern of speaking or writing that has developed socially, that is, from multiple sources; it functions to "circulate a coherent set of meanings about an important topic" (Fiske, 1987, p. 14). Such meanings often influence our understanding of how the world works or should work.

As we saw in the last chapter, examples of such discursive patterns included Gifford Pinchot's discourse of conservation, which helped to justify the utilitarian uses of nature, such as logging. And, in the late 20th century, activists calling for environmental justice criticized the prevailing discourse of environmentalism that overlooked the places where people lived, worked, played, and learned. Each of these discourses arose from multiple sources—essays, news reports, and other symbolic acts—that articulated a coherent view of nature and our relationships to the environment.

When a discourse gains a broad or taken-for-granted status in a culture (for example, growth is good for the economy) or when its meanings help to legitimize certain practices, it can be said to be a **dominant discourse.** Often, these discourses are invisible in the sense that they express naturalized or taken-for-granted assumptions and values about how the world is or should be organized.

Perhaps the best example of a dominant environmental discourse is what biologists Dennis Pirages and Paul Ehrlich (1974) called the **Dominant Social Paradigm (DSP).** Communication scholars would point out that a dominant social paradigm is a specific discursive tradition. As expressed in political speeches, advertising, movies, and so forth, today's DSP affirms society's "belief in abundance and progress, our devotion to growth and prosperity, our faith in science and technology, and our commitment to a laissez-faire economy, limited government planning and private property rights" (quoted in Dunlap & Van Liere, 1978, p. 10). In everyday terms, this dominant discourse is recognized in references to free markets as the source of prosperity and the wise use of natural resources to build a strong economy and so forth.

Other discourses may question society's dominant discourses. These alternative ways of speaking, writing, or portraying nature in art, music, and photographs illustrate **critical discourses.** These are recurring ways of speaking that challenge society's taken-for-granted assumptions and offer alternatives to prevailing discourses. In some ages, critical discourses are muted or absent, whereas in other periods, they may be boisterous and widespread. In our own time, critical discourses have proliferated in mainstream media and online, questioning dominant assumptions about growth and the environment. For example, we saw (earlier) the emergence of a new antagonism, opening space for a discourse of sustainability by scientists and environmentalists who are questioning the business as usual (BAU) model of carbon societies.

Discourses about nature, of course, need not be written or even verbal; they also may be visual, drawing upon powerful images to influence our perceptions. In the final section, I'll identify some of the ways that visual rhetoric functions to *re*-present or construct our views of the natural world or what are environmental problems.

Visual Rhetorics: Portraying Nature

Communication about the environment, of course, is not limited to verbal communication. Visual images have been influential in shaping Americans' perceptions of the environment at least since the 18th and 19th centuries, particularly in paintings and photographs of the American West. Since then, visual portrayals of nature have ranged from the stunning photographs of melting glaciers from global warming (Braasch, 2007) to the dramatic cinematography of oceans, rainforests, wildlife, and the polar ice worlds in the TV series *Planet Earth*. More recently, activists in Appalachia have posted dramatic photographs online (www.ilovemountains.org) to protest mountaintop removal coal mining in West Virginia, Kentucky, Tennessee, and southwest Virginia.

As a result, rhetorical scholars have begun to look more closely at the significance of visual images in the public sphere. Dobrin and Morey (2009), for example, have called for the study of *Ecosee*, the "study and the production of the visual (re)presentation of space, environment, ecology, and nature in photographs, paintings, television, film, video games, computer media, and other forms of image-based media" (p. 2). The purpose, they suggest, is to understand the ways in which visual rhetorics construct or challenge a particular seeing of nature or the environment. As Olson, Finnegan, and Hope (2008) point out in their study *Visual Rhetoric*, "public images often work in ways that are rhetorical; that is, *they function to persuade*" (p. 1; emphasis added). This final section, therefore, describes two ways in which **visual rhetorics** of the environment function to persuade: (1) by influencing our perceptions or the way we see certain aspects of the environment and (2) by constructing what the public believes is an environmental problem.

Visual Images (Re)present Nature

While the natural world surely affects us, our symbolic actions—including images—also affect our perceptions of nature itself. All images, of course, are artifacts; they are human made. They select certain aspects of the world (and not others), certain angles of vision, frames, and ways of composing this larger reality. As a result, visual representations influence meaning; they suggest an orientation to the world.

Let's pursue this insight by looking at 18th- and 19th-century images of the American West. What is seen in these paintings and photos, and what meaning or orientation do they suggest?

Refiguring Nature in Art and Photographs

Earlier, we saw that 18th- and 19th-century artists such as Thomas Cole, Albert Bierstadt, and the Hudson River School painters were significant sources of the public's awareness of the American West. Equally important were the photographers who followed military expeditions and surveyors into western territories and who were among the first to portray the West to many people who lived in eastern cities and towns. Photographs of Yosemite Valley, Yellowstone, the Rocky Mountains, and the Grand Canyon not only popularized these sites but, as they became broadly available in the media, "were factors in building public support for preserving the areas" (DeLuca & Demo, 2000, p. 245).

With such popularization, however, came an orientation and also ideological disposition toward nature and human relationships with the land. On the one hand, the paintings of the Hudson River School aided in constituting natural areas as pristine and as objects of the sublime. Yet, rhetorical scholars Gregory Clark, Michael Halloran, and Allison Woodford (1996) have argued that such portrayals of wilderness depicted nature as separate from human culture; the viewpoint of paintings distanced the human observer by viewing the landscape from above or in control of nature. They concluded that, although expressing a reverence for the land, such depictions functioned "rhetorically to fuel a process of conquest" (p. 274).

More recently, rhetorical critics Kevin DeLuca and Anne Demo (2000) have argued that what was left out of landscape photographs of the West may be as important as what was included. They gave the example of early photos of Yosemite Valley taken in the 1860s by the photographer Carleton Watkins. DeLuca and Demo wrote that, when Watkins portrayed Yosemite Valley as wilderness, devoid of humans, he also helped to construct a national myth of pristine nature that was harmful. In a critique of the implicit rhetoric of such scenes, they argued that the "ability of whites to rhapsodize about Yosemite as paradise, the original Garden of Eden, depended on the forced removal and forgetting of the indigenous inhabitants of the area for the past 3,500 years" (p. 254). Writer Rebecca Solnit (1992) has pointed out, "The West wasn't empty, it was emptied—literally by expeditions like the Mariposa Battalion [which killed and/or relocated the native inhabitants of Yosemite Valley in the 1850s], and figuratively by the sublime images of a virgin paradise created by so many painters, poets, and photographers" (p. 56, quoted in DeLuca & Demo, 2000, p. 256).

Whether or not one agrees with DeLuca and Demo's claim about the impact of Watkins's photos, it is important to note that visual images often play pivotal roles in shaping perceptions of natural areas as well as our awareness of the impacts of pollution and toxic waste on human communities. As DeLuca and Demo (2000) have argued, visual portrayals often are "enmeshed in a turbulent stream of multiple and conflictual discourses that shape what these images mean in particular contexts"; indeed, in many ways, such pictures constitute "the context in which a politics takes place—they are creating a reality" (p. 242).

Seeing Polar Bears and Climate Change

Visual images such as photos do not exist by themselves. They are not simply images of something, such as an eagle, mountain, or polluting factory. Rather, a specific image may evoke other images and texts and, therefore, a multitude of associations and meanings. As DeLuca and Demo (2000) remind us, visual images exist within "a stream of multiple and conflictual discourses that shape what these images mean in particular contexts" (p. 242). It is important then to understand "how that image fits into the larger ecosystem of images and texts" (Dobrin & Morey, 2009, p. 10). Let's take as an example the contexts in which we see images of the polar bear.

"If anything symbolizes the Arctic," writes Tim Flannery (2005), author of *The Weather Makers*, "it is surely *nanuk*, the great white bear" (p. 100). Seen on greeting cards, in environmental groups' appeals, and featured as Lorek Byrnison, the great armored ice bear who aided Lyra in the 2007 film *The Golden Compass*, the images of the polar bear abound in popular culture. Recently, compelling images of polar bears struggling for survival have emerged as a powerful symbol of global warming. As early as 2005, scientists were finding evidence that polar bears have been drowning in the Arctic Sea due to the melting of ice floes from climate change. Polar bears feed from these ice floes, and as they drift farther apart, the bears are being forced to swim longer distances.

In the summer of 2008, observers flying for a whale survey over the Chukchi Sea spotted polar bears swimming in open water. The bears were 15 to 65 miles off the Alaskan shore, "some swimming north, apparently trying to reach the polar ice edge, which on that day was 400 miles away" (As Arctic sea ice melts, 2008, p. A16). "Although polar bears are strong swimmers, they are adapted for swimming close to the shore. Their sea journeys leave them vulnerable to exhaustion, hypothermia or being swamped by waves" (Iredale, 2005, para. 3).

News reports about global warming, therefore, constitute a very different context in which images of polar bears appear than do the contexts of greeting cards or a fantasy–adventure film. Within the context of images of melting ice and news of climate change, images of polar bears function as a visual **condensation symbol.** A condensation symbol is a word or phrase (or, in this case, an image) that "stirs vivid impressions involving the listeners' most basic values" (Graber, 1976, p. 289). Political scientist Murray Edelman (1964) stressed that such symbols are able to "condense into one symbolic event or sign" powerful emotions, memories, or anxieties about some event or situation (p. 6). Images of vulnerable polar bears may be one condensation symbol for our anxieties about the planet's warming. As such, they also help to construct what we understand to be an environmental problem itself.

Visualizing Environmental Problems

Earlier, I suggested that problems are not simply a given, out there waiting in the world. Rather, they are created in the minds of citizens as groups struggle to name a

Figure 3.3   Within the context of images of melting ice floes and news of climate change, polar bears may function as a visual *condensation symbol.*

© istockphoto.com/Josef Friedhuber

set of conditions as an environmental concern. As Anders Hansen (2010) explains, the significance we associate with a public issue such as climate change is the result of a great deal of communicative work. For example,

> images of melting ice-floes, Arctic/ Antarctic landscapes, glaciers, etc. become synony-mous with—come to mean or signify—"threatened environments" and ultimately "global warming" or climate change, where in the past they would have signified something quite different such as "challenge" or a test of human endeavour... or simply "pristine" and aesthetically pleasing environments, as yet untouched and unspoilt ... (p. 3)

In fact, the lack of visual evidence of climate change has been a problem for scientists in educating the public of the problem. On the other hand, documentary films about the coal industry in the United States, such as *The Last Mountain,* an official selection for the Sundance Film Festival, produce powerful, visual evidence of the human and environmental problems created from mountaintop removal, literally the blowing-up of mountains to get at coal.

Finally, visual images can be sites of contestation, that is, opponents may chal-lenge or seek to suppress a powerful image, or they may use a very different image to visualize the same set of conditions. The outcome of these rhetorical struggles often determines the context in which politics take place. Let's look at two examples of the ways that visual images become evidence of an environmental problem: debate about oil drilling in the Arctic National Wildlife Refuge in Alaska and live video from the BP *Deepwater Horizon* oil spill of 2010 showing oil gushing into the Gulf of Mexico.

Act Locally!

"Seeing" Global Climate Change

Some climate scientists and journalists have complained that the public cannot "see" global warming. In fact, apart from occasional TV images of melting glaciers or certain documentaries, the public generally lacks visual evidence of climate change.

How would you solve this problem? How might journalists, scientists, filmmakers, or social media represent visually the occurrence and effects of climate change? Try these experiments by searching online:

(1) To represent the impacts of prolonged drought, locate images of wildfires in the Southwest United States or distressed agriculture and the impacts on farm animals and villages in East Africa.

(2) To represent the problem of rising sea levels, locate images of coastal regions or communities that are facing increased storm surges, saltwater seepage into agricultural fields, eroded shorelines, or flooded roads from high tides.

(3) To represent the problem of disease, locate images of dead or dying forests in Canada and the United States as insect vectors spread and trees become distressed (and susceptible) by a warmer climate.

What other visual images can you imagine that would offer evidence of climate disruption and its effects? What are the features of these images that might invite potential interest or inform viewers of the problems? How do these images represent or connect the viewer to climate change?

Photography and the Arctic National Wildlife Refuge

In October 2000, a 33-year-old physicist named Subhankar Banerjee began a two-year project to photograph the seasons and the biodiversity of Alaska's Arctic National Wildlife Refuge. His project, which took him on a 4,000-mile journey by foot, kayak, and snowmobile through the wildlife refuge culminated in stunning photographs, published in his book *Arctic National Wildlife Refuge: Seasons of Life and Land* (2003). (For a sample of the photographs, see www .subhankarbanerjee.org/.)

Banerjee hoped that his photographs would educate the public about threats to Alaska's remote refuge. The Smithsonian Museum in Washington, DC, had scheduled a major exhibition of Banerjee's photos for 2003. However, the young scientist–photographer suddenly found his photos and the exhibit caught in the midst of a political controversy. During a March 18, 2003, debate in the U.S. Senate about oil drilling in the Arctic National Wildlife Refuge, Senator Barbara Boxer of California urged every Senator to visit Banerjee's exhibit at the Smithsonian "before calling the refuge a frozen wasteland" (Egan, 2003, p. A20). The vote to open the refuge to oil drilling later failed by four votes.

Although Banerjee's photos were not the only influence on the Senate's vote, the controversy over his photos caused a political firestorm and helped to create a context for debate over the refuge itself. *Washington Post* writer Timothy Egan (2003) reported that Banerjee had been told by the Smithsonian that "the museum had been pressured to cancel or sharply revise the exhibit" (p. A20). Documents from the museum give an idea of the revised exhibit. For example, Egan reported that the original caption for a photo of the Romanzof Mountains quoted Mr. Banerjee as saying, "The refuge has the most beautiful landscape I have ever seen and is so remote and untamed that many peaks, valleys and lakes are still without names." However, the new caption simply read: "Unnamed Peak, Romanzof Mountains" (p. A20). After the failed vote, the Smithsonian "sent a letter to the publisher of Banerjee's book, saying that the Smithsonian no longer had any connection to Mr. Banerjee's work" (p. A20).

The Smithsonian's criticism of Banerjee's photographs was revealing. Photographs can be powerful rhetorical statements. As DeLuca and Demo (2000) argued, they can constitute a context for understanding and judgment. Especially when accompanied by captions that encourage a particular meaning, photos can embody a range of symbolic resources that sustain or challenge prevailing viewpoints. Some observers felt that Banerjee's photos of Alaska's wilderness had this potential. A reviewer for the *Planet* in Jackson Hole, Wyoming, observed, "Sometimes pictures have a chance to change history by creating a larger understanding of a subject, thus enlightening the public and bringing greater awareness to an issue" (Review, 2003).

Images of an Oil Spill in the Gulf of Mexico

On April 20, 2010, a fiery explosion erupted on the *Deepwater Horizon* oil platform in the Gulf of Mexico, killing eleven workers. The collapse of the rig and failure of BP oil company's "blowout preventer" allowed crude oil a mile beneath the surface to spew into the Gulf waters. The oil gushed for 87 days until BP temporarily blocked the wellhead. Although BP initially claimed the rate of oil flow was low, U.S. government scientists determined as much as 1.5 to 2.5 million gallons of oil a day were spewing into the Gulf (CNN Wire Staff, June 16, 2010). By September 18, 2010, when BP permanently sealed the well, nearly 5 million barrels or 206 million gallons of oil had spilled into Gulf waters. Oil sheen and tar balls ultimately reached into wetlands, marshy bays, and onto beaches in Louisiana, Mississippi, Alabama, and Florida. The U.S. government declared a fishery disaster off the coasts of Louisiana, Mississippi, and Alabama, and hotels and restaurants reported

| Figure 3.4 | An oil-drenched bird struggles to climb onto a boom in the Gulf of Mexico, near the Louisiana coast; the water was filled with oil from the 2010 BP *Deepwater Horizon* oil spill. |

that business had fallen off sharply for the summer season. The U.S. official in charge of overseeing the cleanup called it "the worst oil spill in U.S. history" (Hayes, 2010, para. 1).

From the day of the oil rig explosion, visual images framed the public's sense of the event as an economic and ecological problem: dramatic film showing the collapse of the Deep Horizon oil rig; satellite images of oil spreading over 40,000 square miles on the surface; interviews with unemployed Louisiana shrimpers; and emotionally gripping photos of oil-soaked seabirds, turtles, and dolphins. TV cameras showed oil-tainted wetlands and workers in white hazmat suits scooping up tar balls that had washed onto beaches. (For photos and videos of the oil spill, see: www.nola.com/news/gulf-oil-spill.)

Despite these compelling images, some worried they were not seeing the real extent of the problem. "I think there's an enormous amount of oil below the surface that unfortunately we can't see," one scientist told an oversight committee (quoted in Froomkin, 2010, para. 7). A partial answer to "seeing" the problem would come from the live video from BP's Remotely Operated Vehicles (ROVs) of the oil gushing from the underwater wellhead. Initially, BP had wanted to block this live feed to news outlets. Under intense pressure from federal officials, however, the company relented and agreed to "make a live video feed from the source of the leak continuously available to the public" (Froomkin, 2010, p. 1).

The real-time images of the oil gushing from the ruptured well were compelling: "The sight of an ecological catastrophe unfolding in real time has gripped the public more than the series finale of 'Lost' " (Fermino, 2010, p.1). Within days, millions of people had viewed the video, with at least 3,000 websites using the live feed (Jonsson, 2010). One reporter observed, "The glimpse into the deep has proved mesmerizing" (Jonsson, 2010, para. 2).The images had become so riveting that "when President Obama spoke about the historic spill, TV news channels showed a split screen of Obama and the gushing oil" (Fermino, 2010, p. 1).

The images of oil gushing into the Gulf of Mexico and drowning polar bears help to constitute a context of meaning and implicitly embody multiple streams of discourses. As a consequence, the ability of visual media to affect our understanding and appreciation of the environment illustrate what I earlier described as rhetoric's constitutive role in orienting us to the natural world.

SUMMARY

In this chapter, I've described a perspective on communication that emphasizes the social–symbolic construction of our views about nature and the environment.

- Central to a social–symbolic approach is the role of language in naming our world and helping to define some conditions as environmental problems.
- Related to this approach is a rhetorical perspective that highlights the purposeful and consequential uses of the resources of language. These resources include (a) rhetorical tropes and genres, (b) communication frames, and (c) the recurring dominant or critical discourses that sustain or challenge society's views of the environment.
- Finally, I explored some of the ways in which visual rhetoric such as art, photographs, and TV news images embody symbolic resources that can influence our perceptions of nature or the environment. Such visual rhetorics function in two ways:

  (1) Images *re*present the natural world to us in selected ways that may invite certain orientations or views, and

  (2) Visual rhetorics sometimes impart specific attitudes toward specific aspects of nature and therefore help to constitute these as environmental problems.

While the examples in this chapter illustrate the social and discursive constructions of nature, these occur in concrete places and contexts in the public sphere. In the next chapter, I'll expand on this view of environmental communication by looking at some of these contexts and the legal guarantees that empower ordinary citizens to speak for or about the environment.

SUGGESTED RESOURCES

- Tema Milstein, "Nature Identification: The Power of Pointing and Naming," *Environmental Communication: A Journal of Nature and Culture, 5* (2011), 3–24.
- *The Last Mountain,* a documentary about mountaintop coal mining and an official selection for the 2011 Sundance Film Festival.
- Finis Dunaway, *Natural Visions: The Power of Images in American Environmental Reform.* Chicago: University of Chicago Press, 2008; and "Seeing Global Warming: Contemporary Art and the Fate of the Planet," *Environmental History 14* (January 2009): 9–31.
- Kevin DeLuca and Anne Tersa Demo, "Imaging Nature: Watkins, Yosemite, and the Birth of Environmentalism," *Critical Studies in Mass Communication, 17* (2000), pp. 241–260.

KEY TERMS

Apocalyptic narrative   66

Condensation symbol   71

Critical discourse   68

Discourse   68

Dominant discourse   68

Dominant Social
   Paradigm (DSP)   68

Environmental melodrama   66

Frames   67

Jeremiad   66

Metaphor   64

Naming   61

Rhetoric   63

Rhetorical genres   65

Rhetorical perspective   63

Social–symbolic perspective   60

Sublime   65

Terministic screens   61

Tropes   64

Visual rhetoric   69

DISCUSSION QUESTIONS

1. What do Herndl and Brown (1996) mean when they claim that, "in a very real sense, there is no objective environment in the phenomenal world, no environment separate from the words we use to represent it"? Do you agree with this assertion?

2. Are apocalyptic warnings about global warming effective, or do such warnings create problems of credibility? How can scientists raise awareness of future, serious effects from climate changes—rising sea levels, deaths from prolonged droughts, and so on—without relying on some vision of catastrophic events?

3. Do environmental problems exist before they are named as a problem? How do you explain the fact that not everybody agrees that global warming is a problem?

4. How do visual images function rhetorically to construct ideological views of nature or the environment? Where is this occurring today?

REFERENCES

Antibiotics and agriculture. (2010, June 30). *The New York Times*, p. A24.

As arctic sea ice melts, experts expect new low. (2008, August 28). *The New York Times*, p. A16.

Banerjee, S. (2003). *Arctic National Wildlife Refuge: Seasons of life and land*. Seattle, WA: Mountaineer Books.

Bercovitch, S. (1978). *The American jeremiad*. Madison: University of Wisconsin Press.

Boulding, K. E. (1965, May 10). Earth as a spaceship. Address at Washington State University. Retrieved September 17, 2010, from www.colorado.edu/

Braasch, G. (2007). *Earth under fire: How global warming is changing the world*. Berkeley: University of California Press.

Burke, K. (1966). *Language as symbolic action: Essays on life, literature, and method*. Berkeley: University of California Press.

Campbell, K. K., & Huxman, S. S. (2008). *The rhetorical act* (4th ed.). Belmont, CA: Thomson Wadsworth.

Carson, R. (1962). *Silent spring*. Boston: Houghton Mifflin.

Clark, G., Halloran, M., & Woodford, A. (1996). Thomas Cole's vision of "nature" and the conquest theme in American culture. In C. G. Herndl & S. C. Brown (Eds.), *Green culture: Environmental rhetoric in contemporary America* (pp. 261–280). Madison: University of Wisconsin Press.

CNN Wire Staff. (2010, June 16). Oil estimate raised to 35,000–60,000 barrels a day. Retrieved September 11, 2010, from http://edition.cnn.com/

DeLuca, K., & Demo, A. T. (2000). Imaging nature: Watkins, Yosemite, and the birth of environmentalism. *Critical Studies in Mass Communication, 17*, 241–260.

Depoe, S. P. (2006). Preface. In S. P. Depoe (Ed.), *The environmental communication yearbook* (Vol. 3, pp. vii–ix). London: Routledge.

Dobrin, S. I., & Morey, S. (Eds.). (2009). *Ecosee: Image, rhetoric, Nature*. Albany, NY: SUNY.

Dunlap, R. E., & Van Liere, K. D. (1978). The "new environmental paradigm": A proposed instrument and preliminary analysis. *Journal of Environmental Education, 9*, 10–19.

Edelman, M. (1964). *The symbolic uses of politics*. Urbana: University of Illinois Press.

Eder, K. (1996a). *The social construction of nature*. London: Sage.

Eder, K. (1996b). The institutionalization of environmentalism: Ecological discourse and the second transformation of the public sphere. In S. Lash, B. Szerszynski, & B. Wynne (Eds.), *Risk, environment, and modernity: Towards a new ecology* (pp. 203–223). London: Sage.

Egan, T. (2003, May 3). Smithsonian is no safe haven for exhibit on Arctic Wildlife Refuge. *The New York Times*, p. A20.

Ehrlich, P. R. (1968). *The population bomb*. San Francisco: Sierra Club Books.

Entman, R. M. (1993). Framing: Toward clarification of a fractured paradigm. *Journal of Communication, 43*(4): 51–58.

Evernden, N. (1992). *The social creation of nature*. Baltimore: Johns Hopkins University Press.

Fermino, J. (2010, September 11). Camera captures BP's PR disaster for all to see.

New York Post. Retrieved September 11, 2010, from http://www.nypost.com/

Fiske, J. (1987). *Television culture.* London: Methuen.

Flannery, T. (2005). *The weather makers: How man is changing the climate and what it means for life on earth.* New York: Grove Press.

Froomkin, D. (2010, June 1). Gulf oil spill: Markey demands BP broadcast live video feed from the source. *Huffpost Social News.* Retrieved September 11, 2010, from http://www.huffingtonpost.com

Fuller, B. (1963). *Operating manual for spaceship earth.* New York: Dutton.

Goffman, E. (1974). *Frame analysis: An essay on the organization of experience.* Cambridge, MA: Harvard University Press.

Graber, D. A. (1976). *Verbal behavior and politics.* Urbana: University of Illinois Press.

Hansen, A. (2010). *Environment, media, and communication.* New York: Routledge.

Haraway, D. (1991). *Simians, cyborgs, and women: The reinvention of nature.* New York: Routledge.

Hayes, K. (2010, September 20). U.S. says BP permanently "kills" Gulf of Mexico well. Reuters. Retrieved September 20, 2010, from http://www.reuters.com/

Headapohl, J. (2011, May 7). Obama touts clean energy jobs in weekly address. Retrieved May 20, 2011, from www.mlive.com/

Herndl, C. G., & Brown, S. C. (1996). Introduction. In C. G. Herndl & S. C. Brown (Eds.), *Green culture: Environmental rhetoric in contemporary America* (pp. 3–20). Madison: University of Wisconsin Press.

Herrick, J. A. (2009). *The history and theory of rhetoric: An introduction.* Boston: Pearson.

Institute for Energy Research. (2010, June 30). New study: Kerry-Lieberman to destroy up to 5.1 million jobs, cost families $1,042 per year, wealthiest Americans to benefit. Retrieved September 16, 2010, from http://www.institutcforenergyresearch .org

Iredale, W. (2005, December 18). Polar bears drown as ice shelf melts. *The Sunday Times* [UK]. Retrieved November 8, 2008, from http://www.timesonline .co.uk

Jamieson, K. H., & Stromer-Galley, J. (2001). Hybrid genres. In T. O. Sloane (Ed.), *Encyclopedia of rhetoric* (pp. 361–363). Oxford, UK: Oxford University Press.

Jasinski, J. (2001). *Sourcebook on rhetoric: Key concepts in contemporary rhetorical studies.* Thousand Oaks, CA: Sage.

Jonsson, P. (2010, May 29). BP "top kill" live feed makes stars out of disaster bots. *The Christian Science Monitor.* Retrieved September 16, 2010, from www.csmonitor .com/

Killingsworth, M. J., & Palmer, J. S. (1996). Millennial ecology: The apocalyptic narrative from *Silent Spring* to Global Warming. In C. G. Herndl & S. C. Brown (Eds.), *Green culture: Environmental rhetoric in contemporary America* (pp. 21–45). Madison: University of Wisconsin Press.

Kinsella, W. J. (2008). Introduction: Narratives, rhetorical genres, and environmental conflict: Responses to Schwarze's "environmental melodrama." *Environmental Communication: A Journal of Nature and Culture, 2,* 78–79.

Latour, B. (2004). *Politics of nature: How to bring science into democracy.* (C. Porter, Trans.). Cambridge, MA: Harvard University Press. (Originally published 1999. Paris: Editions la Découverte)

Lindzen, R. S. (2009, July 26). Resisting climate hysteria. *Quadrant Online.* Retrieved September 15, 2010, from http://www.quadrant.org.

Lovelock, J. (2006, January 16). The earth is about to catch a morbid fever that may last as long as 100,000 years. *The Independent.* Retrieved November 26, 2008, from http://www.independent .co.uk/

Mayer, C. (2009). Precursors of rhetoric culture theory. In I. Strecker & S. Tyler (Eds.), *Culture and rhetoric* (pp. 31–48). New York: Berghahn Books, 2009.

Milstein, T. (2011, March). Nature identification: The power of pointing and naming. *Environmental Communication: A Journal of Nature and Culture, 5*(1), 3–24.

Moyers, B. (2011). *Trade Secrets.* Public Broadcasting Corporation. Retrieved from http://www.pbs.org/tradesecrets

Olson, L. C., Finnegan, C. A., & Hope, D. S. (Eds.). (2008). *Visual rhetoric: A reader in communication and American culture.* Thousand Oaks, CA: Sage.

Oravec, C. L. (2004). Naming, interpretation, policy, and poetry. In S. L. Senecah (Ed.). *Environmental communication yearbook* (Vol. 1, pp. 1–14). Mahwah, NJ: Lawrence Erlbaum.

Park, C. C. (2001). *The environment: Principles and applications.* London: Routledge.

Pirages, D. C., & Ehrlich, P. R. (1974). *Ark II: Social response to environmental imperatives.* San Francisco: Freeman.

Rampton, S. (2002). Sludge, biosolids and the propaganda model of communication. *New Solutions, 12*(4), 347–353. Retrieved September 14, 2010, from http://www.sludgenews.org

Review. (2003, June 5). Subhankar Banerjee, Arctic National Wildlife Refuge: Seasons of Life and Land. *Planet.* Retrieved July 17, 2004, from www.mountaineersbooks .org

Ross, A. (1994). *The Chicago gangster theory of life: Nature's debt to society.* London: Verso.

Russill, C. (2008). Tipping point forewarnings in climate change communication: Some implications of an emerging trend. *Environmental Communication: A Journal of Nature and Culture, 2,* 133–153.

Schwarze, S. (2006). Environmental melodrama. *Quarterly Journal of Speech, 92*(3), 239–261.

Solnit, R. (1992). Up the river of mercy. *Sierra, 77,* 50, 53–58, 78, 81, 83–84.

Spiess, B., & Ruskin, L. (2001, November 4). 2,000-acre query: ANWR bill provision caps development, but what does it mean? *Anchorage Daily News.* Retrieved April 13, 2004, from www.adn.com

Stone, D. (2002). *Policy paradox: The art of political decision making* (Rev. ed.). New York: Norton.

Tindall, D. B. (1995). What is environmental sociology? An inquiry into the paradigmatic status of environmental sociology. In M. D. Mehta & E. Ouellet (Eds.), *Environmental sociology: Theory and practice* (pp. 33–59). North York, Ontario, Canada: Captus Press.

Wolfe, D. (2008). The ecological jeremiad, the American myth, and the vivid force of color in Dr. Seuss's *The Lorax. Environmental Communication: A Journal of Nature and Culture, 2,* 3–24.

PART II

Citizen Voices
and Public Forums

Moms March and rally to Stop the Spray (aerial spraying of pesticide) in Marin County, California

Public Participation in Environmental Decisions

Make diligent efforts to involve the public. . . .

—U.S. National Environmental Policy Act (1970)

Environmental issues are best handled with participation of all concerned citizens. . . . Each individual shall have appropriate access to information concerning the environment that is held by public authorities . . . and the opportunity to participate in decision-making processes.

—Rio Declaration on
Environment and Development (1992)

One of the most striking features of the political landscape has been the increase in participation by ordinary citizens, environmental groups, scientists, businesses, and others in decisions about the environment. Environmental historian Samuel Hays (2000) noted that people have been "enticed, cajoled, educated, and encouraged to become active in learning, voting, and supporting [environmental] legislation . . . as well as to write, call, fax, or e-mail decision makers at every stage of the decision-making process." All this has been "a major contribution to a fundamental aspect of the American political system—public participation" (p. 194).

In this chapter, I'll focus on developments in the United States and other nations that strengthen the public's right to be involved in decisions about their environments. Such involvement by the public often has been the critical element in efforts to protect threatened wildlife habitats, achieve cleaner air and water, and ensure a safer workplace.

Chapter Preview

This chapter describes some of the legal guarantees and public forums for communication that enable citizens to participate actively in decisions about the environment.

- The first three sections of this chapter identify the legal rights and practices that embody the ideal of public participation:

(1) The right to know

(2) The right to comment publicly about proposed environmental projects or rules

(3) The right of *standing* to object in a court to actions that are injurious to the quality of the environment

- The last section of the chapter describes the growth internationally of democratic provisions for public participation.

Public participation is the principle that "those who are affected by a decision have a right to be involved in the decision-making process" (*Core values*, 2008). It is also an assumption that such persons' involvement can have some influence on the decisions affecting them. Public participation, therefore, is viewed as a mode of empowerment and a core characteristic of a democracy. This has been especially true of environmental decisions. Here, I define public participation more specifically in the United States as the ability of individual citizens and groups to influence decisions through: (a) the right to know or access to relevant information, (b) the right to comment to the agency that is responsible for a decision, and (c) the right, through the courts, to hold public agencies and businesses accountable for their environmental decisions and behaviors.

These rights reflect more basic, democratic principles: (a) The right to know reflects the principle of **transparency,** or openness of governmental actions to public scrutiny, (b) the right to comment reflects the principle of *direct participation* in democratic decisions, and (c) the right of standing assumes the principle of *accountability,* that is, the requirement that political authority meet agreed-upon norms and standards. (These principles are summarized in Table 4.1.)

Right to Know: Access to Information

One of the strongest norms of democratic society is the principle of transparency. Simply put, this is a belief in openness in government and a right of citizens to know about information important to their lives. Internationally, the principle of transparency was applied specifically to environmental concerns at the United Nations Conference on Environment and Development, informally known as the Earth Summit, in 1992. Principle 10 of the Rio Declaration (1992) states that "environmental issues are best handled with participation of all concerned citizens" and that individuals "shall have appropriate access to information concerning the environment

Table 4.1	Modes of Public Participation in Environmental Decisions		
Legal Right	**Mode of Participation**	**Authority**	**Democratic Principle**
Right to Know	Written requests for information; access to documents online, and so on	Freedom of Information Act (FOIA), Toxic Release Inventory, Clean Water Act, sunshine laws	Transparency
Right to Comment	Testimony at public hearings, participation in advisory committees; written comment (letters, e-mail, etc.)	National Environmental Policy Act (NEPA)	Direct participation
Right of Standing	Plaintiff in lawsuit, amicus brief (third party) in legal case	Clean Water Act and other statutes; Supreme Court rulings (*Sierra Club v. Morton*, etc.)	Accountability

that is held by public authorities . . . and the opportunity to participate in decision making processes." The principle of transparency gained further recognition in the *Declaration of Bizkaia* (1999), which proclaimed that transparency requires "access to information and the right to be informed. . . . Everyone has the right of access to information on the environment with no obligation to prove a particular interest."

Recognition of the principle of transparency also illustrates the importance of information—and who controls it—in influencing environmental policies. As Hays (2000) observed, political power lies increasingly in an ability to understand the complexities of environmental issues, and "the key to that power is information and the expertise and technologies required to command it" (p. 232).

By the late 20th century, moves to ensure transparency in decision making led to new **sunshine laws**. These laws required open meetings of government bodies in order to shine the light of public scrutiny on their workings. The U.S. Congress threw open the doors to government records more generally. The Clean Water Act of 1972 for the first time required federal agencies to provide information on water pollution to the public. And, as we see later, the National Environmental Policy Act of 1970 required all federal agencies to provide environmental impact statements (EIS) about their proposed actions, such as the filling of wetlands, before making a final decision. These EIS reports proved critically important to groups who monitored government agencies.

Two laws in particular have provided important guarantees of the public's **right to know**—that is, their right of access to information about environmental conditions or actions of government that potentially affect the environment. These are the Freedom of Information Act and the Emergency Planning and Community Right to Know Act, which set up the Toxic Release Inventory.

Freedom of Information Act

The move toward greater transparency in government had its roots in an earlier law, the **Administrative Procedure Act (APA)** of 1946. In response to charges of agency favoritism and corruption, APA laid out new operating standards for U.S. government agencies. It required all regulations that were meant to implement a law be published in the *Federal Register* and that the public be given an opportunity to respond before the action took effect. However, there was no requirement that these agencies make available to the public any records or documents related to their decisions.

As a result of public pressure for greater access to information, the U.S. Congress passed the **Freedom of Information Act (FOIA)** in 1966. The act guarantees that any person has the right to see the records of any executive branch agency (but not the judiciary or Congress). Agencies whose records are typically requested by reporters, scholars, and environmental groups include the U.S. Forest Service, Fish and Wildlife Service, Bureau of Land Management, Department of Energy, and the EPA, among others. Upon written request, an agency is required to disclose records relating to the requested topic unless the agency can claim an exemption from disclosure. (For a description of these exemptions, see www.usdoj.gov.) FOIA also grants requesting parties who are denied their request the right to appear in federal court to seek the enforcement of the act's provisions.

In 1996, the Congress amended FOIA by passing the **Electronic Freedom of Information Amendments**. The amendments require agencies to provide public access to information online. This is done typically by posting a guide for making a FOIA request on the agency's website. (See "FYI: How to Make a Request Under the Freedom of Information Act.") Individual states have adopted similar procedures governing public access to the records of state agencies.

☞ FYI How to Make a Request Under the Freedom of Information Act

For information on FOIA, consult the U.S. Department of Justice guide (www.justice.gov/oip/foia_guide09.htm) or the Reporters Committee for Freedom of the Press's "Draft a FOIA Request" (www.rcfp.org/foia). Also, see the EPA's website (www.epa.gov/foia) for requesting documents under the FOIA.

To request information from another agency, see its website. For example, if you want to know what the U.S. Forest Service office in your area has done to enforce the Endangered Species Act (ESA) in a recent timber sale, go to the Forest Service's website for FOIA requests (www.fs.fed.us/im/foia/). There, you will find instructions for submitting your request for information. The Forest Service site also includes a sample FOIA request letter (www.fs.fed.us/im/foia/samplefoialetter.htm).

Under FOIA, individuals, public interest groups, journalists, and others routinely gather information from public agencies as they monitor their decisions and enforcement of permits. For example, a local River Guardians group might be interested in knowing what a mining company plans to do if its application to mine for gravel near a local river is approved by the Army Corps of Engineers. (The Corps is the federal agency responsible for permits under the Clean Water Act.) Although the application itself is public, the mining company's actual proposal may not be available; as a result, the River Guardians group can request this information by filing a FOIA request.

Citizens living in a community contaminated with toxic chemicals also may use FOIA to gather information for a *tort* or legal action against the polluter. An **environmental tort** is a legal claim for injury or a lawsuit, such as those depicted in the films *Erin Brockovich* and *A Civil Action*. Under federal law, the EPA is required to maintain records for companies that handle hazardous waste, including notices of permit violations. As the group prepares its legal case, it can request these documents from the EPA under the agency's procedures for complying with FOIA.

The Right to Know in the Post-9/11 Era

In the immediate aftermath of terrorist attacks on the United States in 2001, the U.S. Congress and the executive branch moved quickly to give new authority to federal law enforcement agencies and intelligence services. However, civil libertarians, public interest groups, and environmentalists discovered that these actions had troublesome implications for civil society. Historians Gerald Markowitz and David Rosner (2002) reported that "in the wake of the September 11 attacks, the Bush administration acted to restrict public access to information about polluting industries and restricted journalists' and historians' access to government documents previously available through the Freedom of Information Act" (p. 303).

Scholars and individuals seeking information about environmental topics from sources that were available to the public before September 11, 2001, first noticed a shift in response by federal agencies. For example, *USA Today* reported:

> When United Nations analyst Ian Thomas contacted the National Archives . . . to get some 30-year-old maps of Africa to plan a relief mission, he was told the government no longer makes them public. When John Coequyt, an environmentalist, tried to connect to an online database where the Environmental Protection Agency lists chemical plants that violate pollution laws, he was denied access. (Parker, Johnson, & Locy, 2002, 1A)

In fact, in the eight months following the 9/11 attacks, the federal government removed hundreds of thousands of public documents from its websites; in other cases, access to material was made more difficult. For example, documents reporting accidents at chemical plants, previously available online from the EPA, were now to be viewed only in government reading rooms (Parker, Johnson, & Locy, 2002).

When the Obama administration came into office, many journalists and civil libertarians were hopeful that the president would reverse the Bush era trend toward secrecy in government. Indeed, on his first full day in office, January 21, 2009, President Obama issued a memorandum calling on all government agencies, to "usher in a new era of open government." His memo directed the U.S. Attorney

General to issue comprehensive new guidelines for administrating the FOIA that adopted "a presumption in favor of disclosure" (White House, 2009).

As I write, in 2011, however, the Obama administration record under the FOIA has been uneven. Several environmental agencies, such as the EPA and the Departments of Energy and Interior, on the one hand, have moved to reduce the backlog of FOIA requests and increase transparency. In 2010, the EPA began launching online searchable databases for information held by the agency, reducing the need for FOIA requests. For example, it established ToxRefDB, a database allowing scientists and the public to search thousands of toxicity results and the potential health effects of chemicals (see http://epa.gov/ncct/toxrefdb). On the other hand, a study by George Washington University found that only "a minority of agencies" had responded to the president's memorandum with concrete changes in their FOIA practices; less responsive were the CIA, Department of State, and NASA (Sunshine and shadows, 2010).

While the FOIA has a mixed history, it has nevertheless been an invaluable tool for requesting information about the environment for journalists, environmental groups, and particularly residents in communities affected by toxic chemicals. A second U.S. law that provides vital information about industrial pollutants in local communities is the Emergency Planning and Community Right to Know Act.

Emergency Planning and Community Right to Know Act

In 1984, thousands of people were killed when two separate plants released toxic chemicals—one a Union Carbide plant in Bhopal, India, and the other a chemical plant in West Virginia. These two incidents fueled public pressure for accurate information about the production, storage, and release of toxic materials in local communities by such companies. Responding to this pressure, Congress passed the **Emergency Planning and Community Right to Know Act** in 1986, known simply as the Right to Know Act. The law requires industries to report to local and state emergency planners the use and location of specified chemicals at their facilities. (For the text of this law and description of its provisions, see http://www.epa.gov.)

The Toxic Release Inventory

The Right to Know Act also requires the EPA to collect data annually on any releases of toxic materials into the air and water by designated industries and to make this information easily available to the public through an information-reporting tool, the **Toxic Release Inventory (TRI)**. The goal of the TRA "is to empower citizens, through information, to hold companies and local governments accountable in terms of how toxic chemicals are managed" (Environmental Protection Agency, 2010).

In the years since the TRI debuted, the EPA has expanded its reporting and now collects data on approximately 581 different chemicals (Environmental Protection Agency, 2010). The EPA regularly makes these data available through online tools such as its TRI Explorer (www.epa.gov/tri/), although the data tend to lag by two years. Other public interest groups also use the TRI database to offer more user-friendly e-portals for individuals wanting information about the release of toxic materials into the air or water in their local communities. (For an example, see "Act Locally: What Toxic Chemicals Are in Your Community?")

Act Locally!

What Toxic Chemicals Are in Your Community?

Use the TRI to check for the presence of toxic chemicals in the air, soil, or water in the community where you or your family or friends live, work, or attend school.

To access the TRI database, use the EPA's TRI Explorer (www.epa.gov/tri/) or its Envirofacts website (www.epa.gov/enviro) or the more user-friendly Scorecard (www.scorecard.org). Sponsored by Environmental Defense, Scorecard makes it possible for you to contact the polluters in your area or e-mail state and federal decision makers.

Scorecard also links you to volunteer opportunities and environmental organizations in your area. Also see the EPA's Enforcement and Compliance History Online (ECHO) (www.epa.gov/echo). This site allows you to know whether the EPA or state governments have conducted inspections at a specific facility, whether violations were detected or enforcement actions were taken, and whether penalties were assessed in response to environmental law violations.

Many community activists as well as city and state governments believe that the TRI is the single most valuable information tool for ensuring community and industry safety. Sometimes, disclosure of information by itself may be enough to affect polluters' behavior. For example, Stephan (2002) found that public disclosure of information about a factory's chemical releases or violations of its air or water permit may trigger a **shock and shame response**. If community members found out that a local factory was emitting high levels of pollution, their shock could push the community into action. Furthermore, Stephan explained that the polluting facility itself (or those who work there) may feel shame from disclosure of its poor performance. However, he conceded another explanation might be that the company fears a backlash from citizens, interest groups, or the market (p. 194).

Calls for the Right of Independent Expertise

An important supplement to the TRI is communities' access to independent experts to aid their understanding of the chemicals found at hazardous sites. Because the effects from exposure to toxic chemicals involves complex issues, advocates from communities with toxic waste sites long have sought access to sources of expertise to aid them in understanding the effects of these chemicals. Often, there is a disparity in the expertise that is available to government agencies or industry, on the one hand, and what is available to local citizens. That is, citizens—in affected communities—lack training in toxicology or other environmental sciences that would allow them to assess the government's findings.

Figure 4.1	The Toxic Release Inventory (TRI) makes information available on air and water pollution, empowering citizens, through this information, to hold companies and local governments accountable for their use, storage, or discharge of toxic chemicals into the environment.

© istockphoto.com/narvikk

In response to this gap, Congress enacted the **Technical Assistance Grant (TAG) Program** in 1986. The TAG program is intended to help communities at **Superfund sites.** (*Superfund sites* are abandoned chemical waste sites that have qualified for federal funds for their cleanup.) Decisions about the cleanup of these sites are usually based on technical information that includes the types of chemical wastes and the technology available. The purpose of the TAG program is to provide funds for citizen groups to pay for technical advisors to explain these technical reports as well as EPA's cleanup proposals at the sites; the grants also allow these advisors to assist local citizens in participating in public meetings with the EPA.

Overall, the public's access to information about their environments has been greatly aided by such laws as the FOIA and the Emergency Planning and Community Right to Know Act and its TRI. The tools available to the public under these laws are a major advance for the principle of transparency as well as important resources for communities in coping with environmental hazards in the United States.

Right of Public Comment

Town hall meetings and the right of citizens to speak directly to their government are long-standing traditions in the United States. When it comes to the environment, this tradition got a significant boost in 1970, the year millions of citizens first celebrated Earth Day. Signed into law in that year, the **National Environmental Policy Act (NEPA)** guaranteed that the public would have an opportunity to speak directly to U.S. government agencies, such as the Forest Service, before these agencies could proceed with any actions affecting the environment. At its core, this right of "public comment" promised citizens a kind of "pre-decisional communication" would occur between them and the agency responsible for any decision that could potentially harm the environment; that is, before it could act, the agency must first solicit and hear citizens' views (Daniels & Walker, 2001, p. 8).

Public comment typically takes the form of in-person, spoken testimony at public hearings, exchanges of views at open meetings, written communications to agencies (e-mails, letters, and reports), and participation on citizen advisory panels.

In this section, I focus on the right to comment, provided under the National Environmental Policy Act of 1970. I'll also examine one of the most common forums for public participation, the *public hearing*. (I will describe citizens' advisory panels and more informal collaboration approaches for resolving environmental conflicts in Chapter 5.)

National Environmental Policy Act

The core authority for the public's right to comment directly on federal environmental decisions, as I just noted, comes from the NEPA. Political scientists Matthew Lindstrom and Zachary Smith (2001) explained that NEPA's sponsors wanted the public not only to be aware of projects that might be environmentally damaging but also to have an active role in commenting on alternative actions that an agency had proposed. Thus, NEPA and its regulations "act like other 'sunshine' laws . . . in that they require full disclosure to the public as well as extensive public hearings and opportunities for comment on the proposed action" (p. 94).

Two NEPA requirements are intended to inform members of the public and then give them an opportunity to communicate about a proposed federal environmental action. These are (a) a detailed statement of any environmental impacts and (b) concrete procedures for public comment.

Environmental Impact Statements

As implemented by the Council on Environmental Quality, NEPA requires federal agencies to prepare a detailed **environmental impact statement (EIS)** for any proposed legislation or major actions "significantly affecting the quality of the human environment" (Council on Environmental Quality, 1997). Such actions range from constructing a highway to setting standards for greenhouse gas emissions. Regardless of the specific action that is proposed, all EISs must describe three things: (1) the environmental impact of the proposed action, (2) any adverse environmental effects that could not be avoided should the proposal be implemented, and (3) alternatives to the proposed action (Sec. 102 [1][c]). (In some cases, a less detailed environmental assessment may be substituted.) Furthermore, NEPA requires that an EIS clearly communicate its meaning to the public:

> Environmental impact statements shall be written in plain language and may use appropriate graphics so that decision makers and the public can readily understand them. Agencies should employ writers of clear prose or editors to write, review, or edit statements, which will be based upon the analysis and supporting data from the natural and social sciences and the environmental design arts. (Sec. 1502.8)

When federal agencies prepare a flawed EIS, they may be subject to legal action; or worse, they may allow harmful practices to go forward. For example, drilling for oil in deep water poses serious risks of environmental damage, as we discovered in the BP *Deepwater Horizon* oil spill in the Gulf of Mexico in 2010. Some scholars believe this could have been prevented if the federal agency in charge—the Minerals Management Service (MMS)—had fulfilled its NEPA responsibilities. Instead, in the BP *Deepwater Horizon* case, "the MMS approved the drilling and operating permits without undergoing full NEPA analysis," instead accepting the oil company's assurances that "that there was very little risk of a blowout," and if did occur, they had the tools to prevent a disaster. They didn't. In the future, some argue, agencies should require a "realistic worst-case analysis in deepwater drilling" in preparing their EISs (Flatt, 2010, p. 7A).

Public Comment on Draft Proposals

NEPA also requires that, before an agency completes a detailed statement of environmental impact, it must "make diligent efforts to involve the public" (Council on Environmental Quality, 1997, Sec. 1506.6 [a]). That is, the agency must take steps to ensure that interested groups and members of the public are informed and have opportunities for involvement prior to a decision. As a result, each federal agency must implement specific procedures for public participation in any decisions made by that agency that affect the environment. For example, citizens and groups concerned with natural resource policy ordinarily follow the rules for public comment developed in accordance with NEPA by the U.S. Forest Service, the National Park Service, the Bureau of Land Management, or the Fish and Wildlife Service. Community activists who work with human health and pollution issues are normally guided by EPA and state rules. The states are relevant because the EPA delegates to them the authority to issue air and water pollution permits for plants and construction permits and rules for managing waste programs (landfills and the like).

The requirements for public comment or communication under NEPA typically occur in three stages: (1) notification, (2) scoping, and (c) comment on draft decisions. These steps are guided by the rules adopted by the Council on Environmental Quality (CEQ) to ensure that all agencies comply with basic requirements for public participation that are implied in the NEPA statute itself.

The process normally starts with publication of a **Notice of Intent (NOI)** to the public. This announces an agency's intention to prepare an EIS for a proposed action. The NOI is published in the *Federal Register* and provides a brief description of "the proposed action and possible alternatives" (Council on Environmental Quality, 2007). The NOI may also be announced in the media and in special mailings to interested parties.

Typically, a notice describes the proposed regulation, management plan, or action and specifies the location and time of a public meeting or the period during which written comments will be received by the agency (Council on Environmental Quality, 2007, p. 13). An example of an NOI was the U.S. Department of Interior's proposal to list polar bears as a threatened species under the ESA. As you learned in Chapter 3, polar bears have seen their ice habitats shrink as the Arctic Ocean continues to warm. (As I write in 2011, polar bears are officially listed as threatened under this act; however, there are legal efforts to change this listing to endangered, a stronger category that would allow consideration of climate change as a factor in the bears' disappearing habitat.)

Importantly, when a federal agency fails to provide an NOI, courts can overturn any action it may take. For example, a U.S. District Court judge in West Virginia recently rebuked the Army Corps of Engineers for issuing permits for so-called mountaintop removal coal mining operations that "did not follow public notification laws" (Federal court, 2009, para. 1). As we saw in the last chapter, **mountaintop removal** is a particularly damaging form of coal mining. Such coal mining literally blows apart tops of mountains to get at coal seams. Giant machines then push the *overburden,* the former mountaintop, into the narrow mountain valleys, often smothering streams below in what is called *valley fill* operations. In this case, the judge told the Army Corps to issue a new notice, respond to public comments, and "reconsider the issuance of the permits" (para. 3).

The NOI under NEPA also describes an agency's **scoping** process. *Scoping* is a preliminary stage in an agency's development of a proposed rule or action, including any meetings and how the public can get involved. It involves canvassing interested members of the public about some interest—for example, a plan to reallocate permits for water trips down the Colorado River in the Grand Canyon—to determine what the concerns of the affected parties might be (Council on Environmental Quality, 2007). Such scoping might involve public workshops, field trips, letters, and agency personnel speaking one-on-one with members of the public.

Finally, NEPA rules require agencies to actively solicit public comment on the draft proposal or action. Public comments usually occur during public hearings and in written comments to the agency in the form of reports, letters, e-mails, postcards, or faxes. The public also may use this opportunity to comment on the adequacy of any EIS accompanying the proposal, or it may use the information in the EIS to assess the proposal itself.

In response, the agency is required to assess and consider comments received from the public. It must then respond in one of several ways: (a) by modifying the proposed alternatives, (b) by developing and evaluating new alternatives, (c) by making factual corrections, or (d) by "explain[ing] why the [public] comments do not warrant further agency response" (Council on Environmental Quality, 2007, Sec. 1503.4).

The success of NEPA's public participation process obviously depends on how well agencies comply with the law's original intent. For example, in its study of NEPA's effectiveness, the CEQ observed, the "success of a NEPA process heavily depends on whether an agency has systematically reached out to those who will be most affected by a proposal, gathered information . . . from them, and responded to the input by modifying or adding alternatives throughout the entire course of a planning process" (Council on Environmental Quality, 1997, p. 17).

Public Hearings and Citizen Comments

At the heart of NEPA, we've just seen, is the guarantee of the public's right to comment on proposed environmental projects. This often occurs through **public hearings**, as well as through written comments. Public hearings are forums for public comments before an agency takes action that might significantly affect the environment. As we saw earlier, NEPA requires agencies to actively solicit the public's involvement as part of its decision making. In this section, we'll look at the kind of communication that typically occurs in such public hearings.

Communication at Public Hearings

The public hearings required by NEPA usually occur in the states or local communities that may be affected by an agency's action. Typically, the agency will announce its proposed action, notify the public of the times and locations of the planned hearings, and then conduct the hearings, allowing interested parties to express their opinions. Both supporters and opponents of a proposal may attend, and both sides usually speak at public meetings.

For example, I recently attended a public hearing on a permit to construct a new coal-burning power plant in my state. Because of the interest in global warming, the hearing room was crowded—agency staff, lawyers for Duke Energy (the electric utility company), health professionals, students, representatives from environmental groups, parents with their young children, religious leaders, reporters, and many others. As usual, there were sign-in sheets for those of us wishing to speak. Before inviting comments from the public, the presiding official called on agency staff to provide technical information on the proposed permit. Then, others in the audience were given three minutes each to comment orally or to read a statement. Some individuals read from prepared statements; others spoke extemporaneously. In this hearing, the comments were overwhelmingly in opposition to the permit for the power plant.

Figure 4.2 Panel of environmentalists, business leaders, and public officials testifying at a public hearing on an invasive species (the Asian carp) into the Great Lakes on Capitol Hill in Washington, DC, in 2010.

AP Photo/Manuel Balce Ceneta

The comments themselves at public meetings may be polite or passionate, restrained or angry, or informed or highly opinionated and emotional. The range of comments reflects the diversity of opinions and interests of the community itself. Officials may urge members of the public to speak to the specific issue on the agenda, but the actual communication often departs from this, ranging from individuals' calm testimony, emotionally charged remarks, and stories of their families' experiences to criticism of opponents or public officials.

Some people may denounce the actions of the agency or respond noisily, even angrily, to proposals affecting their lives or communities. On the other hand, an individual's quiet testimony may be emotionally powerful. At the public hearing on the coal-burning plant in my state, a young mother told of her and her husband's borrowing money to install a solar panel, so concerned were they about global warming and their children's futures. Weeping quietly, she pleaded with the officials to deny the permit for the power plant.

The communication in public hearings also can be affected by factors other than personal emotions or concerns about an issue. Ordinary citizens find themselves apprehensive about having to speak in front of large groups, perhaps with a microphone, to unfamiliar officials. They may face opponents or others who are hostile to their views. Sometimes, they must wait hours for their turns to speak. Those with jobs or small children face additional constraints because they must take time from work or find (and often pay) someone to watch their children.

I return to these and other constraints in Chapter 9 when I describe some of the barriers to citizen participation in public hearings in low-income communities.

As I noted in Chapter 1, the National Research Council has found that "when done well, public participation improves the quality and legitimacy of a decision and . . . can lead to better results in terms of environmental quality" (Dietz & Stern, 2008). Still, many believe that public hearings are not an effective form of public participation due to the conditions that are typically imposed by crowded hearing rooms, limited time, volatile emotions, and long waiting times for speaking. Daniels and Walker (2001) go further when they contend that some public lands management agencies such as the Forest Service exhibit a "Three-'I' Model . . . inform, invite, and ignore." For example, agency officials will inform the public about a proposed action, such as a timber sale, then "invite the public to a meeting to provide comments on that action, and ignore what members of the public say" (p. 9). I will return to some of these shortcomings in Chapter 5.

Although adversarial and impolite at times, public meetings and hearings do reflect the diverse and messy norms of democratic life. At their best, meetings that invite wide participation by members of the public may generate comments and information that help agencies to shape or modify important decisions affecting the environment. Although they occasionally may be confrontational, such hearings provide many citizens their only opportunity to speak directly to government authority about matters of concern to them, their families, or their communities.

Mobilizing Public Comment: Fracking and the Roadless Rule

Public hearings are also used as forums by diverse groups—environmentalists, hunters, public health officials, or off-road recreationists, for example—who mobilize citizens to attend and speak as part of their groups' campaigns to influence an agency's decision. On controversial issues, such as logging in national forests or a proposal to lift a ban on the hunting of wolves, for example, thousands of citizens may testify at public hearings in support of one side or the other.

A dramatic example of citizen mobilization occurred in the U.S. Forest Service's adoption of its **Roadless Rule** for U.S. national forests. The rule, adopted in 2001, prohibits road building and restricts commercial logging on nearly 60 million acres of national forest lands in 39 states. The final rule reflected a year and a half of public comment under NEPA. (Here, I must admit a personal interest, having participated as president of the Sierra Club in mobilizing individuals to participate in the public comment process. For a more critical review of NEPA's role in the Roadless Rule, see Walker, 2004).

By the end of the process, the Forest Service had held more than 600 public meetings and received an unprecedented two million comments from members of the public, environmentalists, businesspeople, sports groups and motorized recreation associations, local residents, and state and local officials. As a result of the strong public support for protecting wild forests, the rule grew stronger, expanding the amount of protected (roadless) forest land. Forest Service Chief Mike Dombeck reflected, "In my entire career, this is the most extensive outreach of any policy I've observed" (Marston, 2001, p. 12, in Walker, 2004, p. 114).

Following its adoption, the Roadless Rule has been both praised and criticized for its public participation process. Its implementation initially was delayed by court challenges from logging interests and western state officials. In May 2005, the Bush administration dropped the Roadless Rule altogether after a hasty NEPA process. Environmental groups challenged this, and the case continues to be argued in the federal courts. The Obama administration is defending the Roadless Rule as this book goes to press. (For the status of the Roadless Rule, see http://roadless.fs.fed.us.) Part of the controversy has been a debate over the meaning of public participation itself and the goals it is intended to serve. Walker (2004) asked, "Does the *number* of public meetings and *amount* of comment letters received provide sufficient evidence of meaningful public participation?" (p. 115; emphasis added). I will take up this question more generally in the next chapter by describing some of the criticisms of public comment in environmental decision making.

More recently, the EPA has been studying the possible health impacts from **hydraulic fracturing or *fracking***, a controversial method used in drilling for oil and natural gas in many parts of the United States. Fracking involves the injection of large volumes of water, sand, and chemicals, under high pressure, into rock or shale formations to create fissures, which then release the trapped oil or gas. In 2010, the EPA held a series of widely attended public hearings to investigate the complaints of scientists and many citizens that "the chemicals used in fracturing may pose a threat, either underground or when waste fluids are handled and sometimes spilled on the surface" (ProPublica, 2010, para. 1).

| **Figure 4.3** | A Bureau of Land Management official facilitates a focus session on protecting water quality in the Monterey, California, watershed during America's Great Outdoors (AGO) Initiative (2011). |

U.S. Department of Agriculture/Flickr

Environmental and public health groups like Clean Water Action, Sierra Club, and the Gas Accountability Project, among others, seized on the EPA's four public hearings to mobilize thousands of citizens to attend and speak against the dangers from fracking. Typical was the crowd of more than 600 people who attended the Fort Worth, Texas, public hearing. "I'm sending out an SOS to the EPA," fracking critic Sharon Wilson told EPA officials. Wilson, a representative of the Texas Oil and Gas Accountability Project, favored strong regulation of the oil and natural gas industry as well as full disclosure of the chemicals used in fracking (Smith, 2010, para. 4). The EPA is expected to conclude its study of fracking in 2012, possibly issuing new regulations on the oil and gas industry.

Overall, NEPA, and its guarantee of public comment, has proved to be one of the most empowering laws in recent U.S. history. In terms of its scope and involvement of the public, NEPA has been the cornerstone of the principle of direct participation in governance through the right of any citizen to comment directly to agencies responsible for decisions affecting the environment. There remains one other guarantee of public participation, to which I now turn.

Right of Standing in Courts: Citizen Suits

Beyond the right to know and public comment is a third route for citizen participation in environmental decisions: the right of standing. A *right of standing* is based on the presumption that an individual having a sufficient interest in a matter may stand before legal authority to speak and seek protection of that interest in court. In both common law and provisions under U.S. environmental law, citizens—under specific conditions—may have standing to object to an agency's failure to enforce environmental standards or to hold a violator directly accountable.

Standing and Citizen Suits

The right of citizens to standing developed originally from common law, wherein individuals who have suffered an **injury in fact** to a legally protected right could seek redress in court. The definition of *injury* under common law normally meant a concrete, particular injury that an individual had suffered due to the actions of another party. One of the earliest cases of standing in an environmental case involved William Aldred, who in 1611 brought suit against his neighbor Thomas Benton. Benton had built a hog pen on an orchard near Aldred's house. Aldred complained that "the stench and unhealthy odors emanating from the pigs drifted onto [his] land and premises" and were so offensive that he and his family "could not come and go without being subjected to continuous annoyance" (9 Co. Rep. 57, 77 Eng. Rep. 816 [1611], in Steward & Krier, 1978, pp.117–118). Although Benton argued that "one ought not have so delicate a nose, that he cannot bear the smell of hogs," the court sided with Aldred and ordered Benton to pay for the damage caused to Aldred's property.

Aldred was able to pursue his claim before the court as a result of his and his family's injury in fact from the offensive odors. But, in the 20th century, the principle of injury in fact would be expanded in ways that allowed wider access to the courts by environmental interests. Two developments modified the strict common-law requirement of concrete, particular injury, allowing a greater opening for citizens to sue on behalf of environmental values.

First, the 1946 Administrative Procedure Act broadened the right of judicial review for persons "suffering a legal wrong because of agency action, or adversely affected or aggrieved by agency action" (5 U.S.C. A7 702, in Buck, 1996, p. 67). This was so because, under the APA, the courts generally have held that an agency must "weigh all information with fairness and not be 'arbitrary and capricious' " in adopting agency rules (Hays, 2000, p. 133). Thus, when an agency's actions depart from this standard, they are subject to citizen complaints under the APA; that is, because citizens have suffered from an "arbitrary and capricious" action, they have standing to seek protection in the courts. In succeeding years, this provision of the APA would be an important tool enabling environmental groups to hold agencies accountable for their actions toward the environment.

The second expansion of standing came in the form of **citizen suits** in major environmental laws. The provision for such lawsuits enables citizens to go into a federal court to ask that an environmental law be enforced. For example, the Clean Water Act confers standing on any citizen or "persons having an interest which is or may be adversely affected" to challenge violations of clean water permits if the state or federal agency fails to enforce the statutory requirements (*Clean Water Act*, 2007). Using this provision, for example, citizens in West Virginia invoked their right of standing by filing citizen suits against the practice of mountaintop removal, where as we've seen, coal companies literally push earth from the tops of mountains into nearby valleys, filling streams in their search for coal. Other environmental laws that allow citizen suits include the ESA, the Clean Air Act, the Toxic Substances Control Act, and the Comprehensive Environmental Response Compensation and Liability Act (the Superfund law).

The purpose of a citizen suit is to challenge an agency's lack of enforcement of environmental standards; local citizens and public interest groups are empowered to sue the agency directly to enforce the law. Jonathan Adler (2000), a senior fellow at the Competitive Enterprise Institute, explained the rationale behind this. When federal regulators "overlook local environmental deterioration or are compromised by interest group pressure, local groups in affected areas are empowered to trigger enforcement themselves" (para. 48). This is especially important in cases of **agency capture**, in which a regulated industry pressures or influences officials to ignore violations of a corporation's permit for environmental performance (for example, its air or water discharges).

Landmark Cases on Environmental Standing

Citizens' claims to the right of standing are subject not only to the provisions of specific statutes (for example, the Clean Water Act) but also to judicial interpretations of the

cases and controversies clause in Article III of the U.S. Constitution. Despite its arcane title, this requirement serves an important purpose. The cases and controversies clause "ensures that lawsuits are heard only if the parties are true adversaries, because only true adversaries will aggressively present to the courts all issues" (Van Tuyn, 2000, p. 42).

To determine if a party is a "true adversary," the U.S. Supreme Court uses three tests: (1) persons bringing a case must be able to prove an injury in fact; (2) this injury must be "fairly traceable" to an action of the defendant, and (3) the Court must be able to redress the injury through a favorable ruling (p. 42). Although environmental statutes grant a right of standing, citizens still must meet these three constitutional tests before proceeding.

The main question in granting standing in environmental cases is the meaning of *injury in fact.* What qualifies as injury where individual citizens seek to enforce the provisions of an environmental law? The Supreme Court has worked out an uneven and, at times, confusing answer to this question in several landmark cases.

Sierra Club v. Morton (1972)

The Supreme Court's 1972 ruling in **Sierra Club v. Morton** provided the first guidance for determining standing under the Constitution's cases and controversies clause in an environmental case. In this case, the Sierra Club sought to block plans by Walt Disney Enterprises to build a resort in Mineral King Valley in California. Plans for the resort included the building of a road through Sequoia National Park.

In its suit, the Sierra Club argued that a road would "destroy or otherwise adversely affect the scenery, natural and historic objects, and wildlife of the park for future generations" (Lindstrom & Smith, 2001, p. 105). Although the Supreme Court found that such damage could constitute an injury in fact, it noted that the Sierra Club did not allege that any of its members themselves had suffered any actual injury, and therefore, they were not true adversaries. Instead, the Sierra Club had asserted a right to be heard simply on the basis of its interest in protecting the environment. The Court rejected the group's claim of standing in the case, ruling that a long-standing interest in a problem was not enough to constitute an injury in fact (Lindstrom & Smith, 2001, p. 105). (For a dissenting view, see: "Another Viewpoint: Do Trees Have Standing?")

Despite its ruling in *Sierra Club v. Morton,* the Supreme Court spelled out an expansive standard for a successful claim of standing. It observed that, in the future, the Sierra Club need only allege an injury to its members' interests—for example, that its members would no longer be able to enjoy an unspoiled wilderness or their normal recreational pursuits. The Sierra Club immediately and successfully amended its suit against Disney Enterprises, arguing that such injury would occur to its members if the road through Sequoia National Park were to be built. (Subsequently, Mineral King Valley itself was added to Sequoia National Park, and Disney Enterprises withdrew its plans to build the resort.)

Another Viewpoint: Do Trees Have Standing?

In his famous dissent in *Sierra Club v. Morton,* Justice William O. Douglas argued that even trees and rivers should have standing. He noted that U.S. law already gave standing to some inanimate objects and that environmental goals would be enhanced if citizens could sue on behalf of natural objects:

> The critical question of "standing" would be simplified...if we fashioned a federal rule that allowed environmental issues to be litigated before federal agencies or federal courts in the name of the inanimate object about to be despoiled, defaced, or invaded by roads and bulldozers and where injury is the subject of public outrage....

> Inanimate objects are sometimes parties in litigation. A ship has a legal personality, a fiction found useful for maritime purposes....

> So it should be as respects valleys, alpine meadows, rivers, lakes, estuaries, beaches, ridges, [and] groves of trees.... The river, for example, is the living symbol of all the life it sustains or nourishes.... The river as plaintiff speaks for the ecological unit of life that is part of it. Those people who have a meaningful relation to that body of water— whether it be a fisherman, a canoeist, a zoologist, or a logger—must be able to speak for the values which the river represents and which are threatened with destruction....

SOURCE: *Sierra Club v. Morton,* 1972; see also the classic essay, C. Stone, "Should Trees Have Standing?" (1996).

The Court's liberal interpretation of the test for injury in fact in *Sierra Club v. Morton,* along with the right of standing in many environmental laws, produced a 20-year burst of environmental litigation by citizens and environmental groups. This trend continued until the Supreme Court issued a series of conservative rulings that narrowed the basis for citizens' standing.

Lujan v. Defenders of Wildlife (1992)

In the 1990s, the U.S. Supreme Court handed down several rulings that severely limited citizen suits in environmental cases. In perhaps the most important case, **Lujan v. Defenders of Wildlife** (1992), the Court rejected a claim of standing by the conservation group Defenders of Wildlife under the citizen suit provision of the ESA. The ESA declares that "any person may commence a civil suit on his own behalf (A) to enjoin any person, including the United States and any other governmental instrumentality or agency . . . who is alleged to be in violation of any provision" of the act (Endangered Species Act, 1973, A71540 [g] [1].) In its lawsuit, Defenders of Wildlife argued that the secretary of the interior (Lujan) had failed in his duties to ensure that U.S. funding of projects overseas—in this case, in Egypt—did not jeopardize the habitats of endangered species, as the law required (Stearns, 2000, p. 363).

Writing for the majority, Justice Antonin Scalia stated that Defenders had failed to satisfy constitutional requirements for injury in fact that would grant standing under the ESA. He wrote that the Court rejected the view that the citizen suit provision of the statute conferred upon "*all* persons an abstract, self-contained, non-instrumental 'right' to have the Executive observe the procedures required by law" (Lujan v. Defenders of Wildlife, 1992, p. 573). Rather, he explained, the plaintiff must have suffered a tangible and particular harm not unlike the common-law requirement (Adler, 2000, p. 52). This ruling seriously constrained *Sierra Club v. Morton,* in which Sierra Club members needed only to prove injury to their interests—that is, that they couldn't enjoy their recreational pursuits or experience of wilderness.

Consequently, courts began to limit sharply citizen claims of standing under citizen suit provisions of environmental statutes. Writing in the *New York Times,* Glaberson (1999) reported that the Court's rulings in the 1990s were one of the most "profound setbacks for the environmental movement in decades" (p. A1).

Friends of the Earth, Inc. v. Laidlaw Environmental Services, Inc. (2000)

In a more recent case, the Supreme Court appeared to reverse its strict Lujan doctrine, holding that the knowledge of a possible threat to a legally recognized interest (clean water) was enough to establish a "sufficient stake" by a plaintiff in enforcing the law (Adler, 2000, p. 52).

In 1992, Friends of the Earth and CLEAN, a local environmental group, sued Laidlaw Environmental Services in Roebuck, South Carolina, under the Clean Water Act citizen suit provision. Their lawsuit alleged that Laidlaw had repeatedly violated its permit limiting the discharge of pollutants (including mercury, a highly toxic substance) into the nearby North Tyger River. Residents of the area who had lived by or used the river for boating and fishing testified that they were "concerned that the water contained harmful pollutants" (Stearns, 2000, p. 382).

The Supreme Court's majority in **Friends of the Earth, Inc. v. Laidlaw Environmental Services, Inc.** (2000) ruled that Friends of the Earth and CLEAN did not need to prove an actual (particular) harm to residents. Writing for the majority, Justice Ruth Bader Ginsburg stated that injury to the plaintiff came from lessening the "aesthetic and recreational values of the area" for residents and users of the river due to their knowledge of Laidlaw's repeated violations of its clean water permit (Adler, 2000, p. 56). In this case, the plaintiffs were not required to prove that Laidlaw's violations of its water permit had contributed to actual deterioration in water quality. It was sufficient that they showed that residents' knowledge of these violations had discouraged their normal use of the river.

Massachusetts v. EPA (2007): Global Warming and the Clean Air Act

The right of standing arose as a pivotal issue in *Massachusetts et al. v. Environmental Protection Agency et al.* (2007), the Supreme Court's first-ever ruling on global warming. Twelve states, including Massachusetts and the territory of American Samoa, and a number of environmental groups petitioned the Supreme Court to direct the EPA to regulate tailpipe emissions of greenhouse gases from motor vehicles under the Clean Air Act. In a 5–4 ruling, the Court sharply rebuked the Bush administration's claim that the EPA lacked this authority or, if it had the authority, could choose not to exercise it.

The central issue in this case was whether carbon dioxide and other greenhouse gases were an "air pollutant" under the definition of this term in the Clean Air Act: "any air pollution agent . . . including any physical, chemical . . . substance or matter which is emitted into or otherwise enters the ambient air" (Clean Air Act Amendments, 1990, 7602[g]). While the majority ultimately agreed that carbon dioxide did meet this definition, the justices first had to decide the question of the plaintiffs' standing to argue before the Court.

In a strategic move, the petitioners decided to list the coastal state of Massachusetts first as the lead plaintiff. (Only one plaintiff is required to be a true adversary for the case to proceed on its merits.) This proved to be important, because as Massachusetts alleged, rising sea levels threatened the economic interests of its citizens. The state also argued that EPA's failure to set greenhouse gas standards was "arbitrary and capricious" (something prohibited by the APA). Justice John Paul Stevens delivered the opinion of the Court on the question of standing:

> EPA's steadfast refusal to regulate greenhouse gas emissions presents a risk of harm to Massachusetts that is both "actual" and "imminent," *Lujan,* 504 U.S. . . . . and there is a "substantial likelihood that the judicial relief requested" will prompt EPA to take steps to reduce that risk. (*Massachusetts et al. v. Environmental Protection Agency et al.,* 2007, p. 3)

☞ FYI | Do Nations Threatened With Rising Sea Levels From Global Warming Have a Right of Standing?

Do Pacific island nations like Kiribati, Vanuatu, and Tuvalu or low-lying countries such as Bangladesh have standing to sue the U.S., China, and other nations who are the main sources of greenhouse gases that contribute to climate change and rising sea levels? A study by the Foundation for International Environmental Law and Development says "small island nations and other threatened countries have the right and likely the procedural means to pursue an inter-state case before the United Nations' International Court of Justice":

> "Some of these countries are getting increasingly desperate," Chrisoph Schwarte, the paper's lead author, said. . . . Many leaders are looking for ways to make the United States and others understand the threats they face from rising sea levels, droughts and storm surges. . . .

> "If nothing significant happens within the next two or three years, I really wouldn't be surprised if countries go to court."

Suing to force a country to reduce its greenhouse gas emissions is a tricky proposition. If a person is harmed or a livelihood threatened, he or she can take the offender to court for the damages incurred. But, what if the victim is an entire country, and the damages—thousands forced to relocate or the loss of tourism dollars because of coral bleaching—are expected but not yet seen? More complicated still is pinpointing the perpetrator. A smokestack in China? The 24-7 air conditioner blasting from a shopping mall in Iowa? Emissions-belching SUVs in Sydney, Australia?

SOURCE: Adapted from Friedman, L. (2010, October 4).

Finally, responding to the EPA's objection that a favorable ruling for the plaintiffs would not solve the problem, Justice Stevens wrote, "While regulating motor-vehicle emissions may not by itself *reverse* global warming, it does not follow that the Court lacks jurisdiction to decide whether EPA has a duty to take steps to *slow* or *reduce* it" (*Massachusetts et al. v. Environmental Protection Agency et al.,* 2007, p. 4).

With these rulings, the Supreme Court reaffirmed the rationale that citizens, as well as states, have an interest in the enforcement of environmental quality under the provisions of specific laws such as the Clean Water Act or the Clean Air Act. However, disagreement over the criteria for standing in environmental cases is likely to continue. (See "FYI: Do Nations Threatened With Rising Sea Levels From Global Warming Have a Right of Standing?") At stake are differing interpretations of injury in fact and the rights of citizens to compel the government to enforce environmental laws.

Growth of Public Participation Internationally

The expansion of rights of the public to participate actively in decisions about the environment has occurred not only in the United States. At its 2008 meeting in Latvia, European nations reaffirmed the goals of the Aarhus Convention, guaranteeing the rights of access to information and participation in decisions about the environment. Marek Belka, executive secretary of the UN Economic Commission for Europe, observed that the convention's core principles "empower ordinary members of the public to hold governments accountable and to play a greater role in promoting more sustainable forms of development" (*Aarhus Parties*, 2008). Similar moves to implement or strengthen the role of the public in decisions affecting the environment are actively underway in China and central Asia, as well as in many parts of Africa and South America.

In the past decade, in fact, more and more nations have begun to guarantee public access to information and implement various forms of public participation in governmental decisions about the environment. Clearly, the European Union, the United Nations Economic Commission for Europe (UNECE), and many of the former nations of the Soviet Union have taken the lead in this area. For example, UNECE has successfully negotiated five environmental treaties, governing trans-boundaries environmental protections in Europe for air pollution and watercourses and lakes and extending guarantees for environmental impact assessments.

Of these five treaties, the Convention on Access to Information, Public Participation, and Access to Justice in Environmental Matters—often called the Aarhus Convention—is unprecedented for its guarantees of public participation. Adopted in 1998 in the Danish city of Aarhus, the **Aarhus Convention** is a "new kind" of agreement, linking environmental rights and human rights (United Nations Economic Commission for Europe, 2008). Article 1 clearly announces its goal:

> In order to contribute to the protection of the right of every person of present and future generations to live in an environment adequate to his or her health and well-being, each party shall guarantee the rights of access to information, public participation in decision-making, and access to justice in environmental matters.

These three principles—access to information, public participation, and access to justice—are developed in detail, with concrete procedures for ensuring citizen access to these rights.

In many ways, the approach of the Aarhus Convention goes further than U.S. environmental law under NEPA by granting a "right" to public information and to review by public authorities. For example, the right of *access to justice* in Article 9 ensures that "any person who considers that his or her request for information . . . has been ignored, [or] wrongfully refused . . . has access to a review procedure before a court of law or another independent and impartial body" (United Nations Economic Commission for Europe, 2008, para. 13).

The idea of transparency, particularly, is gaining in popularity internationally. For example, in addition to the Aarhus Convention, the UNECE also tracks changes in the U.S. TRI for programs in Europe and nations of the former Soviet Union. And, programs similar to the TRI have been established or are being implemented not only in Europe but Asia, Australia, Canada, and some countries in South America and Africa. These TRI-like initiatives range from emission inventories, which collect data on specific chemical releases, to more comprehensive programs known as **Pollutant Release and Transfer Register** (PRTR) that expand on this data collection. Like the TRI, PRTR programs require not only the collection of data but mandatory reporting of a facility's chemical releases as well as public access to this data. PRTR programs also differ in some nations. For example, Japan collects information on automobile emissions, while Mexico's PRTR is voluntary for industries.

Clearly, demands for public participation in environmental matters are increasing worldwide. For example, in early 2008, the Carter Center in Atlanta convened an International Conference on the Right to Public Information. More than 125 representatives from 40 nations gathered to "identify the necessary steps and measures to ensure the effective creation, implementation, and exercise of the right of access to public information" (Carter Center, 2008, para. 2). Elsewhere, new initiatives for public participation are emerging in Asia, Africa, and Latin America, with a vigorous movement for environmental protection and public access to information growing in China, particularly. (For updates on recent initiatives to strengthen public participation guarantees in China, see www.greenlaw.org.cn/enblog; this blog is a joint project of the Natural Resources Defense Council and the China Environmental Culture Promotion Association.)

SUMMARY

In this chapter, I've identified some of the legal rights and forums that enable you and other citizens to participate directly and publicly in decisions about the environment.

- In the introduction, I defined *public participation* as the ability of citizens and groups to influence environmental decisions through (a) the right to know or access to relevant information, (b) the right to comment to the agency that is responsible for a decision, and (c) the right, through the courts, to hold public agencies and businesses accountable for their environmental decisions and behaviors.

- Basic to effective public participation is a *right to know,* to have access to information. In the first section, I described two powerful tools for citizens' right to know: (1) the Freedom of Information Act (FOIA), and (2) the Toxic Release Inventory (TRI).
- In the second section, I explored the right of public comment that is guaranteed by the National Environmental Policy Act (NEPA) and its requirements for: (a) an environmental impact statement about a proposed action and (b) concrete procedures for public comment on this action.
- The third section described a third basic right of public participation—the right of *standing* of citizens to enforce major environmental laws in court.
- Finally, initiatives guaranteeing public participation are expanding in Europe, Asia, and other nations. The most comprehensive of these rights-based approaches is Europe's Aarhus Convention, which seeks to implement rights of access to information, public comment on environmental matters, and review by the courts.

SUGGESTED RESOURCES

- Thomas Dietz and Paul C. Stern (Editors), *Public Participation in Environmental Assessment and Decision Making.* National Research Council. Washington, DC: National Academies Press, 2008.
- An online summary *Massachusetts et al. v. Environmental Protection Agency et al.* (2007), the U.S. Supreme Court ruling on global warming, 2008: www.pewclimate .org/epavsma.cfm
- *Rio Declaration on Environment and Development,* adopted at the United Nations Conference on Environment and Development (Earth Summit) in Rio de Janeiro, 1992.

KEY TERMS

DISCUSSION QUESTIONS

1. Are there limits to what the public has a right to know? For example, should the U.S. government have a right to restrict the public's access to information about oil refineries, pipelines, nuclear plants, or other environmental facilities to prevent potential terrorists from exploiting vulnerabilities in these facilities?

2. Do public hearings merely allow angry citizens to blow off steam about controversial environmental actions? Do such forums serve an important role for public comment, or are they just window dressing?

3. Do trees have standing? How about streams, plants, and animals? What about Pacific island nations and low-lying villages threatened with a rise in sea levels? Do they have standing to sue the U.S. and other nations who emit greenhouse gases for contributing to global warming?

4. How would these island nations meet the test for *true adversaries,* that is, that they suffer: (a) an injury in fact, (b) that this injury be *fairly traceable* to an action of the defendant, and (c) that a court is able to redress the injury through a favorable ruling?

REFERENCES

Aarhus Parties commit to strengthening environmental democracy in the UNECE region and beyond. (2008, June 11–13). UN Economic Commission for Europe. Retrieved August 31, 2008, from http://www.unece.org

Adler, J. H. (2000, March 2–3). *Stand or deliver: Citizen suits, standing, and environmental protection.* Paper presented at the Duke University Law and Policy Forum Symposium on Citizen Suits and the Future of Standing in the

21st Century. Retrieved August 20, 2003, from www.law.duke.edu/journals

Buck, S. J. (1996). *Understanding environmental administration and law.* Washington, DC: Island Press.

Carter Center. (2008, February 27–29). *International Conference on the Right to Public Information.* Retrieved December 30, 2008, from http://www.cartercenter.org

Clean Air Act Amendments. (1990). U.S.C. Title 42. Chapter 85. Subsection III. 7602 [g]. Retrieved November 2, 2011, from http://www.law.cornell.edu/uscode

Clean Water Act–Citizen Suits. (2007, July 30). Washington, DC: U.S. Environmental Protection Agency. Retrieved September 5, 2008, from http://www.epa.gov

Core values for the practice of public participation. (2008). The International Association for Public Participation. Retrieved from http://www.iap2.org

Council on Environmental Quality. (1997, January). *The national environmental policy act: A study of its effectiveness after twenty-five years.* Washington, DC: Council on Environmental Quality, Executive Office of the President. Retrieved from http://ceq.eh.doe.gov

Council on Environmental Quality (CEQ). (2007, December). *A citizen's guide to the NEPA: Having your voice heard.* Retrieved December 29, 2008, from http://ceq.hss .doe.gov

Daniels, S. E., & Walker, G. B. (2001). *Working through environmental conflict: The collaborative learning approach.* Westport, CT: Praeger.

Declaration of Bizkaia on the Right to the Environment. (1999, February 10–13). International Seminar on the Right to the Environment, held in Bilbao, Spain, under the auspices of UNESCO and the United Nations High Commissioner for Human Rights. Retrieved from http:// unesdoc.unesco.org

Dietz, T., & Stern, P. C. (2008). *Public participation in environmental assessment and decision making.* National Research Council. Washington, DC: National Academies Press.

Environmental Protection Agency. (2010, October 7). *What is the Toxic Release Inventory (TRI) program?* Retrieved October 12, 2010, from http://www.epa .gov

Federal court says Army Corps of Engineers ignored public process in issuing permits for mountaintop removal coal mining in WV. (2009, November 25). Sierra Club Press Room. Retrieved October 14, 2010, from http://action .sierraclub.org

Flatt, V. B. (2010, June 5). What if drilling goes really wrong? *The News & Observer,* p. 7A.

Friedman, L. (2010, October 4). Developing countries could sue for climate action— study. *New York Times.* Retrieved November 2, 2011, from http://www .nytimes.com

Glaberson, W. (1999, June 5). Novel antipollution tool is being upset by courts. *The New York Times.* Retrieved March 1, 2009, from http://query.nytimes.com

Hays, S. P. (2000). *A history of environmental politics since 1945.* Pittsburgh, PA: University of Pittsburgh Press.

Lindstrom, M. J., & Smith, Z. A. (2001). *The national environmental policy act: Judicial misconstruction, legislative indifference, & executive neglect.* College Station: Texas A&M University Press.

Lujan v. Defenders of Wildlife, 504 U.S. 555 (1992).

Markowitz, G., & Rosner, D. (2002). *Deceit and denial: The deadly politics of industrial pollution.* Berkeley: University of California Press.

Marston, B. (2001, May 7). A modest chief moved the Forest Service miles down the road. *High Country News, 33*(9). Retrieved August 25, 2003, from www .hcn.org

Massachusetts et al. v. Environmental Protection Agency et al. (2007). Supreme

Court of the United States. Retrieved December 30, 2008, from www.supreme courtus.gov

National Environmental Policy Act, 42 U.S.C.A. A7 4321 *et seq.* (1969).

Parker, L., Johnson, K., & Locy, T. (2002, May 15). Post-9/11, government stingy with information. *USA Today,* p. 1A. Retrieved March 12, 2005, from www .usatoday.com/ news/nation

ProPublica. (2010). Hydraulic fracturing: What is hydraulic fracturing? Retrieved October 23, 2010, from http://www .propublica.org/

Rio Declaration on Environment and Development. (1992). United Nations Conference on Environment and Development. Rio de Janeiro. Retrieved October 4, 2010, from www.unep.org/

Sierra Club v. Morton, 405 U.S. 727. (1972). FindLaw. Retrieved December 29, 2008, from http://caselaw.lp.findlaw.com

Smith. J. Z. (2010, July 9). Fort Worth meeting on gas drilling process draws heated response. *Star-Telegram.* Retrieved October 23, 2010, from www.star-tele gram.com/

Stearns, M. L. (2000, March 2–3). *From Lujan to Laidlaw: A preliminary model of environmental standing.* Paper presented at the Duke University Law and Policy Forum Symposium on Citizen Suits and the Future of Standing in the 21st Century. Retrieved from www.law .duke.edu/journals

Stephan, M. (2002). Environmental information disclosure programs: They work, but why? *Social Science Quarterly, 83*(1), 190–205.

Steward, R. B., & Krier, J. (Eds.). (1978). *Environmental law and public policy.* New York: Bobbs-Merrill.

Stone, C. (1996). *Should trees have standing? And other essays on law, morals and the environment* (Rev. ed.). Dobbs Ferry, NY: Oceana.

Sunshine and shadows: The national security archive FOIA audit. (2010, March 15). Retrieved October 11, 2010, from http:// www.gwu.edu

United Nations Conference on Environment and Development. (1992, June 3–14). Rio de Janeiro, Brazil.

United Nations Economic Commission for Europe. (2008, March 12). *Text of the [Aarhus] convention.* Retrieved December 31, 2008, from http://www .unece.org

Van Tuyn, P. (2000). "Who do you think you are?" Tales from the trenches of the environmental standing battle. *Environmental Law, 30*(1): 41–49.

Walker, G. B. (2004). The roadless areas initiative as national policy: Is public participation an oxymoron? In S. P. Depoe, J. W. Delicath, & M-F. A. Elsenbeer (Eds.), *Communication and public participation in environmental decision making* (pp. 113–135). Albany: State University of New York Press.

White House. (2009, January 21). Memorandum for the heads of executive departments and agencies. Press Office. Retrieved October 11, 2010, from http:// www.whitehouse.gov/

Citizens rally against hydraulic fracturing for natural gas in the Marcellus Shale region of New York, at the Capitol in Albany, 2011. Fracking has produced intense controversy in many areas of the United States.

AP Photo/Mike Groll

CHAPTER 5

Managing Conflict: Collaboration and Environmental Disputes

Many citizens, environmentalists, business leaders, and others have become increasingly frustrated with public hearings and traditional forms of public participation. Some have turned to other ways to resolve conflicts over environmental issues—conflicts, for example, over logging in Canada's Great Bear Rainforest, feuds between ranchers and conservationists over prairie dogs, opposition to dams that impede salmon runs on the Klamath River in Oregon and northern California, and more. The purpose of this chapter is to describe the adoption by many community leaders, environmentalists, natural resource industries, and others of some form of collaboration to resolve environmental disputes.

Chapter Preview

- In the first section of this chapter, I describe the dissatisfaction with some forms of public participation, such as public hearings, and I identify a range of alternatives for managing environmental conflicts: citizens' advisory committees, natural resource partnerships, and community-based collaboration.
- In the second section, I ask, When is collaboration appropriate? And, what communication skills are required for successful collaboration? We explore two areas: requirements for successful collaboration and two case studies of collaboration about water quality and the Great Bear Rainforest.
- Finally, in the third section, I consider criticisms of collaboration and identify some of the circumstances in which collaboration may not be appropriate for resolving environmental conflicts.

(Continued)

(Continued)

When you've finished this chapter, you should be familiar with the benefits of collaborative approaches to resolving environmental disputes and with the communication skills needed for successful collaboration. You should also be aware of barriers to effective collaboration and circumstances under which collaborative approaches may not be appropriate.

In hundreds of communities across the country, citizens, environmentalists, business leaders, and public officials are experimenting with new approaches to public participation in environmental disputes. They are talking with their opponents across the table, working through their differences, and in many cases resolving conflicts that have festered for years. These innovative forms of conflict management have been called by different names: community-based collaboration, citizen advisory boards, consensus decision making, and alternative dispute resolution models. Usually, they involve a form of communication called collaboration.

Collaboration is defined as "constructive, open, civil communication, generally as dialogue; a focus on the future; an emphasis on learning; and some degree of power sharing and leveling of the playing field" (Walker, 2004, p. 123). In many cases, participants will strive to reach agreement by *consensus,* which usually means that discussions will not end until everyone has had a chance to share his or her differences and find common ground. For example, after years of conflict, ranchers, environmentalists, and off-road vehicle recreationalists (who often fought over public lands in the West) came together in an unprecedented agreement over Idaho's Owyhee Canyonlands; the agreement's designation of wilderness and wild rivers is one of the largest additions in recent years to the U.S. wild and scenic river system (Barker, 2010; Eilperin, 2004). (See "FYI: Idaho at Forefront of Collaboration on Public Land Use.")

☞ FYI "Idaho at Forefront of Collaboration on Public Land Use" (excerpt from the *Idaho Statesman*, May 2, 2010)

Private property rights Fred Grant said he lost longtime friends over his willingness to sit down with environmentalists and forge a bill to protect the Owyhee Canyonlands and the ranching culture [in Idaho].

But the 2009 law which established...money for ranchers, more than 517,000 acres of wilderness, and 315 miles of wild rivers was worth the effort, he said. "I don't think there is anybody I trust more than the conservationists on the Owyhee Initiative Board," Grant said.

Similar collaborations have changed the dynamics of public land management across the American West....

Successes in the Owyhees [and other areas]...are putting Idaho at the forefront in a national shift from confrontational conservation to collaboration...." This may be the best opportunity for conservation since (Theodore Roosevelt's) time," said [U.S. Forest Service Chief Tom] Tidwell.

New Approaches to Environmental Disputes

Since the passage of the National Environmental Policy Act (NEPA), the public's right to comment on government actions affecting the environment has been widely recognized, and forums for public involvement have proliferated. As we learned in the previous chapter, public comment on an environmental proposal typically takes the form of public hearings, citizen testimony, and written comments. Yet, citizens and public officials alike feel that these processes sometimes produce more frustration and division than they do reasoned decision making. Officials and consultants often speak in technical jargon, using such phrases as *parts per billion* of chemical substances, and nonexpert members of a community sometimes feel that their concerns do not matter, that their efforts to speak are dismissed by public officials and experts. In this section, I examine some of the criticisms of traditional public hearings and identify some of the emerging alternatives for public involvement.

Criticism of Public Hearings

Several years ago, public officials in a town near a mine announced a public hearing after they had decided informally to build a hazardous waste facility near residential homes and a hospital. Many of the town's residents and patients' advocates understandably were upset at this. The atmosphere at the public hearing was electric; many voiced their anger at officials who sat stone-faced in the front of the auditorium. While some testified, other members of the audience shouted at the officials. One young man rushed to the front of the auditorium and dumped a bag of garbage in front of the officials to dramatize his objection to hazardous waste. Area TV stations and news editorials denounced the "irrational" behavior of residents and the heavy reliance on emotion.

Are ordinary citizens really irrational? Or are public officials insensitive to the concerns of ordinary citizens, dismissing citizens' fears because they lack technical expertise? Certainly, some officials feel that the behavior of citizens is "overdramatized and hysterical" and that they must endure "the public gauntlet" of angry, shouting, sign-waving protesters (Senecah, 2004, pp. 17, 18). Yet, environmental communication scholar Susan L. Senecah (2004) poses the question differently: Are public hearings sometimes divisive or unproductive because of the way the public acts, or is there something wrong with the process itself? She suggests that, in many local conflicts, a gap exists between what the public expects and their "actual experiences" from participating in these forums (p. 18). Although NEPA procedures require officials to solicit the views of the public, formal mechanisms for public participation are sometimes simply ritualistic processes that give members of the public little opportunity to influence decisions. It's no surprise, then, that ordinary citizens so often experience "frustration, disillusionment, skepticism, and anger" (Senecah, 2004, p. 18).

What has gone wrong? Stephen Depoe, director of the University of Cincinnati's Center for Environmental Communication Studies, and John Delicath (2004) of the

U.S. General Accounting Office surveyed the extensive research on traditional modes of public participation, such as written comments and public hearings. They identified five primary shortcomings:

1. Public participation typically operates on technocratic models of rationality, in which policy makers, administrative officials, and experts see their roles as educating and persuading the public of the legitimacy of their decisions.

2. Public participation often occurs too late in the decision-making process, sometimes even after decisions have already been made.

3. Public participation often follows an adversarial trajectory, especially when public participation processes are conducted in a decide–announce–defend mode on the part of officials.

4. Public participation often lacks adequate mechanisms and forums for informed dialogue among stakeholders.

5. Public participation often lacks adequate provisions to ensure that input gained through public participation makes a real impact on decisions' outcomes. (pp. 2–3)

Although formal mechanisms for citizens' involvement in influencing environmental decisions have been effective on some occasions, on others, they have fallen far short of citizens' expectations. Too often, disputes over local land use or the cleanup of communities contaminated by chemical pollution linger for years. In many of these cases, citizens, businesses, government agencies, and environmentalists have turned to alternatives to public hearings to resolve conflicts over environmental problems.

Emergence of Alternative Forms of Public Participation

Starting in the 1990s, new forms of public involvement in environmental decisions began to emerge—from local, neighborhood initiatives to Environmental Protection Agency (EPA) collaborations with cities over new standards for safe drinking water. As citizens, public officials, businesses, and some environmentalists grew frustrated with traditional forms, they began to experiment with new ways of organizing public participation: scoping meetings, listening sessions, advisory committees, blue-ribbon commissions, citizen juries, negotiated rule making, consensus-building exercises, and professional facilitation, among others (Dietz & Stern, 2008). For example, the U.S. Institute for Environmental Conflict Resolution, an independent federal program, works with local groups and public officials to "find workable solutions to tough environmental conflicts" (www.erc.gov), while the EPA provides alternative dispute resolution (ADR) services to deal with environmental disputes and potential conflicts through its Conflict Prevention and Resolution Center (www.epa.gov/adr/cprc_adratepa.html).

At the heart of these experiments is some version of community or place-based collaboration among the relevant parties. Later in this chapter, I'll identify characteristics of collaboration that help to explain its success or failure. But first, let's look at three forms that collaboration about environmental conflicts can take: (1) citizens' advisory committees, (2) natural resource partnerships, and (3) community-based collaborations.

Citizens' Advisory Committees

One of the most common types of collaboration is the **citizens' advisory committee.** Also called citizens' advisory panels or boards, these usually are groups that a local or even national government agency appoints to solicit input from diverse interests—citizens, businesses, environmentalists—in a community about a project or problem. For example, the Department of Defense uses Restoration Advisory Boards (RABs) to advise military officials on the social, economic, and environmental impacts of military base closings and the restoration of military lands. The purpose of RABs, which were initiated in 1994, is to "achieve dialogue between the installation and affected stakeholders; provide a vehicle for two-way communication; and provide a mechanism for earlier public input" (Santos & Chess, 2003, p. 270). One successful RAB, composed of local interests and military officials, collaborated in helping the Department of Defense to convert the former Rocky Mountain Arsenal, a chemical weapons facility, into the Rocky Mountain Arsenal National Wildlife Refuge, where today, bison and other wildlife adapted to the high plains browse (www.fws.gov/rockymountainarsenal).

The impetus for involving communities in the work of federal agencies is a result of the Federal Advisory Committee Act of 1972. The impact of this act can be seen in other agencies that also use citizen advisory panels. For example, the EPA uses citizen advisory panels to involve citizens in ongoing projects to clean up abandoned toxic waste sites. Similarly, the Department of Energy (DOE) relies on site-specific advisory boards to involve nearby residents during the cleanup of toxic waste at former energy sites, such as the nuclear weapons production facility in Fernald, Ohio. (For case studies of the troubled collaboration between citizens and the DOE at the Fernald nuclear site, see Depoe, 2004; Hamilton, 2004, 2008.)

For most citizen advisory committees, the government agency selects participants to represent various interests or points of view or to be "representative, that is, a microcosm of the socioeconomic characteristics and the issue orientation of the public in [a] particular area" (Beierle & Cayford, 2002, pp. 45–46). The committee's work normally takes place over time in meetings of the participants. The committee's decision-making process may or may not assume that consensus will be achieved, although that is often the stated objective. Typically, the outcome of collaboration is a set of recommendations to the agency (Beierle & Cayford, 2002).

Natural Resource Partnerships

Particularly in western states, the idea of collaboration has taken off as diverse groups seek ways to manage differences over the uses of watersheds, public lands, and other natural features. As early as the 1990s, Colorado's *High Country News* observed

| Figure 5.1 | Intense differences among logging companies, First Nations people, local businesses, and environmentalists blocked agreement over management of the Great Bear Rainforest for many years. |

Dogwood Initiative/Flickr

that, "coalitions of ranchers, environmentalists, county commissioners, government officials, loggers, skiers, and jeepers are popping up as often as wood ticks across the Western landscape" (Jones, 1996, p. 1). Sometimes called **natural resource partnerships**, these coalitions include private landowners, local officials, businesses, and environmentalists, as well as state and federal agencies. They are organized around an identifiable region—such as a watershed, forest, or rangeland—with natural resource concerns (for example, water quality, timber, agriculture, wildlife). Such partnerships operate collaboratively to integrate their differing values and approaches to the management of natural resource issues.

One of the earliest and longest-running models of natural resource collaboration is the Applegate Partnership, organized in 1992. It was formed after years of conflict among ranchers, local government, loggers, environmentalists, and the U.S. Bureau of Land Management (BLM) in the watershed of southwestern Oregon and northern California. Feuding parties finally decided to take a different approach. Local BLM official John Lloyd explained, "We got to the point where we just had to sit down and start talking" (Wondolleck & Yaffee, 2000, p. 7).

As they talked, it became apparent that conservationists, loggers, and community leaders all shared a love of the land and a concern for the sustainability of local communities. At its first meeting, the partnership agreed on a vision statement that foreshadowed a model later adopted by other communities in the West:

> The Applegate Partnership is a community-based project involving industry, conservation groups, natural resource agencies, and residents cooperating to encourage and facilitate the use of natural resource principles that promote ecosystem health and diversity. Through community involvement and education, the partnership supports the management of all lands within the watershed in a manner that sustains natural resources and that will, in turn, contribute to economic and community stability within the Applegate Valley. (Wondolleck & Yaffee, 2000, pp. 140–141)

Similar natural resource partnerships addressing different issues have grown up across the United States but particularly in the West. Among these are:

- Ponderosa Pine Partnership in Southwest Colorado, a coalition of citizens, loggers, local colleges, and the U.S. Forest Service, working to enhance wildlife habitat and sustainable approaches to forestry;
- Henry's Fork Watershed Council in Eastern Idaho and western Wyoming that has brought together scientists, nonprofit groups, and state and federal land management agencies to do research and build consensus about projects in the watershed; and
- Kiowa National Grasslands in New Mexico, a collaborative partnership among ranchers, the Forest Service, and the state's Natural Resource Conservation Service that has "greatly improved the quality of the area's rangeland" by addressing the "needs of wildlife, cattle, and environmental restoration . . . as a whole" (Ecosystem Management Initiative, 2009, para. 1).

Collaboration in natural resource partnerships differs somewhat from the agency-appointed citizens' advisory committee. Partnerships usually are voluntary, although officials from government agencies like the BLM or Forest Service may be among the partners. They focus on a geographical region and a wider range of ecological concerns. And, unlike a citizens' advisory committee, a natural resource partnership usually works on an ongoing basis to respond to new challenges and concerns in its region.

Community-Based Collaboration

Occasions for local disputes over the environment are numerous: the loss of green space, contamination of well water, tensions between automobile drivers and bicyclists, and so forth. Increasingly, local government and courts are encouraging the use of collaborative processes to avoid long, contentious conflicts that can drain resources, divide groups, and weaken the relationships in a community. **Community-based collaboration** involves individuals and representatives of affected groups, businesses, or other agencies in addressing a specific or short-term problem in the local community. Often operating by consensus, this kind of collaborative group identifies issues of concern, forms subgroups to investigate alternatives, and seeks support for specific solutions. Besides being court-appointed or agency-sponsored associations, these community-based groups may be voluntary associations without legal sanction or regulatory power.

Although they have some features in common with natural resource partnerships, community-based collaborations tend to focus on specific, local problems that involve shorter time frames. For example, in Sherman County, Oregon, a conflict arose over a proposal by Northwest Wind Power (NWWP) to locate a 24-megawatt wind farm in the community. A farming community with a population of 1,900, Sherman County lies directly in the path of relentless winds from the Pacific Ocean; for this reason, the area was proposed as a site for harvesting wind energy. In other communities, proposals for wind farms had generated considerable conflict—powerful, 200-foot-tall turbines can affect aviation, bird populations, cultural and historical sites, weed control, and other ecological matters (Policy Consensus Initiative, 2004b).

In the face of potential controversy, Oregon's governor invited local farmers, citizens' groups, landowners, the Audubon Society, and representatives from local, state, and federal agencies, NWWP, and other business concerns to engage in a collaborative process to decide the fate of the proposed wind farm. Working together, the group identified possible wind-farm sites and related issues of concern, then formed subgroups to address each issue. Their efforts eventually led to an agreement on a site that would have "minimal negative impacts on the community and environment" (Policy Consensus Initiative, 2004b).

Each of these forms of participation—citizens' advisory committees, natural resource partnerships, and community-based collaboration—share certain characteristics that contribute to their eventual success (or failure). Therefore, in the next section of this chapter, I identify some of the conditions that must be in place for successful collaboration as well as the requirements for building trust among the participants and sustaining open, civil dialogue.

☞ **FYI** | **Case Studies of Successful Collaboration in Environmental Disputes**

- *The Fire Next Time:* www.pbs.org/pov

  A film about the way residents in the Flathead Valley, Montana, came together to resolve conflicts over loss of jobs and the environment that threatened to tear their community apart. For a copy of this film for local showing and discussion, see http://www.pbs.org/pov.

- *Cultivating Common Ground:* www.youtube.com

  The participants in the Lakeview Stewardship Group, a natural resource partnership, tell their story of successful collaboration to restore the 500,000-acre Lakeview Federal Stewardship Unit in the Fremont-Winema National Forest in Oregon in this brief YouTube video.

- *A River Reborn: The Restoration of Fossil Creek:* www.mpcer.nau.edu/riverreborn

  A film documenting environmental conflict and collaboration in an Arizona community as it struggled to protect Fossil Creek by removing a 100-year-old hydroelectric dam in the high desert country. The DVD, narrated by actor Ted Danson, is available at http://www.mpcer.nau.edu/riverreborn.

For more case studies of successful resolution of environmental conflicts, see these online sites:

(1) The University of Michigan's Ecosystem Management Initiative site for collaboration, "Case Studies and Lessons Learned" at www.snre.umich.edu/ecomgt//collaboration.htm.

(2) The National Policy Consensus Center's "Policy Consensus Initiative" and its archive of case studies at http://www.policyconsensus.org/casestudies.

Collaborating to Resolve Environmental Conflicts

As we've seen in the previous examples, collaboration clearly differs from the forms of public participation that I reviewed in Chapter 4. Collaboration is also sharply distinguished from more adversarial forms of managing environmental conflict, such as litigation or advocacy campaigns, although sometimes, these have led adversaries to put aside their differences and talk to each other. (I'll describe how this conflict–collaboration dynamic worked in the controversy over the Great Bear Rainforest later in this chapter.) One of the field's leading scholars in collaboration, Gregg Walker (2004) identifies eight attributes that distinguish collaboration from traditional forms of public participation:

1. Collaboration is less competitive.

2. Collaboration features mutual learning and fact finding.

3. Collaboration allows underlying value differences to be explored.

4. Collaboration resembles principled negotiation, focusing on interests rather than positions.

5. Collaboration allocates the responsibility for implementation across many parties.

6. Collaboration's conclusions are generated by participants through an interactive, iterative, and reflective process.

7. Collaboration is often an ongoing process.

8. Collaboration has the potential to build individual and community capacity in such areas as conflict management, leadership, decision making, and communications. (p. 124)

Walker's list helps us understand collaboration as a process that is distinct from more adversarial forms of public participation in environmental decisions.

In this section, I build on Walker's observations to describe some of the characteristics of successful collaboration. However, before going further, it may be helpful to distinguish collaboration from two other, closely related forms of conflict resolution: arbitration and mediation. *Arbitration* is usually court ordered and involves the presentation of opposing views to a neutral, third-party individual or panel that, in turn, renders a judgment about the conflict. *Mediation* is a facilitated effort entered into voluntarily or at the suggestion of a court, counselors, or other institution. Most important, this form of conflict management involves an active mediator who helps the disputing parties find common ground and a solution on which they agree. Whereas collaboration may use a mediator on occasion, it requires active contributions from all participants.

With these distinctions in mind, let's look at the minimum, core conditions that are typically present when collaboration succeeds.

Requirements for Successful Collaboration

Most scholars and those who participate in effective collaborations cite a number of conditions and participant characteristics that must be present for collaboration to succeed. (See Table 5.1.)

Table 5.1   Requirements of Successful Collaboration
1. Relevant stakeholders are at the table.
2. Participants adopt a problem-solving approach.
3. All participants have access to necessary resources and opportunities to participate in discussions.
4. Decisions usually are reached by consensus.
5. Relevant agencies are guided by the recommendations of the collaboration.

1. *Relevant stakeholders are at the table.* Collaboration begins when the relevant "stakeholders" agree to participate in "constructive, open, civil communication" (Walker, 2004, p. 123) to address some problem. **Stakeholders** are those parties to a dispute who have a real or discernible interest (a stake) in the outcome. Sometimes, they're selected by a sponsoring agency to sit at the table, usually to represent certain interests or constituents, such as local businesses, residents, environmental groups, the timber industry, and so forth. In other cases, stakeholders self-identify and volunteer to participate. In most collaborations, stakeholders are place-based; that is, they live or work in the affected community or region. (For more information about the concept of the stakeholder in environmental decision making, see Dietz & Stern, 2008.)

2. *Participants adopt a problem-solving approach.* Communication among participants strives to solve problems instead of being adversarial or manipulative. Problem solving uses discussion, conversation, and information, seeking to define the concrete problem, the relevant concerns, the criteria for appropriate solutions, and finally a solution that addresses the concerns of all parties. Although conflict is expected in the discussion, collaboration keeps the focus on the interests or issues rather than on the people. It discourages adversarial or overtly persuasive stances and instead favors listening, learning, and trying to agree on workable solutions.

3. *All participants have access to necessary resources and opportunities to participate in discussions.* In a collaborative effort, solutions cannot be imposed. If agreement is to be reached by all parties, all participants must have an opportunity to be heard, to challenge others' views, to question, and to provide input to the solution. Each party must also have access to the same information as others do, including reports, expert briefings, and so on. Finally, the group must guard against the effects of different levels of power or privilege among the participants to ensure that all voices are respected and have opportunities to contribute to and influence the solution.

4. *Decisions usually are reached by consensus.* Most collaborative groups aim to reach decisions by *consensus,* which usually means *general agreement* or that discussions will not end until everyone has had a chance to share their differences and find common ground. Consensus often means that all participants agree with the final decision. Daniels and Walker (2001) note, however, that some define consensus in a way that leaves room for some differences of opinion. In this use, consensus is an agreement that tries to identify the interests of all stakeholders and craft a decision that addresses as many of these concerns as possible (p. 72).

Consensus can also be distinguished from *compromise,* another form of collaboration that groups use in reaching decisions. As interpersonal communication scholar Julia Wood (2009) observes, in consensus, "members may differ in how enthusiastically they support a decision, but everyone agrees to it"; whereas, in a **compromise**, "members work out a solution that satisfies each person's minimum criteria but may not fully satisfy all members" (pp. 270, 271). In either case, a decision assumes some form of cooperation, requiring opposing interests to work together, a process that can take the form of "internal negotiations among participants" (Beierle & Cayford, 2002, p. 46).

5. *Relevant agencies are guided by the recommendations of the collaboration.* The results of a collaborative effort usually are advisory to the agency that appointed the group, for example, the report of a citizens' advisory committee to the governmental agency handling the cleanup of a toxic waste site. The recommendations are not legally binding in most cases. However, in some cases, an agency may agree to implement the results of a consensus-based process. The prospect of their solution's implementation is a powerful incentive for participants to invest the time and work required for successful collaboration. When a group's recommendations are not implemented, those who participated in the collaboration often feel frustrated or

angry at the energy wasted in a process the outcome of which was ignored. (For an excellent case study illustrating this problem and the requirements for successful collaboration, see Depoe, 2004.)

Successful collaboration among parties with diverse interests is not always possible, particularly in environmental disputes where the stakes are high or the parties are too deeply divided by a history of discord or entrenched opposition. Guy Burgess and Heidi Burgess (1996), codirectors of the Conflict Research Consortium at the University of Colorado at Boulder, observed, "While consensus building can be very effective in low-stakes disputes . . . it does not work as well when the issues involve deep-rooted value differences, very high stakes, or irreducible win-lose confrontations" (p. 1). Those who have worked with environmental conflicts generally agree that collaboration succeeds only when the adversaries come to feel that something must change and can identify a shared vision of the future.

Collaborating About Water Quality and Rainforests

It may be helpful to look at two case studies of successful collaboration—a citizens' advisory committee and a natural resource partnership. The first is a successful case in Ohio that resolved a dispute over water quality standards. The second case illustrates a long-running conflict over logging in Canada's Great Bear Rainforest that led to a successful model of collaboration among environmentalists, First Nations, the timber industry, and local communities. In each case, I identify the presence of the minimum, core requirements for effective collaboration and illustrate the importance of these to a successful outcome.

Reaching Consensus on Water Quality in the Great Lakes

The state of Ohio borders on Lake Erie and is therefore one of eight states subject to a stringent agreement called the Great Lakes Water Quality Initiative. For years, large portions of the Great Lakes have been dying biologically. Pollution runoff from factories, agricultural fields, and urban sources surrounding the Great Lakes has contaminated the water and led to high levels of toxins in fish. Starting in 1995, the EPA issued a far-reaching Great Lakes Water Quality Initiative, requiring the states to adopt strict standards for waste disposal and discharge into the lakes. Although the EPA gave states such as Ohio two years to come up with rules to implement the new standards, the initiative caused considerable controversy among affected industries, environmentalists, and the states' governors (Policy Consensus Initiative, 2004a).

In an attempt to reach an agreement, Ohio's governor appointed a group of 25 diverse stakeholders as a citizens' advisory committee. The members included representatives of business and industry, environmental groups, universities, local and state government, and the Ohio EPA. The charge to this external advisory group (EAG) was to seek consensus on the new water quality rules that would satisfy the requirements of the Great Lakes Water Quality Initiative.

The task before the advisory group was daunting. In addition to the diverse interests among the 25-member group, the EAG had to resolve a total of 99 issues, many technically complicated. For example, they had to establish the numerical levels, or parts per billion, of chemicals that could be present in waters discharged into Lake Erie (Policy Consensus Initiative, 2004a, para. 1) as well as the mix of aquatic species that would indicate a healthy recovery of the Great Lakes. The director of the Ohio EPA gave the EAG a strong incentive: "If the group achieved consensus on an issue, and if the recommendation was consistent with state and federal law, [the Ohio EPA] would implement it. If the group could not reach consensus, [the director] would make a decision," taking into account the recommendations of both the agency's technical staff and the majority of the advisory group (Policy Consensus Initiative, 2004a, para. 1).

As they started, EAG members agreed on the ground rules to guide their deliberations. At first, the level of trust among participants was not high enough to make progress on the issues facing them. As a result, they formed subcommittees, each with a facilitator, to begin discussions. As the subcommittees made progress, they reported their recommendations to the full group, and when agreement was reached with the Ohio EPA staff on a specific issue, the issue was crossed off the list. As progress continued, the relationships among group members improved. In the end, the State of Ohio adopted new rules for waste disposal and discharge into the Great Lakes. One facilitator summed up the two-year process: "All perspectives had been thoroughly aired, and the interest groups were confident that they had been heard" (Policy Consensus Initiative, 2004a).

The conditions for successful collaboration clearly were present in the Ohio experience. At the outset, all parties were motivated to reach agreement on the rules for water quality. If they failed, the state EPA office would decide the rules. The two-year deadline also served to motivate the search for agreement. In addition, the requirements for effective collaboration were satisfied:

1. Relevant stakeholders were invited to the table (and nonrelevant people were absent).

2. EAG members agreed to use a problem-solving approach rather than advocacy. They agreed early on ground rules for discussion and had the assistance of "impartial, skilled facilitators" (Policy Consensus Initiative, 2004a, para. 2).

3. As a result of these ground rules, the presence of facilitators, and use of subcommittees in the early period, the participants learned to work with one another and felt they had an equal opportunity to participate in discussions.

4. Most of the recommendations of the EAG were reached by consensus.

5. The relevant agency, the Ohio EPA in this case, honored its pledge to implement the committee's recommendations.

While the Ohio citizens' advisory group addressed the disagreements between industry and environmentalists in a timely fashion, other conflicts do not so easily come to the negotiating table. In fact, our next case study illustrates the role that conflict itself sometimes plays in persuading opponents that a shift in viewpoint may be needed before a turn to collaboration is even possible.

From Conflict to Collaboration in the Great Bear Rainforest

The area that stretches 250 miles along Canada's Pacific Coast, known as the Great Bear Rainforest, is the largest remaining, temperate rainforest in the world. It encompasses more than 28,000 square miles. Its mountains, streams, fjords, forests, and estuaries are home to tremendous biodiversity, including grizzly bears, the white Kermode bear (known as Spirit Bears), wolves, salmon, and millions of migratory birds as well as 1,000-year-old trees. This region is also home to First Nations—pre-European, indigenous peoples—whose communities often are accessible only by air or water (Armstrong, 2009; Smith, Sterritt, & Armstrong, 2007). The old-growth forests of the Great Bear Rainforest were also the scene of intense conflict between logging companies and First Nations and environmentalists for many years. This conflict, nevertheless, evolved into a model of collaboration by unlikely groups, resulting in an unprecedented agreement to protect forests, indigenous rights, and local communities.

| Figure 5.2 | British Columbia Premier Gordon Campbell announces an initial agreement by the BC government, First Nations, environmentalists, and industry over the Great Bear Rainforest at a news conference in Vancouver, Canada, February 7, 2006. |

In the 1990s, the Great Bear Rainforest witnessed a sharp increase in logging and other extractive activities, often in First Nations's traditional territories. These activities also brought an era of conflict as environmental activists joined with First Nations's elders in protests and direct actions to protect the region's forests and watersheds. In 1993, in Clayoquot Sound on Vancouver Island, more than 900 people were arrested in nonviolent, direct-action protests, including blockades of logging roads, in "the largest mass arrest in Canadian history" (Smith, Sterritt, & Armstrong, 2007, p. 2). The protests were the start of 15 years of conflict and an international campaign, what newspapers called "the war in the woods" (p. 4), to preserve one of the planet's last, temperate rainforests.

As logging blockades continued, environmental groups launched an international campaign, using blogs and social networking sites, to target the industry's markets. Greenpeace, Forest Ethics, Rainforest Action Network, and other groups aimed to "tell the world's pulp and paper customers exactly what was happening to British Columbia's coastal rainforests and to urge wood product buyers to change their procurement practices" (Conflict and protest, n.d., para. 4). Many businesses began to cancel their contracts. Ultimately, over 80 companies, including well-known brands like Ikea, Home Depot, Staples, and IBM, responded, and "committed to stop selling wood and paper products" from the region (Markets campaign, n.d., para. 3).

As the markets campaign grew, other changes were starting in British Columbia. In 1999, senior industry leaders began a discussion about ways to resolve the controversy with environmentalists and First Nations. It was, they decided, "time to travel in new direction," including "sitting down face to face with environmental groups" (Armstrong, 2009, pp. 8–9). Old assumptions were "replaced by a recognition that the environment represents a core social value," that environmentalists were seen by the public "as both credible and influential," and that "customers expect their [forest industry] suppliers to resolve conflict, not simply rationalize it" (Smith, Sterritt, & Armstrong, 2007, p. 4). The Chief Forester for Western Forests Products, Bill Dumont, put it more succinctly, "Customers don't want their two-by-fours with a protester attached to it. If we don't end it, they will buy their products elsewhere" (p. 4).

The shift to dialogue received a significant boost in 2000 when the forest companies—joining together as the Coast Forest Conservation Initiative—agreed to halt logging in more than 100 watersheds in the Great Bear Rainforest. Smith, Sterritt, and Armstrong (2007) describe what happened next: "In return, ForestEthics, Greenpeace, and Rainforest Action Network modified their market campaigns," no longer asking customers to cancel their contracts. "This 'mutual standstill' created the conditions for a new beginning between the parties" (p. 5).

At the same time, the environmental groups, ForestEthics, Greenpeace, RAN, and Sierra Club of British Columbia, came together as the Rainforest Solution Project to develop shared proposals for protecting the Great Bear Rainforest. Shortly afterward, this group and industry's Coast Forest Conservation Initiative formed a coalition called the Joint Solutions Project. The new coalition would be "a structure for communications and negotiations" among the former opponents and would serve to facilitate "a broader dialogue with First Nations, the BC government, labour groups, and local communities" (Smith, Sterritt, & Armstrong, 2007, p. 5). The way was opened finally for collaboration among all of the major parties to begin crafting a far-reaching set of agreements for the Great Bear Rainforest.

Much work remained. By 2006, however, forest companies, First Nations, environmentalists, and the BC government had negotiated a set of consensus recommendations which, if fully implemented, would protect key areas, manage other areas in a sustainable manner, and invest in local communities. On March 31, 2009, the parties announced the deadline had been met for implementation of these recommendations, including completion of a land use plan for an ecosystem-based management (EBM) of the Great Bear Rainforest. The agreements included:

1. *Protected Areas Network:* More than one third of the rainforest (8,150 square miles) would be protected in a new network of conservancies. These areas include old-growth forests, estuaries, wetlands, salmon streams, and habitat for key species, "representing the full diversity of habitat types," and quadrupling the total protected areas within the Great Bear Rainforest (Smith, Sterritt, & Armstrong, 2007, p. 8).

2. *Ecosystem-Based Management:* Logging or other development occurring within the other areas of the Great Bear Rainforest would be subject to "ecosystem-based management (EBM) rules and guidance for governing resource use in the region" (Armstrong, 2009, p. 13). The EBM guidelines will attempt to ensure "high degrees of ecological integrity," including the goal of maintaining 70% of natural, old-growth forests across the region (p. 13).

3. *Coast Opportunities Fund:* An important aspect of the new agreement was economic investment in First Nations communities in the region. The newly created Coast Opportunities Fund, endowed by public and private sources with an initial $120 million, "is designed to support conservation and environmentally responsible economic development initiatives for First Nations in the Great Bear Rainforest" (Armstrong, 2009, p. 15).

An agreement of this scale could not have happened without a number of key elements that sustained the Great Bear Rainforest collaboration. The five core minimum requirements for a successful collaboration were clearly present, but most of the parties acknowledged that the final discussions would not have occurred without other, distinctive factors as well. Recently, Merran Smith of Forest Ethics, Art Sterritt from the Coastal First Nations, and Patrick Armstrong, a consultant who worked with companies in the Coast Forest Conservation Initiative reflected on several, key dynamics of change. Among these were four dynamics:

Persistent Vision: The vision cocreated by environmentalists and First Nations of "a protected, globally significant rainforest with healthy indigenous communities and a diverse economy . . . played an integral role in inspiring new people, keeping the process on track, and reminding participants of what they were trying to achieve" (Smith, Sterritt, & Armstrong, 2007, p. 12).

Power Shift: As a result of the international market campaigns, the region's revenue from sales of forest products "hung in the balance"; Smith, Sterritt, and

Armstrong (2007) noted that, "when forest companies and ultimately the BC government acknowledged this power, negotiations . . . experienced a fundamental shift" (p. 12). This shift was important, and it was "one of the most critical elements to achieving the eventual outcome in the Great Bear Rainforest" (p. 12). This is because, when all parties—environmentalists, First Nations, forest companies, and the BC government—held power that was needed to achieve a lasting solution, "all parties stayed at the table" (p. 12).

Collaboration and Relationships: The principal groups—environmentalists, First Nations, and forest companies—each formed an informal entity to resolve internal conflicts and represent their interests to the other groups. As a result, those in the Joint Solutions Project and in the broader communications with First Nations and the BC government "were empowered by their constituencies to move the dialogue forward" (p. 13).

Leadership: While some in each group resisted the idea of collaborating with their opponents, leaders within the forest industry, in First Nations, and among environmentalists arose to counter the resistance in their own ranks. As Smith Sterritt, and Armstrong (2007) observed, "Leadership meant standing up to critics—and even to traditional allies—who disagreed with building solutions with one's opponents" (p. 14).

The Great Bear Rainforest agreements appear to be becoming a reality, though as this book goes to press, an important milestone remains. The parties were still collaborating to ensure that, by 2014, "low ecological risks" in managing forests and "high levels of human wellbeing" in local communities would be achieved (Armstrong, 2009, p. 15).

Limits of Collaboration and Consensus

Not all attempts at collaboration and consensus-based solutions are successful. Following, I will describe a case that initially appeared to be a very successful experiment in bringing together loggers, environmentalists, and local business and community leaders but that was criticized almost immediately for excluding relevant stakeholders. However, before we look at this case, it may be helpful to identify some benchmarks by which to evaluate collaborative efforts and assess the reasons for their failures, where these occur.

Evaluating Collaboration and Consensus-Based Decisions

In recent years, environmental scholars have addressed the recurring problems not only in traditional forums for public participation but in the newer models of consensus-based decisions. For example, Senecah (2004) has offered a three-part model for assessing the different forms of public participation in environmental decisions, called the **Trinity of Voices (TOV)**. The model builds on the importance of the stakeholder and on many of the characteristics we identified earlier for effective collaboration. Let's use the TOV model, then, as a guide to assess some of the strengths and limitations consensus-based approaches.

Specifically, the TOV model refers to three elements that most effective participatory processes seem to share and that empower a stakeholder. These are: access, standing, and influence. Senecah explains that **access** refers to the minimum resources that citizens need to exercise fully their opportunity to participate, including convenient times and places, readily available information and technical assistance to help them understand the issues, and continuing opportunities for public involvement. By **standing**, Senecah (2004) does not mean the right to bring a legal complaint in court (see Chapter 4). Instead, she explains, standing is "the civic legitimacy, the respect, the esteem, and the consideration that all stakeholders' perspectives should be given" (p. 24). Finally, **influence** is the element felt by many to be most often missing in traditional models of public participation. Influence refers to participants' opportunities to be part of a "transparent process that considers all alternatives, opportunities to meaningfully scope alternatives, opportunities to inform the decision criteria, and thoughtful response to stakeholder concerns and ideas" (p. 25).

Let's use Senecah's TOV model to evaluate one of the most highly touted examples of collaboration, an effort by a local community to develop a consensus approach for managing national forest lands in northern California. Though initially successful, the efforts of the **Quincy Library Group (QLG)**, as the participants called themselves, ended in conflict and by moving in a different, more adversarial direction.

The Quincy Library Group: Conflict in the Sierra Nevada Mountains

The rural town of Quincy (fewer than 50,000 residents) is located 100 miles northeast of Sacramento, California. More important, it lies in the geographical center of the timber wars in the Plumas, Lassen, and Tahoe National Forests of the Sierra Nevada Mountains. Although logging increased from the 1960s through the 1980s in the three national forests around Quincy, the timber cut fell sharply in the 1990s due to shifting market demands and to Forest Service restrictions that protected old-growth trees and habitat for spotted owls and other endangered species.

As logging declined and local sawmills shut down, the area began to experience sharp conflicts between timber interests and environmentalists. For example, loggers and their families blamed the Forest Service for restricting the level of timber cuts and organized the Yellow Ribbon Coalition to lobby for their interests. Charges and countercharges also flew between the coalition and environmentalists over instances of tree spiking (see Chapter 2) and the use of nail clusters on forest roads to stop logging trucks (Wondolleck & Yaffee, 2000, p. 71). Plumas County Supervisor Bill Coates expressed the fears of many in local communities: "Our small towns were already endangered. This [decline in logging] was going to wipe them out" (Wondolleck & Yaffee, 2000, p. 71).

Initial Success: Collaboration in Quincy

Despite the controversy, some in the community suggested that opponents might share a larger set of interests and values. Michael Jackson, an environmental attorney and member of Friends of Plumas Wilderness, was one of the earliest. In 1989, he wrote a letter to the local newspaper, the *Feather River Bulletin,* "arguing that environmentalists, loggers, and business needed to work together for 'our mutual future'" (quoted in Wondolleck & Yaffee, 2000, p. 71). In his letter, Jackson invited loggers to work with environmentalists toward a set of common goals:

> What do environmentalists believe we have in common with the Yellow Ribbon Coalition? We believe that we are all honest people who want to continue our way of life. We believe that we all love the area in which we live. We believe that we all enjoy beautiful views, hunting and fishing and living in a rural area. We believe that we are being misled by the Forest Service and by large timber, which controls the Forest Service, into believing that we are enemies when we are not. (quoted in Wondolleck & Yaffee, 2000, pp. 71–72)

By 1992, a few individuals in each of the warring camps—forest industry, community and business leaders, and environmentalists—began to talk about the effects of declining timber production on the community. Initially, three men agreed to talk among themselves: Bill Coates (Plumas County supervisor and a business owner who supported the timber industry), Tom Nelson (a forester for Sierra Pacific Industries), and Michael Jackson (the environmental attorney and a passionate environmentalist). The three "found more common ground than they had expected, and decided to try to build at least a truce, maybe even a full peace treaty, based upon that common ground" (Terhune & Terhune, 1998, para. 8).

Soon, other people joined the discussions of Coates, Nelson, and Jackson. Later observers recalled that these "early meetings had some very tense moments, and some participants were very uncomfortable at times" (Terhune & Terhune, 1998, p. 8). Meeting in the public library, they began calling themselves the QLG. "Some only half-jokingly [noted] that meeting in a library would prevent participants from yelling at each other" (Wondolleck & Yaffee, 2000, p. 72).

By 1993, members of the QLG (www.qlg.org) had agreed among themselves on the Community Stability Plan, which the group hoped would guide management practices in the Plumas, Lassen, and Tahoe National Forests. Although this plan had no official status—the Forest Service was not involved in the discussions—it reflected the group's belief that "a healthy forest and a stable community are interdependent; we cannot have one without the other" (Terhune & Terhune, 1998, p. 11). The purpose of the Community Stability Plan was to integrate these values into a common vision: "to promote the objectives of forest health, ecological integrity, adequate timber supply, and local economic stability" (Wondolleck & Yaffee, 2000, p. 72). The group's plan set forth a series of recommendations to the Forest Service for implementing its vision:

> The plan would . . . prevent clear-cutting on Forest Service land or in wide protection zones around rivers and streams and would require group and single tree selection [logging] intended to produce an "all-age, multi-storied, fire-resistant forest approximating pre-settlement conditions." Under the plan, local timber mills would process all harvested logs. The plan also included provisions to reduce the amount of dead or dying plant material, which the group believed was posing a significant threat of fire to the area. (Wondolleck & Yaffee, 2000, p. 72)

The Community Stability Proposal was the result of many meetings, difficult conversations, and the desire of all participants to reach consensus where possible. Their agreement was unusual among the (previously) contentious parties in Quincy and its surrounding communities. Nevertheless, the QLG confronted resistance from others that would shift it to a more adversarial process. Most important, the Forest Service—which had not participated in the collaborative process—refused to entertain the group's Community Stability Proposal.

Frustrated by resistance from the Forest Service and criticized by other environmentalists, QLG members turned to the legislative process in Washington, DC. After successive lobbying trips in 1998, they persuaded Congress to enact a version of the Community Stability Proposal. In an unprecedented move, the Quincy Library Group Forest Recovery Act overrode the usual Forest Service decision-making process and directed it to include this version in its management planning for the three national forests in the Quincy area.

Although I return to some of the criticisms of this experience, it is important to observe that, initially, the QLG received considerable praise for its collaborative work. Prompted by the feeling that something had to change, individuals in Quincy believed that conditions were ripe for some alternative mechanism for resolving the long-simmering dispute over logging in the area's national forests.

Using Senecah's (2004) TOV model, we can assess favorably the group's effort to find consensus: Participants felt they had full *access* to all meetings, information, and ongoing opportunities to participate. Despite their initial suspicions, business and community leaders, timber industry personnel, and local environmentalists learned to respect and work with each other. In Senecah's (2004) term, they had acquired *standing* in one another's eyes. And, throughout the process, participants themselves exercised *influence* in determining the vision, the criteria to be used in their deliberations, and the final set of recommendations in the Community Stability Plan.

As they looked at their work, QLG members Pat and George Terhune (1998) stressed the importance of consensus in keeping the group together and focused. "Votes are not taken until the group is pretty well convinced that the decision will be unanimous. If it isn't, then more discussion takes place, and if anybody is still opposed, the decision is either dropped or postponed for still more discussion" (p. 32).

Criticisms of the Quincy Library Group

Not everyone was pleased with the QLG's process or with its vision for management of the national forests. "Although the group attracted widespread public participation at first, most outsiders who had offered new ideas said they got the cold shoulder and stopped attending. When the QLG chose to go the legislative route, others dropped out" (Red Lodge Clearinghouse, 2008). Some objected that the process used by the Quincy group excluded key stakeholders—particularly environmental groups concerned with the national forests—therefore evading the NEPA process (Chapter 4) and allowing local interests to set national standards for managing natural resources. (See "Another Viewpoint: A Skeptic Looks at Collaboration.") Some that had been excluded, for example, were upset that the QLG's proposal would double the levels of logging in the Lassen, Plumas, and Tahoe National Forests (Brower & Hanson, 1999).

Indeed, by 2009, it had become clear that the QLG was frustrated in its aims. Environmental groups continued to block implementation of many projects by filing lawsuits as well as appeals with the Forest Service. (The QLG has developed a set of responses to the environmental concerns on its website; see http://www.qlg.org.)

Based on these criticisms, community-based collaborations such as the QLG would seem to violate the principle of access in Senecah's (2004) TOV model: Certain citizens (outside the local area) were not a part of the process for setting standards for these natural resources. Such exclusions can lead to mistrust of the collaboration's outcomes by those excluded as well as prevent access to the resources that these other (outside) citizens can provide. For example, environmentalists David Brower and Chad Hanson (1999) charged that the QLG had allowed industry interests to capture the decision process: "The Quincy plan is based on the premise of letting industry groups in rural timber towns dictate the fate of federally owned lands, essentially transferring decision-making power from the American people and into the hands of extractive industries" (p. A25). Similar criticism came from other environmentalists, editorials, and scholars studying collaborative processes. For example, Wondolleck and Yaffee (2000) observed that, instead of being "a model collaborative effort, the QLG suddenly became the focus of an acrimonious debate" (p. 265).

Another Viewpoint: A Skeptic Looks at Collaboration

In a well-publicized article in the western *High Country News,* the Sierra Club's former executive director, Michael McCloskey (1996), argued that collaborative processes such as the QLG give small local groups "an effective veto" over entire national forests. McCloskey cited two shortcomings of local or place-based collaboration:

1. Placed-based collaboration excludes key stakeholders. They ignore "the disparate geographical distribution of constituencies" (p. 7). That is, those who are sympathetic to environmental values often live in urban areas; therefore, they are not invited to participate in collaborative processes in the communities near the national forests where there is a dispute.

2. Placed-based collaboration undermines national standards for managing natural resources such as national forests. By transferring the power to decide the direction for public lands to small, local groups, local collaboration evades the need to hammer out "national rules to reflect majority rule in the nation" (p. 7).

As a result, McCloskey argued, such models are abdications of the role of government to represent the national (public) interest.

The Red Lodge Clearinghouse (2008), a project of the Natural Resources Law Center at the University of Colorado, summarized the QLG collaboration this way:

> It is as a collaborative that the Quincy Library Group is troubling. Many who have tried to participate have felt ostracized. And although it is developing policy for managing federal lands, the coalition has demonstrated little concern for involving the broader public in its process. . . . No one knows what would be happening now if QLG had stuck with consensus and insisted on trying to include everyone. Instead . . . the QLG took a top-down, federally mandated approach that has limited participation in the program.

The charge by Brower and Hanson that local groups can capture the decision-making process affecting U.S. public lands also illustrates a dilemma posed by place-based collaboration. To what extent do such models provide mechanisms for resolving contentious disputes, and to what extent do they exclude key stakeholders and ignore national standards? The Quincy experience is not encouraging in this regard.

Act Locally!

Is Collaboration Always Possible?

Successful collaboration among differing parties—environmentalists, developers, and so on—can be difficult to achieve. Where a conflict has been resolved, there may be important lessons to be learned. One way to gain an appreciation for the challenges to successful collaboration is to investigate a local environmental conflict by interviewing some of its participants.

Identify a successful case of conflict resolution in your community or a current conflict in which efforts are being made to bring the parties together, and invite one or more representatives from each side of the conflict to your class or group:

1. Ask the different participants to describe the nature of the conflict, their goals, and concerns.

2. In successful cases, ask the participants how they managed to come together and to collaborate despite their differences; what kept them talking? How would they characterize their communication with one another?

3. In an ongoing conflict, have attempts been made to try to have the sides sit down with each other to explore the possibility of collaboration? Ask the different parties about what they perceive to be the obstacles to a more collaborative process.

Alternatively, arrange for your class or group to screen one of the videos from the (above) "FYI: Case Studies of Successful Collaboration in Environmental Disputes." Were the basic requirements for effective collaboration present? What communication features helped to explain the willingness of the feuding parties to talk with one another and to reach an agreement?

Common Criticisms of Collaboration

Although community-based collaborations have many advantages, Daniels and Walker (2001) have observed that they have not been universally accepted as a model for handling conflicts over natural resources. In closing, it may be useful to review some of the common criticisms of the use of collaboration and consensus decision making in environmental conflicts. Environmental scholars and facilitators who work with such disputes have found seven basic complaints or occasions for which collaboration may not be appropriate:

1. *Stakeholders may be unrepresentative of wider publics.* Some scholars have suggested that the more intensive modes of alternative participation, such as citizens' advisory councils and consensus-seeking groups, may be able to reach agreement, but they often do so only by excluding wider publics. For example, Beierle and Cayford (2002) report that "the exclusion of certain groups, the departure of dissenting parties, or the avoidance of issues ultimately made consensus possible—or at least easier—in 33%" of the cases they studied involving consensus-based efforts in which conflict was reported (p. 48). Environmental communication scholar William Kinsella (2004) also observes that highly involved individuals who serve on citizens' advisory boards "do not necessarily represent the larger public" (p. 90). In other situations, the questions of who is a stakeholder and who should set environmental policy lie at the heart of many local, national, and global environmental controversies.

2. *Place-based collaboration may encourage exceptionalism or a compromise of national standards.* As we witnessed in the QLG case, the exclusion of national environmental groups gave local interests greater control over the management of national resources. Daniels and Walker (2001) reported that such cases may "preclude meaningful opportunities for non-parties to review and comment on proposals" (p. 274), encouraging a kind of **exceptionalism,** or the view that, because a region has unique or distinctive features, it is exempt from the general rule. The concern by some critics is that, if place-based decisions reached at the local level in one area become a precedent for exempting other geographical areas, they may compromise more uniform, national standards for environmental policy.

3. *Power inequities may lead to co-optation.* One of the most common complaints about collaboration and consensus approaches is that power inequities among the participants may lead to the co-optation of environmental interests. The greater resources in training, information, and negotiation skills often brought to collaboration processes by industry representatives and government officials may make it harder for ordinary citizens and environmentalists to defend their interests. Environmentalists such as McCloskey (1996) are especially critical of such inequities in power and resources: "Industry thinks its odds are better in these forums [place-based collaboration]. . . . It believes it can dominate them over time and relieve itself of the burden of tough national rules" (p. 7).

4. *Pressure for consensus may lead to the lowest common denominator.* In cases of successful collaboration, groups striving for consensus may drop contentious issues or defer them until later. However, some critics fear that this tendency can go too far, that vocal minorities are given an effective veto over the process. "Any recalcitrant stakeholder can paralyze the process. . . . Only lowest common denominator ideas survive the process" (McCloskey, 1996, p. 7). Instead of a win-win solution, agreement on the least contentious parts is simply a deferral of the real sources of conflict to other forums or other times.

Conversely, a pressure for conformity among the group's members can lead to what psychologist Irving Janis (1977) called **groupthink,** that is, excessive cohesion that impedes critical or independent thinking. Indeed, in a broad survey, Robert S. Baron (2005) found that the symptoms of groupthink are widespread with the result of groupthink often being an uninformed consensus.

5. *Consensus tends to delegitimize conflict and advocacy.* Conflict can be unpleasant. For many people, civil dialogue in forums where collaboration is the rule may be a safe harbor from controversy. The desire to avoid disagreement, however, is closely related to groupthink and may lead to a premature compromise, thus postponing the

Figure 5.3	Can disputing parties reach agreement when an environmental conflict involves sharp differences? Demonstrators block the entrance of Chevron Corporation, in San Ramon, CA, in 2009 to protest the company's activities in Ecuador.

AP Photo/Paul Sakuma

search for long-term solutions. As a result, some charge that the desire for consensus "may serve to de-legitimize conflict and co-opt environmental advocates" (Daniels & Walker, 2001, p. 274).

6. *Collaborative groups may lack authority to implement their decisions.* In the Ohio water quality standards case discussed earlier, the state pledged to implement any recommendation that the Great Lakes External Advisory Group reached by consensus. But, this is not always the case. Many citizens' advisory committees deliberate for extended periods without the assurance that their decisions will be accepted or implemented by federal agencies. The QLG, for example, ran into resistance from the Forest Service when it presented its proposal. The simple fact is that most collaborative groups are composed of nonelected citizens and other individuals whose authority—when present—is contingent upon the very governmental agency they are seeking to influence.

7. *Irreconcilable values may hinder agreement.* I suggested earlier that collaborative approaches do not work well when the issues involve deep-rooted value differences, very high stakes, or irreducible, win–lose confrontations. Each of us has values that we believe we cannot or should not compromise—for example, the health of our children, liberty, biodiversity, private property rights, or the right of people to be safe from industrial poisons. And, many wilderness advocates believe that the natural environment has been compromised enough. For them, further compromises presumably are nonnegotiable.

Most successful instances of collaboration assume that not all conflict is bad and not all controversy should be avoided in group deliberations. Indeed, what communication scholar Thomas Goodnight and others have called *dissensus* may serve an important communication role (Fritch, Palczewski, Farrell, & Short, 2006; Goodnight, 1991). **Dissensus** is a questioning of or disagreement with a claim or a premise of a speaker's argument. Rather than bringing a discussion to a halt, dissensus can be generative. If properly handled, it may invite more communication about the areas of disagreement between the differing parties. The attractiveness of collaboration and consensus models for managing environmental conflicts should not, therefore, overshadow the difficulties these processes may involve.

SUMMARY

This chapter has explored an important alternative approach for resolving environmental conflicts. At the heart of these approaches is the idea of *collaboration* and the search for consensus among the relevant parties.

- In the first section, I described the dissatisfaction of many with traditional forms of public participation, and I identified a range of alternatives for managing environmental conflicts: citizens' advisory committees, natural resource partnerships, and community-based collaboration.

- In the second section of this chapter, I identified five conditions for successful collaboration:

  (1) All relevant stakeholders are at the table

  (2) Participants adopt a problem-solving approach

  (3) All participants have equal access to resources and opportunities to participate in discussions

  (4) Decisions usually are reached by consensus, and

  (5) The relevant agencies are guided by the recommendations of the collaborating group.

- Finally, I described a number of recurring complaints and problems from those who have worked with collaboration and consensus approaches, ranging from a failure to include key stakeholders to pressure by some participants toward the lowest common denominator in order to reach consensus, and I noted that collaboration may not always be possible when a conflict involves deep differences over values or irreducible win–lose confrontations.

Neither collaboration nor more adversarial forms of public participation provide a magic answer to conflicts arising from complex human–environment relationships. In the end, disputes over deeply held values about the environment may require both conflict and conversation—collaboration with opponents and, at other times, advocacy of values that cannot or should not be compromised. Collaboration—like advocacy—has a place in managing environmental conflicts, but no single mode is always the most appropriate or effective path to a solution.

SUGGESTED RESOURCES

- Resources and case studies at the U.S. Institute for Environmental Conflict Resolution (www.ecr.gov).
- Patrick Armstrong, *Conflict Resolution and British Columbia's Great Bear Rainforest: Lessons Learned 1995–2009,* July 30, 2009 (www.coastforestconservationinitiative .com/pdf7/GBR_PDF.pdf)
- Steven E. Daniels and Gregg B. Walker, *Working Through Environmental Conflict: The Collaborative Learning Approach.* Westport, CT: Praeger, 2001.
- Julia M. Wondolleck and Steven L. Yaffee, *Making Collaboration Work: Lessons From Innovation in Natural Resource Management.* Washington, DC: Island Press, 2000.

KEY TERMS

Access   128

Arbitration   120

Citizens' advisory committee   115

Collaboration   112

DISCUSSION QUESTIONS

1. Is conflict always needed to force opponents to the negotiating table, or can collaboration be used at the start when an environmental concern is first identified?

2. Would you feel comfortable disagreeing with the majority in a collaborative process? Would you still support a group consensus even if your preferred solution was not adopted as long as you felt that the group had fairly considered your views before it reached its decision?

3. Some critics feel that the inequities in power and resources between representatives of industry and citizens make true consensus between these two groups impossible. "Industry thinks its odds are better in these forums. . . . It believes it can dominate them over time" (McCloskey, 1996, p. 7). Do you agree?

4. Should "outside" interests, like national environmental groups, be stakeholders in local, place-based collaborations about natural resources? How about local representatives of an industry that is headquartered elsewhere?

5. Is compromise or consensus possible in all environmental conflicts? How about in cases such as oil or natural gas drilling in wilderness areas (like the Arctic National Wildlife Refuge) or near community water sources?

REFERENCES

Armstrong, P. (2009, July 30). Conflict resolution and British Columbia's Great Bear Rainforest: Lessons learned 1995–2009. Retrieved November 2, 2010, from www .coastforestconservationinitiative.com/

Barker, R. (2010, May 2). Idaho at forefront of collaboration on public land use. *Idaho Statesman.* Retrieved November 4, 2010, from http://www.idahostatesman.com/

Baron, R. S. (2005). So right it's wrong: Groupthink and the ubiquitous nature of polarized group decision making. In M. P. Zanna (Ed.), *Advances in experimental social psychology* (Vol. 37, pp. 219–253). San Diego, CA. Elsevier Academic.

Beierle, T. C., & Cayford, J. (2002). *Democracy in practice: Public participation in environmental decisions.* Washington, DC: Resources for the Future.

Brower, D., & Hanson, C. (1999, September 1). Logging plan deceptively marketed, sold. *The San Francisco Chronicle*, p. A25.

Burgess, G., & Burgess, H. (1996). *Consensus building for environmental advocates.* (Working Paper #96–1). Boulder: University of Colorado Conflict Research Consortium.

Conflict and protest. (n.d.). The Rainforest Solutions Project. Retrieved November 12, 2010, from www.savethegreatbear.org/

Daniels, S. E., & Walker, G. B. (2001). *Working through environmental conflict: The collaborative learning approach.* Westport, CT: Praeger.

Depoe, S. P. (2004). Public involvement, civic discovery, and the formation of environmental policy: A comparative analysis of the Fernald citizens task force and the Fernald health effects subcommittee. In S. P. Depoe, J. W. Delicath, & M-F. A. Elsenbeer (Eds.), *Communication and public participation in environmental decision making* (pp. 157–173). Albany: State University of New York Press.

Depoe, S. P., & Delicath, J. W. (2004). Introduction. In S. P. Depoe, J. W. Delicath, & M-F. A. Elsenbeer (Eds.), *Communication and public participation in environmental decision making* (pp. 1–10). Albany: State University of New York Press.

Dietz, T., & Stern, P. C. (Eds.). (2008). *Public participation in environmental assessment and decision making.* National Research Council of the National Academies. Washington, DC: National Academies Press.

Ecosystem Management Initiative. (2009). The collaborative dimension of EM. University of Michigan. Retrieved November 10, 2010, from www.snre.umich.edu/

Eilperin, J. (2004, April 14). Groups unite behind plan to protect Idaho wilderness. *Washington Post,* p. A2.

Fritch, J., Palczewski, C. H., Farrell, J., & Short, E. (2006). Disingenuous controversy: Responses to Ward Churchill's 9/11 essay. *Argumentation and Advocacy, 42*(4), 190–205.

Goodnight, G. T. (1991). Controversy. In D. Parson (Ed.), *Argument in controversy* (pp. 1–12). Annandale, VA: Speech Communication Association.

Hamilton, J. D. (2004). Competing and converging values of public participation: A case study of participant views in Department of Energy nuclear weapons cleanup. In S. P. Depoe, J. W. Delicath, & M-F. A. Elsenbeer (Eds.), *Communication and public participation in environmental decision making* (pp. 59–81). Albany: State University of New York Press.

Hamilton, J. D. (2008). Convergence and divergence in the public dialogue on nuclear weapons cleanup. In B. C. Taylor, W. J. Kinsella, S. P. Depoe, & M. S. Metzler (Eds.), *Nuclear legacies: Communication, controversy, and the U.S. nuclear weapons complex* (pp. 41–72). Lanham, MD: Lexington Books.

Janis, I. L. (1977). *Victims of groupthink.* Boston: Houghton Mifflin.

Jones, L. (1996, May 13). "Howdy, Neighbor!" As a last resort, Westerners start talking to each other. *High Country News, 28,* pp. 1, 6, 8.

Kinsella, W. J. (2004). Public expertise: A foundation for citizen participation in energy and environmental decisions. In S. P. Depoe, J. W. Delicath, & M-F. A. Elsenbeer (Eds.), *Communication and public participation in environmental decision making* (pp. 83–95). Albany: State University of New York Press.

Markets campaign. (n.d.). The rainforest Solutions Project. Retrieved November 12, 2010, from www.savethegreatbear.org/

McCloskey, M. (1996, May 13). The skeptic: Collaboration has its limits. *High Country News, 28,* p. 7.

Policy Consensus Initiative. (2004a). Reaching *consensus in Ohio on water quality standards.* Retrieved September 4, 2004, from http://www.policyconsensus.org

Policy Consensus Initiative. (2004b). *State collaboration leads to successful wind farm siting.* Retrieved September 6, 2004, from http://www.policyconsensus.org

Red Lodge Clearinghouse. (2008, April 11). *Quincy library group.* A project of the Natural Resources Law Center at the University of Colorado Law School. Retrieved November 22, 2008, from http://rlch.org

Santos, S. L., & Chess, C. (2003). Evaluating citizen advisory boards: The importance of theory and participant-based criteria and practical implications. *Risk Analysis, 23,* 269–279.

Senecah, S. L. (2004). The trinity of voice: The role of practical theory in planning and evaluating the effectiveness of environmental participatory processes. In S. P. Depoe, J. W. Delicath, & M-F. A. Elsenbeer (Eds.), *Communication and public participation in environmental decision making* (pp. 13–33). Albany: State University of New York Press.

Smith, M., Sterritt, A., & Armstrong, P. (2007, May 14). From conflict to collaboration: The story of the Great Bear Rainforest. Retrieved November 15, 2010, from www.forestethics.org/

Terhune, P., & Terhune, G. (1998, October 8–10). *QLG case study.* Prepared for Engaging, Empowering, and Negotiating Community: Strategies for Conservation and Development workshop. Sponsored by the Conservation and Development Forum, West Virginia University, and the Center for Economic Options. Retrieved August 12, 2004, from http://www.qlg .org/pub

Walker, G. B. (2004). The roadless area initiative as national policy: Is public participation an oxymoron? In S. P. Depoe, J. W. Delicath, & M-F. A. Elsenbeer (Eds.), *Communication and public participation in environmental decision making* (pp. 113–135). Albany: State University of New York Press.

Wondolleck, J. M., & Yaffee, S. L. (2000). *Making collaboration work: Lessons from innovation in natural resource management.* Washington, DC: Island Press.

Wood, J. T. (2009). *Communication in our lives* (5th ed.). Boston: Wadsworth Cengage Learning.

PART III

Media and the Environment

Environmental activists, left, hold a press conference on beach during the United Nations Climate Change Conference in Cancun, Mexico, 2010.

AP Photo/Eduardo Verdugo

CHAPTER 6

News Media and Environmental Journalism

News about the environment, environmental disasters, and environmental issues or problems does not happen by itself, but is rather "produced," "manufactured," or "constructed."

—Hansen (2010, p. 72)

By now, we've seen that our perceptions of nature and environmental controversies are mediated by many sources—films, political debate, news media, and so forth. Among the important sources of information about the environment are journalists and the mainstream news media. (I'll describe the role of social media in Chapter 7.) In this chapter, I'll explore the nature of news production and the constraints on environmental journalists working in traditional media.

Chapter Preview

- The first section of this chapter describes the growth and nature of traditional news media and the differing views of *nature* in environmental media.
- The second section identifies some of the journalistic norms and constraints on news production, including: newsworthiness, media frames, norms of objectivity and balance, political economy, and gatekeeping and newsroom routines.
- The third section explores the case study of climate change to illustrate the challenges of meeting a newsworthiness standard in news media.
- In the fourth section, I describe the research on media effects and the debate over the influence of media on our attitudes and behavior related to the environment. I identify three theories: (1) agenda setting, (2) narrative framing, and (3) cultivation analysis.
- Finally, I describe changes in traditional news media, including the so-called death of newspapers (and their migration online), and what these changes might mean for the future of environmental journalism.

In referring to *news media,* however, it is important to distinguish between traditional print and electronic media, on the one hand, and online news sites and social media on the other. By **traditional news media,** I mean newspapers, news magazines, network television news, and radio news programs. In this chapter, I'll describe the role of these traditional sources in covering environmental stories. In the next chapter, I'll explore the explosive growth of online news sites (blogs and environmental news services) as well as social media (e.g., Facebook, Twitter, and mobile applications) that are arising to supplement—and substitute for—mainstream media's role in producing news and information about the environment.

Apart from technological advances, there is another reason to distinguish traditional and online media. At the heart of traditional environmental journalism is a dilemma. Journalism professor Sharon Friedman (2004) observed that environmental journalists working in traditional media today must deal with a "shrinking news hole while facing a growing need to tell longer, complicated and more in-depth stories" (p. 176).

In journalistic parlance, a **news hole** is the amount of space that is available in a newspaper or TV news story relative to other demands for the same space. Friedman argues that competition for shrinking news space has increased the pressure on journalists to simplify or dramatize issues to ensure that a story gets printed or aired. As a result, many journalists are also using online media, particularly blogs, which offer greater freedom and news space. (I'll explore this and related trends in online and social media in the next chapter.)

When you have finished this chapter, you'll be aware of some of the factors that influence the production of news about the environment as well as news media's "construction" of nature and environmental problems. You should also be able to raise questions about the possible influence of news media in shaping our perceptions and behavior as well as the media's potential for public education about important environmental concerns.

Growth and Nature of Environmental News

By the 1960s, news stories and visual images of environmental concerns began to appear prominently in the media—from the photo of the Earth taken by astronauts on Apollo 8 in 1968 and TV film of an oil spill off the coast of Santa Barbara to *Time* magazine's story of Ohio's Cuyahoga River bursting into flames from pollution in 1969. During the next decades, the media's interest would periodically expand and wane, portraying environmental problems in multidimensional and often dramatic ways.

In this section, I describe the origins of environmental reporting and some of the characteristics of news coverage of the environment. I'll also describe the episodic nature—the rise and fall—of media interest in environmental stories over the years, as well as the diverse, even conflicting depictions of nature that appear in mainstream news.

Characteristics of Environmental News

News coverage of environmental problems began on a sustained basis in the 1960s at "a handful of news organizations" (Wyss, 2008, p. ix). As environmentalism became a formidable force after Rachel Carson's *Silent Spring* (1962), "environmental journalism grew with it"; some newspapers began an environmental beat, but beat or no beat, reporters found themselves covering issues like dioxin, smog, and endangered species, as well as oil spills, air pollution, and nuclear fallout (Palen, 1998, para. 1). In 1990, the field of environmental journalism was given a boost by the creation of the Society of Environmental Journalists (SEJ), whose mission "is to strengthen the quality, reach and viability of journalism across all media to advance public understanding of environmental issues" (www.sej.org). By the first decade of the 21st century, more than 1,400 journalists identified as environmental reporters in the U.S., with more than 7,500 journalists in other countries covering the environment (Wyss, 2008, p. ix).

Even as news coverage of environmental issues has grown, the characteristics of this coverage—and the demands on journalists—are not unlike other areas of journalism. That is, news stories about the environment often are driven by specific events or by the release of reports by scientific or governmental bodies, and like other topics, environmental stories must compete with news of war, unemployment, terrorism, and other breaking news.

Event-Driven Coverage

Inevitably, contemporary news "is largely event focused and event driven," and it is this norm that is important in determining "which environmental issues get news coverage and which don't" (Hansen, 2010, p. 95). Indeed, environmental news thrives on dramatic events such as oil spills, forest fires, hurricanes, and accidents at nuclear power plants. Yet, as veteran environmental journalist Bob Wyss (2008) points out, environmental issues rarely are as dramatic as Hurricane Katrina, for example. "Rather than striking with a fury, some [stories] ooze, seep, or bubble silently . . . or the story might change so imperceptibly as to be nearly invisible, such as the disappearance of another animal or plant species" (p. 8). Nor are the long-term effects of global climate change "immediately observable"; nor is the link between pollution and respiratory diseases obvious to observers (Hansen, 2010, pp. 95–96).

This invisibility of many environmental phenomena presents a challenge for journalists. As media scholar Anders Hansen (2010) reminds us,

> the timescale of most environmental problems is ill-suited to the 24-hour cycle of news production: Many environmental problems take a long time to develop; there is often uncertainty for years about the causes and wider effects of environmental problems . . . and even where a scientific and political consensus may emerge, the "visualization" for a wider public audience of what is happening requires a great deal of communicative "work." (p. 96)

As a result, many environmental news stories—like news stories about health care, education, or the economy—present a *snapshot,* a specific moment, event, or action from a larger phenomenon.

Added to this challenge is another difficulty. Many environmental reporters, themselves, lack training in the issues they're covering. These issues are often complex, ranging from depletion of the ozone layer around the Earth to the health effects of genetically modified organisms. The Knight Center for Environmental Journalism, for example, reported that "only 12 percent of environmental journalists had degrees in scientific or environmental fields" (Wyss, 2008, p. 18). Still, some journalists, such as Andrew Revkin, formerly of the *New York Times,* have excelled in reporting complex issues like climate change in a manner that has informed readers about the causes, long-term impacts, and even the science behind these important subjects.

The event-driven nature of news and the invisibility of many environmental issues, nevertheless, have meant that an environmental story must compete with other breaking news. Even an in-depth, but complicated story about the shortage of water globally may be shoved aside in favor of a more dramatic news event. Indeed, over the years, the frequency of environmental news has risen and fallen as wars, economic recession, terrorism, and other concerns have seized TV and newspaper headlines.

Rise and Fall of Environmental News

With the rise of an ecology movement in the late 1960s, environmental news grew in coverage and reached an early peak after Earth Day during the early 1970s. After declining in the 1980s, the mainstream media's interest in the environment saw another high point in 1989, the year of the *Exxon Valdez* oil spill in Alaska. Film of oil-soaked birds and otters and oil-blackened coastlines of Alaska's Prince William Sound filled TV screens nightly. The Tyndall Report, which tracks network news minutes, reported that, in 1989, environmental stories saw an unprecedented 774 minutes, combined, on the *CBS Evening News, NBC Nightly News,* and *ABC World News Tonight* (Hall, 2001).

The years following the *Exxon Valdez* oil spill, however, would see a marked difference. Shabecoff (2000) reports that, not only did environmental stories not grow in the 1990s during President Bill Clinton's administration, but the total number of news stories about the environment carried by newspapers and television networks declined substantially. The Tyndall Report tracked a low of 174 minutes in 1996 for the major TV news reports and 195 minutes in 1998 (Hall, 2001). By the end of the 1990s decade, environmental reporters were citing shrinking news holes as one of the most frequent barriers to coverage of environmental news (Sachsman, Simon, & Valenti, 2002).

A resurgence in environmental coverage began after President George W. Bush came into office in 2001. Hall (2001) observed that the controversial policies of the Bush administration—such as the relaxing of rules for arsenic in drinking water—put the environment back on page one. This green trend, however, was interrupted by the terrorist attacks on the World Trade Center and Pentagon on September 11, 2001; with these attacks, news turned to the war on terror and, later, the wars in Iraq and Afghanistan. Friedman (2004) reports that nearly all the environmental journalists with whom she consulted agreed that "the events of September 11 have shrunk the [environmental] news hole even further" (p. 179).

By 2006, coverage of the environment had expanded again, across all media—newspapers, TV, online news sites, and green business stories. For example, popular magazines like *Glamour, Time, Vanity Fair,* and *Sports Illustrated* flooded newsstands with special "green" cover issues such as "The 10 Easiest Things You Can Do to Help the Planet" and "Sports and Global Warming," as well as the cover of *Time* magazine in April 3, 2006, warning, "Be Worried. Be Very Worried" (about global warming).

Newspaper reporting on global warming, particularly, spiked during this period (Brainard, 2008, para. 10). Roger Cohn, editor of the new *Yale Environment 360* online magazine, explained that the increased coverage of environmental issues was "strictly a reflection of heightened interest based on the implications of climate change" (quoted in Juskalian, 2008, para. 5). Two factors contributing to this interest were the popular reception of former Vice President Al Gore's documentary film *An Inconvenient Truth* (2006), warning of the dangers of global climate change, and the United Nation's Intergovernmental Panel on Climate Change (IPCC) report in early 2007, concluding that the observed increases in global temperatures since mid-20th century were "very likely" due to human-caused greenhouse gases (Sec. 2.2). (The IPCC's next report, scheduled for 2014, will undoubtedly produce another spurt of news coverage.)

Despite the renewed interest, especially in climate change, this trend would not last, and by the second decade of the 21st century, news coverage of the environment had begun to decline again. (See "FYI: Frequency of News Stories About Global Warming" later in this chapter.)

As I write in 2011, news stories about the environment are not first-tier stories in the traditional media. Yet, this will last only until a new natural disaster strikes, a major scientific report is released, or some other dramatic event occurs. As Friedman (2004) reminds us, "The environmental beat has never really been stable, riding a cycle of ups and downs like an elevator. These cycles . . . appear to be driven by public interest and events, as well as economic conditions" (p. 177).

Even as news about the environment goes through bursts of coverage, it is important to note that public interest in environmental problems has likely not disappeared. Political scientists Norman Vig and Michael Kraft (2003) found that, although events such as a terrorist attacks may divert the public's interest from environmental problems for a while, over time "one can see the continuity of strong public support for environmental protection and [for] expanding environmental authority" (p. 10).

Differing Views of Nature in Media

Beyond the frequency of stories in traditional news media, what is actually said or shown about the environment itself? The media's portrayal of nature is hardly uniform: Film and photographs of polar bears and melting glaciers clash with splashy ads for "clean coal" or those showing sports utility vehicles climbing rugged mountain ridges. And, while local TV news covers tree-planting ceremonies, the Weather Channel showcases images of devastating forest fires and tornados.

Do these depictions of nature invite concern for environmental values or a desire to exploit or manage nature for our own purposes? In Chapter 2, we saw that, rhetorically, nature can be presented in different ways, from the fearsome sermons of early colonial preachers to the passion for wild areas of preservationists such as John Muir. British philosopher Kate Soper (1995) observed in her book *What Is Nature?* that mainstream media construct contradictory images of nature—treacherous and sublime, and more:

> Nature is . . . represented as both savage and noble, polluted and wholesome, lewd and innocent, carnal and pure, chaotic and ordered. Conceived as a feminine principle, nature is equally lover, mother and virago: a source of sensual delight, a nurturing bosom, a site of treacherous and vindictive forces bent on retribution for her human violation. Sublime and pastoral, indifferent to human purposes and willing servant of them, nature awes as she consoles, strikes terror as she pacifies, presents herself as both the best of friends and the worst of foes. (p. 71)

If popular media images depict nature as both "the best of friends and the worst of foes," does this mean that there are no problems in the media's representations of nature? Or are there stable and recurring trends in media's depictions?

The research is somewhat mixed, as might be expected. For example, Meisner (2005) surveyed images of nature in a comprehensive study of Canadian media that included newspapers, magazines, and prime-time television shows (news, drama, documentaries, comedy, science fiction, and current affairs). He reported that the most prominent representations of nature found in these media could be classified according to four major themes: (1) nature as a victim, (2) nature as a sick patient, (3) nature as a problem (threat, annoyance, and so forth), and (4) nature as a resource.

Meisner found that, not unlike Soper's account, these themes offered two competing views of nature: "Sometimes there seems to be a strong admiration and desire for Nature. At other times there is a hatred. Sometimes there is a strong injunction to connect with or care for Nature. At other times the injunction is to fight or exploit it" (p. 432). Overall, however, he found that the frequency of images valuing nature positively outweighed negative images by a ratio of three to one.

A related example of such representations of nature can be seen in *The Simpsons*, the longest-running cartoon show on television, as well as *The Simpsons Movie* (2007). *Entertainment Weekly* has called *The Simpsons* television series "guerrilla TV, a wicked satire masquerading as a prime-time cartoon" (Korte, 1997, p. 9). We could also say that, from the perspective of environmental communication, the show borrows themes in the news media about the environment for its satiric commentary in its episodes. This is the view of Anne Marie Todd (2002) in her critical study of *The Simpsons*. Todd argues that *The Simpsons* "presents a strong ideological message about nature as a symbol—as an object for human exploitation" (p. 77).

In particular, Todd singles out the character of Lisa, the brainy daughter whose concern for the environment often emerges as a humorous counterpoint to the **anthropocentricism** of her father, Homer. (As used by many environmentalists, *anthropocentricism* is the belief that nature exists solely for the benefit of humans.) For example, "When Lisa bemoans the crashing of an oil tanker on Baby Seal Beach, Homer comforts her. . . . 'It'll be okay, honey. There's lots more oil where that came from'" (Appel, 1996, in Todd, 2002, p. 78). Todd notes that Homer's only concern about the oil tanker's wreck is whether there will be enough oil left for his and his family's usual lifestyle.

But, why are there certain portrayals of nature and not others? One reason is the struggle reporters experience in trying to convey a subject's importance to viewers or readers who may know or care little about it. The challenge is that many environmental problems are both complex and *unobtrusive*—that is, they are remote—it's not easy to link their relevance concretely to our lives. This makes it difficult to fit these concerns into the media's conventions for reporting. Let's examine this further.

News Production and the Environment

Environmental news stories do not write themselves. As we learned in Chapter 3, an environmental problem becomes recognized as a *problem* as a result of the constitutive nature of communication itself. As Hansen (2010) reminds us, "News about the environment, environmental disasters, and environmental issues or problems does not happen by itself, but is rather 'produced,' 'manufactured,' or 'constructed'" (p. 72). This production of news depends upon a number of factors, including journalistic norms, editorial policy, and ownership of media, as well as the need to sell newspapers or increase market share for TV news (Anderson, 1997).

In this section, I'll describe the influences that shape or constrain the production of news and environmental news in particular. I'll describe some of the journalistic norms that guide reporters, including newsworthiness, media frames, and the norms of objectivity and balance in news stories, as well as other forces that may impact journalists, such as media ownership and the role of gatekeeping and newsroom routines.

Journalistic Norms and Constraints

Newsworthiness

One of the most important of the practices that affect environmental news reporting is the value or *newsworthiness* of a story. **Newsworthiness** is the ability of a news story to attract readers or viewers. In their popular guide to news reporting, *Reaching Audiences: A Guide to Media Writing,* Yopp, McAdams, and Thornburg (2009) identify the criteria, found in most U.S. media guidelines, that determine the newsworthiness of a particular story. Reporters are also likely to draw on one or more of these for selecting and reporting environmental news: (a) prominence, (b) timeliness, (c) proximity, (d) impact, (e) magnitude, (f) conflict, (g), oddity, and (h) emotional impact.

As a result, reporters and editors feel they must strive to fit or package environmental problems according to these news values. For example, a March 14, 2011, front-page headline, "Japan Faces Potential Nuclear Disaster as Radiation Levels Rise," in the *New York Times,* stressed the potential *impact* and *magnitude* of the crisis at the Fukushima Daiichi nuclear plant, which burned, following an earthquake and tsunami that struck Japan four days earlier. These criteria were reinforced immediately in the lead paragraph:

> Japan's nuclear crisis verged toward catastrophe on Tuesday after an explosion damaged the vessel containing the nuclear core at one reactor and a fire at another spewed large amounts of radioactive material into the air, according to the statements of Japanese government and industry officials. (Tabuchi, Sanger, & Bradsher, 2011, p. A1)

Later in the story, a criterion of *proximity,* or nearness to readers, emerged to guide the story's narrative: "After an emergency cabinet meeting, the Japanese government told people living within 30 kilometers, about 18 miles, of the Daiichi plant to stay indoors, keep their windows closed and stop using air conditioning" (p. A1).

| **Figure 6.1** | Japanese NTV newscast during the crisis at the Fukushima Daiichi nuclear power station after the 2011 earthquake and tsunami. |

Another criterion—*conflict*—is an especially influential factor in news stories about the environment: environmentalists versus loggers, climate scientists versus global warming skeptics, angry residents versus chemical companies, and so forth. Conflict may also account for the front-page placement of stories. For example, stories about global warming are usually not on the front page of newspapers; however, "the global warming stories that do make it onto the front page tend to concern the most contentious aspects of climate science" (Brainard, 2008, para. 13). *New York Times* reporter Andrew Revkin (2011) noted that, unfortunately, reserving the front page for stories exhibiting conflict or "hot conclusions" can lead to a glossing over of the climate science behind the controversy (quoted in Brainard, 2008, para. 13).

Overall, Anderson (1997) found that environmental news coverage tends to feature stories that are (a) event centered (for example, oil spills and publicity stunts), (b) characterized by strong visual elements (pictures or film), and (c) closely tied into a 24-hour daily cycle. An event-centered approach focusing on disasters such as the Bhopal chemical accident in India and the *Exxon Valdez* oil spill seemed to characterize environmental news coverage in the 1970s and 1980s in particular. However, Friedman (2004) suggested that this pattern may be changing as "the obvious stories [give] way to more complex issues like particulate air pollution, climate change, endocrine disruption, and non-point water pollution" (p. 179).

Anderson (1997) emphasizes, however, that a bias toward visual elements and the 24-hour news cycle still characterize environmental news coverage and can be a particular challenge for reporting environmental stories on television. She cites the example of a BBC News correspondent who complained, "We're about pictures. . . . Above all environment stories need good pictures. . . . Global warming is very difficult because you can't actually see global warming" (pp. 121–122). As we've seen, many environmental problems don't fit these requirements for newsworthiness either because they lack visual quality or they involve slower, more diffuse, and drawn-out processes.

☞ **FYI** **Image Events and the Environment**

Despite the resistance of environmental stories to visual images, some have found that the news media's reliance on film or photos provides an opening for environmentalists and journalists alike. By offering dramatic visual events as part of a story, groups like Greenpeace, for example, have been able to fulfill the newsworthiness criterion and have excelled in gaining coverage for their campaigns. Greenpeace pioneered this tactic with its dramatic film of activists in small Zodiac boats, interposing themselves between ships' harpoons and whales in the Pacific Ocean in the 1970s. Today, Captain Paul Watson's ships (featured in *Whale Wars* on TV's Animal Planet channel) provide compelling film as they track the Japanese whaling fleet in frigid, Antarctic waters (http://animal.discovery.com/tv/whale-wars/about).

Environmental communication scholar Kevin DeLuca (2005) has called these **image events**. Image events fully take advantage of television's hunger for pictures, such as footage of large banners draped from a corporate headquarters proclaiming, "End clear-cutting of rain forests!" DeLuca quotes a veteran Greenpeace campaigner who explained that such image events succeed by "reducing a complex set of issues to symbols that break people's comfortable equilibrium, get them asking whether there are better ways to do things" (p. 3).

Despite the occasional success of image events, criteria for newsworthiness have periodically come under fire. For example, some have asked, Why are environmental stories expected to meet standards like conflict, oddity, or emotional impact, when these seem more relevant to entertainment than to news? One reason that many editors give is that they believe there is little or no interest among the public in environmental stories. Yet, as I reported earlier, evidence suggests that, while the public supports environmental protection over time, short-term developments often divert the public's interest. In the end, then, many reporters believe the challenge of environmental journalism remains to make environmental news both accurate and newsworthy in the face of other pressures for news space.

Media Frames

In his classic study, *Public Opinion,* Walter Lippmann (1922) was perhaps the first to grasp a basic dilemma of news reporting when he wrote:

> The real environment is altogether too big, too complex, and too fleeting for direct acquaintance. We are not equipped to deal with so much subtlety, so much variety, so many permutations and combinations. And although we have to act in that environment, we have to reconstruct it on a simpler model before we can manage it. *To traverse the world men [sic] must have maps of the world.* (p. 16, emphasis added)

As a result, journalists have sought ways to simplify, frame, or make "maps of the world" to communicate their stories.

The term **frame** was first popularized by Erving Goffman (1974) in his book *Frame Analysis: An Essay on the Organization of Experience.* Goffman defined *frames* as the cognitive maps or patterns of interpretation that people use to organize their understandings of reality. Others have defined frames as principles of selection or emphasis about the world and what matters (Gitlin, 1980) and the act of framing as the selection of "some aspects of a perceived reality and [making] them more salient in a communicating text" (Entman, 1993, p. 56). Hansen (2010) says, "Frames, in other words, draw attention—like a frame around a painting or photograph—to particular dimensions or perspectives, and they set the boundaries for how we should interpret or perceive what is presented" (p. 31).

Building on the idea of a frame, Pan and Kosicki (1993) defined **media frames** as the "central organizing themes . . . that connect different semantic elements of a news story (headlines, quotes, leads, visual representations, and narrative structure) into a coherent whole to suggest what is at issue" (Rodríguez, 2003, p. 80). By providing this coherence, media frames help people make sense of new experiences, relating them to familiar assumptions about the way the world works.

Consider, for example, a news story in the *Washington Post* on efforts by environmentalists in California to protect endangered desert tortoises. The *Post's* headline stated: "Desert Tortoise Advocates Fight Solar Energy Backers in Environmental Feud." The lead sentence reinforced this theme: "A federal assessment shows more than 3,000 desert tortoises that are threatened with extinction would be disturbed by a California solar project, and up to 700 of the young turtles would be killed during construction" (Associated Press, 2011, para. 1). Both the headline and lead introduced a central organizing theme or frame of *conflict*—environmentalists against solar developers—with the fate of the desert tortoise hanging in the balance. This frame is reinforced throughout the news article: "Questions over the California tortoises highlight tensions in the U.S. between wilderness conservation and the quest for cleaner power" (para. 3). (As I write in 2011, the federal government has ordered the solar project to halt construction for some of the project.)

A news story also can be viewed quite differently if an editor chooses a different media frame for it. An example of this occurred in newspapers after the crisis at the Fukushima Daiichi nuclear plant in Japan in 2011. As journalists raised the question of the safety of U.S. nuclear plants, newspapers framed the story in strikingly different ways. Charleston's *Post and Courier* carried the disturbing headline, "New Report Details Safety Issues at U.S. Nuclear Plants" (Fretwell, 2011). The opening paragraph reinforced a frame that raised concerns about safety: "Inspectors studying safety questions at more than a dozen U.S. nuclear plants last year found the most serious concerns in South Carolina—at a 40-year-old Darlington County power station that experienced two fires and equipment failures" (para. 1). A different headline, from the Reuters (2011) news agency a few days later, declared, "Most Americans Say U.S. Nuclear Plants Safe." The headline and lead sentences clearly framed nuclear safety in the U.S. in a more reassuring way: "Fifty-eight percent of Americans think U.S. nuclear power plants are safe" (paras. 1, 2).

The two stories oriented readers in very different ways. The first story organized the subject of nuclear power around a worrisome report and problems at U.S. nuclear plants, drawing upon a reason-to-worry or concerns-about-safety frame. The second story framed the subject in light of the public's reassuring opinion about nuclear power—a public-confidence frame.

Because different frames orient us to different meanings, the parties to an environmental controversy sometimes compete to influence the framing of a news story. Miller and Riechert (2000) explain that opposing stakeholders try to gain public support for their positions, often "not by offering new facts or by changing evaluations of the facts, but *by altering the frames or interpretive dimensions for evaluating the facts*" (p. 45, emphasis added).

An example of the reframing of a story occurred in a controversy over a new runway at Boston's Logan Airport near a working-class neighborhood. In this case, opponents of the runway succeeded in challenging the journalistic frame in newspapers' coverage. In her study of the conflict, Marchi (2005) found that, early in the controversy, news articles used sources such as the airline industry and businesses; these sources framed the project as essential to the economic health of the region. As the controversy dragged on, however, opponents succeeded in introducing a new frame in news coverage, one that recognized the problematic aspects of the runway, such as noise pollution and health and environmental impacts.

Figure 6.2	Image events take advantage of news media's desire for pictures, particularly images of conflict (protest at the White House during a rally on Offshore Drilling in Washington, June 25, 2011).

AP Photos/Luis M. Alvarez

Finally, some scholars have observed that media frames often function rhetorically to sustain dominant discourses about the economy, nature, or environmentalists. For example, in *Image Politics*, DeLuca (2005) argues that commercial news programs such as *ABC World News Tonight* tended to negatively frame—and thus marginalize—radical environmental groups such as Earth First! that criticize timber and mining interests and challenge the U.S. Forest Service.

Similarly, Wagner (2008) argues that national newspapers have successfully reframed acts of *ecotage* through the frightening lens of terrorism (p. 25). **Ecotage** is controversial in itself, of course. It refers to acts such as vandalism and arson that are undertaken by activists for the purpose of protecting nature or certain species; while clearly illegal, these acts are not intended to harm human beings. Yet, in his study of newspapers, from 1984 to 2006, Wagner found "a marked shift in framing ecotage as terrorism starting in 2001"; although the volume of stories using the ecoterrorist frame increased afterward, the number of actual incidences of ectoage steadily declined during this same period (p. 25). This reframing, Wagner reports, helped to construct a "discourse of fear," a kind of "moral panic . . . that a widespread threat to society exists" (p. 28).

Clearly, the choice of a frame in a story matters. Indeed, the history of environmentalism in the United States can be understood partly to be a struggle over quite different but powerful frames for nature and our relationship to the environment. For example, news media now refer more often to *rainforests* instead of *jungles* and to *wetlands* instead of *swamps*.

Norms of Objectivity and Balance

The values of **objectivity and balance** have been bedrock norms of journalism for almost a century. In principle, these are the commitments by journalists to provide information that is accurate and without reporter bias and, where there is uncertainty or controversy, to balance news stories with statements from all sides of the issue. Additionally, the latter norm has been relied upon when a reporter lacks the expertise or time to determine where "truth" lies (Cunningham, 2003).

Objectivity

In practice, however, the norms of objectivity and balance run into difficulty. Particularly in environmental journalism, reporters struggle to maintain genuine objectivity. For example, while a story on oil drilling or the shooting of wolves may be accurate on one level, a kind of bias already has occurred in the selection of this story versus others; this occurs also in its framing and the choice of sources that are interviewed. For example, environmental media scholar Anabela Carvalho (2007) found in her study of British newspapers that the discursive constructions of climate change are "strongly entangled with ideological standpoints." That is, the ideas and values underlying different political views or orientations work as a "powerful selection device in deciding what is scientific news, i.e., what the relevant 'facts' are, and who are the authorized 'agents of definition' of science matters" (p. 223).

As a consequence, a challenge for "objective" reporting is the need for journalists to rely upon credible sources, that is, sources whose understanding or insight readers and viewers will trust as the basis for "truth." Often, these individuals are those whom Ericson, Baranek, and Chan (1987) have called the "authorized knowers" of society—scientists, experts in a field, government and industry leaders, and so on (quoted in Hansen, 2010, p. 91). Later, I'll describe some of the difficulties that victims of environmental harms, such as residents of low-income communities, have experienced in being interviewed or recognized as "credible" sources in environmental news stories.

Balance

Related to objectivity sometimes is the norm of balance in reporting a story. *Balance* usually is taken to mean a responsibility to report all sides of story, particularly when there is a controversy. Yet, this also can be problematic. As Wyss (2008) points out, "Getting both sides of a story, while generally desirable in journalism, does not always work in science and environmental coverage" (p. 62). He cites the long-time science editor for the *Dallas Morning News* who quipped that, "balance in space stories would require that every story about satellites would require a comment from the Flat Earth Society" (p. 62).

Nevertheless, when environmental issues are controversial, or when reporters lack the expertise to judge conflicting claims, the tendency in journalism has been to balance stories by quoting differing viewpoints. This refers to the pairing of a disputed report or statement from a scientist or public official with an opposing viewpoint. For example, balance was a common practice in much of the early coverage of global warming. Boykoff and Boykoff (2004) cite the following example from a Los Angeles article in 1992:

> The ability to study climatic patterns has been critical to the debate over the phenomenon called "global warming." *Some scientists believe*—and some ice core studies seem to indicate—that humanity's production of carbon dioxide is leading to a potentially dangerous overheating of the planet. *But skeptics contend* there is no evidence the warning exceeds the climate's natural variations. (Abramson, 1992, p. A1; emphasis added)

In recent years, the norm of balance has been sharply criticized. (See "Another Viewpoint: Objectivity and Balance in News Reporting.") Some media critics have challenged the assumption that there are always two sides of an issue, particularly when empirical data or scientific research strongly supports one side. For example, climatologist Stephen H. Schneider (2009) complained, "A mainstream, well-established consensus of hundreds of experts may be 'balanced' against the opposing views of a few special-interest PhDs. To the uninformed, each position seems equally credible" (pp. 203–204). As a result, balance will be misleading. Boykoff and Boykoff (2004) found that "balancing" in the reporting of global warming in U.S. newspapers actually led to "biased coverage" of the science of climate change and the findings of anthropogenic (human) contributions to global warming (p. 125).

Another Viewpoint: Objectivity and Balance in News Reporting

Veteran reporter and Director of the Center for Environmental Communication at Loyola University, New Orleans, Robert A. Thomas describes the responsibility of journalists this way:

> A reporter should use balance in researching all sides of a story, but in drawing conclusions and reporting the results of this research, a reporter must be guided by fairness and objectivity. As an example, the evidence for global climate change is solid and scientists who specialize in this arena overwhelmingly are supporters. There is a school of thought, call The Deniers, largely composed of the freemarket policy community and others whose best interests are served by denying the impacts of carbon on climate, who cast doubt into the equation by raising anecdotal arguments and using fragments of data sets. Good journalists will acquaint themselves with these disparate arguments, but give credence to the arguments of climate scientists who follow the scientific method in their quest for truth.

SOURCE: Robert A. Thomas, PhD, Director, Center for Environmental Communication, School of Mass Communication, Loyola University, New Orleans (personal communication, April 5, 2011).

The trend of balancing science and skepticism in reports of global warming may be changing. Brainard (2008), for example, reports that the news media seem to be "slowly but surely eliminating false balance when addressing human activity's role in global warming" (para. 6). Boykoff (2007) also has found that "balanced" coverage of global warming science has tapered off in recent years in major U.S. newspapers.

Other Influences on Environmental Journalists

Political Economy of News Media

The term *media political economy* refers to the influence of ownership and the economic interests of the owners of newspapers and television networks on the news content of these media sources. In her critical study of corporate influence on the media, Australian environmental scholar Sharon Beder (2002) noted that most commercial media organizations are owned by multinational corporations with financial interests in other businesses—such as forestry, energy companies, pulp and paper mills, oil wells, real estate, electric utilities, and so forth—that are often affected by environmental regulations. With increasing consolidation of media ownership, some media managers and editors may feel pressure from owners to choose (or avoid) stories and to report news in ways that ensure a favorable political climate for these business concerns. In turn, such editors and managers "become the proprietor's 'voice' within the newsroom, ensuring that journalistic 'independence' conforms to the preferred editorial line" (McNair, 1994, p. 42).

Consider the example of General Electric (GE), one of the world's largest corporations and owner of NBC television and its business channel CNBC. Beder (2002) found that GE is by no means a hands-off owner of its networks. Instead, she reported, GE officials regularly insert the business's interests into network editorial decisions. Although GE has had environmental problems, "NBC journalists have not been particularly keen to expose GE's environmental record" (p. 224). For example, when the Environmental Protection Agency (EPA) found GE responsible for discharging more than a million pounds of polychlorinated biphenols (PCBs) into New York's Hudson River and proposed that GE pay for a massive cleanup, "the company responded with an aggressive campaign aimed at killing the plan," spending, by its own estimates, $10 to $15 million on advertising (Mann, 2001, para. 2). (Eventually, GE agreed to fund a cleanup plan for the river.)

A more subtle form of ideological influence also may be present in some newsrooms. This is the case when economic interests determine the size of the news hole available for certain kinds of stories. Corbett (2006) points out that research also has found a form of social control in many newsrooms. This control takes the form of a "conditioned belief" where "a reporter does not realize that he or she is submitting to the organization's norms" (p. 225).

Finally, another effect of media political economy may result from the shifting of ownership of major U.S. newspapers. The Pew Research Center's *The State of the News Media* recently reported, "As a result of bankruptcies [of newspapers], private equity funds now own and operate a substantial portion of the industry," including some of the nation's largest newspapers—the *Los Angeles Times, Chicago Tribune, Philadelphia Inquirer, Denver Post,* and others (Edmunds, Guskin, & Rosenstiel, 2011, para. 59). Some fear the greater pressures for profit from such investors will affect the quality or even the number of reporters at newspapers.

Gatekeeping and Newsroom Routines

The decisions of editors and media managers to cover or not cover certain environmental stories illustrates what has been called the **gatekeeping** role of news production. Simply put, the metaphor of gatekeeping is used to suggest that certain individuals in newsrooms decide what gets through the "gate" and what stays out. White's (1950) classic study "The 'Gatekeeper': A Case Study in the Selection of News" launched the tradition in media research of tracking the structure and routines of the newsroom and the informal forces that set priorities for and help shape news stories. Gatekeeper studies thus focus on the routines, habits, and informal relationships among editors and reporters and among reporters' backgrounds, training, and sources.

Many editors and newsrooms find it particularly difficult to deal with the environmental beat for two reasons: First, the unobtrusive or "invisible" nature of many environmental problems makes it hard for reporters to fit these stories into conventional news formats. Second, as we've seen, environmental issues can be difficult to report because few reporters have training in science or knowledge of complex environmental problems such as groundwater pollution, animal waste, urban sprawl, genetically modified crops, or cancer and disease clusters. And few news organizations have the financial resources to hire such talent. As a result, Corbett (2006) observes, "Newsrooms may be at a loss as to how to best fit stories about the environment into newsroom organizations and routines" (p. 217).

Reporters and editors, therefore, face a dilemma: "As the public becomes increasingly aware of and worried about the environment, editors and reporters cannot rely on a 'seat-of-the-pants' approach when reporting on environmental issues. Stories must be technically accurate. . . . Yet few newspapers or broadcast stations can assign a full-time reporter to environmental stories" (West, Lewis, Greenberg, Sachsman, & Rogers, 2003, p. vii). For example, "on any given day, an environmental story may be assigned to a science specialist, a health reporter, a general assignment reporter, or even a business reporter" (Corbett, 2006, p. 217).

As a result of these constraints, reporters and editors have been turning to online news services such as the Environmental News Network (www.enn.com). Other databases useful to reporters are maintained by the Society of Environmental Journalists (SEJ). (I discuss these newer, online sources in the next chapter.)

The influences on news production that we've reviewed—newsworthiness, media frames, the norms of objectivity and balance, political economy, and gatekeepers—both enable and limit traditional news media in different ways. One way, perhaps, to appreciate these influences is to take up a case study. In the next section, I'll describe some of the challenges that reporters face in covering climate change.

Climate Change in the News (or Not)

Since the testimony of scientists before the U.S. Congress in the late 1980s, the question of how to communicate the importance of climate change to the general public has consumed the attention of educators, journalists, media consultants, and scientists themselves. Although "much of the early communication was relatively narrowly focused on scientific findings," global warming soon became a subject of general public interest, controversy, and policy debates (Moser, 2010, p. 32). Despite this interest, many scientists today fear the public's understanding, particularly in the U.S., lags behind the scientific understanding of climate change and its impacts (Krugman, 2009; Moser, 2010).

In this section, I describe some of the challenges that journalists, especially, face in covering climate change. And, I'll describe briefly some of the ways in which the media (and others) are attempting to reframe the problem of climate change in order to create a sense of urgency and support for action to mitigate its harmful impacts. Finally, in Chapter 11 ("Science Communication"), I'll also review initiatives by climate scientists to work with journalists in communicating better the evidence for the accelerating warming of the planet.

Is Climate Change Newsworthy?

As I write, the award-winning journalist Andrew Revkin (2011), is reporting that news coverage of climate change has again declined in the United States: "After several years of heavy [media] exposure, global warming, the greatest story rarely told, [has] reverted to its near perpetual position on the far back shelf of the public consciousness—if not back in the freezer" (para. 2). But, why is this? Why is "the greatest story rarely told" so difficult to sustain as a newsworthy subject in the media?

One reason is that social scientists and communication specialists are finding that the nature of climate change is more difficult to communicate than other environmental or health issues. "Indeed," Moser (2010) says, "a number of challenging traits make climate change a tough issue to engage with" (p. 33). Among the challenges she identifies are: (a) its invisible causes and distant impacts, (b) our insulation from the environment, (c) delayed or absent gratification for taking action, (d) the complexity and uncertainty of climate science, and (e) inadequate signals for the need to change.

Other reasons for the declining number of news stories may be the lack of staff at news organizations or views of news directors themselves. Recently, the Center for Climate Change Communication at George Mason University released the results of its survey of news directors at radio and TV stations. Among its chief findings were:

- Television news directors are interested in running science stories, but few have staff dedicated to this beat.
- Climate change is covered relatively infrequently on local TV news.

- Most news directors are comfortable with their weathercasters reporting on climate science.
- TV news directors appear less skeptical about the science of climate change than are TV weathercasters, although many still question the scientific consensus.
- Despite the scientific consensus that climate change is happening and is human caused, nearly all news directors (90%) believe that, like coverage of other issues, coverage of climate change must reflect a "balance" of viewpoints (Maibach, Wilson, & Witte, 2010, pp. 4, 5).

Earlier, we also saw how the journalistic norm of balance, that is, quoting climate skeptics along with scientists, helped to cause uncertainty among the public about climate change. Although this practice has waned, the number of stories themselves has declined. And, as Moser (2010) points out, the impacts of climate change are often distant, subtle, or outside the personal experience of readers or viewers, while the public's sense of urgency to take action has weakened in the face of joblessness, wars, and a sluggish economy.

Still, news media have covered climate change since the late 1980s, although unevenly. At times, this coverage has been intense, peaking in 2006 with the showing

Figure 6.3	Can global warming be visually illustrated? During recent droughts in East Africa, scenes of carcasses of dead sheep and goats outside of villages could be seen on U.S. and European TV.

Oxfam East Africa/Flickr

of Al Gore's documentary film *An Inconvenient Truth.* Yet, in the years since then, coverage has steadily declined. By late 2008, sociologist Robert Brulle observed, "Global warming is no longer a new story. . . . In the never-ending search for novelty and the unique, global warming no longer supplies new or dramatic headlines." The first collapse of an ice shelf, he noted, is "big news," but by the third or fourth collapse, "it becomes pretty regular and normal. . . . We get used to these occurrences" (quoted in Ward, 2008).

As a result, Brulle concluded, "I think it is fair to say that the cycle of media interest in climate change has run its course, and this story is no longer considered newsworthy" (quoted in Revkin, 2011, para. 6). How, then, might environmental journalists adapt to the loss of interest or a shrinking news hole, when the subject of global climate disruption is still significant in its own right?

One response by some has been to reframe the subject of climate change, using, instead, frames about health or national security. For example, a U.S. naval admiral made news headlines when he warned, "Global warming and a race for resources could spark a new 'cold war' in the Arctic"; in sounding this alert, the admiral invoked a national-security frame, citing the potential conflict over minerals in an unfrozen Arctic (Macalister, 2010, para. 1). Other news stories have put in the foreground frames of clean energy, green jobs, and the health impacts from coal-burning power plants. Similarly, many European newspapers are reframing climate change in terms of responsibility (for solving the problem) and consequences, that is, how climate change will affect people (Dirikx & Gelders, 2009; Hansen, 2011, pp. 16).

Act Locally!

Frequency of News Stories About Global Warming

How well do U.S. and world newspapers cover global warming? One measure of how well newspapers are doing is the frequency of articles about global warming or climate change. Dr. Maxwell Boykoff, at the University of Colorado, and Dr. Maria Mansfield, at Exeter University in the UK, track newspaper coverage of this subject in the United States and in 50 newspapers in 20 different nations and on 6 continents. What do their trends show?

For an up-to-date look at how well the largest five U.S. newspapers are covering global warming, check out the current Boykoff and Maxwell graph at: http://sciencepolicy .colorado.edu/media_coverage. (The newspapers included in this graph are the *Washington Post, Wall Street Journal, New York Times, USA Today,* and *Los Angeles Times.*)

Also, check how well the world's newspapers are covering this subject today at this same site.

Our above discussions of newsworthiness, frames, and the frequency of news coverage have implicitly assumed that news media have effects, that is, that news about the environment matters; news media affect our perceptions or behaviors. Do they? In the next section, I describe some of the research on media effects and the debate over whether (and how) news media influence our views about the environment.

Media Effects

Earlier, in Chapter 1, I said that our understanding and behavior toward the environment depend not only on environmental sciences but also on media representations and public debate as well as ordinary conversation. Nevertheless, there is also intense controversy about the possibility of **media effects.** By this phrase, I mean the influence of different media content, frequency, and forms of communication on audiences' attitudes, perceptions, and behaviors.

Early theories assumed that media effects are the result of direct transmission of information from a sender (source) to a receiver. This early theory viewed audiences as highly susceptible to manipulation and typically viewed people "as a homogenous mass of damp sponges, uniformly soaking up messages from the media" (Anderson, 1997, pp. 18–19). This approach received little support, and because it has not proved particularly useful in explaining the influence of environmental media, other accounts have emerged. These accounts move beyond the study of specific effects on individuals to broader influences of media in shaping perceptions of issues and in constructing social narratives about the environment.

In this section, I review three broad theories of the effects of news coverage on the public's attitudes and behavior. These theories are (a) agenda setting, (b) narrative framing, and (c) cultivation theory. While these approaches provide little evidence of direct, causal effects, they do suggest media's impact is both cumulative and a part of a wider context of social influences that help to construct our interest in, and our understanding of, the environment.

Agenda Setting

Perhaps the most influential theory of media effects that applies to environmental news is **agenda setting.** Cohen (1963) first suggested the idea of agenda setting to distinguish between individual opinion (what people believe) and the public's perception of the salience or importance of an issue. News reporting, he said, "may not be successful much of the time in telling people *what to think,* but it is stunningly successful in telling its readers *what to think about*" (p. 13, emphasis added; see also McCombs & Shaw, 1972). In their study of television, Iyengar and Kinder (1987) defined agenda setting this way: "Those problems that receive prominent attention on the national news become the problems the viewing public regards as the nation's most important" (p. 16).

The agenda-setting hypothesis has been influential in much environmental communication research. Such studies "have confirmed that the media can play a potentially powerful role in setting the agenda for public concern about and awareness of environmental issues" (Hansen, 2011, p. 18; Soroka, 2002). Nevertheless, the results sometimes have been conflicting. On the one hand, Iyengar and Kinder (1987) found firm evidence of the agenda-setting effect in their study of evening news on television, in which viewers rated the importance of the environment higher after viewing increased coverage of news of environmental pollution (p. 19). And, Eyal, Winter, and DeGeorge (1981), Ader (1995), and Soroka (2002) discovered that the agenda-setting effect is especially strong for unobtrusive issues or those to which readers or viewers have little personal access. This effect is most apparent in media's enhancement of the public's perceptions of risk or danger from environmental sources.

On the other hand, Iyengar and Kinder (1987) found no support for the vividness of news reports in affecting television viewers' perceptions of the importance of environmental issues. In this case, a story that featured a link between a toxic waste site and a stormy interview with a mother and her sick child produced no more viewer concern than a pallid version in which a reporter merely discussed a possible connection between the chemical site and catastrophic illness.

Environmental communication scholars, however, caution against a rejection of agenda-setting effects based on these findings. Ader (1995) pointed out, for example, that real-world conditions may affect perceptions of the seriousness of a problem independently of news coverage of these concerns. Anderson (1997) also points out that other influences, such as friends and family, may affect the public's perception of the importance of environmental issues and that agenda-setting research should take these factors into consideration.

In an attempt to refine agenda-setting theory, Ader (1995) investigated the influence of real-world conditions, public opinion, and the media's agenda in a study of news reports about the environment in the *New York Times* from 1970 to 1990. As this is considered by some as a definitive study, let's explore it further:

Adler asked two questions: (1) Is the public's concern about environmental problems driven by real-world conditions rather than media coverage? And, (2) Do public attitudes influence the amount of media coverage of an issue rather than the media's setting of the agenda? Using data from Gallup polls during this period, Ader identified problems that the public periodically rated as the "most important problem facing the nation today." To control for the influence of public opinion and real-world conditions on media coverage, Ader examined the length and prominence of news reports of pollution in the *Times* for three months before and three months after each Gallup poll was conducted as well as data from independent sources documenting real-world conditions for disposal of wastes, air quality, and water quality in these same periods.

Ader's findings affirmed the presence of a strong agenda-setting effect, even when real-world conditions and prior public opinion both were taken into account. That is, even though objective measures showed that overall pollution had declined for the period studied, the *Times* increased its coverage of news stories about pollution; furthermore, the greater length and prominence of these stories correlated positively with a subsequent increase in readers' concerns about this issue. However, the opposite was not true; that is, the media did not appear to be mirroring public opinion. Ader concluded, "The findings suggest that the amount of media attention devoted to pollution influenced the degree of public salience for the issue" (p. 309).

While the agenda-setting hypothesis may explain the importance of an issue to the public, it doesn't claim to account for what people think about this issue. Therefore, it is important for us to look at other theories that focus on the role of the media in constructing meaning or ways of understanding environmental concerns.

Narrative Framing

As I noted earlier, news media communicate not only facts about the environment but also wider frames or guides for understanding and making sense of these facts. Theories of media effects, therefore, have begun to focus on such sense-making or frames to help explain the role of news reporting in organizing our experiences of the world and our relationships to the environment. Such theories do not argue that media reports cause public opinion; rather, they claim that "media discourse is part of the process by which individuals construct meaning" (Gamson & Modigliani, 1989, p. 2). In this section, I describe the specific role of framing in providing a narrative or coherent story line about the world.

A narrative approach takes seriously the role of media frames that provide organizing themes that connect different elements of a news story into a coherent whole. *Narrative framing,* then, refers to the ways in which media organize the bits and facts of phenomena through stories to aid audiences' understanding and the potential for this organization to affect our relationships to the phenomena being represented. Such a view of framing builds upon communication scholar Robert Entman's (1993) definition of frames: "To frame is to select some aspects of a perceived reality and make them more salient . . . in such a way as to promote a particular problem definition, causal interpretation, moral evaluation, and/or treatment recommendation" (p. 52). In other words, media frames can organize the "facts" of a news story in ways that provide a narrative structure—what is the problem, who is responsible, what is the solution, and so on.

The principal proponents of a narrative framing approach, James Shanahan and Katherine McComas (1999), observe that environmental media coverage is "hardly ever the simple communication of a 'fact;' " instead, "journalists use narrative structures to build interesting environmental coverage. . . . [B]ecause journalists and media programmers must interest audiences, they must present their information in narrative packages" (pp. 34–35). Sometimes, such frames may also evoke deeper "interpretive packages" that reflect cultural images, beliefs, or values that convey "particular ideological interpretations of nature and the environment" (Hansen, 2010, p. 105).

A case in point is Schlechtweg's (1992) early study of narrative framing in a Public Broadcasting Service (PBS) report on Earth First! protesters. In May 1990, the *Earth First! Journal* announced the start of Redwood Summer, a mobilization of activists who would flood into California's northern redwood forests and "non-violently blockade logging roads, [and] climb giant trees to prevent their being logged" (Cherney, 1990, p. 1). Earth First! organizers stressed that anyone who disagreed with nonviolence would be barred from Redwood Summer. Earth First!

also tried to open a dialogue with loggers, suggesting they shared a common interest in sustainable logging from new-growth forests rather than the older-growth areas (Schlechtweg, 1992).

Nevertheless, that summer tensions grew among loggers, Earth First! activists, and rural communities. On July 20, 1990, the PBS program *The MacNeil-Lehrer NewsHour* aired "Focus–Logjam," a report about the protests. It is this report and its narrative framing of loggers, Earth First! protesters, community people, and violence that Schlechtweg explored.

In his analysis of "Focus–Logjam," Schlechtweg (1992) identified key visual and verbal terms that disclosed the broadcast's thematic frame. These included scenes of pristine forests, references to "small-town economies" that depended on "lumber," close-up shots of an ax or hatchet pounding a spike into a tree, and the PBS reporter's voiceover announcing that "Earth First! has a record of civil disobedience, injuring private timberlands, sabotaging logging machinery, and . . . writing about putting metal spikes in trees so they can't be logged" (pp. 266–267). By the end of the 9-minute, 40-second news report, "Focus–Logjam" had established clear identities for protagonists and antagonists in a tense confrontation that suggested the real prospect of violence.

Protagonists in the broadcast were portrayed through key identity and value terms: The report introduced "workers, "timber people," and "regular people" who depended on "timber harvests" and "small-town economies" for "jobs," "livelihood," and their "way of life" (p. 273). Conversely, the report identified Earth First! protesters as "apocalyptic," "radical," "wrong people," "terrorists," and "violent" people who engaged in "confrontation," "tree spiking," "sabotage," and "civil disobedience" to save "tall, beautiful" trees (p. 273). Schlechtweg argued that, as a result of these and other verbal and visual terms, "Focus–Logjam" implicitly constructed a narrative that pitted "regular people" against a "violent terrorist organization, willing to use sabotage . . . and tree spiking to save redwood forests" (pp. 273–274).

Cultivation Analysis

Akin to narrative theory is a cultivation model of media influence. Shanahan (1993) describes **cultivation analysis** as "a theory of story-telling, which assumes that repeated exposure to a set of messages is likely to produce agreement in an audience with opinions expressed in . . . those messages" (pp. 186–187). As its name implies, cultivation is not a claim about immediate or specific effects on an audience; instead, it is a process of gradual influence or cumulative effect. The model is associated with the work of media scholar George Gerbner (1990), who stated:

> Cultivation is what a culture does. That is not simple causation, though culture is the basic medium in which humans live and learn. . . . Strictly speaking, cultivation means the specific independent (though not isolated) contribution that a particularly consistent and compelling symbolic stream makes to the complex process of socialization and enculturation. (p. 249)

Gerbner's own research looked exclusively at the long-term effects of viewing violence on television—the cultivation of a worldview that he called the "mean world syndrome." This is a view of society as a dangerous place, peopled by others who want to harm us (Gerbner, Gross, Morgan, & Signorielli, 1986).

Similarly, environmental communication scholars who use cultivation analysis are interested in the longer-term effects of media on environmental attitudes and behavior. Perhaps surprisingly, this research suggests that heavy media exposure is sometimes correlated with lower levels of environmental concern (Novic & Sandman, 1974; Ostman & Parker, 1987; Shanahan & McComas, 1999). In a study of college students' television viewing, Shanahan and McComas (1999) report that heavy exposure to television may retard the cultivation of proenvironmental attitudes: "This tends to go against the suggestion that media attention to the environment results in greater socio-environmental concerns. That television's heavy viewers tended to be less environmentally concerned suggests the opposite: Television's messages place a kind of 'brake' on the development of environmental concern, especially for heavy viewers" (p. 125).

Interestingly, Shanahan and McComas (1999) found that the decrease in environmental concern among heavy television viewers is stronger among politically active students. This finding appears to contradict what we said earlier about the effects of agenda setting; that is, the more frequent the coverage of a subject, the more salience it gained. How is this explained? Cultivation researchers explain this pattern as *main-streaming,* or a narrowing of differences toward a cultural norm. Shanahan and McComas (1999) suggested that, in the case of environmental media, television's consistent stream of messages may draw groups closer to the cultural mainstream, with the mainstream (as represented by television programs) being "closer to the lower end of the environmental concern scale" (p. 130).

A second explanation for the decrease in environmental concern among heavy viewers of television is sometimes termed *cultivation in reverse* (Besley & Shanahan, 2004; Shanahan, 1993). In other words, media may cultivate an anti-environmental attitude through a persistent lack of environmental images or by directing viewers' attention to other, nonenvironmental stories. Thus, by ignoring or passively depicting the natural environment, television tends to marginalize its importance. Cultivation theorists (Shanahan & McComas, 1999) also call this phenomenon *symbolic annihilation*—the media's erasure of the importance of a theme by the indirect or passive deemphasizing of that theme.

An exception to the general findings of a mainstreaming effect from frequent exposure to television is a recent study of TV viewers' perceptions about environment risks. This study sought to improve cultivation analysis by more carefully identifying the diversity of TV channels being viewed, from CNN, Discovery, and Fox News to Comedy Central. As a result, they found that exposure to a wider diversity of TV channels "is associated with concern [about] environmental risks above and beyond both the effects of the amount [frequency] of television watched and individual differences [of viewers]" (Dahlstrom & Scheufele, 2010, p. 54).

It can be difficult to detect specific effects of news media on public opinion or behaviors, at least in the short run. Media effects can be complex and nonlinear. Nevertheless, theories such as agenda setting, narrative framing, and the longer-term cultivation of viewers' outlooks do suggest broader influences. In the end, the media may provide, as Hansen (2011), observes, "an important cultural context from which various publics draw both vocabularies and frames of understanding for making sense of the environment generally, and of claims about environmental problems more specifically" (p. 20).

Challenges to Traditional (Environmental) News Media

Although traditional news media continue to play an important role in coverage of environmental stories, this may be changing as a result of an ongoing crisis in the business model of traditional media.

The Pew Research Center's (2011) annual *The State of the News Media* gives us some insight into what's happened to the industry lately. While revenue for some media, after years of decline, has begun to bounce back, income for newspapers continues to drop, falling almost 50% in the last four years.

The sharp drop in revenue has left newspapers downsizing everything—daily circulation, newspaper size, space devoted to news, and the number of reporters. This is not to say that environmental journalism has disappeared. In any given year, there are still remarkable efforts, such as James Astill's (2010) eight-part series investigating the state of the world's forests in *The Economist*. (Astill won the 2011 Grantham Prize for the best environmental journalism.) Nevertheless, newspapers' revenues are in decline, and the resources available for environmental journalism are increasingly scarce.

Overall, Pew Research Center (2011) found that newspapers have lost over 25% in daily circulation since 2000, while newsrooms—reporters, editors, and so on—are now 30% smaller than in 2000. Pew concludes that this has left "the largest newsrooms in most American cities bruised and necessarily less ambitious than they were a decade ago" (p. 6). As Bud Ward, editor of the *Yale Forum on Climate Change and the Media,* said, "It's hard for reporters to focus on ambitious climate reporting . . . when their ranks are being 'carnaged' " (Ward, 2008, para. 28). Ward was referring not simply to the so-called death of newspapers but specifically to the downsizing of news staff and expertise as newspapers lose revenue, cut circulation, and migrate online.

And, while online versions are springing up, these still depend on news staff to produce content, and therein lies a potential problem. When the Seattle *Post-Intelligencer* newspaper moved online, for example, it slashed its news staff of 165 reporters and began operating online with only 20 (Yardley & Pérez-Pena, 2009). As a consequence, online daily papers depend increasingly on content aggregators for much of their

Figure 6.4	With the so-called death of newspapers in the United States, many newsrooms are losing science and environmental reporters.

national reporting. Pew Research Center's (2010) *State of the News Media* report found that, even the best of the online media sites have limited ability to produce content without a revenue model larger than what newspapers had in the past.

And, as media cut staff, there is inevitably a loss of science expertise. Some are eliminating entire beats: The San Jose *Mercury News* reports that, "two decades ago nearly 150 papers had a science section. Now fewer than 20 are left, and [these] . . . usually dedicate their scarce column inches to lifestyle and health" (Daley, 2010, para. 16). Veteran TV reporter John Daley (2010) put it bluntly: "The ranks of reporters best equipped to cover . . . major environmental and climate change stories at most news outlets, particularly in local markets, are being decimated" (para. 6).

And, as Daley noted, the trend is similar in network and cable TV. In 2008, for example, CNN cut its entire science, technology, and environment news staff, and the Weather Channel cancelled its weekly climate program "Forecast Earth." With its news staff cut, cable TV news is increasingly filling its time slots with opinion journalism.

By the first decade of the 21st century, Pew Research Center's (2004) *State of the News Media* had concluded, "journalism was in the midst of an epochal transition, as momentous as the invention of the telegraph or television" (p. 4). In the next chapter, I'll describe some of these changes, including the rise of social media and their role in this new epoch of environmental communication.

SUMMARY

Because few of us directly encounter problems such as global warming or mercury poisoning, we rely on the reports and representations of others, including the traditional media: television, newspapers, and radio. Yet, these media are neither innocent nor neutral in their representations of the environment.

- In the first section of this chapter, I described the growth and nature of traditional news media and the differing views of nature in environmental media.
- In the second section, I described some of the journalistic norms and constraints on news production, including: newsworthiness, media frames, norms of objectivity and balance, political economy, and gatekeeping and newsroom routines.
- The third section looked at the case study of reporting on climate change to illustrate the difficulties in meeting a newsworthiness standard in news media.
- In the fourth section, I described *media effects,* the influence of environmental media on our attitudes and behavior, and identified three theories: (1) agenda setting, (2) narrative framing, and (3) cultivation analysis. For example, agenda-setting theory has enabled researchers to appreciate media's ability to affect the public's perception of the importance of an issue.

Finally, I described changes in traditional news media, including the death of newspapers phenomenon and what these changes might mean for the future of environmental journalism. News media generally have undergone major changes as newspapers continue to reduce their daily circulations, lay off reporters, and migrate online. In the next chapter, I will describe the explosive growth of online news as well as the growing use of social media in environmental affairs.

SUGGESTED RESOURCES

- Anders Hansen, *Environment, Media, and Communication.* London and New York: Routledge, 2010.
- Libby Lester, *Media and Environment: Conflict, Politics and the News.* Cambridge, UK: Polity Press, 2010.
- Tammy Boyce and Justin Lewis, *Climate Change and the Media.* New York: Peter Lang, 2009.
- Bob Wyss, *Covering the Environment: How Journalists Work the Green Beat.* London and New York: Routledge, 2008.

- The Society of Environmental Journalists (SEJ) website (www.sej.org). How well does it strengthen the quality, reach, and viability of journalism across all media to advance public understanding of environmental issues (its mission)?

KEY TERMS

Agenda setting   162

Anthropocentricism   149

Cultivation analysis   165

Cultivation in reverse   166

Ecotage   154

Frame   152

Gatekeeping   158

Image events   151

Mainstreaming   166

Media effects   162

Media frames   152

Media political economy   157

Narrative framing   164

News hole   144

Newsworthiness   149

Objectivity and balance   155

Symbolic annihilation   166

Traditional news media   144

DISCUSSION QUESTIONS

1. Can you identify the frames that influence you when reading an environmental news story? What are some of the different media frames used in news stories in campus or local newspapers or on a local radio or television station?

2. How do you feel about the journalistic norm of objectivity? Do you agree with journalists who argue for reporters' rights to evaluate the competing arguments in an environmental controversy? Or should they be objective? Is this possible?

3. Do media affect your attitudes about and behavior toward the environment? Has an online or mainstream news report altered your attitude about a specific issue, such as nuclear power, vegetarianism, or global warming? Can you identify characteristics of this report that particularly influenced you?

4. To what extent are dominant ideologies reproduced by commercial news and entertainment media? Can you identify mainstream media that question or challenge these ideologies?

REFERENCES

Abramson, R. (1992, December 2). Ice cores may hold clues to weather 200,000 years ago. *Los Angeles Times,* p. A1.

Ader, C. (1995). A longitudinal study of agenda setting for the issue of environmental pollution. *Journalism and Mass Communication Quarterly, 72,* 300–311.

Anderson, A. (1997). *Media, culture, and the environment.* New Brunswick, NJ: Rutgers University Press.

Associated Press. (2011, April 27). Desert tortoise advocates fight solar energy backers in environmental feud. *Washington Post*. Retrieved April 30, 2011, from www.washingtonpost.com

Astill, J. (2010, September 23). Seeing the wood. *The Economist*. Retrieved July 16, 2011, from http://www.economist.com

Beder, S. (2002). *Global spin: The corporate assault on environmentalism* (Rev. ed.). White River Junction, VT: Chelsea Green.

Besley, J. C., & Shanahan, J. (2004). Skepticism about media effects concerning the environment: Examining Lomborg's hypothesis. *Society and Natural Resources, 17*(10), 861–880.

Boykoff, M. T. (2007). Flogging a dead norm? Newspaper coverage of anthropogenic climate change in the United States and United Kingdom from 2003 to 2006. *Area 39*(4), 470–481. Retrieved December 23, 2008, from http://www.eci.ox.ac.uk

Boykoff, M. T., & Boykoff, J. M. (2004). Bias as balance: Global warming and the US prestige press. *Global Environmental Change, 14*(2), 125–136.

Brainard, C. (2008, August 27). Public opinion and climate: Part II. *Columbia Journalism Review.* [Electronic version]. Retrieved December 22, 2008, from http://www.cjr.org

Carson, R. (1962). *Silent spring*. Boston: Houghton Mifflin.

Carvalho, A. (2007). Ideological cultures and media discourses on scientific knowledge: Re-reading news on climate change. *Public Understanding of Science, 16*, 223–243.

Cherney, D. (1990, May 1). Freedom riders needed to save the forest: Mississippi summer in the California redwoods. *Earth First! Journal, 1*, 6.

Cohen, B. C. (1963). *The press and foreign policy.* Princeton, NJ: Princeton University Press.

Corbett J. B. (2006). *Communicating nature: How we create and understand environmental messages.* Washington, DC: Island Press.

Cunningham, B. (2003). Re-thinking objectivity. *Columbia Journalism Review, 42,* 24–32.

Dahlstrom, M. F., & Scheufele, D. A. (2010). Diversity of television exposure and its association with the cultivation of concern for environmental risks. *Environmental Communication: A Journal of Nature and Culture, 4*(1), 54–65.

Daley, J. (2010, January 7). Why the decline and rebirth of environmental journalism matters. *Yale Forum on Climate Change and the Media*. Retrieved October 5, 2010, from www.yaleclimatemediaforum.org/

DeLuca, K. M. (2005). *Image politics: The new rhetoric of environmental activism.* London: Routledge.

Dirikx, A., & Gelders, D. (2009). Global warming through the same lens: An exploratory framing study in Dutch and French newspapers. In T. Boyce & J. Lewis (Eds.), *Media and climate change* (pp. 200–210). Oxford, UK: Peter Lang.

Edmonds, R., Guskin, R., & Rosenstiel, T. (2011). Newspapers: Missed the 2010 media rally. Pew Research Center. *The State of the News Media.* Retrieved May 3, 2011, from http://stateofthemedia.org

Entman, R. M. (1993). Framing: Toward clarification of a fractured paradigm. *Journal of Communication 43*(4), 51–8.

Ericson, R. V., Baranek, P. M., & Chan, J. B. L. (1989). *Negotiating control: A study of news sources.* Milton Keynes, UK: Open University Press.

Eyal, C. H., Winter, J. P., & DeGeorge, W. F. (1981). The concept of time frame in agenda setting. In G. C. Wilhoit (Ed.), *Mass communication yearbook* (pp. 212–218). Beverly Hills, CA: Sage.

Fretwell, S. (2011, March 20). New report details safety issues at U.S. nuclear plants, the most serious in South Carolina. *The Post and Courier*. Retrieved April 29, 2011, from www.postandcourier.com

Friedman, S. M. (2004). And the beat goes on: The third decade of environmental journalism. In S. Senecah (Ed.), *The environmental communication yearbook* (Vol. 1, pp. 175–187). Mahwah, NJ: Erlbaum.

Gamson, W. A., & Modigliani, A. (1989). Media discourse and public opinion on nuclear power: A constructionist approach. *American Journal of Sociology, 95,* 1–37.

Gerbner, G. (1990). Advancing on the path to righteousness, maybe. In N. Signorielli & M. Morgan (Eds.), *Cultivation analysis: New directions in research* (pp. 249–262). Newbury Park, CA: Sage.

Gerbner, G., Gross, L., Morgan, M., & Signorielli, N. (1986). Living with television: The dynamics of the cultivation process. In J. Bryant & D. Zillmann (Eds.), *Perspectives on media effects* (pp. 17–40). Mahwah, NJ: Erlbaum.

Gitlin, T. (1980). *The whole world is watching: Mass media in the making and unmaking of the new left.* Berkeley, Los Angeles, and London, UK: University of California Press.

Goffman, E. (1974). *Frame analysis: An essay on the organization of experience.* Cambridge, MA: Harvard University Press.

Hall, J. (2001, May/June). How the environmental beat got its grove back. *Columbia Journalism Review* [Electronic version]. Retrieved December 22, 2008, from http://backissues.cjrarchives.org

Hansen, A. (2010). *Environment, media, and communication.* London and New York: Routledge.

Hansen, A. (2011, February). Towards reconnecting research on the production, content and social implications of environmental communication. *International Communication Gazette, 73*(1–2), 7–25.

Intergovernmental Panel on Climate Change. (2007). *Climate change 2007: Synthesis report.* United Nations Environment Program. Retrieved April 26, 2011, from http://www.ipcc.ch/

Iyengar, S., & Kinder, D. R. (1987). *News that matters: Television and American opinion.* Chicago: University of Chicago Press.

Juskalian, R. (2008, June 6). *Launch: Yale Environment 360: Roger Cohn endeavors to make ends meet online.* Retrieved December 27, 2008, from http://www.cjr.org

Korte, D. (1997). The Simpsons as quality television. *The Simpsons archive.* Retrieved April 23, 2004, from www.snpp.com

Krugman, P. (2009, September 27). Cassandras of climate. *New York Times,* p. A21.

Lippmann, W. (1922). *Public opinion.* New York: Harcourt, Brace.

Macalister, T. (2010, October 11). Climate change could lead to Arctic conflict, warns senior NATO commander. *The Guardian.* Retrieved May 22, 2011, from www.guardian.co.uk

Maibach, E., Wilson, K., & Witte, J. (2010). A national survey of news directors about climate change: Preliminary findings. George Mason University. Fairfax, VA: Center for Climate Change Communication. Retrieved July 9, 2011, from www.climatechangecommunication.org

Mann, B. (2001, May 26). Bringing good things to life? *On the media.* New York: WNYC. Retrieved May 3, 2004, from www.onthemedia.org

Marchi, R. M. (2005). Reframing the runway: A case study on the impact of community organizing on news and politics, *Journalism, 6*(4), 465–485.

McCombs, M., & Shaw, D. (1972). The agenda setting function of the mass media. *Public Opinion Quarterly, 36,* 176–187.

McNair, B. (1994). *News and journalism in the UK.* London and New York: Routledge.

Meisner, M. (2005). Knowing nature through the media: An examination of mainstream print and television representations of the non-human world. In G. B. Walker & W. J. Kinsella (Eds.), *Finding our way(s) in environmental communication: Proceedings of the Seventh Biennial Conference on Communication and the Environment* (pp. 425–437). Corvallis: Oregon State University Department of Speech Communication.

Miller, M. M., & Riechert, B. P. (2000). Interest group strategies and journalistic norms: News media framing of environmental issues. In S. Allan, B. Adam, & C. Carter (Eds.), *Environmental risks and the media* (pp. 45–54). London: Routledge.

Moser, S. C. (2010). Communicating climate change: History, challenges, process and future directions. *Wiley Interdisciplinary Reviews—Climate Change 1*(1): 31–53.

Novic, K., & Sandman, P. M. (1974). How use of mass media affects views on solutions to environmental problems. *Journalism Quarterly, 51,* 448–452.

Ostman, R. E., & Parker, J. L. (1987). Impacts of education, age, newspaper, and television on environmental knowledge, concerns, and behaviors. *Journal of Environmental Education, 19,* 3–9.

Palen, J. (1998, August). SEJ's origin. Paper presented at the national convention of the Association for Education in Journalism and Mass Communications, Baltimore, MD. Retrieved August 4, 2011, from www.sej.org/sejs-history

Pan, Z., & Kosicki, G. M. (1993). Framing analysis: An approach to news discourse. *Political Communication, 10,* 55–76.

Pew Research Center. (2004). *The State of the News Media 2004.* Retrieved November 8, 2011, from www.stateofthemedia .org/files/2011/01/execsum.pdf

Pew Research Center. (2010, March 1). *The State of the News Media.* Retrieved May 19, 2011, from http://pewresearch.org.

Pew Research Center. (2011, March 14). *The State of the News Media.* Retrieved May 19, 2011, from http://pewresearch.org

Reuters. (2011, April 4). Most Americans say U.S. nuclear plants safe: poll." Retrieved April 29, 2011, from www.reuters.com

Revkin, A. C. (2011, January 5). Climate news snooze? *Dot Earth.* Retrieved May 4, 2011, from http://dotearth.blogs .nytimes.com

Rodríguez, I. (2003). Mapping the emerging global order in news discourse: The meanings of globalization in news magazines in the early 1990s. In A. Opel & D. Pompper (Eds.), *Representing resistance: Media, civil disobedience, and the global justice movement* (pp. 77–94). Westport, CT: Praeger.

Sachsman, D. B., Simon, J., & Valenti, J. (2002, June). The environment reporters of New England. *Science Communication, 23,* 410–441.

Schlechtweg, H. P. (1992). Framing Earth First! The *MacNeil-Lehrer NewsHour* and redwood summer. In C. L. Oravec & J. G. Cantrill (Eds.), *The conference on the discourse of environmental advocacy* (pp. 262–287). Salt Lake City: University of Utah Humanities Center.

Schneider, S. H. (2009). *Science as a contact sport: Inside the battle to save earth's climate.* Washington, DC: National Geographic.

Shabecoff, P. (2000). *Earth rising: American environmentalism in the 21st century.* Washington, DC: Island Press.

Shanahan, J. (1993). Television and the cultivation of environmental concern: 1988–92. In A. Hansen (Ed.), *The mass media and environmental issues* (pp. 181–197). Leicester, UK: Leicester University Press.

Shanahan, J., & McComas, K. (1999). *Nature stories: Depictions of the environment and their effects.* Cresskill, NJ: Hampton Press.

Soper, K. (1995). *What is nature?* Oxford, UK: Blackwell.

Soroka, S. N. (2002). Issue attributes and agenda-setting by media, the public, and policy-makers in Canada. *International Journal of Public Opinion Research, 14*(3), 264–285.

Tabuchi, H., Sanger, D. E., & Bradsher, K. (2011, March 14). Japan faces potential nuclear disaster as radiation levels rise. *New York Times,* p. A1.

Todd, A. M. (2002). Prime-time subversion: The environmental rhetoric of the Simpsons. In M. Meister & P. M. Japp

(Eds.), *Enviropop: Studies in environmental rhetoric and popular culture* (pp. 63–80). Westport, CT: Praeger.

Vig, N. J., & Kraft, M. E. (2003). Environmental policy from the 1970s to the twenty-first century. In N. J. Vig & M. E. Kraft (Eds.), *Environmental policy: New directions in the 21st century* (5th ed., pp. 1–32). Washington, DC: CQ Press.

Wagner, T. (2008). Reframing ecotage as ecoterrorism: News and the discourse of fear. *Environmental Communication: A Journal of Nature and Culture, 2*(1), 25–39.

Ward, B. (2008, December 18). 2008's year-long fall-off in climate coverage. *The Yale Forum on Climate Change and The Media.* Retrieved February 13, 2009, from www.yaleclimatemediaforum.org

West, B. M., Lewis, M. J., Greenberg, M. R., Sachsman, D. B., & Rogers, R. M. (2003). *The reporter's environmental handbook.* New Brunswick, NJ: Rutgers University Press.

White, D. M. (1950). The "gatekeeper": A case study in the selection of news. *Journalism Quarterly, 27*(4), 383–390.

Wyss, B. (2008). *Covering the environment: How journalists work the green beat.* London and New York: Routledge.

Yardley, W., & Pérez-Pena, R. (2009, March 16). Seattle paper shifts entirely to the web. *New York Times.* Retrieved March 28, 2009, from www.nytimes.com

Yopp, J. J., McAdams, K. C., & Thornburg, R. M. (2009). *Reaching audiences: A guide to media writing* (5th ed.). Boston: Allyn & Bacon.

Our mobile phones and other social media become extensions of ourselves, "the structures by which [we] connect to the world and other people" (new media pioneer, Jaron Lanier, 2010, pp. 5–6).

CHAPTER 7

Social Media and the Environment Online

Too often, we consider news and social networking as an either/or proposi-
tion. The circulation of powerful environmental symbols and images will, in
the future . . . rely on both.

—L. Lester, *Media &*
Environment (2010, p. 182)

We make up extensions to your being, like remote eyes and ears (web-cams
and mobile phones) and expanded memory (the world of details you can
search for online). These become the structures by which you connect to the
world and other people. These structures in turn can change how you con-
ceive of yourself and the world.

—Jaron Lanier, *You Are Not a*
Gadget (2010, pp. 5–6)

W hen Captain Paul Watson's ship the *Steve Erwin* harassed the Japanese
whaling fleet in icy seas near Antarctica recently, news of the encounter
was instantly (through satellite links) reported, tweeted, blogged,
tagged, and digitally posted on blogs and news websites worldwide (Lester, 2011;
Yamaguchi, 2011). The images were later shown on an episode of *The Discovery
Channel's Whale Wars.* The antiwhaling crew's use of media illustrates the altered
landscape of environmental communication. Social media, digital cameras, and Web
2.0 applications have changed forever the relationships between those who are the
producers of news and those who are receivers or what journalism critic Jay Rosen
calls, "the people formally known as the audience" (quoted in Wyss, 2008, p. 222).

Chapter Preview

In this chapter, I'll describe this new landscape and some of the uses of social media and Web 2.0 sites by journalists, environmentalists, climate activists, the Environmental Protection Agency (EPA), and others. I'll also identify some of the challenges that new media pose for environmental advocacy.

- The first section of this chapter describes the migration of environmental news online as well as the explosive growth of the green blogosphere.
- The second section introduces the landscape of social media—Facebook, Twitter, Ning, smartphones, other mobile devices, and Web 2.0 applications. It also describes six ways that social media are changing environmental communication:

  (1) Environmental information and buzz

  (2) Green communities and social networking

  (3) Reporting and documenting

  (4) Public criticism and accountability

  (5) Mobilizing

  (6) Microvolunteering and self-organizing

- The third section presents a case study of social media use for environmental advocacy; it also identifies some of the challenges and limitations of social media for this purpose.
- Finally, the last section identifies future trends that pose both opportunities and obstacles to environmental uses of social media.

On finishing this chapter, you will have a better understanding of the rich range of social media use by environmental interests as well as the dramatic growth of online platforms and Web 2.0 applications available for journalists, public agencies, educators, and individuals. You may also have a better appreciation for some of the challenges of using social media for environmental advocacy.

Environmental Journalism Migrates Online

Two forces came together in the late 1990s and early 2000s to produce a dramatic shift in the production and dissemination of environmental news: First, as I noted in Chapter 6, print newspapers and broadcast television faced a continuing decline in revenues as well as loss of readers and viewers. Newspaper circulation especially "continues to deteriorate as people increasingly go online for news that is timelier and free" (Krol, 2009, para. 3).

Second, environmentally interested readers and working journalists themselves grew frustrated with the insufficient depth, range, and accuracy of commercial media, along with the *shrinking news hole* (Chapter 6) of mainstream news. And, even as newspapers and TV migrated online, the websites they built in the late 1990s "usually were simply digests of what had already appeared in print or on the air. Such formats were quickly called 'shovelware' " (Wyss, 2008, p. 216).

By the first decade of the 21st century, however, online platforms featured a wide range of news and information, including journalists' blogs, videos, news forums, and websites of scientists, environmental groups, and governmental agencies, such as the EPA. Among the earliest and most influential of the online platforms were **environmental news services,** such as Greenwire and the nonprofit EnviroLink Network, and it is these online services to which I now turn.

Environmental News Services

Almost from the start, the online environmental news services offered the widest access to both working journalists and readers looking for more in-depth environmental news and timely information. Early on, Friedman (2004) observed that many of the changes related to improved sources for journalists could be traced to these platforms. One senior environmental reporter claimed that such web services, including regularly updated news feeds, "drastically changed the way journalists do their job" (p. 183).

The first of this new genre was the Environmental News Service (ENS), the original daily, international wire service reporting environmental news. ENS stories are indexed by Reuters, Dow Jones, and other newswires, and they cover a range of topics: environmental politics, science and technology, air quality, drinking water, oceans and marine life, land use, wildlife, natural disasters, toxics, and nuclear issues.

ENS was soon followed by other online news services devoted to specialized areas such as public lands or climate change. Specialty coverage is of particular interest to environmental and business groups, policy makers, and others who follow environmental legislation in the U.S. Congress. One of the most prominent of these services is Environment and Energy Publishing (E&E, at eenews.net). It offers online newsletters, a wire service, E&E TV, and special reports providing detailed coverage of energy, public lands issues, water, climate change, and other issues being addressed by the courts or U.S. Congress. Its Land Letter (eenews.net/11), for example, specializes in natural resources (e.g., wilderness, oil and gas drilling on public lands, etc.), while E&E Daily (eenews.net/eed) focuses on air, water, and energy issues. E&E Publishing also hosts Greenwire (eenews.net/gw), one of the earliest news services online and which many journalists consider the leading daily news source for environmental stories.

More recently, E&E Publishing launched Climate Wire (eenews.net/cw), a premier source for daily news reports on energy and climate-related stories. Also, Climate Central (climatecentral.org), a nonprofit science and media site, provides news and information about climate change and renewable energy with rich media—informative stories with video, images, links, and high-quality content available for print media, television, and other online sites.

While many of the above news services are subscription based, other environmental news and analysis websites are available free. The choices are wide ranging and seemingly endless:

- EnviroLink Network (envirolink.org) is a nonprofit organization that provides access online to a comprehensive set of environmental news and information.
- *Grist magazine* (grist.org) features biting commentary, analyses of developments within the environmental movement, and breaking news.

- Environmental News Network's (enn.com) mission is "to publish information that will help people understand and communicate the environmental issues and solutions that face us and hopefully inspire them to get involved."

In many ways, online news sites such as Greenwire or ENS are challenging conventional media theory about topics such as political economy and the gatekeeper function that I described in the last chapter. With the wide availability and interconnectivity of blogs, news, and other sites, media scholars are rethinking who—if anyone—controls access to news and information and what determines newsworthiness.

Other online news platforms are also redefining the traditional roles of news sources and readers in what Technorati (2008) called the "active Blogosphere," that is, the "interconnected community of bloggers and readers at the convergence of journalism and conversation" (para. 7). Environmental and climate bloggers are among those leading the way in the restructuring of the political economy of news and information in the new media era.

Journalists' Blogs and the Green Blogosphere

The fastest-growing source for online news and analyses of environmental topics actually has not been the environmental news services but the blogosphere. A *blog,* of course, is an online site that is authored by an individual (usually) or collective authors and that posts information or commentary about specific topics; blogs also feature video and graphics. BlogPulse, which tracks blog traffic, put the total number of blogs on the web at 168,059,462 worldwide when I last checked in 2011. However, this estimate is meaningless because nearly 10,000 new blogs were being added daily (see blogpulse.com).

Environmentally themed blogs are, not surprisingly, among the more active in the blogosphere. A leading authority on blogs, Technorati (technorati.com) lists over 9,000 green blogs. These range from the Oil Drum (theoildrum.com), a blog about energy and the future, to Yale Environmental 360 (e360.yale.edu/), which blogs about climate change and the media.

While many blogs began as online, personal journals, they have clearly evolved as a new generation of journalists, climate scientists, environmentalists, and individuals has developed expertise in specific subject areas within a wider ecology of news and commentary. As a result, environmental bloggers—including online journalists— have played influential roles in a number of areas in the last decade. Let's look at four of these areas:

Environmental Authority

Quite a few in the green blogosphere have attained the standing and authority previously accorded to the traditional news media. For example, Dr. Michael Mann, a prominent climate scientist at Pennsylvania State University, blogs at Real Climate (realclimate.org). Dr. Mann and other science bloggers at this site are authoritative sources for visitors, including other scientists, who want to understand specific areas of the science of climate change or are interested in scientists' responses to criticisms from climate skeptics. They are perceived by many as the go-to place online for authoritative posts on the more technical aspects of climate science.

Amplifying and Popularizing

From the start, environmental bloggers have played major roles in amplifying issues and enabling the viral spread of news and information about environmental topics, ranging from acid rain and threats to weaken the Endangered Species Act (ESA) to the latest scientific reports about climate change. Often these bloggers, including science reporters, function to translate or popularize technical science reports in their blogs, enabling them to be posted on more popular media sites or blogs such as Huffington Post or Treehugger.com.

One of the most influential bloggers who has popularized environmental science is former *New York Times* reporter Andrew Revkin who still blogs at Dot Earth blog (dotearth.blogs.nytimes.com). Revkin, who received the prestigious John Chancellor Award for Excellence in Journalism, has been recognized for his insightful reporting on climate change and energy issues for many years at the *Times*. Launched in 2007, Dot Earth allowed Revkin to expand on his print stories, post breaking news and content from other websites, share videos, and generally facilitate a growing conversation about climate change among readers worldwide.

Conversely, the blogosphere has also been the source of viral, antiscience criticism and commentary, particularly regarding climate change. Obviously, bloggers can be favorable to the environmental sciences or critical of them. I'll describe the role of more critical bloggers in the so-called Climategate controversy in Chapter 11.

Augmenting News

As newspapers continue to migrate online, many reporters have launched their own blog sites as well. More than 95% of the top 100 U.S. newspapers now have such blogs (Technorati, 2008). Recently, I had a chance to speak with the New Orleans *Times-Picayune's* environmental reporter Mark Schleifstein about his blog. Mark covers coastal environmental issues and, in 2006, he received the Pulitzer Prize for his coverage of the devastating impact of Hurricane Katrina. There is little difference, he told me, between his work today as a reporter for the print newspaper and being a blogger, posting stories in more depth on the *Times-Picayune* website daily. Such detailed and timely information has not only earned Mark numerous followers but augments the environmental coverage that the newspaper provides.

Environmental Eyewitnesses

As news staff is cut at newspapers and network TV news programs, bloggers are now supplementing news coverage in the field and at remote locations. Scientists are blogging about glacier studies in Greenland, environmentalists are blogging from the locations of oil spills and remote protests against mountaintop removal coal mining in Appalachia, while others travel to international climate summits or scientific expeditions. For example, Philippe Cousteau, explorer and CNN International's environmental correspondent, accompanied scientists to the Arctic, where daily, he blogged and posted video blogs (cnn.com/environment) about the impact of climate change on one of the coldest places on the planet. His blog posts from the Gulf Coast during the BP oil disaster also appeared at Planet Green.com, Treehugger.com, and other environmental sites.

Finally, as the blogosphere expands, the lines between what is a blog and what is a mainstream news site is becoming less clear. Technorati 's *State of the Blogosphere* reported that, "larger blogs are taking on more characteristics of mainstream [news media] sites and mainstream sites are incorporating styles and formats from the Blogosphere" (2008, para. 5). Some blogs, such as the popular Treehugger blog (treehugger.com), have even launched web TV sites. (For an analysis of Treehugger TV, see Slawter, 2008.) Finally, many blogs routinely post videos and news feeds from other sources. For example, HuffPost Green (huffingtonpost.com/green), the environmental blog at the popular *Huffington Post,* features stunning photos, video stories, news briefs, and links to original news sources.

As I write in 2011, blogs are in transition. No longer are they an upstart community. Instead, blogs now exert influence on mainstream narratives about the environment and compete with established, traditional news media outlets (Sobel, 2010,

Figure 7.1   Philippe Cousteau, explorer and environmental correspondent for CNN International, was a frequent blogger for CNN from the Arctic during a scientific study of climate change.

Photo provided courtesy of CNN

para. 3). And, along the way, bloggers have brought "changes in how news is generated, compiled, and disseminated," transforming journalism from "a one-way system where reporters and editors talked to readers" to a two-way system in which an abundance of green bloggers, scientists, and individuals are expanding the available news and analysis about environmental topics (Wyss, 2008, p. 216).

Nowhere has the blogosphere changed more than in its use of social media with the sharing of blog posts increasingly through social networks (Sobel, 2010). And, as bloggers like Mark Schleifstein and Philippe Cousteau include Twitter and really simple syndication (RSS) feeds in their blogs, "the lines between blogs, micro-blogs, and social networks are disappearing" (Sobel, 2010, para. 3). It is to this expanding landscape of environmental social media that I now turn.

Social Media and the Environment

In the last five to seven years, social media have dramatically altered the landscape for environmental communication. Today, "tens of millions of individuals are engaging with the networked public sphere, using online tools and platforms to find, rank, tag, create, and distribute, mock and recommend content" (Clark & Slyke, 2011, p. 239).

In this section, I will describe this networked public sphere and the uses of social media for environmental communication by journalists, green groups, science educators, public agencies, citizens' groups, and others. Then, in the next section, I'll illustrate some of the uses of social media specifically for advocacy campaigns as well as some limitations that green groups have experienced. Finally, I'll look at future trends in social media that pose both opportunities and challenges for environmental communication.

Let's start at the beginning: *Social media* can be defined as the use of web-based technologies and mobile applications for personal interactions, including use of Web 2.0 platforms that enable the creating and sharing of user-generated content (Kaplan & Haenlein, 2010). Social media are a change in the ways that we learn, share, create, and interact with others. The digital tools by which we are doing this are seemingly infinite—social networking (Facebook, LinkedIn, Ning), microblogging (Twitter, Tumblr, etc.), smartphones (and endless apps), wikis, vlogs, social news sites (Digg, Reddit, etc.), YouTube, location-based services like MyTown and Gowalla, and many more. Importantly, social media have also democratized who it is that generates and disseminates "news." At its core, Web 2.0 is a shift from a one-way, elite news media to a participatory model of content generation and sharing.

It is hardly surprising, then, that environmental interests are using this array of technologies from alerts, microblogging, Facebook, online campaigning, publishing, and custom social networking service like Ning to uses of Gowalla to encourage attendance at rallies. Journalists, environmental groups, and green celebrities are gaining followers on Twitter as well. As I wrote this chapter, Twitter was reporting its users were generating over 200 million tweets per day while adding almost half a million new accounts each month (blog.twitter.com). (A *tweet* is a short text message, up to 140 characters, sent through the online Twitter service.)

It is inevitable that, in a world mediated by online and mobile connections with others, such media influence what we learn, perceive, and think about the environment. As new media pioneer Jaron Lanier (2010) explains, our mobile phones and other social media become extensions of ourselves, "the structures by which [we] connect to the world and other people" (pp. 5–6). And, these in turn influence how we conceive of ourselves and the world around us.

How, then, does this mediated world influence how we think about the natural world or about environment problems? In answering, it may be useful to identify not so much the specific technologies but some of the major functions or uses of social media to communicate about the environment. In this section, then, I will describe six of these functions.

Environmental Information and Buzz

The most basic use of environmental social media, undoubtedly, is sharing of news and information by environmental groups, journalists, authors, and users on Twitter, Facebook, LinkedIn, YouTube, and other media. In the past few days, for example, I've received numerous alerts and updates via Twitter, e-mail, and RSS feeds that were particularly of interest to me:

- Al Gore's tweet (@algore) called attention to the e-book app for his *Our Choice: A Plan to Solve the Climate Crisis,* available with rich data, interactive graphics, photos, and video.
- Social news sites buzzed about a new technology story posted on Climatecentral .com about splitting water to produce a new energy source by releasing hydrogen.
- A Sierra Club tweet (@Sierra_Club) announced *SIERRA* magazine's fifth annual ranking of the greenest colleges in the United States.

Social news sources (e.g., Digg) and RSS feeds are ways that individuals increasingly can easily access environmental information or stories in a timely manner. Social news sites like Digg and Reddit, particularly, have subsections for sharing and finding environmental content, and RSS feeds have replaced older methods for bookmarking and manually returning to a site to keep track of updates that you're interested in following. You could subscribe, for example, to an RSS feed for updates and stories from Andrew Revkin's Dot Earth blog or EPA's Facebook, or you could link to ecorazzi.com, a fashionable site for "the latest in green gossip" and video on film, fashion, music, cars, animals, and houses.

In addition, government agencies, nonprofit groups, and environmental organizations routinely use social media tools to post, disseminate, and invite timely information. For example, the National Oceanic and Atmospheric Administration (NOAA) website provides RSS feeds from its newsroom and weather service as well links to its Twitter, Facebook, and YouTube sites. It also has biweekly audio podcasts about NOAA's latest scientific work with oceans, fisheries, climate, atmosphere, and weather sciences.

And, when the Appalachian Mountains Advocates (appalmad.org) overhauled its website, it embedded an array of social media—a blog, LinkedIn, Twitter (@AppalCenter), Facebook, and a link to its "AppMountainAdvocates" channel on YouTube. (Appalachian Mountain Advocates is a leading law and policy nonprofit center that fights mountaintop removal coal mining in West Virginia and other Appalachian states.)

Green Communities and Social Networking

One of the most robust applications of Web 2.0 technology has been the creation of online **social networking** sites or *communities* that allow users to interact with each other, post content, and receive updates and information relevant to their interests. With more than 750 million active users (and growing), Facebook, particularly, has become a major tool for many environmental groups' online personae or *faces,* portals for sharing information and interactions and links to other social media.

Indeed, large and small environmental organizations, from Greenpeace International to the Dogwood Alliance—a regional forest protection group in the Southern Appalachian mountains—are on Facebook or other social networking sites. The Nature Conservancy (TNC) also facilitates a green community. Its MyNature.org site enables its members to share photos and tips for living green or explore TNC's interactive maps of its conservancy work with water or endangered species habitat.

Similarly, public environmental agencies like EPA, the U.S. Fish and Wildlife, and even the White House Council on Environmental Quality (CEQ) use Facebook along with other social media. The Obama Administration's EPA has been particularly enthusiastic about social media, including social networking. Its Facebook site, for example, serves as a bridge for local communities and citizens who rely upon the EPA for guidance, information, and technical help; the site also invites comments on EPA policies and programs.

Act Locally!

Finding Interesting and Helpful Environmental Sources Online

Today, the sources online for environmental news, information, and opinion are seemingly infinite: environmental news services, countless listings for the top green blogs, climate blogs, social news sites, and more. What are your particular interests in the environment? Are you currently following any Twitter feeds? Do you read any green blogs such as Treehugger, Dot Earth, or HuffPost Green? Do you follow with bookmarks or RSS feeds?

Go online and identify five to seven environmental blogs, Twitter feeds, or RSS feeds from news sites or blogs that address your concerns. (For environmental blogs, check out Technorati's updated list of over 9,000 green blogs at http://technorati.com/blogs/directory/green.) Then, follow these sources for the next week.

- Which sources provided the most relevant, interesting, or substantive information?
- Which mode of following proved to be the most convenient for you: bookmarking, an RSS, Facebook, or Twitter feed?
- Finally, how media rich were the sites? That is, did they post videos, images, interactive graphics, or links to further information and other sites?

Not just Facebook but other platforms for social networking have appeared, making it easier for groups, campaigns, or other green causes to organize their presence online. Ning (ning.com), for example, is a platform that allows a group to create customized social networking or community websites that feature videos, discussion forums, and blog posts that can be promoted on Twitter, LinkedIn, or even Facebook. Even the financier T. Boone Pickens used Ning to develop support for the Pickens Plan, promoting the use of natural gas and wind power instead of oil. His site last had over 200,000 followers, living in 91 U.S. Congressional Districts, able to help promote the plan (Quain, 2010, para. 7).

Finally, activist groups like the climate justice organization 350.0rg have been among the innovative developers of social networking sites. The small group of students from Middlebury College, along with Professor Bill McKibben, launched 350.0rg's site as their main portal for organizing students, civil society groups, and activists globally to call attention to climate change and the urgent need for solutions. Social networking is so central to 350.0rg's organizing activities that some observers have described the site as "more of a social media network than an activist group" (DeLuca, Sun, & Peeples, 2011, p. 153). I will describe 350.0rg's role in organizing climate justice protests in the next chapter.

Reporting and Documenting

One of the most interesting uses of social media in recent years has been the ability of ordinary citizens to document, report, or even expose conditions on the ground—whether it's monitoring species, reporting oil spills, or alerting officials to toxic waste sites. Citizens, researchers, and environmental groups are using mobile apps, digital cameras, smartphones, iPads, and online registries to document their observations of the natural world or report environmental problems to others.

The location-based services MyTown, Loopt, Foursquare, and Gowalla, for example, are starting to offer opportunities for environmental and other groups to visit and document events at critical sites. Such services allow users to locate designated sites on any smartphone with a global positioning system (GPS). Gowalla, particularly with its apps for iPhone, Android, Blackberry, and iPad, proved a useful tool for environmental groups in the aftermath of the BP *Deepwater Horizon* oil spill in the Gulf of Mexico by tagging locations affected by the spill (Quain, 2010, para. 13)

One of the promising uses of social media for documenting changes in the natural world is the use of mobile apps and links to online registries to enable citizen–volunteers to help scientists or public officials. Such applications enable "naturalist armies" to act on behalf of ecologists and other natural scientists by "monitoring species, observing behavioral patterns, and reporting the presence of changes in climate, vegetation, and populations" (Fraser, 2011, para. 3).

Cornell University's Citizen Science Central maintains an ambitious citizen–volunteer online registry. It acts as a clearinghouse for more than 130 natural science projects. Many of these "offer training in species identification and invite the public to post targeted observations: the number of gray vs. fox squirrels (Project Squirrel), the appearance of buds in spring . . . [or] the migratory behavior of Monarch butterflies (Monarch Watch)" (para. 7).

More urgently, community activists in the Coachella Valley of Southern California are using Web 2.0 applications to document abandoned waste dumps and shoddy migrant housing conditions in this region with a large population of poor, farmworker families. As a result of a newly formed task force, residents now are able to log online and report environmental hazards, including unexplained fumes or pollution, to environmental officials (Flaccus, 2011). The citizen complaints have begun to pay off. In 2011, the EPA and state regulators "cracked down on a soil recycling plant that was blamed by air quality officials for a putrid stench that sickened dozens of children and teachers at a nearby school" (para. 2).

Finally, in New Orleans, middle and high school students are learning to use digital media to document and report their sightings of water pollution, oil sheens, or other environmental hazards in their coastal communities. The program, STREAM (Students Reporting Environmental Action through Media) was begun after the BP oil spill in the Gulf by Earth Echo International, a nonprofit organization founded by Philippe and Alexandra Cousteau. The goal of STREAM is to support youth-focused citizen journalism in the students' communities by providing them with training, online workshops, and a multimedia digital platform for their stories (carthecho.org).

As a result of the ability of social media to document and easily share with wider outlets, more and more citizens, activists, students, and researchers are expanding our awareness of changes in the world that are often out of sight of the mainstream media or environmental officials. Such uses of media broaden our scientific understanding and also enable ordinary citizens to bear witness to environmental dangers in their communities.

Public Criticism and Accountability

Throughout history, media all of types—from broadsides to television—have been used to criticize corrupt politicians and other powerful interests. With Facebook, Twitter, and other social media, the reach of public scrutiny and criticism has accelerated dramatically. This scrutiny has shamed environmental villains, criticized inept officials, and held accountable corporations, governments, and illegal operators for everything from air pollution to destruction of rainforests.

Greenpeace has been especially active in using social media as part of its campaigns to protect endangered species and rally against global warming. In 2011, Greenpeace mounted an Unfriend Coal campaign on Facebook itself (facebook.com/unfriendcoal). The idea was to unfriend coal on countless Facebook pages as a way of signaling to Facebook employees that they should end the company's reliance on coal and lead the industry toward renewable energy (Carus, 2011).

More recently, Greenpeace initiated a social media campaign against the large toy companies of Disney, Hasbro, Lego, and Mattel (the maker of Barbie) for their use of product packaging from endangered rainforests. Through its use of

Facebook, YouTube, and Twitter, the group hoped to rally public support to pressure the companies to end their harmful practices. Greenpeace's main target was Mattel. It used Barbie's boyfriend Ken as its virtual spokesperson, by releasing a spoof video on YouTube:

> The spoof plays on Mattel's [then] current advertising campaign which involves Ken winning Barbie back after seven years apart. In the YouTube video, Ken discovers Barbie's deforestation habits in Indonesia and dramatically ends their recently renewed relationship. Ten days after it was first uploaded, the YouTube clip was viewed over a million times in multiple languages, according to Greenpeace in July 2011. (Stine, 2011, paras. 5–6)

After its launch on YouTube and a huge banner at Mattel's corporate offices, Greenpeace then turned to Facebook and Twitter to enlist the public to protest the toy companies, and "directed users on the social media sites to confront Mattel via Barbie's pages and also send e-mails directly to Bob Eckert, Mattel's CEO" (Stine, 2011, para. 8).

Within a matter of months, Greenpeace's campaign was showing signs of success. Responding to public criticism, Mattel announced in June 2011 that it was directing its suppliers to stop buying products from a Singapore company that had clear-cut vast areas of Indonesian rainforests and, further, was investigating the deforestation allegations (Roosevelt, 2011). Overall, Stine (2011) noted, "The relative success of Greenpeace's campaign during its first two months reveals the potential of social media in ethical campaigns" (para. 4).

Other groups have also taken on the coal industry with social media campaigns. Several activists, calling their group Coal Is Killing Kids, recently embarrassed Peabody Energy, the giant coal corporation, with a satiric site called Coal Cares on Facebook and Twitter. The mock company's website (coalcares.org) declares:

> Coal Cares is a brand-new initiative from Peabody Energy, the world's largest private-sector coal company, to reach out to American youngsters with asthma and to help them keep their heads high in the face of those who would treat them with less than full dignity. For kids who have no choice but to use an inhaler, Coal Cares™ lets them inhale with pride. (Hecht, 2011, para. 2)

The site's images feature a young boy, stretching his arms wide at the beach, and the words, "Breathe *easier* with a Free INHALER FOR YOUR CHILD!"

The Coal Is Killing Kids site also announces satirically: "Puff-Puff™ inhalers are available free to any family living within 200 miles of a coal plant." A link takes you to Coal Cares's list of inhalers with cartoon images, including Dora the Explorer (ages 0–3), Batman (ages 3–8), and Justin Bieber ("The Bieber") for ages 9–13. After its launch, the website quickly went viral on other sites and blogs.

A spokesperson for the activist group explained that the site was created "to highlight . . . that pollution that comes from coal plants hurts kids. Something that wasn't doom and gloom" (Palevsky, 2011, para. 7). The spoof site was created in collaboration with the Yes Men's online lab at yeslab.org.

Mobilizing

Social media also are regularly used to mobilize supporters and the general public in support of various environmental causes. Greenpeace's campaign against toy makers (above) enlisted the public to e-mail Mattel and post on Barbie's Facebook page as well as publicly shame the company. Also, we saw in the successful Great Bear Rainforest campaign (Chapter 5) the use of blogs and social networking sites "to fire up [an] online campaign" to deny markets for the wood products exporters in British Columbia (Johnson, 2008). A spokesperson for Forest Ethics, at the time, said that social media proved effective in spreading the Great Bear Rainforest campaign's message:

> The campaign has appeared on dozens of popular blogs and networking sites around the world. They include Facebook and Twitter. . . . In the United States, we're finding this is getting picked up even on religious blogs, which are wanting to save Creation. . . . Supporters have been sending about 100 e-mails per day to the BC government through the group's website. (Johnson, 2008, paras. 9–10, 12–13)

Today, environmental, climate, and social justice activists are using the full suite of social media in their organizing efforts. This approach was evident in the International Day of Action campaign in 2011, waged by environmental and other civil society groups. The campaign urged people to demand that the World Bank reduce its funding of fossil fuel projects around the world. In addition to holding rallies outside of World Bank offices in London, Paris, Berlin, Johannesburg, and other major cities, the campaign also coordinated a worldwide effort online and on smartphones.

The International day of Action, for example, asked people to tweet @WorldBank and use the hashtag #WBDayOfAction, e-mail their friends, and post comments on the World Bank's Facebook and its blog demanding that the bank phase out its lending for coal plants and other projects. Sample tweets calling on the World Bank included: "'Free Us From #fossilfuels' #WBDayOfAction" and "How long until @ WorldBank updates its energy strategy to live up to its pro-poor, pro-climate rhetoric? #WBDayOfAction." The campaign is ongoing as I write in 2011 and involves hundreds of civil society groups, landless cooperatives, and climate change activists around the world.

Finally, an innovative Twitter–Facebook campaign in Texas may illustrates some of the ways in which social media is coordinating with more traditional methods like e-mail to mobilize supporters. In Texas, the Sierra Club and Environment Texas, a coalition of state organizations, have waged a long-running, successful campaign against coal-burning power plants. Recently, I had the chance to talk with Flavia de la Fuente, a conservation organizer for the Sierra Club, who helped to lead the campaign's social media efforts.

Working out of Environment Texas' office in Austin, Flavia was given access to the group's Twitter account. An official told her to "go crazy on Twitter" in building support for the coal campaign. (Flavia told me that she had been on Twitter for years as a DREAM Act activist.[1]) Initially, her objective was to generate more followers on the group's Twitter feed and hold their interest. This was made easier due to breaking news about the BP oil spill in the Gulf and incidents of electricity outages in Texas at the time. Flavia, therefore, started with updates about these events and tweeted sources for getting help or more information.

Gradually, Flavia began to inform her Twitter followers about the underlying cause of many of these problems—Texans' reliance on fossil fuels, oil and, particularly, coal-burning power plants. At this point, she began to test how many potentially active followers were out there, asking, for example, "Would you be willing to take action?" She followed up each Twitter reply with a personal e-mail and directed people to the Sierra Club's Facebook campaign page for more information in their local areas. As the campaign grew, Environment Texas and the Sierra Club were able to target these supporters via e-mail for turnout at rallies, public hearings, and so forth

Building a Twitter following, nurturing the relationships with personal e-mails, and providing followers with information and opportunities for participation all contributed to support for the ongoing campaign. Of course, other measures were also used to mobilize supporters in the coalition's campaign to shut down or block the construction of new coal-burning plants in Texas. (For more information, see beyondcoal.org.)

Microvolunteering and Self-Organizing

Microvolunteering refers to sites that allow people to do small, bite-sized tasks via mobile apps, which sponsors believe will have meaningful results for different environmental groups or charitable causes. For example, Sparked (sparked.com), created by the Extraordinaries, has mobile apps for microvolunteering, and its online site coordinates other sites and matches volunteers with them. For example, when I clicked on *environment* and my interest in *social media*, I was matched with 15 projects with 13,080 people currently volunteering for them.

Other nonprofit groups like Social Actions bring together opportunities to "make a difference" (socialactions.com). The site has over 50 online platforms for issues ranging from health care, poverty, and climate change, to homelessness, HIV/AIDS, animals, and other issues. When I checked, it had 2,342 links for environmental actions, including volunteering, downloading an energy-saving program for your laptop, and signing a petition.

Mobile apps may be the most-used portals for microvolunteering. For example, the Sierra Club released an Earth Day iPhone application that allowed its users to become Eco Heroes by pledging to take action for the environment. The application also had a map feature that showed users which areas of the U.S. had received a lot of pledges and which areas needed more pledges. The idea of the map was to encourage users to share real-time information through Facebook, Twitter, and e-mail and challenge their friends to make their own pledges.

Indeed, there are seemingly infinite ways to green your iPhone or Android. Smartphone apps for microvolunteering for environmental causes include, for example, green shopping guides, checking on pollution in your area, reducing your carbon footprint, or receiving a daily EPA environmental *widget*. A **widget** is a short programming code that enables something interesting to appear on your blog, wiki, or smartphone. For example, the EPA's Daily Actions widget might provide, on any one day, tips for taking steps to address climate change, while one of the EPA's Envirofacts widgets lets users search for hazardous waste sites in that person's region.

Finally, social media also have spawned an entirely different type of microvolunteering through self-organizing. *Self-organizing* refers to the ability of individuals, through what are often called *bottom-up* websites, to initiate actions via social media that actively engage others. **Bottom-up sites** provide online tools that enable users to start petitions on platforms like Facebook and Twitter, for example. Dedicated sites at Moveon.org (Signon.org), Care2 (thepetitionsite.com), and Change.org also have bottom-up tools. For example, Change.org claims that more than a million people and groups are using its online start-a-petition tool. One recent Change.org petition seeks to bring pressure on the Food Network television program to stop featuring shark as food:

> Sadly, according to the International Union for the Conservation of Nature, as many as one-third of all shark species are threatened with extinction or are close to becoming threatened. Because shark populations are in such dire straits, there's no reason for people to be eating these threatened swimmers. Food Network and its properties are the predominant places to find food television programming. . . . Tell Food Network that you want a policy stating that shark will not be featured as an ingredient on air, in the magazine, or in recipes posted on Food Network-owned Web sites.

By Day 16 in the online drive, more than 31,000 people had signed the "Stop Featuring Shark" petition to the Food Network.

☞ **FYI** **iTunes and Environmental Causes**

Perhaps the easiest, self-interested, bite-sized step in microvolunteering that one can take simply involves downloading a song. For example, blues singer–songwriter Bonnie Raitt worked with the Patagonia Music Collective to persuade musicians to donate unreleased tracks, like Raitt's own "So Damn Good," to benefit environmental groups and activists (Bonnie Raitt Q/A, 2011, p. 12). Other artists give a percentage of money from every song of theirs that is downloaded from iTunes.

While each of these activities and social media tools is interesting in its own, it might be useful to see how environmental organizations put it all together in a campaign or how an advocacy group coordinates social media within its overall communication program.

Social Media and Environmental Advocacy

In drawing attention to, criticizing, or mobilizing around a specific environmental problem, activists today rarely rely on one social media tool. Rather, individuals and advocacy campaigns put it all together by using an array of media. In this section, I'll describe some of the ways that social media are being used in opposition to offshore oil drilling and, particularly, the BP oil disaster in the Gulf of Mexico in 2010. The oil spill also illustrates the difference between spontaneous, individual uses of social media and a more coordinated use in advocacy campaigns. Finally, I'll discuss some of the challenges of specific types of social media for environmental advocacy.

Opposing Offshore Oil Drilling

When the *Deepwater Horizon* oil rig exploded in 2010, killing 11 workers and spewing oil into the Gulf of Mexico, the world's attention was riveted. Some people vented their frustration by demonstrating at gas stations and BP's corporate offices. Others expressed their anger and outrage online. In addition to newspapers and television, "social networking sites like Facebook and Twitter [were] alight with posts from government, the oil industry and citizens around the globe" (Rudolf, 2010, para. 2). And, as I described in Chapter 3, real-time images of gushing oil from the wellhead were streamed on countless blogs.

One of the principal uses of social media during the Gulf oil spill was the airing of public criticism of BP officials who seemed incompetent or uncaring. Individuals, environmental groups, customers, and others hammered BP "all over the Web, with thousands of posts on Twitter and Facebook slamming the company for its failure to prevent the disaster and its inability to stanch the flow of oil from their well nearly two weeks after the accident" (Rudolf, 2010, para. 4). One person tweeted BP, "You can rest assured that I will walk before I would ever buy a gallon of your gasoline," while another tweeted, "BP must not be let off the hook" (para. 5, 3).

There was also a spoof Twitter feed, @BPGlobalPR, that pretended to be the oil company's "online persona" (Zabarenko & Whitcomb, 2010, para. 1). The feed mocked BP officials' reassurances and claims of effective cleanup. At its height, the Twitter feed had more than 114,000 followers, far more than the official BP feed. Those behind the feed also donated $10,000 to the Gulf Restoration Network from their sales of T-shirts making fun of BP's slogan that "BP cares" (paras. 10–11). On April 20, 2011, the one-year anniversary of the BP *Deepwater Horizon* oil spill, @BPGlobalPR tweeted, "Today is the one year anniversary of something happening off the Gulf of Mexico. Looking into it (http://twitter.com/-%21/search?q=%23bpcares)."

While social media made possible an outpouring of criticism (and mockery) of BP and oil drilling, it is, nevertheless, important to note that this communication likely had a very limited effect on the company or on energy policy. In this sense, it is useful to distinguish between what Karpf (2011) calls *political activity* in the social media environment and the *political organizing* that occurs through more coordinated campaigns.

The latter, while also using social media, enables a more sustained and strategic effort versus one-off or momentary tactics. Let's look at this difference in the debate over offshore oil drilling.

Social media played a major but somewhat different role in the advocacy campaigns against offshore oil drilling by environmental and other civic groups. These campaigns mounted more coordinated and sustained efforts using social media but aimed at having an impact on energy. When the Gulf oil spill occurred, for example, one U.S. environmental group, the Sierra Club, responded by initiating a campaign to go Beyond Oil. Using an array of online and social media to inform and mobilize its members, the campaign aimed to organize their public comments and expressions of concern in a way that built political pressure on political leaders who had the power to bring change.

In mobilizing and coordinating the activities of its members, the Beyond Oil campaign made use of social media and its online resources in a number of ways:

- Tweeting and live blogging during the weeks of the ruptured and spewing well-head to alert and inform members
- Using the location-based platform Gowalla to create a trip, "BP Oil Disaster," to catalog sites impacted by the spill and coordinate these locations with activists visiting the Gulf Coast.
- Launching a new website (beyondoil.org) that generated thousands of comments to President Obama, with thousands more Facebook hits
- Building a separate website housing photos and stories from events protesting the spill around the U.S. to sustain interest and enthusiasm
- Publishing news feeds urging reform of offshore drilling to media outlets, later quoted in newspaper editorials, news blogs, and the business sections of papers like the *New York Times*
- Using its Convio system (a constituent services application) to organize house parties around the U.S., recruiting new supporters and generating comments to public officials.

A major part of the Beyond Oil campaign was the Sierra Club's participation in a broader coalition called Hands Across the Sands, a cooperative effort of local, national, and international groups protesting the dangers of deepwater, offshore oil drilling.

The Hands Across the Sands campaign pivoted off public awareness of the Gulf oil spill—fueled by social media and the visual images on TV and numerous websites of the oil gushing from the wellhead. Beyond opposition to oil drilling, the campaign sought to communicate a message of "NO to Offshore Oil Drilling, YES to Clean Energy." Using e-mail, Facebook, Twitter, and a dedicated website (handsacrossthe-sand.com), the campaign, in only four weeks, mobilized large numbers of supporters who organized more than 1,000 same-day events in the United States and 42 other countries.

Supporters of the campaigns gathered on June 26, 2010, on beaches and along coastlines. The event's organizers hoped the participation of ordinary citizens—joining hands—would visually convey a message of human solidarity: "Every time we join hands that message is reinforced. . . . Embrace clean energy. A line in the sand is a powerful thing" (handsacrossthesand.com). During and after the beach events, participants shared photos of local protests via YouTube and Flickr and on the campaign's own website.

In the months and year following the 2010 oil spill, the Obama administration imposed a moratorium on permits for deepwater oil drilling in the Gulf of Mexico. Before issuing new permits a year later, a newly organized Bureau of Ocean Energy Management Regulation and Enforcement had put in place tougher standards for drilling, reviews, and inspection of sites.

Many causal factors, of course, were involved in bringing about reform of offshore oil policies. Nevertheless, the public criticisms and coordinated advocacy campaigns illustrate the expanding capacity of social media and Web 2.0 applications to generate news and political pressure. As Cottle and Lester (2011) have observed in another context, "It is in and through this fast-evolving complex of interpenetrating communications networks and media systems . . . that protests and demonstrations today principally become transacted around the world" (p. 5).

Challenges for Social Media Advocacy

Despite the widespread use of social media, it may come as a surprise that environmental and other nongovernmental organizations recognize that there are challenges (and some limitations) in its use for advocacy. This became clearer to me when I participated in a symposium recently with social media and digital strategists from Moveon.org, Jumo, Organizing for America, EchoDitto, Media Matters, the New Organizing Institute, Sierra Club, and others. In exploring new directions in organizing advocacy campaigns, the participants observed that advocacy groups face a number of challenges in using social media and other online resources. I'll identify briefly four of these challenges.

Unbundling Green Content

A common concern for environmental organizations has been how to disseminate their messages, alerts, information on issues, and appeals for support to wider audiences. Unfortunately, much of this content is found only on a group's webpage. As a consequence, unless it is e-mailed, tweeted, or broadcast to potential audiences, this information may be difficult to find elsewhere on the web. The challenge for such groups, therefore, has been finding ways to *unbundle* this content. **Unbundling** is freeing of content from a single portal for information, such as a website, ensuring that it is available at other places online where people are going. If a group does not already have an adequate audience, it will need to gain exposure for its content elsewhere online; that is, a group will need to find its audience and stand in front of it, figuratively.

One of the most successful examples of the unbundling of environmental content is the National Aeronautics and Space Administration (NASA). Although NASA has several core missions, it is also a premier source of information about environmental and climate phenomena. And while its main website (nasa.gov) has extraordinarily rich media, NASA's visuals, interactive data, and news about climate change are disseminated widely online. For example, the research report by NASA's Goddard Institute showing that the year 2010 tied 2005 as the warmest year on record was reposted widely at online news sites such as CNN.com, on dedicated climate websites such as Climatecentreal.org, and on numerous science and environmental blogs. (Of course, rumor is that NASA has a larger budget for media than most nonprofit, advocacy groups.)

Many environmental groups, with more limited budgets, are expanding the distribution of their content particularly through Facebook and the use of RSS feeds, Digg, and so on. For example, the Environmental Defense Fund (EDF), like most groups, has a media-rich Facebook page and numerous blogs for news and analysis on climate, health, ecosystems, oceans, transportation, and other issues. Nevertheless, unless users receive updates via RSS feeds, they must first visit these (still limited) sites, available largely through the group's webpage. One exception to this, however, is EDF's ability to produces video news and feed this content to other media outlets.

Working With a Network Model

Similar to the challenge of unbundling content, environmental groups—like other membership-based organizations—are also working to transform themselves "from a broadcast communication model to a networked model in order to interact with their members" (Clark & Slyke, 2011, p. 245). By **networked,** I mean the multiple, intersecting flows of communication, "using online tools and platforms to find, rank, tag, create, distribute, mock, and recommend content" (p. 239). The challenge for green groups is their need to discover more ways to interact directly with these networks, engaging members and potential supporters in the social media spaces where they are gathering.

The challenge of working with a networked model is similar to what Clark and Slyke (2011) have observed about news media online. Environmental groups are going to have to go where their members are conversing rather than waiting for users to find them:

> There are thousands of Facebook groups, blogs, Twitter feeds, listservs, and more where self-organized groups virtually gather. [Environmental groups] will have to figure out how to authentically interact with these groups. . . . Last, but not least, they will have to use this interaction to bring some of those users back into their web sites and integrate them into those community spaces. (p. 244)

There are other challenges as well in accessing such networks if the main purpose is advocacy. While social media are good tools for nurturing networks, there are many things that networks don't do well, particularly for advocacy. Journalist Malcolm Gladwell (2010) has argued, for example, that because networks don't have clear lines of authority, "they have real difficulty reaching consensus and setting goals. They can't think strategically. . . . How do you make difficult choices about tactics or strategy or philosophical direction when everyone has an equal say?" (para. 24).

Gladwell's criticisms of social media have occasionally been harsh and have not been shared by all social media enthusiasts. (See "Another Viewpoint: 'The Revolution Will Not Be Tweeted.' ") Still, his observations are a useful caution for those who design environmental advocacy campaigns (Chapter 8). If, as he fears, social media make it "easier for activists to express themselves," relying on social networking alone may also make it "harder for that expression to have any impact" (para. 32).

A Light Lift for Mobilizing?

A more serious challenge arises from the experience of some environmental and civil society leaders who believe that Facebook, Twitter, and other social media are not the first-choice tools for initially mobilizing supporters for an advocacy campaign. While *mobilizing* is one of the six functions of social media I've described above, many feel that such tools are not the primary or most effective tools for targeting potential activists in the beginning of a campaign. (I'll discuss the role of Twitter in the Texas coal campaign and in Hands Across the Sands below.) Let me explain.

For all of its popularity, Facebook, for example, is generally not viewed as a first-line tool in building constituent support for campaigns. At the symposium of digital strategists I attended (mentioned earlier), the political director for a major online organizing group cautioned, "Facebook is not 'pixie dust.' "[2] The expectations of what Facebook can do, he warned, are unrealistic, at least as far as mobilizing or organizing (A. Ruben, personal communication, July 14, 2011.)

As a result, many environmental groups acknowledge that e-mail is still their preferred tool for targeting or proactive outreach, especially for an initial communication to a group's members. In these cases, Facebook is used as a secondary platform or as a repository for information about the campaign. (In the Hands Across the Sands effort, discussed earlier, e-mail was used to drive potential supporters to the campaign's Facebook page and website.) As the online organizing director (above) explained, "If we don't have the space in our initial e-mail blast to cover all of the content we would like, we'll use social media as a backup, posting it on our Facebook page."

A further reason e-mail is relied upon by advocacy groups is its ability to follow up with responses that are generated through Twitter and by other means, such as signing or clicking on an online e-petition. This latter action is called **clicktivism,** the taking of action simply by clicking on a response link online. In itself, such clicktivism is often inconsequential; Sometimes called *slacktivism,* it can give the (misleading) impression that one is having an effect simply by clicking on an online link (Good, 2011, p. 1). By contrast, the Twitter coal campaign organizer, Flavia, credited her success partly to *following up* on responses to her Twitter request with personal e-mails. Rutgers University Media Professor David Karp explains that such follow-up enables an advocacy group to encourage a "ladder-of-engagement" that leads to more and heavier volunteer involvement and actions as a campaign goes forward (Karpf, 2010).

Twitter's reputation, on the other hand, would seem to contradict such doubts about social media as a mobilizing tool. Gladwell (2009), for example, has argued that, from fundraising for a new classroom in Tanzania to Ashton Kutcher's tweeting two million followers about ending malaria, Twitter has "become the *de facto* tool for organizing and taking action" (para. 8).

While Twitter is a terrific tool for charity fundraising, especially when celebrities tweet or during a natural disaster, many environmental leaders, nevertheless, believe it also has limits as a mobilizing tool. Twitter is a "light lift" for such purposes, one participant in the digital symposium that I attended said (J. Danzig, personal communication July 14, 2011). This light lift may be true, particularly, for environmental groups with a small number of Twitter followers or those with inactive followers who may lack incentive to follow up or take action.

In saying this, it is helpful to remember that, in both the Texas Twitter campaign and the Hands Across the Sands campaign, a key to their success was the breaking news about the BP oil spill. Eager to follow information about this disaster, thousands flocked to the campaigns' Twitter feeds, which in turn, directed many of them to the groups' websites for more information. It appears to be important, therefore, for a major news event to be present for the optimal effect of some social media campaigns, for example, a natural disaster, nuclear plant accident, or an oil spill. In other words, if the subject of the tweets is not on the front page, it can be difficult to get mass engagement with social media alone.

Another Viewpoint: "The Revolution Will Not Be Tweeted"

Malcom Gladwell (2010) has argued that "the revolution will not be tweeted." His criticism derived from his comparison of the U.S. civil rights movement with the activism of social media today. He described the commitment of the students who practiced nonviolent civil disobedience in the lunch counter sit-ins in Greensboro, NC, and in Mississippi Freedom Summer in the 1960s. Such actions, Gladwell argued, depended upon strong, personal relationships, trust, and endurance in the face of overwhelming obstacles. He then said:

> The kind of activism associated with social media isn't like this at all. The platforms of social media are built around weak ties. Twitter is a way of following (or being followed by) people you may never have met. Facebook is a tool for efficiently managing your acquaintances, for keeping up with the people you would not otherwise be able to stay in touch with. That's why you can have a thousand "friends" on Facebook, as you never could in real life.... In other words, Facebook activism succeeds not by motivating people to make a real sacrifice but by motivating them to do the things that people do when they are not motivated enough to make a real sacrifice. We are a long way from the lunch counters of Greensboro.

SOURCE: Malcolm Gladwell, "Small Change: Why the Revolution Will Not Be Tweeted." *The New Yorker,* October 4, 2010.

Irony of "Efficient" Media

Finally, there may be an irony in the "efficiency" of social media to connect with intensely committed followers. Being able to narrowly target small-issue publics (i.e., those interested in a particular issue) via Twitter or LISTSERVs, advocacy groups can directly connect with their supporters. Nevertheless, at least one media scholar points out that, in doing so, there is little or no spillover awareness of that issue to wider publics. As a result, only a weak or small political constituency is mobilized (D. Karpf, new media professor at Rutgers University, personal communication, January 17, 2011). And, therein may be an irony: Social media is clearly an efficient tool for targeting key groups but may be constrained by this very advantage. Let me explain.

In an earlier, "inefficient" media era dominated by mass media newspapers and TV, advocacy groups had to educate a broader public in order to reach a smaller number of activists for a planned event. This allowed a spillover or "beneficial inefficiency" of information for this wider audience (Karpf, 2011).

With a new media landscape, it has become easier to communicate via Twitter or Facebook with small, committed publics. Although environmental groups should continue to do so, Karpf argues, such groups also need to be aware, if this is their only communication, that the rest of the nation won't hear their mobilizing call or learn about the issue. The challenge of social media, therefore, is that it may require a wider strategic repertoire of media, enabling activists to communicate beyond the choir when necessary.

Future Trends: Challenges and Obstacles for Environmental Social Media

As new developments in social media and related technologies occur, there are a number of opportunities, as well as obstacles, for environmental communication. Given the speed at which many of these are occurring, environmental leaders and educators are already grappling with their implications. Let's look at four trends that will affect the way environmental sources will be communicating in a green public sphere in the near future.

Content Flood

Several developments have converged in recent years to produce what one new media advisor has called a potential "content flood" for users of social media and the Internet (T. Matzzie, personal communication, July 14, 2011). With hundreds of thousands of mobile applications now being developed across multiple platforms and a faster, one-gigabyte pipeline coming soon, the resulting content flood will be huge. (Apple's iPhone alone already has more than 425,000 apps.)

| **Figure 7.2** | We are entering an app-centric world where mobile applications will be our main portals for information online. |

http://www.epa.gov/appsfortheenvironment/

Already, the volume of content available online and via smartphone apps is enormous. The web and social media monitoring service, Pingdom.com (2011), reported these numbers for the year 2010:

- 25 billion sent tweets on Twitter
- 2 billion videos watched per day on YouTube
- 255 million websites
- 600 million people on Facebook
- 107 trillion e-mails sent on the Internet
- 5 billion photos hosted by Flickr

And, as we learned earlier, there were 168,059,462 blogs on the Internet (as tracked by BlogPulse), when I last checked.

Also contributing to this flood of content, search engine giant Google announced in 2011 that it was ready to deliver a new broadband service for the Internet at 1 gigabit per second. One gig is about 100 times faster than what most of us have had available until now (Goldman, 2011). This ability, combined with a 4G or higher mobile network, promises to deliver a seemingly infinite amount of information at faster speeds to social media and online users.

The implications of such a content flood for environmental communication are real. For environmental advocacy groups, for example, online organizing space is getting crowded. One group's call to action is increasingly competing with thousands of other communications almost daily. In addition, there is a real potential for further fracturing of media outlets for environmental sources generally and, therefore, further fragmentation of audiences. Even as new technologies get more robust, environmental producers of content will find the playing field quite busy.

App-Centric Environment

Along with the large number of mobile applications, there is a related development. Increasingly, people are using their smartphones to search the Internet. As I write in 2011, however, only 35% of Americans have smartphones (Inman News, 2011), but this number is growing. By 2015, almost 50% will be using them, and the number of iPad users is also growing (EMarketer, 2011). As a result, with the number of apps available, the primary way of searching online will be from mobile devices. In fact, by 2015, "almost half the total US population will be using the mobile internet" (EMarketer, 2011, para. 2). As a consequence, we are entering an **app-centric** world, where mobile applications on smartphones, Twitter, iPads, notebooks, and so on, will be our main portals for information online.

The implications of this development for environmental communication are significant. How does an environmental advocacy group, for example, get inside users' mobile platforms? Such sources are potentially facing two obstacles: First, while an environmental group may have developed a green app, there is still the challenge of getting onto a user's smartphone or iPad. With only 20 apps on a typical smartphone (out of hundreds of thousands of apps available), what incentives must a group use to be in this select list?

A second challenge for environmental sources may be the need to develop different apps for the different operating systems (OS) that smartphones currently use (e.g., Android, RIM, Apple, Symbian). An environmental app developed for the iPhone, for example, may not be compatible with an Android device. These are not insurmountable obstacles, of course, but staying in the game of making environmental content easily accessible to audiences will require more media savvy and quicker adaptation than before.

Environmental Video Networks

With the faster, one-gigabit pipeline coming, there is the potential for environmental media, educators, governmental agencies, and advocacy groups to introduce their own video networks (over broadband). Even as such groups today often have their own YouTube channels, with the enhanced capacity of broadband, new (noncommercial) independent sources can also broadcast longer or more sophisticated content. The dilemma, of course, is such networks will have to compete in the content flood mentioned earlier.

Gamification

A final development is the trend to *gamify* actions or efforts online to motivate individuals to engage in something. **Gamification** is a term originating from digital media developers and is defined as "the use of game design elements in non-game contexts" (Dixon, 2011, para. 1). Although the concept itself is from behavioral economics and marketing, gamification only gained widespread adoption by social media and general web use in late 2010 (para. 2).

The idea behind gamification is that one can apply the elements of a game—competition, fun, and social engagement with others—to something that typically isn't considered a game. There also is a reward (usually) and an element of transparency; that is, you receive feedback on your performance and (usually) that of your competitors. In engaging people in this manner, it's possible—so the theory goes—that one can encourage people to act or respond in ways they ordinarily would not, such as attending a rally or changing their environmental behaviors.

The idea of gamifying behavior was first used in marketing initiatives like frequent flyer programs. More recently, Nissan has adapted the interactive features of new technologies by gamifying the driving performance of their Leaf line of electric vehicles: The Eco Mode feature keeps track of variables such as power usage and provides "constant feedback so drivers can improve upon efficiency. The car even provides online profiles so people can compete with other drivers" (Gamification of environment, 2011, para. 1).

While used principally in commercial marketing, gamification is gradually being adopted by some environmental interests. The concept may be especially good for microvolunteering sites or requests for people to participate in environmental actions. Often, gamifying such actions occurs on location-based platforms like Gowalla or maps showing locations of members of a "team" or other competitors.

An interesting example of the use of Web 2.0 and social media tools for environmental gamifying is Carbonrally.com. Carbonrally invites users to take a challenge by teaming with others "to save energy and prevent climate change." The challenges run the gamut from "Lonely Light Love" (turn off the lights in an empty room) to "Get Off the Bottle" (give up drinking bottled water). Each contestant is given feedback showing the amount of carbon dioxide reduction that completing the challenge achieves, the location of other players, and tools to communicate with others or follow on Twitter. As I write, Carbonrally.com boasts that "45,172 Rallyers have reduced CO_2 emissions by over 7,998.4 tons so far" by completing the challenges, equal to taking 1,591 cars off the road for about one year.

Whether gamification is a useful practice for every environmental interest is an open question. Some environmental leaders may fear that gamifying issues like climate change or pollution trivializes these issues. Others question whether playing the games can achieve results at a scale that justifies the effort invested in the construction of such sites. Clearly, the application of game design is not for all purposes or users.

SUMMARY

In this chapter, I've tried to describe the social media landscape and some of its uses for environmental communication by journalists, environmentalists, the EPA, and others. I have also identified some of the challenges that new media pose for environmental advocacy.

- This chapter began by describing the migration of news online, especially environmental news services, as well as the explosive growth of the green blogosphere.
- The second section introduced the landscape of social media and described six ways such media are changing environmental communication: (1) environmental information and buzz, (2) green communities and social networking, (3) reporting and documenting, (4) public criticism and accountability, (5) mobilizing, and (6) microvolunteering and self-organizing.
- The third section surveyed the uses of social media for environmental advocacy during the 2010 Gulf of Mexico oil spill; it also identified some of the challenges of social media for this purpose.
- Finally, the last section looked at some of future trends that pose both opportunities and possible obstacles to environmental uses of social media.

In reading this chapter, I hope you have a better understanding of the wide range of social media and Web 2.0 applications being used by journalists, public agencies, environmental groups, and individuals as well as an appreciation for the challenges of using social media for environmental advocacy. In the next chapter, I'll explore in more detail the nature of advocacy campaigns themselves.

SUGGESTED RESOURCES

- *Social Media Today* (socialmediatoday.com) for good articles on social media and (sometimes) the environment.
- David A. Karpf, *The MoveOn Effect: The Unexpected Transformation of American Political Advocacy.* New York: Oxford, 2011.
- Malcolm Gladwell, "Why the Revolution Will Not Be Tweeted." *The New Yorker,* October 4, 2010.
- *The Social Network,* 2010, Academy Award and Golden Globe-winning film about the founding of Facebook, with background at thesocialnetwork-movie.com.

KEY TERMS

App-centric   200   Bottom-up sites   191

Blog   180   Clicktivism   196

DISCUSSION QUESTIONS

1. Do social media change the ground rules for environmental communication; that is, do such tools enable qualitatively different kinds of communication or effects? How?

2. Do you agree with Malcolm Gladwell when he argues "the revolution will not be tweeted"? Why or why not? Relatedly, is social media a "light lift" for environmental groups' organizing?

3. What uses have you made of social media to initiate communication about an environmental concern?

4. What social media trends seem most promising to you for groups or individuals in strengthening their abilities to communicate about environmental concerns?

5. Some environmental leaders believe that *gamification* will trivialize environmental issues like climate change. Do you agree? How could gamifying avoid these charges?

NOTES

1. The DREAM Act grants conditional residency to illegal immigrant students, in good standing, who arrived in the United States as children and who graduated from a U.S. high school.

2. According to the Disney story, Tinker Bell could enable others to fly by sprinkling them with fairy dust or "pixie dust."

REFERENCES

Bonnie Raitt Q/A. (2011, Summer). *Earthjustice,* pp. 12–13.

Carus, F. (2011, March 30). Greenpeace targets Facebook employees in clean energy campaign. Retrieved August 18, 2011, from www.guardian.co.uk

Clark, J., & Slyke, T. V. (2011). How journalists must operate in a new networked media environment. In R. W. McChesney & V. Pickard (Eds.), *Will the last reporter please turn out the lights* (pp. 238–248). New York and London: The New Press.

Cottle, S., & Lester, L. (2011). Introduction. In S. Cottle & L. Lester (Eds.), *Transnational protests and the media* (pp. 3–16). New York: Peter Lang.

DeLuca, K. M., Sun, Y., & Peeples, J. (2011). Wild public screens and image events from Seattle to China. In S. Cottle & L. Lester (Eds.), *Transnational protests and the media* (pp. 143–158). New York: Peter Lang.

Dixon, D. (2011, May 7–12). Gamification: Toward a definition. Retrieved August 28, 2011, from http://hci.usask.ca

EMarketer. (2011, August 24). Two in five mobile owners use internet on the go. Retrieved September 3, 2011, from www.emarketer.com

Flaccus, G. (2011, June 17). Sewage pile, illegal dump on Calif toxic tour list. *CNSNews .com*. retrieved August 18, 2011, from http://www.cnsnews.com

Fraser, C. (2011, July 11). Tapping social media's potential to muster a vast green army. *Yale Environment 360*. Retrieved August 18, 2011, from http://e360.yale .edu

Friedman, S. M. (2004). And the beat goes on: The third decade of environmental journalism. In S. Senecah (Ed.), *The environmental communication yearbook* (Vol. 1, pp. 175–187). Mahwah, NJ: Erlbaum.

Gamification of environment. (2011, August 23). *Gamification wiki.* Retrieved August 28, 2011, from http://gamifi cation.org/wiki/Gamification_of_ Environment

Gladwell, M. (2009, May 12). 10 ways to change the world thru social media. Retrieved August 27, 2011, from http:// mashable.com

Gladwell, M. (2010, October 4). Small change: Why the revolution will not be tweeted. *The New Yorker.* Retrieved August 12, 2011, from http://www .newyorker.com

Goldman, D. (2011, March 30). Google chooses Kansas City for ultra-fast Internet. *CNN Money.* Retrieved August 28, 2011, from http://money.cnn.com

Good, J. (2011, November 18). On strategizing, leveraging, and not losing the miraculous. Paper presented at the National Communication Association meeting, New Orleans, LA.

Hecht, S. (2011, May 11). Anti-coal satire (with My First Inhaler) punks Peabody Energy. Retrieved August 18, 2011, from http://legalplanet.wordpress.com

Inman News. (2011, August 30). Number of smartphone users jumps 10%. Retrieved September 3, 2011, from www.inman .com/news

Johnson, L. (2008, November 28). Environmentalist turns to online campaign to protect B.C. forest. *CBC News.* Retrieved April 28, 2011, from www .cbc.ca/news

Kaplan, A. M., & Haenlein, M. (2010). Users of the world, unite! The challenges and opportunities of social media. *Business Horizons 53*(1), 59–68.

Karpf, D. (2010). Online political mobilization from the advocacy group's perspective: Looking beyond clicktivism. *Policy & Internet, 2*(4), Article 2.

Karpf, D. A. (2011). *The MoveOn effect: The unexpected transformation of American political advocacy.* New York: Oxford.

Krol, C. (2009, January). Newspapers in crisis: Migrating online. Retrieved August 13, 2011, from www.emarketer.com

Lanier, J. (2010). *You are not a gadget.* New York: Knopf.

Lester, L. (2010). *Media and environment: Conflict, politics and the news.* Cambridge, UK: Polity.

Lester, L. (2011, March). Species of the month: Anti-whaling, mediated visibility, and the news. *Environmental Communication: A Journal of Nature and Culture, 5*(1): 124–139.

Palevsky, M. (2011, May 12). Yes Men hoax uses Twitter, Facebook to put Peabody Energy on the defensive. Retrieved August 18, 2011, from www.poynter.org

Pingdom.com. (2011, January 12). Internet 2010 in numbers. Retrieved August 28, 2011, from http://royal.pingdom.com

Quain, J. R. (2010, October 15). How social networking is changing politics and public service. *U.S. News and World Report*. Retrieved August 11, 2011, from www.usnews.com

Roosevelt, M. (2011, June 10). Pressured by Greenpeace, Mattel cuts off sub-supplier APP. *Los Angeles Times*. Retrieved September 3, 2011, from http://articles .latimes.com

Rudolf, J. C. (2010, May 3). Social media and the spill. The *New York Times'* Green Blog. Retrieved August 25, 2011, from http://green.blogs.nytimes.com

Slawter, L. D. (2008). TreeHuggerTV: Re-visualizing environmental activism in the post-network era. *Environmental Communication: A Journal of Nature and Culture, 2*(2), 212–228.

Sobel, J. (2010, November 3). State of the blogosphere. *Technorati*. Retrieved August 15, 2011, from http://technorati .com/

Stine, R. (2011, August 5). Social media and environmental campaigning: Brand lessons from Barbie. Retrieved August 18, 2011, from www.ethical corp.com

Technorati. (2008). State of the Blogosphere /2008. Retrieved December 23, 2008, from http://technorati.com

Wyss, B. (2008). *Covering the environment: How journalists work the green beat.* London and New York: Routledge.

Yamaguchi, M. (2011, February 16). Sea Shepherd activists prompt Japan to suspend whaling. *Huffington Post*. Retrieved August 14, 2011, from www.huffington post.com

Zabarenko, D., & Whitcomb, D. (2010, June 6). A groundswell against BP on Facebook and Twitter. *The Washington Post*. Retrieved July 30, 2011, from www .washingtonpost.com

PART IV

Environmental Movements and Campaigns

Advocacy campaigns are a uniquely democratic form of communication, offering a collective voice for those who lack the means or power to affect change themselves.

CHAPTER 8

Advocacy Campaigns and Message Construction

The grassroots campaign to move beyond coal has seen an outpouring of support and victories that no one thought possible just a few years ago. Hundreds of thousands of people around the country, talking to their neighbors ... media outlets, and most importantly, decision-makers, have successfully stopped over 150 coal plants to date.

—Sierra Club, Beyond Coal
Campaign (2011, paras. 1–2)

T he Beyond Coal campaign (above) illustrates a form of environmental communication called *advocacy*, the act of persuading or arguing in support of a specific cause, policy, idea, or set of values. Campaigns are just one form of advocacy. Used by businesses, candidates for public office, and public relations firms, as well as environmental groups, advocacy takes many forms; these include advertising, political campaigning, community organizing, marches and demonstrations, legal argument, and so forth. In this chapter, however, I will focus on one major form of advocacy—the *environmental advocacy* campaign. (We'll look at other forms in the chapters to follow.)

Chapter Preview

- In the first section of this chapter, I describe *advocacy* in general and distinguish *advocacy campaigns* and *critical rhetorics*, the questioning or criticism of the status quo.
- In the second section, I explore the basic elements of advocacy campaigns, focusing on: (a) objectives, (b) audiences, and (c) strategies.

(Continued)

(Continued)

- I'll go behind the scenes, in the third section by describing the design of a successful advocacy campaign—the Zuni Salt Lake Coalition's campaign against plans to strip-mine for coal near sacred Native American lands.
- In the final section, I describe the role of *message construction* in campaigns and identify two challenges: (1) overcoming the *attitude-behavior gap* and (2) the use of values in the construction of messages that seek to motivate supporters.

My hope is that, when you have finished this chapter, you'll be more aware of the wide range of communication that environmental advocates engage in and that you'll also appreciate the challenges they face in questioning strongly held values and ideologies in building public demand for environmental protection.

Environmental Advocacy

Advocacy is a powerful tool for a wide range of social change organizations. Organizations whose goals range from support for the homeless to the stopping of sweatshop labor provide forums for newly emerging voices and concerns. The Humane Society (animal protection), the Center for Health, Environment, and Justice (an antitoxics group), 350.0rg (a climate justice social networking site), It Gets Better (supporting lesbian, gay, bisexual, and transsexual [LGBT] youth), and other groups offer collective voices and advocate for those who lack the means or power to effect change themselves. Such groups help to hold more powerful institutions accountable to democratic and humane principles and have often achieved changes that protect vulnerable populations and interests, such as new medicines for people living with HIV/AIDS, or the agreement by some universities not to buy clothing from companies using sweatshop labor in third-world countries.

In providing a voice for those who may have no means of expression, advocacy groups act as intermediaries between individuals and the large, often impersonal institutions of public life. This has been particularly true of environmental groups. Former *New York Times* writer Philip Shabecoff (2000) argues that a chief role of environmental groups is to act as "intermediaries between science and the public, the media, and lawmakers" (p. 152). For example, students at the University of North Carolina at Chapel Hill, my campus, drew on alumni, state environmental groups, and the expertise of economics and physics professors to press the university to end its reliance on a campus coal-burning power plant. As intermediaries, this Beyond Coal campus group enabled other students to gain expertise and express their concerns to university administrators.

Modes of Environmental Advocacy

Environmentalists engage in a wide variety of advocacy modes or forms of communication. These modes may differ in their goals, the media they use, and the audiences they target. They may include public education, campaigns to influence environmental legislation in Congress, community organizing, boycotts, and direct action protests such as sit-ins and hanging banners from corporate buildings. (See Table 8.1.)

Here and in following chapters, I'll describe some of these modes of advocacy in more detail. In Chapter 9, for example, I will describe the use of toxic tours hosted by environmental justice groups who invite people to visit communities that are contaminated by toxic chemicals to see, smell, and feel what daily life is like for those who live there (Pezzullo, 2007). For now, I describe two broad forms of advocacy: advocacy campaigns and critical rhetoric. I did not include these in Table 8.1 because they are much broader than the forms of advocacy listed there. Indeed, campaigns, especially, will use a range of these specific types of advocacy—such as media events or community organizing—in implementing the campaign strategy.

Campaigns Differ From Critical Rhetoric

Before an environmental advocacy campaign starts, there is often a period in which the status quo is questioned and a desire to find a better way is expressed. This is the role of critical rhetoric. For example, Rachael Carson's (1962) classic book *Silent Spring* sharply criticized the practices of the pesticide industry and

Table 8.1 Modes of Environmental Advocacy

Mode of Advocacy	Objective
Political and Legal Channels:	
1. Political advocacy	To influence legislation or regulations
2. Litigation	To seek compliance with environmental standards by agencies and businesses
3. Electoral politics	To mobilize voters for candidates and referenda
Direct Appeal to Public Audiences:	
4. Public education	To influence societal attitudes and behavior
5. Direct action	To influence specific behaviors through acts of protest, including civil disobedience
6. Media events	To create publicity or news coverage to broaden advocacy effects
7. Community organizing	To mobilize citizens or residents to act
Consumers and the Market:	
8. Green consumerism	To use consumers' purchasing power to influence corporate behavior
9. Corporate accountability	To influence corporate behavior through consumer boycotts and shareholder actions

government agencies that exposed the public to harmful chemicals. As a result of this questioning, public health advocates and groups such as Environmental Action began campaigns for federal legislation to curb the pesticide dichloro-diphenyl-trichloroethane (DDT) and for stronger laws to protect air and water. Although they are different in some ways, campaigns and critical rhetorics can function in complementary ways, and it is therefore important to understand each of these modes of advocacy in more detail.

Critical Rhetoric

Critical rhetoric is the questioning or denunciation of a behavior, policy, societal value, or ideology; such rhetoric may also include the articulation of an alternate policy, vision, or ideology. Throughout the modern environmental movement, many voices—not part of any particular campaign—have questioned or criticized the taken-for-granted views of society and its behavior toward nature. For example, Greenpeace activists have released *mind bombs* in the media since the 1970s to raise the world's consciousness of the cruelty of modern whaling. Greenpeace Cofounder Robert Hunter defines **mind bombs** as simple images, such as scenes of Greenpeace activists on small, inflatable boats interposing themselves between whales and their harpooners, that "explode in people's minds" to create a new awareness (quoted in Weyler, 2004, p. 73).

A critical rhetoric may also include the articulation of an alternate policy, vision, or ideology. The Foundation for Deep Ecology urges such a vision, arguing that the basic economic and technological structures of society must change to the point that "the resulting state of affairs will be deeply different from the present" (Naess & Sessions, n.d.). And, advocates for Just Sustainability are initiating a critique of modern development, the burden of whose growth-oriented economies falls most heavily on the poor and disenfranchised. In arguing for a truly sustainable society, this critical rhetoric prioritizes justice and envisions "a better quality of life for all, now and into the future, in a just and equitable manner, whilst living within the limits of supporting ecosystem" (Agyeman, Bullard, & Evans, 2003, p. 5). As a result, critical rhetorics frequently serve to expand the range of social choices and visions that are eclipsed in the day-to-day political struggles of a campaign.

Although Just Sustainability advocates and the Foundation for Deep Ecology stated their criticisms of society in polite language, critical rhetorics also have gained attention as a result of sharp denunciation and not-so-decorous challenges to existing norms. Sometimes, this has taken the form of what communication scholars Robert Scott and Donald Smith (1969) originally termed *confrontational rhetoric,* the use of strident language, obscenity, and actions such as sit-ins and the occupation of buildings to critique racism, war, or exploitation of the environment. Despite the controversy often surrounding such rhetoric or actions, Scott and Smith urge us to take seriously the criticisms they raise. Sometimes, society's calls for "civility and decorum serve as masks for the preservation of injustice," they explain. "They become the instrumentalities of power for those who 'have'" (p. 7).

In the context of environmental advocacy, scholars of confrontational rhetoric have examined marches, demonstrations, sit-ins, and other visual rhetoric, as well as highly symbolic acts such as the destruction of logging equipment, SUVs, and animal research laboratories. Environmental communication scholar Kevin DeLuca (2005) has called these acts of destruction "ecotage" (p. 6).

Advocacy Campaigns

Although campaigns may advocate for major social changes, they differ from critical rhetorics in their approach. Most important, campaigns are organized around concrete, strategic actions that move us closer to those larger goals. In this sense, an **advocacy campaign** can be defined broadly as a strategic course of action, involving communication, which is undertaken for a specific purpose. That is, a campaign is waged to win a victory or bring about a concrete outcome; it therefore goes beyond simply questioning or criticism of a policy. This is an important point. For example, local citizens might question or criticize plans to build a toxic waste landfill in their neighborhood. A campaign, however, will go further; it might pursue the objective of blocking a permit for the construction of the landfill by organizing local residents, businesses, and church and synagogue leaders to call, visit, and lobby city council members who have the power to decide for or against the landfill's permit. The difference between a campaign and critical rhetoric, then, is not the goal (blocking the toxic landfill), but the strategic course of action by which a campaign pursues such goals.

In contemporary society, the advocacy campaign is a mode of communication used by many groups, agencies, and institutions for a wide range of purposes. In *information campaigns*, for example, the basic campaign form is used, among other purposes, to reduce health risks from smoking, promote family planning, encourage the use of designated drivers, and encourage people to conserve energy by properly inflating their tires or turning down their thermostats. Environmental advocacy campaigns share some characteristics of these information campaigns, and it is important to recognize these similarities before looking at their differences.

☞ FYI   Features of Campaigns

In their classic study of campaigns, Everett Rogers and Douglas Storey (1987) identified four features shared by most campaigns:

1. *A campaign is purposeful.* That is, "specific outcomes are intended to result from the communication efforts of a campaign" (p. 818).

2. *A campaign is aimed at a large audience.* A campaign's purpose usually requires an organized effort that goes beyond the interpersonal efforts of one or a few people to persuade another person or a small number of others.

(Continued)

(Continued)

3. *A campaign has a more or less specifically defined time limit.* A target audience's response to a campaign—a vote, a change in one's diet, or passage of a law, for example—should be made by some date, and the window for any further response will close.

4. *A campaign involves an organized set of communication activities.* The communication activities in a campaign are particularly evident in construction of the campaign's message.

SOURCE: Everett M. Rogers and Douglas D. Storey, "Communication Campaigns," in C. R. Berger & S. H. Chaffee (Eds.), *Handbook of Communication Science* (pp. 817–846). Newbury Park, CA: Sage, 1987.

Although they share these features with public health and other issue campaigns, environmental advocacy campaigns sometimes differ from them in basic ways. Two differences in particular stand out:

First, most campaigns that aim to reduce risk or influence individual behavior are *institutionally sponsored;* that is, they are initiated by a government health agency, the American Lung Association, United Nations, or a university. Environmental advocacy campaigns, on the other hand, are usually waged by *noninstitutional* sources—concerned individuals, environmental organizations, or small community action groups.

Second, most public relations (PR) and public health campaigns seek to change individuals' attitudes or behaviors (for example, personal lifestyle, consumer choices, diet, drug or alcohol use, or sexual practices) rather than broader changes in laws or corporate practices. Most environmental advocacy campaigns, on the other hand, seek to change *external conditions*—for example, the cleanup of an abandoned toxic waste site—or aim at more *systemic change,* that is, the policies or practices of a governmental or corporate body.

Campaigns draw upon several of the advocacy forms listed in Table 8.1. For example, many environmental advocacy campaigns will involve legislative and electoral politics; they also might engage in public education, community organizing, and corporate accountability campaigns. And, in Chapter 10, I'll illustrate corporations' use of different forms of advocacy—such as lobbying and *issue advertising*—in their campaigns to influence environmental legislation. The important idea is that a campaign may rely on multiple forms of advocacy as part of a strategic and time-limited course of action for a specific purpose.

From my own experience in the U.S. environmental movement, I've been convinced that campaigns are increasingly important in shaping public debate and decisions about environmental policy. Therefore, in the following sections, I will describe in more detail the basic design that many advocacy campaigns use. I'll also provide two examples of successful campaigns.

Environmental Advocacy Campaigns

By the time of the first Earth Day in 1970, the ecology movement had begun to change the way citizens communicated with public officials about the environment. Not content to rely simply on magazine articles or nature programs on television to educate the public, many environmental groups began to design advocacy campaigns to achieve specific changes. One architect of this new strategy was Michael McCloskey, the former executive director of the Sierra Club. In an interview, McCloskey reflected on his role in the environmental movement's turn to campaigns:

> What I have emphasized has been a serious approach toward achieving our ends. I thought that we were not here just to bear witness or to pledge allegiance to the faith, but in fact we were here to bring that faith into reality. . . . That means we could not rest content with having said the right things . . . but we also had to plan to achieve them. We had to know how the political system worked, how to identify the decision makers. . . . We had to have people concerned with all the practical details of getting our programs accomplished. (Gendlin, 1982, p. 41)

The shift described by McCloskey echoes the basic difference between critical rhetoric and a campaign, that is, between "having said the right things" and having "to plan to achieve them." Having a plan means that advocates will need to ask, "What do we need to do to implement a strategic course of action, involving communication, to achieve our purpose?" From my observations of successful campaigns in the past three decades,[1] I've found that environmental leaders usually ask themselves, and then attempt to answer, three fundamental questions:

(1) What exactly do you want to accomplish?

(2) Which decision makers have the ability to respond?

(3) What will persuade these decision makers to act on your objectives?

These three questions ask, respectively, about a campaign's (1) objectives, (2) audiences, and (3) strategies. (I will discuss each of these questions below.)

In answering these three questions, advocacy campaigns also pursue three corresponding **communication tasks**. First, effective campaigns seek to create broader support or demand for their objectives, whether the objective is to block construction of a hazardous waste incinerator or to get funds approved to build a bicycle path. Second, campaigns strive to mobilize this support from relevant constituencies (audiences) to demand accountability from decision makers. And, third, campaigns identify strategies to influence these decision makers to grant their objectives. Finally, it is important to be aware that campaigns take place in the context of other, competing voices and countercampaigns. Successful campaigns adapt their communication in this plural, ever-changing, communication environment.

In the remainder of this section, I describe these three questions and their corresponding communication tasks. (See Figure 8.1 for a model of the advocacy campaign.)

Creating Demand: Campaigns' Objectives

Successful advocacy campaigns require a clear-eyed focus on a concrete objective. For example, John Muir's preservation campaign to protect Yosemite Valley focused on the passage of a single bill in the U.S. Congress in 1890 that designated the mountains around Yosemite Valley as a national park. Thus, the first question in designing an advocacy campaign is about a group's objectives. It asks, first, "What exactly do you want to accomplish?"

Goals Versus Objectives

Campaigns flounder when their objectives are unclear or when they confuse a broad goal or vision with near-term, achievable, and specific actions or decisions. It is one thing to declare, "The United States should protect old-growth forests," and

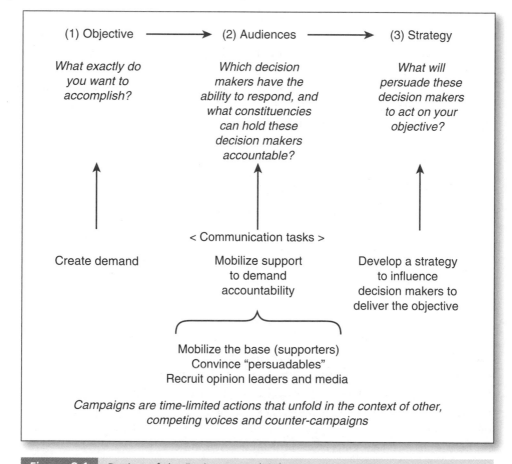

Figure 8.1   Design of the Environmental Advocacy Campaign

quite another to mobilize citizens to persuade the U.S. Forest Service to issue a specific ruling to halt the building of roads into these native forests. While stopping roads in national forests contributed to the broader goal of protecting America's wild lands, it is important to distinguish this objective from the broader effort that is presumably needed to protect permanently the remaining old-growth areas.

What, then, does it mean to answer the first question, "What exactly do you want to accomplish?" First, it is important to distinguish between a campaign's long-term *goals* and its specific *objectives*. As it is used here, the term **goal** refers to a long-term vision or value, such as the desire to protect old-growth forests, reduce arsenic in drinking water, or reduce the levels of greenhouse gases entering the atmosphere. Critical rhetorics are often important in articulating these broader visions, but they are not campaigns.

On the other hand, the term **objective** refers to a specific action, event, or decision that moves a group closer to its broader goal. An objective is a concrete and time-limited decision or action. For example, the Environmental Protection Agency (EPA) can issue a regulation imposing stricter limits on the number of parts per billion of arsenic allowed in drinking water. That's why the emphasis in this first question is to ask, "What exactly do you want?"

Most successful campaigns answer this question by identifying an objective that is a concrete, specific, and time-limited action or decision. Typical objectives from past campaigns have included the passage of a referendum in support of clean water bonds, a city council's vote for a zoning ordinance that banned hazardous waste facilities within 10 miles of a school, and a state utility commission decision to deny a permit for a coal-burning power plant. Each of these objectives—once achieved—furthered a broader goal but, in themselves, were concrete, achievable decisions or actions.

Creating a Public Demand

A campaign also has an important communication task to perform once it identifies its objective. It must create a broader *public demand* for its objective. A **public demand** is an active demonstration of support for the campaign's objective by key constituency groups, such as voters in a key swing district, families with small children, persons with respiratory problems, commuters, or members of a sports club. Although the American public generally supports clean air, clean water, and protection of natural resources, particular events and controversies often require the public's attention and active support. (As I cautioned earlier, other voices and constituencies may be competing for the same support.)

As a result, many environmental groups' training programs stress that the challenge of a campaign is to translate the public's passive support for environmental values into an active demand for action protecting those values (personal communication from Sierra Club training staff, January 6, 2009). Creating such a public demand requires persuading the public that there is a specific and imminent threat to an environmental value, ecosystem, or human community that will motivate people to demand that it be protected and to demonstrate their concern to key decision makers.

Figure 8.2	Among its communication tasks, an advocacy campaign seeks to create broader support for its objectives, whether to secure funds for clean energy or win approval to build a bicycle path.

© istockphoto.com/apatrimonio

Creating public demand forces a campaign to address a second core question, "Who has the ability to respond?" And that, in turn, suggests the relevant constituencies and supporters whom a campaign must educate and mobilize as part of its strategy.

Mobilizing Support

Once a campaign decides what exactly it wants to achieve, it must ask, second, "Which decision makers have the ability to respond?" In answering this question, campaign organizers must identify the decision makers who have the authority to act as well as relevant constituencies (audiences) who are able to hold these leaders accountable.

Primary Versus Secondary Audiences

Here, it is important to distinguish between two different types of audiences: (1) the *primary audience* is the decision maker who has the authority to act or implement the objectives of a campaign, and (2) the *secondary audiences* (also called *public audiences*) are the various segments of the public, coalition partners, opinion leaders, and news media; the support of these constituencies is often pivotal in holding a primary audience or decision maker accountable for the campaign's objectives.

A campaign cannot achieve an objective until someone with the ability or authority to decide on the objective responds favorably. This decision maker is a campaign's primary audience. For example, if the campaign's objective is to prohibit flashing (digital) billboards along state highways, then the primary audience is most likely to be the members of the state legislature's budget or commerce committee. On the other hand, if a campaign wants tighter regulation of emissions of mercury from coal-burning power plants, then the primary audience will be the EPA, which administers the Clean Air Act.

Mobilizing Constituencies

Once a campaign has answered the second question, it faces an important communication task: Campaigns must, first, identify and then mobilize the support of relevant constituencies who can help to influence the primary audience or decision maker. The ability to fulfill this second task assumes that decision makers, in fact, are ultimately accountable to voters, the media, or other groups. (This assumption goes to the heart of democratic politics and is, itself, a subject of much debate.) On the other hand, some decision makers may not be public officeholders and hence may be less susceptible to being held accountable by others. (For example, movements generally find it hard to influence corporate behavior, which is not directly accountable to the public constituencies.)

In mobilizing the support of relevant constituencies to hold decision makers accountable, it is useful to distinguish between the media and opinion leaders, on one hand, and members of the general public, on the other. Opinion leaders are those whose statements often are influential with the media and members of the primary audience. For example, the Natural Resources Defense Council relies upon the well-known environmentalist Robert F. Kennedy, Jr. in many of its campaigns, while a local environmental group may turn to a respected member of that community—a business, sports, or religious leader—to speak for the group publicly.

When campaigns turn to the public, they distinguish among three types of audiences: (1) the campaign's **base** (its core supporters and potential coalition partners), (2) *opponents,* and (3) **persuadables,** members of the public who are undecided but potentially sympathetic to a campaign's objectives. Normally, a campaign does not try to persuade its opponents as they are committed already to their own objectives. But persuadables constitute the heart of a campaign's communication because they often make the difference in the outcome of the campaign.

It's important to note that, although persuadables may be potential supporters of a campaign, they may be undecided or unmotivated by its objectives at first. This appeared to be the case with the Sierra Club's Beyond Coal campaign (http://beyond coal.org). Residents, parents, and others in local communities were initially unaware of the impacts of coal plant emissions, either on their families' health or the global climate. Nevertheless, the Beyond Coal campaign viewed them as potentially open to information about the campaign's objective and, hence, were ultimately persuaded to attend public hearings about coal plant permits.

Therefore, a campaign answers the second question by mobilizing a network of supporters—particularly its base and persuadable audiences, opinion leaders, and the media—until sufficient resources are mobilized for the campaign. At this point, successful campaigns usually seek to align public support with a plan to influence the primary decision maker(s). Campaigns therefore ask, "What strategy is most likely to persuade this primary audience to act on the group's objective?"

Developing a Strategy to Influence Decision Makers

The third question a campaign answers is, "What will persuade these decision makers to act on your objective?" This is a quintessential question about strategy. Strategy can be a surprisingly slippery concept, and it is often confused with a campaign's tactics, so let's look more closely at this important term.

Strategy Versus Tactics

Environmental educator David Orr (1992) once said that questions about strategy land us squarely in the realm of *praxis,* the study of efficient action or the best means to achieve an objective. Whereas critical rhetorics may help us to imagine a desired future, a campaign goes further and asks, "How do we actually get to this future?" Answering this is the heart of strategy.

The idea of strategy can be confusing, so it might be best to begin with a definition and an example. Simply defined, a **strategy** is a critical source of influence or *leverage* to persuade a primary decision maker to act on a campaign's objective. Sometimes, the specific actions of a campaign—lobbying, protests, and so forth—are mistaken for strategy. These are tactics and not the wider leverage a campaign may be using. **Tactics** are the concrete acts that carry out or implement the broader strategy.

An interesting example of a strategy is the leverage used by environmental and health groups to persuade McDonald's to change its food purchasing policies. In 2003, the fast-food chain acknowledged that the use of growth-stimulating antibiotics by large factory farms that raise and sell poultry and beef threatens human health. Many scientists believe that overuse of growth hormones in animals encourages the development of resistant strains of bacteria that may affect human immunity to disease. In its 2003 announcement, McDonald's agreed to phase out its purchase of poultry raised in this manner; this added pressure to the poultry industry to begin to change its practices. (The company's agreement was less specific for hogs and cattle.) (Greider, 2003, p. 8).

What brought about this change not only at McDonald's but in the practices of some of the nation's largest providers of meat products? In the McDonald's case, a coalition of 13 environmental, religious, and public health organizations, including Environmental Defense, the Humane Society, and National Catholic Rural Life Conference, did not rely upon a campaign to target public officials; rather, they made innovative use of market forces. Their campaign pursued a strategy that drew on the power of consumers to change industry behavior, "not by one purchase at a time, but on a grand scale by targeting large brands in the middleman position" (Greider, 2003, p. 8). That is, they chose to influence the behavior of the meat industry by targeting one of the largest purchasers of its products: McDonald's.

Journalist William Greider (2003) closely studied the shift in strategy that occurred in this campaign. He observed that traditional, buy green campaigns that rely on individual consumer purchases have had an exceedingly modest effect on corporate practices. "What has changed is an essential strategic insight" (p. 10). He explained:

> Consumers are in a weak position and have very little actual leverage over the content of what they buy or how it is produced.... Instead of browbeating individual consumers, new reform campaigns focus on the structure of industry itself and attempt to leverage entire sectors. The activists identify and target the larger corporate "consumers" who buy an industrial sector's output and sell it at retail under popular brand names. They can't stand the heat so easily, since they regularly proclaim that the customer is king. When one of these big names folds to consumer pressure, it sends a tremor through the supplier base, much as McDonald's has. (p. 10)

In the case of McDonald's, the campaign's strategy sought to use the purchasing power of the fast-food giant itself rather than individual consumers to influence the poultry industry. By targeting the famous brand and familiar logo of this global icon, the campaign was able to leverage the buying power of McDonald's to influence the behavior of its suppliers. If the factory farms that sold meat products to McDonald's wanted to continue to do business, they would have to reduce their use of growth hormones in poultry and perhaps in other animals as well.

The campaign to persuade McDonald's and the poultry industry also clearly illustrates the difference between strategy and tactics. In this case, strategy, as a source of influence or leverage, was the use of a powerful corporation's brand and buying power to affect the meat industry's decisions about the use of growth hormones in chicken. The tactics that carried out this strategy included the materials distributed to McDonald's, meetings with company officials, organizing of protests outside the restaurants, and so forth. Each of these was important, but their critical function was to implement the wider strategy—using the vulnerability of McDonald's brand to public pressure and, subsequently, its purchasing power to affect changes in the meat industry.

Strategy is often the weak link of a campaign, and it is often overlooked. When its strategy is unclear, a campaign often suffers as a result. In his discussion of this problem, Orr (1992) recalled the cartoon shown as Figure 8.3, which appeared in the journal *American Scientist*. The cartoon shows a scientist who, in balancing an equation on the chalkboard, has inserted this curious step: "then a miracle occurs." Orr observed, "Most strategies of social change have similar dependence on the miraculous" (p. 61).

Political theorist Douglas Torgerson (1999) has claimed that a dependence on the miraculous is particularly true of environmental strategies. He argued that a simple, although cynical assumption sometimes underlies green strategic thought. It assumes, "Environmental problems are sure to get worse . . . and when they do,

"I think you should be more explicit here in step two."

| Figure 8.3 | A miracle needed? |

Reprinted with permission from Sidney Harris, © www.ScienceCartoonsPlus.com

more and more people will be moved to join the green cause, thus enhancing its power and its chance of making a real difference" (p. 22). Torgerson believed that such an assumption borders on belief in the miraculous. I agree. Environmental campaigns more often succeed when they identify a source of influence or leverage that is able to affect a larger power or decision maker. Exercising that leverage, rather than waiting for a miracle, is the meaning of strategy. Let's look at a creative example of such leverage in environmentalists' campaigns to stop coal-burning power plants.

Strategy as Leverage: Stopping the Coal Rush

Since 2007, growing numbers of citizens and public health and environmental groups have succeeded at the local level in blocking, delaying, or cancelling permits for coal-fired power plants, one of the principal sources of global CO_2 emissions. At the start of 2007, the U.S. Department of Energy had announced that more than 150 new coal-fired plants were being proposed; yet that year alone, "59 of those proposed plants were either refused licenses by state governments or quietly abandoned" (Brown, 2008). As I write in 2011, almost all new coal-burning power plants proposed in the United States have been delayed or halted; recently, electric utility companies have announced plans to close a number of their existing coal plants.

| Figure 8.4 | Since 2007, coalitions of citizens and public health and environmental groups have succeeded in blocking, delaying, or canceling numerous coal-fired power plants, a principal source of global carbon dioxide emissions. |

Kim Steele/Photodisc/Thinkstock

The movement to go Beyond Coal, as some call it, has had real consequences for the U.S. energy economy. The cancellation of coal-burning power plants has begun to signal an increased risk for the sources—capital markets—that underwrite our carbon-based energy economy, and this, in turn, has had the potential to shift greater investments toward other, renewable energy sources. But, this outcome has not happened by chance. It was, at least partly, due to a strategic choice by environmental groups in designing their campaigns. Let me explain.

Construction of a new coal-fired power plant is expensive. Usually, the energy company borrows large amounts of private capital to build the plant. As a result, the slowing or cancellations of permits to build plants has particular meaning in this sector. Investment firms may have to wait longer for a return; their capital is tied up. Environmental groups, therefore, saw an opportunity to affect the flow of these investments to other, cleaner energy sources; that is, by delaying or halting the permits of individual coal plants, they might be able to alter (leverage) what signals were being sent to capital markets, for example, that coal plants are a risky investment.

There is some evidence the Beyond Coal strategy had begun to have an effect. In 2008, three of the nation's largest investment firms—Citigroup, Morgan Stanley, and J.P. Morgan Chase & Co.—announced they were imposing new requirements for financing construction that "will make it harder for companies to build coal-fired power plants in the U.S." (Ball, 2008, 1). Such stricter rules, in turn, sent a further, "potent signal to the energy sector that it views dirty coal as [a] shaky financial [prospect] and that the smart money is heading toward cleaner, more sustainable energy options" (Beinecke, 2008, 1). Ultimately, environmentalists hope, this has the potential, amplified by the continuing efforts of multiple, local battles over coal permits, to build an agenda for a more comprehensive shift in energy policy in the United States.

A Campaign's Message

Finally, in designing its strategy, a campaign also has an important communication task. This is the identification of the appropriate educational and persuasive messages, spokespersons, materials, and media for communicating with the campaign's primary audience of decision makers and the campaign's supporters. These materials help to mobilize the campaign's base and also convince its persuadable audiences, opinion leaders, and media to help persuade the primary audience to act on the campaign's objective. For example, in the McDonald's campaign, supporters circulated scientific research on the overuse of antibiotics in farm animals, made persuasive appeals to consumers to protest outside McDonald's restaurants, issued reports to the news media, and briefed officials at McDonald's corporate headquarters.

An important element of a campaign's strategic communication is its message. As developed by many advocacy groups, a **message** is usually a phrase or sentence that concisely expresses a campaign's objective and the values at stake in the goals it seeks. Although campaigns develop considerable information and arguments, the message itself is usually short, compelling, and memorable and accompanies all of a campaign's communication materials. Messages from the world of advertising are familiar to us for this reason: "Imagination at work" (General Electric), "The Real Thing" (Coca-Cola), and "The ultimate driving machine" (BMW). A message is not the complete communication, of course, but it opens the door of attention from a target audience to a campaign's other materials.

Messages are only one part of a campaign's communication, but they serve an important purpose. Messages summarize a campaign's objective, state its central values, and provide a frame for audiences' understanding and reception of the details of its other informational materials. In developing such messages, campaigns often attempt to identify values and language that resonate with their base and persuadables—those sympathetic to their objectives but undecided. Because the choice of a message is so important to advocacy campaigns, I will return to this topic and the role of values in mobilizing supporters later in this chapter.

In summary, advocacy campaigns usually succeed by building public demand for a concrete, achievable objective, by mobilizing support, and by identifying a strategy to hold public officials, corporations, or other decision makers accountable for this objective. When they are designed well, advocacy campaigns have several advantages over simple protests or critical rhetorics:

- By planning a strategic course of action, campaigns increase the chances of achieving their objectives.
- Campaigns draw on the collective strength of people and resources for both planning and implementing a course of action.
- Campaigns serve as intermediaries between individuals in their private lives and the large, often impersonal, institutions of public life.

Each of the core elements of an environmental advocacy campaign was demonstrated by a coalition of Native Americans, religious groups, and environmental groups in their campaign to oppose plans for a massive coal strip mine near a sacred tribal lake in New Mexico. Let's look at this successful campaign in more depth.

The Campaign to Protect Zuni Salt Lake

On August 4, 2003, the Salt River Project (SRP), the third-largest electric power company in the United States, announced it was dropping plans for a coal mine located near the Zuni Salt Lake in western New Mexico. The company's announcement was a victory for a coalition of Native American tribes, environmental and religious groups, and the Zuni people themselves who waged a multiyear campaign to protect the sacred Zuni Salt Lake and surrounding lands from mining and other environmental threats.

I use this example because it clearly illustrates the three core elements of design that campaigns must consider: (1) a clear *objective*, (2) a clearly identified *decision maker*, and (3) a *strategy* to persuade the primary decision maker to act on this objective. The Zuni Salt Lake campaign also illustrates the ability of a small group, working with allies and coalition partners, to use the principles of an advocacy campaign to achieve an important objective—safeguarding a sacred, tribal site.

Zuni Salt Lake and a Coal Mine

The SRP company's plans called for strip-mining more than 80 million tons of coal from 18,000 acres of federal, state, and private lands. (Strip-mining is the removal of surface land to expose the underlying coal seams.) To settle the coal dust from strip-mining, SRP planned to pump 85 gallons of water per minute from underground aquifers (Valtin, 2003). The New Mexico Department of Energy, Minerals, and Natural Resources had granted permits for the company to begin construction of the mine in 1996, although work did not immediately begin. By June 22, 2001, opposition to the mine had grown.

To the Zunis and area tribes, the Salt Lake is sacred. It is home to the Zunis' deity *Ma'l Oyattsik'i*, the Salt Mother, who, Zunis believe, has provided salt for centuries for tribal religious ceremonies. (In dry season, the water evaporates, leaving behind salt flats, which is the source of salt for the Zunis and neighboring tribes.)

The region surrounding the Zuni Salt Lake is known as the Sanctuary or *A:shiwi A:wan Ma'k'yay'a dap an'ullapna Dek'ohannan Dehyakya Dehwanne*. It has burial grounds and other sacred sites and is laced with trails that are used by the Zunis, Navajos, Acomas, Hopis, Lagunas, Apaches, and other Southwestern tribes to reach the Zuni Salt Lake. By tradition, the Sanctuary is a neutral zone where warring tribes put their weapons down and share in the gathering of "the salt which embodies the flesh of the Salt Mother herself" (Sacred Land Film Project, 2003, p. 1).

The strip mine would have been located in the heart of the Sanctuary, 10 miles from Zuni Salt Lake. Although the mine itself would not be on Zuni land, tribal leaders feared that the company's plans to pump large volumes of groundwater from the same desert aquifer that feeds the Salt Lake would dry up the lake. Malcolm Bowekaty, former Zuni Pueblo governor, told reporters, "If they vent a lot of pressure that's forcing the water up, we will no longer have the salt" (Valtin, 2003, p. 3).

A Coalition's Campaign

By 2001, Zuni leaders had assembled a coalition that would work together to protect Zuni Salt Lake and the Sanctuary. For two days, the group met informally in the kitchen of a Zuni leader to design a two-year advocacy campaign plan.[2] On November 30, 2001, leaders from the Zuni tribe, Water Information Network, Center for Biological Diversity, Citizens Coal Council, Tonatierra (an indigenous group), Friends of the Earth, Sierra Club, and Seventh Generation Fund for Indian Development publicly announced the formation of the Zuni Salt Lake Coalition. In what follows, I describe how this campaign embodied the core elements of an advocacy campaign.

Campaign Objectives: Creating Demand

From the beginning, the Zuni Salt Lake Coalition saw its long-term goal as to "get SRP to drop its plans for the Fence Lake Coal Mine [and to] protect Zuni Salt Lake for the long-term" (Zuni Salt Lake Coalition, 2001). More immediately, the coalition was faced with the prospect of SRP's imminent preparation of the mine site, including plans to drill into the Dakota Aquifer that fed Zuni Salt Lake.

Therefore, the coalition identified two immediate objectives: (1) to "make sure that SRP does not tap Dakota Aquifer," and (2) persuade the State of New Mexico and the Department of the Interior to deny the permits needed to open the coal mine; if these permits were granted, then the objective would be to appeal these decisions in order to delay actual construction of the mine (Zuni Salt Lake Coalition, 2001). Coalition members felt that, if they were successful in achieving either of these two objectives, they could persuade SRP, in turn, to cancel its plans for the project.

Audiences: Mobilizing Support to Demand Accountability

The Zuni Salt Lake Coalition identified two sets of primary decision makers. Ultimately, they sought to persuade SRP officials to withdraw plans for the coal mine. Related to this goal and the campaign's two more concrete objectives, the coalition targeted the Department of the Interior and New Mexico officials who oversaw the state's permitting process.

Key to influencing these decision makers was the Zuni Salt Lake Coalition's ability to mobilize support from the appropriate constituencies to hold the primary decision makers accountable for their actions. Holding a powerful utility company accountable may seem unrealistic. SRP officials were not publicly elected; therefore, they were unaffected by voters. Nevertheless, the coalition believed that the company's credibility and ability to secure cooperation (including its permits) depended on a number of constituencies, including public officials, opinion leaders, and the media, and that some of these groups could be mobilized.

At the start, the coalition had to reach out to its base—the Zuni people themselves and their allies among area tribes. In addition, it targeted several persuadable groups—area churches, environmental groups, and people of faith generally (Zuni Salt Lake Coalition, 2001). In turn, support from these groups would draw support from opinion leaders, the media, and ultimately, key elected officials.

In creating a public demand for its objectives, and for mobilizing secondary audiences, the coalition developed communication materials that drew on several sources of persuasion. Especially relevant to mobilizing its base and other key supporters, the coalition highlighted: (a) the spiritual and cultural values associated with the Zuni Salt Lake, the Zuni tribe's history, and the indigenous cultures of this region; and (b) an appeal to the *irreparable* nature of threats to the Zuni Salt Lake. Elsewhere, I've defined the **irreparable** as a warning to act before it is too late (Cox, 1982, 2001). Such a forewarning identifies: (a) something that is unique or rare and therefore of great value; (b) the existence of which is threatened or precarious; (c) its loss or destruction cannot be reversed; (d) therefore, action to protect it is timely or urgent.

The campaign materials developed by the coalition reflected these persuasive appeals. For the area's indigenous peoples, the Zuni Salt Lake and nearby Sanctuary are very powerful places. Zuni Council Member Arden Kucate reminded the coalitions' supporters of these values when he warned of the challenge before them: "We have to start thinking in the traditional way. It is not the earth, it is Mother Earth. Zuni people will not sacrifice our Salt Woman for cheap coal to serve Arizona or California, because she is irreplaceable" (LaDuke, 2002).

Finally, the Zuni Salt Lake Coalition reached out to other secondary audiences. Most important, the campaign used the growing support of tribal and public constituencies to gain the attention of news media and to enlist the support of public officials in New Mexico. The importance of these groups will become clearer as I describe the coalition's strategy.

Strategy: Influencing the Primary Decision Makers

Given its goal to persuade SRP officials to withdraw their plans for the mine, the Zuni Salt Lake Coalition decided the best strategy would be to raise the costs to the company as it pursued permits for the mine. At its very first meeting, the coalition pledged to hold SRP accountable by making "it so hard for them [SRP officials] that they want to drop it. Make them feel that the Fence Lake project is a fruitless effort" (Zuni Salt Lake Coalition, 2001). This core strategy, to raise the costs to SRP, would guide subsequent decisions and activities of the coalition.

Specifically, the coalition sought ways to influence SRP and the federal officials responsible for issuing the mine's permits (a) by introducing scientific evidence of the ecological effects on the Zuni Salt Lake of pumping water from the aquifer and (b) by launching an aggressive outreach to opinion leaders, news media, and New Mexico public officials. By organizing around these actions, the coalition intended to place continual roadblocks in SRP's path and thereby raise the costs to SRP, increasing the pressure on the company to cancel its plans for the coal mine.

The first element of the coalition's strategy was to introduce evidence of environmental damage to Zuni Salt Lake as a basis for challenging the state and federal permits that had been issued.[3] New research was a critical part of the effort to hold the Department of Interior accountable to the National Environmental Policy Act (NEPA) requirement for an environmental impact statement. (I described the importance of NEPA in Chapter 4.) For example, the coalition argued that "every hydrological study, except SRP's own, shows that this pumping will detrimentally affect the lake" (Zuni Salt Lake Coalition, 2003). Based on its hydrological information (pumping tests), the coalition requested that Interior conduct a supplemental environmental impact study. Similarly, it appealed the state's water permit pending completion of further pumping tests on the aquifer.

Also, the threat to file a challenge also to Interior's failure to consider possible impacts of pumping water from the underground aquifers promised to add delay and therefore more costs to SRP's plans to start construction of the coal mine.

The Zuni Coalition also turned to a second element of its strategy—an aggressive outreach to the news media and New Mexico public officials. In part, this was to respond directly to SRP's counterpublicity. It was also to supplement the coalition's work on the permits by keeping the threat to Zuni Salt Lake before the wider public. From the outset of the campaign, the coalition members sought creative ways to keep the issue alive.

At the heart of this strategy were efforts to generate "lots of publicity" (Zuni Salt Lake Coalition, 2001). From 2001 to 2003, the Zuni Salt Lake campaign generated thousands of letters to newspapers, public officials, and allied groups. It placed multilanguage ads on local radio stations and sent traditional runners from Zuni Pueblo to SRP's corporate headquarters in Phoenix. The coalition publicized resolutions of support from other tribal councils and from the New Mexico Conference of Churches, and it mounted two *fax attacks*—deluges of fax messages—to the Department of the Interior to urge delays in its approval of the permits. Finally, the coalition won the National Trust for Historic Preservation's listing of the area as one of America's most endangered places (Victory, 2003, p. 6).

Communication Message

In all of its communication materials, the campaign reiterated its basic message: "SRP Is Targeting Our Sacred Lands. Save Zuni Salt Lake." The campaign also adapted this message in speaking to key secondary audiences—church members and people of faith. Particularly in the American Southwest, many people are sensitive to the historical mistreatment of Native Americans. One example of an appeal based on these sensitivities was a postcard that supporters mailed to the SRP president, emphasizing respect for sacred sites and the irreparable nature of the potential harm to Zuni Salt Lake. The text of the postcard read: "People of faith don't want any sacred areas to be desecrated by a strip mine . . . for cheap electricity from dirty coal: Not the Vatican, not Mecca, not Temple Square in Salt Lake City . . . and not Zuni Salt Lake."

One of the campaign's creative ways of getting out its message was a truck with space on its panel side. Valtin (2003) reports that, after companies in Phoenix refused to accept the coalition's billboard ad, organizers contacted a mobile company that placed the billboard on the side of its truck. The billboard had a large photo of Zuni Salt Lake with a rifle's crosshairs on it, and it prominently displayed the campaign's message, "SRP Is Targeting Our Sacred Lands. Save Zuni Salt Lake" (see Figure 8.5). Coalition organizer Andy Bessler recalled, "We drove the truck around SRP headquarters and all over Arizona and New Mexico to tribal pueblos, and we got a lot of people to sign petitions" (quoted in Valtin, 2003, p. 3).

| **Figure 8.5** | Members of the Zuni Salt Lake Coalition pose beside the mobile billboard truck used in their campaign. |

Photo courtesy of the Zuni Salt Lake Coalition

In an effort to keep the threat to Zuni Salt Lake before the public, the campaign also sought creative ways to generate coverage by the news media. Bessler explained:

> Tribal members have a different approach, which made us think "outside the box." Where the Sierra Club might air a radio spot to convey our message, the Zuni suggested sending runners. And where we did run radio ads, we had scripts in English, Spanish, Zuni, Navajo, Hopi, and Apache so the spots could run on tribal radio stations as well as on mainstream stations in Phoenix and Albuquerque. (quoted in Valtin, 2003, p. 3)

Examples of such thinking "outside the box" included the use of traditional runners from Zuni Pueblo to SRP's corporate headquarters in Phoenix to generate public pressure for the power company to withdraw its plans for the coal mine. Another example, on July 19, 2003, was the campaign's scheduling of a people's hearing on Zuni Salt Lake in Zuni Pueblo. The event included the showing of a video, updates on the campaign, and a people's hearing. More than 500 people attended the informal public hearing and offered their own testimony. "At the conclusion of the hearing, the sky opened up and let loose a torrential downpour, which the Zuni took as a blessing from heaven" (Valtin, 2003, p. 1).

The campaign's effort to frame news coverage (Chapter 6) of the controversy as a struggle over spiritual and ecological values began to pay dividends. In July 2003, the entire U.S. Congressional delegation from New Mexico sent a letter to Secretary of the Interior Gale Norton, asking her to stop the mining permit until new studies of the aquifer could be completed. Their letter also announced that they were planning to bring a lawsuit under NEPA if the department refused to prepare a supplemental environmental impact statement. The prospect of a federal lawsuit threatened to delay SRP's plans even further, carrying out the campaign's strategy of making it "so hard for them that they want to drop" plans for the strip mine.

Success for Zuni Salt Lake

On August 4, 2003, SRP announced that the company had canceled its plans for the coal mine and would also relinquish its permits and the coal leases it had acquired for the mine. This was a rare victory for indigenous peoples and environmental groups, as such development projects usually proceed, and it is one of the reasons that study of this campaign is noteworthy.

After the announcement by SRP, Zuni Tribal Councilman Arden Kucate led a delegation to the edge of Zuni Salt Lake to pray and to make an offering of turquoise and bread to *Ma'l Oyattsik'i*, the Salt Mother. Back at Zuni Pueblo, the tribe's Head Councilman Carlton Albert expressed his feelings of relief and appreciation to coalition partners who had worked with the Zuni Salt Lake campaign: "It has been a long 20 year struggle . . . but we have had our voices heard. . . . If there is a lesson to be learned it is to never give up and [to] stay focused on what you want to accomplish" (Seciwa, 2003, p. 2).

**Design an Environmental Advocacy
Campaign for Your Campus or Community**

Recently, students at my campus—the University of North Carolina (UNC) at Chapel Hill—and
other campuses across the United States have succeeded in persuading their universities to
forgo or end their reliance on coal-burning power plants on their campuses. These victories
were the result of their well-planned advocacy campaigns, and they have placed their universities on a path to alternative, clean energy sources and conservation measures that will
lower energy use.

What is one important step that your own campus or community can take to support
environmental values? Convert the university's fleet of cars and trucks to biofuels? Reduce
the use of paper? Disinvest or sell stock shares in companies that have poor environmental
performance?

Working with a small group, design an advocacy campaign plan to pursue a specific
objective (for example, the UNC students proposed that their chancellor commit to phasing
out the use of coal in generating energy by the year 2020). How would you answer the following core questions about this campaign?

1. What *exactly* do you want to accomplish?

2. Who has the ability to respond?

3. What will influence this person or authority to respond?

What groups are likely to be your base of support? Who will be your coalition partners?
Who are your persuadables? What message and other communication materials would be
required to perform the related communication tasks of creating demand, mobilizing support to hold decision makers accountable, and designing a course of action to influence
these authorities?

As an exercise in designing a campaign, work with several friends or classmates to draft
a proposal to submit to a group that is interested in pursuing such a campaign.

Message Construction

The Zuni Salt Lake campaign succeeded in mobilizing area tribes, churches, elected
officials, and others whose support was critical to the campaign. Yet, this is not always
possible. In some cases, advocates may succeed in changing audiences' beliefs or attitudes but fail to mobilize them or change their behaviors. This disconnection between
one's beliefs or attitudes, on the one hand, and their behaviors, on the other, is called
the *attitude–behavior gap* and is a major challenge facing advocacy campaigns.

In this final section, therefore, I describe the attitude–behavior gap and the question that environmental campaigns must address: How can advocates construct messages or persuasive appeals that will mobilize or influence their audiences' behaviors?
In answering this question, campaigns usually do two things: (1) They identify the

important values related to the campaign's goals, and (2) they frame the campaign's messages in light of these values. I'll describe each of these steps and look at examples of successful campaign messages.

The Attitude–Behavior Gap and the Importance of Values

The Attitude–Behavior Gap

Public concern about environmental issues has grown in the past decades in the United States. People generally have high regard for environmental amenities such as clean air and water, chemical-free food, parks, and open space. Yet, these attitudes are not always a good prediction of what people do or the actions they take. Literary critic Stanley Fish (2008) provides a self-confessed example of this attitude–behavior gap:

> Now don't get me wrong. I am wholly persuaded by the arguments in support of the practices I resist. I believe that recycling is good and that disposable paper products are bad. I believe in global warming. . . . But it is possible to believe something and still resist taking the actions your belief seems to require. (I believe that seat belts save lives, but I never wear them, even on airplanes.) I know that in the great Book of Environmentalism my name will be on the page reserved for serial polluters. But I just can't get too worked up about it. (para. 9)

Social scientists who study environmental campaigns call this phenomenon the **attitude–behavior gap** (Kollmuss & Agyeman, 2002). The gap refers to the fact that, although individuals may have favorable attitudes or beliefs about environmental issues, they may not take any action. Individuals may believe recycling is good or global warming is real but do nothing to change their behaviors (e.g., recycle, drive a fuel-efficient car). Their attitudes, therefore, are disconnected from their behaviors. For example, Moser (2010) reports that, while many individuals believe global warming is real and happening now, they may not feel any urgency to change their own behaviors or speak out. This gap is also seen in consumer behavior. For example, research by OgilvyEarth (2011) found a "green gap" in Americans' buying behavior; while "82% of Americans have good green intentions . . . only 16% are dedicated to fulfilling these intentions" (para. 3).

The difficulty in changing people's behavior has been a concern recently in public education campaigns to persuade consumers to take steps to save energy or install energy-efficient appliances in their homes. Local utility companies and the U.S. government have expended enormous time and energy in recent years trying to improve energy efficiency in homes and businesses, often with limited success. A study by researchers at the Lawrence Berkeley National Laboratory found that changing individuals' energy consumption behaviors has proven difficult. Merrian Fuller, an author of the Berkeley study, explained, "Convincing millions of Americans to divert their time and resources into upgrading their homes to eliminate energy waste, avoid high utility bills and help stimulate the economy is one of the great challenges facing energy efficiency programs around the country" (quoted in Mandel, 2010, para. 8). (I'll return to recommendations of this study below.)

One of the reasons campaigns often fail is that they assume that providing information—educating people—is enough. Simply knowing that better insulation in our attics will save us money on our energy bills is usually not enough to persuade us to purchase (and install) higher R-rated (energy-efficient) insulation. The reason, Fuller explained, is that, when public education campaigns "address the issue of energy efficiency benefits, they . . . neglect the issue of *how to motivate consumers* to take advantage of home energy upgrade programs" (quoted in Mandel, 2010, para. 9; emphasis added).

Campaigns do succeed (sometimes) in persuading people to change their behaviors, or they succeed in mobilizing their supporters, as we saw in the example of the Zuni Salt Lake campaign. Although many factors are involved, an important component in successful campaigns is the construction of messages that are framed in terms of values that are important to those the campaign is aiming to reach.

Values and Proenvironment Behavior

Clearly, our attitudes are related to our behavior in some way. The point is that there is not always a strong causal relationship; that is, our beliefs or attitudes often do not directly influence our behaviors. In fact, research in this area finds it is our behavior that often influences our attitudes and not the other way (Rose & Dade, 2007). (We sometimes call this *rationalizing*.) Because behavior is generally a strong determinant of peoples' attitudes, advocacy campaigns cannot influence behavior changes only by trying to change our attitudes toward something.

On the other hand, peoples' values do influence their behavior. Indeed, there is a great deal of evidence that proenvironmental behaviors are related to certain values (Crompton, 2008; Schultz & Zelezny 2003). For this reason, some social change strategists are urging a rethinking of advocacy campaigns to take into greater account the role of values. (See, for example, *Weathercocks and Signposts* at wwf.org.uk/strategies forchange.) Let's look, therefore, at the different types of values that advocacy campaigns sometimes consider in their messages.

Recent research suggests that there are three broad categories of values associated with environmental behaviors:

1. Egoistic concerns focusing on the self (e.g., health, quality of life, prosperity, convenience)

2. Social–altruistic concerns focusing on other people (e.g., children, family, community, humanity)

3. Biospheric concerns focusing on the well-being of living things (e.g., plants, animals, trees) (Farrior, 2005, p. 11; see also Stern, Dietz, & Kalof, 1993)

Some people may be concerned about water pollution because of the dangers to themselves (for example, "I don't want to drink polluted water"). Others may be motivated by social–altruistic concerns about their children or communities ("I don't want my children to drink polluted water"). For example, an ad by the Sierra Club urged parents to take simple steps to help curb greenhouse gases by appealing to social–altruistic concerns. The ad included a photo of television and film star Eva La Rue holding her young daughter Kaya and this message:

> Our kids are counting on us to help protect their world. Scientists say that we can curb the most dangerous effects of global warming if we cut our carbon emissions by 80% by the year 2050. That's an achievable 2% reduction a year—the 2% Solution! LEARN WHAT YOU CAN DO, VISIT www.sierraclub.org/twopercent.

Finally, others may be concerned about the effects of polluted water on plants and animals; that is, they are motivated by wider, biospheric concerns.

An international survey of values among college students found that social–altruistic values rated the highest. The survey, however, found that students in different countries differed about the importance of other values. In the United States, a majority rated egoistic concerns higher than biospheric; students in Latin American countries, however, placed biospheric concerns higher than egoistic (Schultz & Zelezny, 2003, pp. 129–130). The researchers concluded, "A person who scores high on self-enhancement will care about environmental problems when the problem affects them directly" (p. 130).

This finding presents an interesting dilemma for some advocates in choosing the values they'll use in their campaign's messages. For example, in arguing for the value of wilderness, the radical group Earth First! (2011) rejects all self-interested rationales for wilderness, such as recreation or medicines from native plants. Instead, the group voices a clear, biospheric value in its messaging. In stating there should be "No Compromise in Defense of Mother Earth," the group explains:

> Guided by a philosophy of deep ecology, Earth First! does not accept a human-centered worldview of "nature for people's sake." Instead, we believe that life exists for its own sake, that industrial civilization and its philosophy are anti-Earth, anti-woman and anti-liberty. . . . To put it simply, the Earth must come first. (paras. 5–6)

Earth First!, therefore, faces a dilemma: Can it appeal to biospheric values and still gain a hearing from those it must persuade? Or, must wilderness advocates appeal to the egoistic concerns of individuals or to their social–altruistic values to gain a hearing and begin to mobilize support from a wider public?

Responses to the dilemma about values have varied. Canadian environmental studies scholar Neil Evernden (1985) has offered the classic defense of biospheric concerns. In *The Natural Alien,* Evernden warned that persuasion based on self-interest ("What is useful to me?") is shortsighted and dangerous: "By basing all arguments on enlightened self-interest . . . environmentalists have ensured their own failure whenever self-interest can be perceived as lying elsewhere" (p. 10). Evernden cautioned, "As soon as [a mountain]'s worth is greater as tin cans than as scenery, the case for the mountain vanishes" (p. 11).

On the other hand, the Biodiversity Project (Farrior, 2005) has recommended, based on the Schultz and Zelezny research (above), that campaigns in support of biodiversity be based on "messages that address socio–altruistic concerns or make biodiversity relevant to everyday life" (p. 11). The key is "targeting audiences and using a 'diversity of messages that will appeal to people with a different range of value orientation' " (Farrior, 2005, p. 11, quoting Schultz & Zelezny, 2003, p. 134).

As the Biodiversity Project makes clear, a campaign must choose values that potentially motivate or influence an audience, and it does this in the construction of its message.

Message Construction: Values and Framing

As I noted earlier in this chapter, a campaign's strategy has an important communication task—the identification of the appropriate educational and persuasive messages, spokespersons, and media for communicating with the campaign's supporters and primary audience. I described a *message* as a phrase or sentence that succinctly expresses the campaign's objective and, sometimes, the values that are at stake. It is usually compelling, memorable, and is used in all of a campaign's communication materials.

Messages serve an important function in campaign communication. In addition to providing a frame for its audiences' understanding of the issue, messages also seek to mobilize or influence the actions of the campaign's base and its persuadable audiences, opinion leaders, and media. A campaign's message, therefore, can play a pivotal role in addressing the attitude–behavior gap that occurs for many audiences. This is particularly true when a campaign refers in its message to an important value that its audience perceives as threatened, such as their health or a natural area that has special meaning. Let's look more closely, therefore, at the role of values in a campaign's messaging and the ways in which campaigns frame these messages.

Framing and a Campaign's Values

The role of values in a campaign's communication was illustrated recently when environmental groups reframed their messages in defense of the EPA's authority to regulate greenhouse gases. With the U.S. Congress posed recently to restrict the EPA's authority, the *New York Times* reported that environmentalists were "stepping up their transition toward a new health-centric message" to persuade lawmakers to back away from limits on the EPA (Schor, 2011, para. 1). A spokesperson for the group Health Care Without Harm, for example, told reporters: "Failure to allow EPA to safeguard our air . . . exposes thousands of people with chronic illnesses, including our children, to increased health episodes" (quoted in Schor, 2011, para. 2).

As an advisor to one of the groups in the campaign to defend the EPA, I was aware of the importance of this shift in the campaign's messaging. Words such as *health, chronic illness, our children,* and *increased health* episodes were intended to evoke a fundamental frame in the minds of the campaign's target audiences. In Chapter 6, I described a *frame* as the cognitive maps or patterns of interpretation that people use to organize their understanding of reality. It is important to understand that frames are not just words but are deeper, often unconscious, conceptual structures. As cognitive linguist George Lakoff (2010) explains, frames "are physically realized in neutral circuits in the brain. All of our knowledge makes use of frames, and every word is defined through the frames it neutrally activates" (p. 71). Moreover, many of our "frame-circuits have direct connections to the emotional regions of the brain" (p. 72), and the campaign's message must be able to evoke or activate these deeper connections in the minds of its audience.

The language that a campaign uses in its message, therefore, "must make sense in terms of *the existing system of frames*" of its audience (Lakoff, p. 72; emphasis added). Lakoff is using *frame* in a different sense than media researchers do when speaking about *media frames*—the headlines, lead sentences, and other cues that help readers understand the point of a news story. Media frames are thematic guides to what a story is about; they are not (usually) intended to activate deeper neutral circuits that have been reinforced over time and are linked to more basic emotions or values. Hence, in Lakoff's meaning, we cannot easily or simply create a new frame. Nevertheless, while words themselves are not frames, he explains, "under the right conditions, words can be chosen to activate desired frames" (p. 73). A campaign's message, to be successful, attempts to evoke an existing and emotionally relevant frame. Environmentalists' campaigns to defend the EPA, as we saw, used words that were designed to evoke an existing, powerful frame for many Americans—a concern for their health and, especially, the health of their children.

Another Viewpoint: Framing or Organizing?

Sociologists Robert Brulle and Craig Jenkins disagree with George Lakoff and others' views of framing and its importance for environmental advocacy. In their article, "Spinning Our Way to Sustainability?" they argue that simply reframing an issue without addressing the basic causes of political and economic change won't alter entrenched power. Summarizing Lakoff's views, they write:

Social reality is defined simply in terms of how we *perceive* reality. If we just get the right frames out there, it will create political consensus, and the progressive alliance can then take power. However comforting this idea might sound, it is a form of linguistic mysticism that assumes that social institutions can be transformed by cultural redefinition alone. . . . The structure of power has to be changed as part of the process, and any rhetorical strategy that promises to be effective must link its rhetoric to a broader political strategy that includes grassroots organizing at its base. . . . Although better framing would be useful, alone it can do little. We need to move beyond simplistic analyses and clever spin tactics. What is needed is a new organizational strategy that engages citizens and fosters the development of enlightened self-interest and an awareness of long-term community interests. (pp. 84, 86).

SOURCE: Robert J. Brulle and J. Craig Jenkins. (2006, March). Spinning our way to sustainability? *Organization & Environment, 19*(1): 82–87.

Let's look at two examples of messages that evoke powerful mental frames. First, a number of civil society groups in the United States, Europe, Asia, South America, and Africa have joined together in a Water Is Life campaign. The campaign opposes the move to turn over the world's water resources to the private sector through commercialization, privatization, and large-scale development. By explicitly identifying water with *life*, the message signals the urgency of the campaign's work for many people in drought-prone areas. And a second, classic message is Extinction Is Forever. Although adopted many years ago by the Center for Environmental Education (n.d.) for its campaign for a ban on commercial hunting of whales, it has since been adopted by numerous groups that campaign to protect endangered species. By appealing to the *irreparable* (see definition of this term in the section on the Zuni Salt Lake campaign), the phrase "Extinction Is Forever" evokes powerful feelings about mortality and life itself.

More recently, the framing of a campaign's message in light of key values is seen in the Lawrence Berkeley National Laboratory's study on home energy consumption in the United States. After surveying the best practices of 14 home energy-efficiency programs in the United States, researchers at the Berkeley Lab concluded that it is not enough just to provide information; the communication must address something people want or value, such as "health benefits, improved comfort, community pride, or other benefits that consumers tend to care about" (Fuller, Kunkel, Zimring, Hoffman, Soroye, & Goldman, 2010, p. 2). Researchers, therefore, recommended that the energy campaigns spend time studying their audience—residential customers— and "tailor messages to this audience" (Fuller et al., p. 2). In constructing their messages, they advised the programs to "avoid meaningless or negatively associated words like 'retrofit' and 'audit.' [Instead,] use words and ways of communicating that *tap into customer's existing mental frames*" (Fuller et al., p. 2, emphasis added).

One of the successful programs studied by the Berkeley Lab was an experiment in rural, conservative Kansas, urging people to save energy.

Framing an Energy Savings Message

"Don't mention global warming," Nancy Jackson warned. "And don't mention Al Gore. People out here just hate him" (quoted in Kaufman, 2010, p. A1). Jackson heads the Climate Action and Energy Project, a nonprofit group in Kansas whose goal is to persuade people to reduce fossil fuel emissions that contribute to climate change. But, any talk about climate change or global warming is very unpopular in rural Kansas. So, how could the project go about constructing a message to persuade people to cut their use of oil or coal-generated electricity?

Jackson felt that saving energy was a different matter. The project's message could separate this from appeals about stopping global warming. She explained, "If the goal was to persuade people to reduce their use of fossil fuels, why not identify issues that motivated them instead of getting stuck on something that did not?" (Kaufman, 2010, p. A4). The project, therefore, commissioned a study of independent voters and Republicans in the area around Wichita and Kansas City to identify what people cared about, what worried them, or what values motivated them.

Based on its study, the project ran an experiment "to see if by focusing [its messages] on thrift, patriotism, spiritual conviction, and economic prosperity, it could rally residents of six Kansas towns to take meaningful steps to conserve energy and consider fossil fuels" (Kaufman, 2010, p. A4). It adapted its message in a number of ways as it worked with civic leaders, churches, and schools. For example, Jackson talked with civic leaders about jobs in renewable energy, such as wind power, as a way of boosting local economies.

Jackson also spoke to Kansas ministers about "Creation Care," the duty of Christians "to act as stewards of the world that God gave them" (Kaufman, 2010, p. A4). And, importantly, Jackson used the appeal of thrift to persuade the six towns to compete to see which could save the most energy and money. As part of the competition, for example, schoolchildren "searched for 'vampire' electric loads, or appliances that sap energy even when they seem to be off," and towns' restaurants served meals by candlelight for Valentine's Day. The project discovered, while many of the towns' residents believed global warming was a "hoax," they cared about "saving money"; as one man explained, "That's what really motivated them" (quoted in Kaufman, p. A4).

By the end of the first year of the experiment, the project saw signs of success. Overall, the six towns experienced energy savings of more than 6 million kilowatt-hours (Fuller et al., 2010, p. 13). This amounted to a decline in energy use in the towns "by as much as 5 percent relative to other areas—a giant step in the world of energy conservation" (Kaufman, 2010, p. A4).

Finally, here's a reminder: While constructing the campaign's message is important, a message, even if powerful, cannot alone succeed in achieving a group's ultimate objectives. Messages must always be aligned with other aspects of the campaign's strategy. For example, is the message aligned with the specific values held by key audiences? Do these audiences have influence with the primary decision makers? In other words, messages help to implement a campaign's strategy—its mode of leverage or influence—that is designed to persuade the primary decision makers who are able to act on the campaign's objective (Cox, 2010).

SUMMARY

In this chapter, I've focused on the environmental advocacy campaign, its key characteristics, and the importance of constructing campaign messages that resonate with the values of a campaign's audience.

- In the first section, I defined the *advocacy campaign* as a strategic course of action, involving communication, which is undertaken for a specific purpose, and I distinguished campaigns from *critical rhetorics*, the questioning or criticism of the status quo.
- In the second section, I outlined the basic elements of advocacy campaigns and their communication tasks:

    (1) Goals and objectives and creation of public demand

(2) Audiences and mobilizing of support

(3) Campaign strategies and the construction of messages

- In the third section, I described the design of a successful advocacy campaign—the Zuni Salt Lake Coalition's campaign against plans to strip mine for coal near sacred Native American lands.
- Finally, I discussed the role of message construction in campaigns, including the importance of key values of an audience; I also identified two challenges:

  (1) overcoming the attitude–behavior gap

  (2) the use of values in the construction of messages that seek to motivate supporters

It is my hope that, when you have finished reading this chapter, you will appreciate some of the elements important in designing an advocacy campaign, as well as the role of critical rhetorics in questioning existing practices and ideologies. As a result, I hope you will feel inspired to work with others on your campus or in your community to do extraordinary things.

SUGGESTED RESOURCES

- Roger Kaye, *Last Great Wilderness: The Campaign to Establish the Arctic National Wildlife Refuge.* Fairbanks: University of Alaska Press, 2006.
- Simon Cottle and Libby Lester (Eds.), *Transnational Protests and the Media.* New York: Peter Lang, 2011.
- Bill McKibben, *Fight Global Warming Now: The Handbook for Taking Action in Your Community.* New York: St. Martin's Press, 2007.
- For images, film, and history of the Zuni Salt lake and the campaign to protect it, see www.sacredland.org/zuni-salt-lake

KEY TERMS

DISCUSSION QUESTIONS

1. A common perception of strategy is that, with the worsening of environmental problems, people will wake up and begin to take action. Is this an accurate view? What would it take to wake people up to be really effective?

2. Do you as a consumer have power to affect environmental change? Journalist William Greider (2003) says that consumers are in a weak position and have very little actual leverage over the actions of large corporations. Do you agree?

3. Can advocates for wilderness or endangered species appeal to biospheric values and still gain acceptance from the audiences it must persuade? Or, must they appeal to the egoistic concerns of individuals or to their social–altruistic values to gain a hearing or mobilize support?

4. How effective is the framing of a campaign's message? Do you agree with Brulle and Jenkins ("Another Viewpoint" on page 236) that simply reframing an issue without addressing political and economic change won't alter entrenched power?

NOTES

1. I am indebted to the many leaders in the U.S. environmental movement with whom I've worked in describing this approach to the design of an environmental advocacy campaign.

2. In describing the Zuni Salt Lake Coalition's campaign, I am indebted to the meeting notes of the coalition and its campaign materials and to Andy Bessler, a coalition member and organizer with the Sierra Club, who generously shared his recollections of the campaign in a personal interview, September 24, 2003.

3. By May 31, 2002, the Department of Interior had approved SRP's plan for the mine, while New Mexico officials had previously given their permission. Unless challenged, mining at the Fence Lake site was expected to begin by spring 2003.

REFERENCES

Agyeman, J., Bullard, R. D., & Evans, B. (Eds.). (2003). *Just sustainabilities: Development in an unequal world.* London: Earthscan/MIT Press. Retrieved December 19, 2008, from http://www.appropedia.org/Just_sustainability

Ball, J. (2008, February 4). Wall Street shows skepticism over coal: Banks push utilities to plan for impact of emissions caps. *Wall Street Journal.* Retrieved July 26, 2008, from http://online.wsj.com

Beinecke, F. (2008, February 11). The twilight of dirty coal. *NRDC Switchboard.* Retrieved July 26, 2008, from http://switchboard.nrdc.org/blogs/fbeinecke/the_twilight_of_dirty_coal.html

Brown, L. R. (2008, February 14). *U.S. moving toward ban on new coal-fired power plants.* Earth Policy Institute. Retrieved August 13, 2008, from http://www.earth-policy.org

Brulle, R. J., & Jenkins, J. C. (2006, March). Spinning our way to sustainability?

Organization & Environment, 19(1): 82–87.

Carson, R. (1962). *Silent spring.* Boston: Houghton Mifflin.

Center for Environmental Education. (n.d.). *Will the whales survive?* [Brochure]. Author.

Cox, J. R. (1982). The die is cast: Topical and ontological dimensions of the locus of the irreparable. *Quarterly Journal of Speech, 68,* 227–239.

Cox, J. R. (2001). The irreparable. In T. O. Sloane (Ed.), *Encyclopedia of rhetoric* (pp. 406–409). Oxford, UK, and New York: Oxford University Press.

Cox, R. (2010). Beyond frames: Recovering the strategic in climate communication. *Environmental Communication: A Journal of Nature and Culture, 4*(1), pp. 122–133.

Crompton, T. (2008). *Weathercocks and signposts: The environment movement at a crossroads.* World Wildlife Fund-UK. Retrieved December 17, 2008, from wwf.org.uk/strategiesforchange

DeLuca, K. M. (2005). *Image politics: The new rhetoric of environmental activism.* London: Routledge.

Earth First! (2011). No compromise in defense of mother earth. *Earth First! Journal.* Retrieved June 14, 2011, from www.earthfirstjournal.org

Evernden, N. (1985). *The natural alien: Humankind and the environment.* Toronto, ON: University of Toronto Press.

Farrior, M. (2005, February). *Breakthrough strategies for engaging the public: Emerging trends in communications and social science for biodiversity project.* Retrieved December 18, 2008, from http://www.biodiversityproject.org

Fish, S. (2008, August 3). *Think again: I am therefore I pollute.* Retrieved August 15, 2008, from http://fish.blogs.nytimes.com

Fuller, M. C., Kunkel, C., Zimring, M., Hoffman, I., Soroye, K. L., & Goldman, C. (2010, September). *Driving demand for home energy improvements.* Environmental Energies Technology Division, Lawrence Berkeley National Laboratory. Retrieved July 17, 2011, from http://eetd.lbl.gov/EAP/EMP/reports/lbnl-3960e-web.pdf

Gendlin, F. (1982). A talk with Mike McCloskey: Executive director of the Sierra Club. *Sierra, 67,* 36–41.

Greider, W. (2003, August 5). Victory at McDonald's. *The Nation,* pp. 8, 10, 36.

Harris, S. (1977). *What's so funny about science?* Los Altos, CA: Wm. Kaufmann.

Kaufman, L. (2010, October 19). Kansans scoff at global warming but embrace cleaner energy. *New York Times,* pp. A1, 4.

Kollmuss, A., & Agyeman, J. (2002). Mind the gap: Why do people act environmentally and what are the barriers to pro-environmental behavior? *Environmental Education Research, 8*(3), 96–119.

LaDuke, W. (2002, November/December). The salt woman and the coal mine. *Sierra,* pp. 44–47, 73.

Lakoff, G. (2010). Why it matters how we frame the environment. *Environmental Communication: A Journal of Nature and Culture, 4*(1), 70–81.

Mandel, J. (2010, October 5). Don't say "retrofit," say "upgrade"—study. *Greenwire.* Retrieved October 5, 2010, from www.eenews.net/gw

Moser, S. C. (2010). Communicating climate change: History, challenges, process and future directions. *Wiley Interdisciplinary Reviews—Climate Change 1*(1): 31–53.

Naess, A., & Sessions, G. (n.d.). *Deep ecology platform.* Foundation for Deep Ecology. Retrieved October 8, 2003, from www.deepecology.org

OgilvyEarth. (2011). *Mainstream Green: Moving sustainability from niche to normal.* Retrieved June 14, 2011, from www.ogilvyearth.com

Orr, D. W. (1992). *Ecological literacy: Education and the transition to a postmodern world.* Albany: State University of New York Press.

Pezzullo, P. C. (2007). *Toxic tours: Rhetorics of pollution, travel and environmental justice.* Tuscaloosa: University of Alabama Press.

Rogers, E. M., & Storey, J. D. (1987). Communication campaigns. In C. R. Berger & S. H. Chaffee (Eds.), *Handbook of communication science* (pp. 817–846). Newbury Park, CA: Sage.

Rose, C., & Dade, P. (2007). *Using values modes.* Retrieved December 18, 2008, from www.campaignstrategy.org

Sacred Land Film Project. (2003). *Zuni salt lake.* Retrieved September 24, 2003, from www.sacredland.org/zuni_salt_lake

Schor, E. (2011, February 1). Enviro groups' public health pivot in support of EPA regs hitting red states too. *New York Times.* Retrieved June 14, 2011, from www.nytimes.com/

Schultz, P. W., & Zelezny, L. (2003). Reframing environmental messages to be congruent with American values. *Research in Human Ecology, 10,* 126–136.

Scott, R. L., & Smith, D. K. (1969). The rhetoric of confrontation. *Quarterly Journal of Speech, 55,* 1–8.

Seciwa, C. (2003, August 5). *Zuni Salt Lake and sanctuary zone protected for future generations.* [News release]. Zuni Pueblo, NM: Zuni Salt Lake Coalition.

Shabecoff, P. (2000). *Earth rising: American environmentalism in the 21st century.* Washington, DC: Island Press.

Sierra Club. (2011). Beyond coal. Retrieved Augist 31, 2011, from http://beyond-coal.org/act-now/

Stern, P. C., Dietz, T., & Kalof, L. (1993). Value orientations, gender, and environmental concerns. *Environment & Behavior, 25,* 322–348.

Torgerson, D. (1999). *The promise of green politics: Environmentalism and the public sphere.* Durham, NC: Duke University Press.

Valtin, T. (2003, November). Zuni Salt Lake saved. *Planet: The Sierra Club Activist Resource* [Newsletter], 1.

Victory and new threats at Zuni Salt Lake, New Mexico. (2003, Winter). *The Citizen* [Newsletter of the Citizens Coal Council], 6.

Weyler, R. (2004). *Greenpeace: How a group of journalists, ecologists, and visionaries changed the world.* New York: Rodale.

Zuni Salt Lake Coalition. (2001, October 6–7). [Zuni Salt Lake Coalition's campaign plan: Edward's kitchen. Notes from first meeting of coalition members]. Unpublished raw data.

Zuni Salt Lake Coalition. (2003). Background. Retrieved September 23, 2003, from www.zunisaltlakecoalition.org/

Kids play on a merry-go-round near an oil refinery at the Carver Terrace housing project playground in west Port Arthur, Texas. The Port Arthur area is part of one of the United States's most polluted regions.

CHAPTER 9

Environmental Justice, Climate Justice, and the Green Jobs Movement

We, representatives of the poor and the marginalized of the world . . . resolve to actively build a movement from the communities that will address the issue of climate change from a human rights, social justice and labour perspective.

—Delhi Climate Justice Declaration
(November 1, 2002)

O
n the margins of urban areas, in Appalachian valleys, in the polluted corridor in Louisiana called Cancer Alley, on Native American reservations, and in villages in poor nations, grassroots voices have been speaking against environmental racism and demanding environmental justice and climate justice.

Chapter Preview

- The first section of this chapter[1] examines the challenges to a dominant discourse that views environment as a place apart from the places where people live and work. In this section, I describe:

  (1) The voices that called the disproportionate hazards in low-income neighborhoods and communities of color a form of environmental racism, and

  (2) The emergence of a new movement and a discourse of environmental justice and some of its successes.

(Continued)

(Continued)

- The second section introduces the concept of *indecorous voices,* and identifies barriers faced by residents in at-risk communities who attempt to speak out against the hazards they face. This sections considers:

  (1) The communication practices that dismiss the voices of some as inappropriate or emotional, and

  (2) Use of toxic tours by low-income neighborhoods and communities of color to call attention to the sights, sounds, and smells of environmental racism.

- In the third section of the chapter, I describe the global movement for climate justice, whose discourse seeks to frame global climate change ethically in terms of human rights and environmental justice.
- In the final section, I describe the related movement for green jobs in the United States and its discourse of renewable energy, jobs, people, and communities.

Nowhere are efforts to redefine the meaning of *environment* more striking than the grassroots, multiracial struggles for social justice as well as environmental protection. As used by community activists and scholars studying the movement, the term **environmental justice** refers to (a) calls to recognize and halt the disproportionate burdens imposed on poor and minority communities by environmentally harmful conditions, (b) more inclusive opportunities for those who are most affected to be heard in the decisions affecting their communities, and (c) a vision of environmentally healthy and economically sustainable communities. As we'll see later in this chapter, a climate justice movement has also arisen, borrowing from the discourse of this symbolically potent movement.

My hope is that when you have finished reading the chapter, you'll sense a more robust meaning of *environment,* one that includes places where people live, work, and play. You'll also understand some of the barriers that citizens from poor and minority communities often face when they call attention to environmental hazards, and you will understand why, in the end, the movements for environmental justice and climate justice are also movements for a more democratically inclusive world.

Environmental Justice: Challenging *a Place Apart*

The environmental movement in the United States—historically associated with white Euro-Americans—had been concerned with wild places and the natural world. The 1960s, however, saw a widening focus of the movement to include human health and environmental quality. Nevertheless, the movement continued to offer "disjointed and at times contradictory" accounts of humans' place in nature, accounts that assumed a "long-standing separation of the social from the ecological" (Gottlieb, 2002, p. 5).

Partly in response, by the 1980s, activists in minority and low-income communities had opened a new antagonism by challenging society's view of nature as a place apart from the places where people live. (In Chapter 2, I defined *antagonism* as the recognition of the limits of an idea or prevailing viewpoint; recognizing a limit creates an opening for alternative voices to redefine a condition or state of affairs.) This opening for new voices also fueled efforts to ensure that processes for environmental decision making are more inclusive, democratic, and just.

The Toxic Sea Around Us

By the 1960s, concerns had begun to emerge in the United States about the health and effects related to new developments in large-scale chemical manufacturing and disposal of toxic wastes. Some scientists and citizens were skeptical of public institutions' ability to safeguard citizens' health in this new petrochemical society. Rachel Carson's (1962) best-selling book *Silent Spring* became the most influential questioning of the use of powerful chemicals, such as dichloro-diphenyl-trichloroethane (DDT), by agricultural businesses and public health agencies. Her book set off a national debate over the pesticide industry. Two decades later, the small, upstate New York community of Love Canal became a metaphor for the nation's consciousness of the hazards of its chemical culture.[2]

Increasingly, citizens had begun to feel themselves surrounded by what environmental historian Samuel Hays (1987) termed *the toxic "sea around us"* (p. 171).[3] Many feared that the new synthetic chemicals were having devastating health effects—cancer, birth defects, respiratory illness, and neurological disorders—adding to the public's fears of "an environmental threat that was out of control" (p. 200). It also became clear that certain communities—largely low-income and minority communities—were most affected by toxic pollutants and the resulting health and social problems.

Questioning the Discourse of Environmentalism

Some attempts to call attention to the specific impacts of these environmental hazards occurred before a movement for environmental justice arose. In the late 1960s and 1970s, a few civil rights groups, churches, and environmental leaders tried to call attention to the particular problems of urban communities and the workplace. Dr. Martin Luther King, Jr., went to Memphis, Tennessee, in 1968 to join with African-American sanitation workers who were striking for wages and better work conditions—an event that sociologist and environmental justice scholar Robert Bullard (1993) called one of the earliest efforts to link civil rights and environmental health concerns. Also addressing the workplace environment was Congress's passage of the federal Occupational Safety and Health Act (OSHA) in 1970. This landmark law helped "stimulate the budding workplace environmental movements . . . as well as community-based organizations of activists and professionals" (Gottlieb, 1993, pp. 283, 285).

Other early efforts included the 1971 Urban Environment Conference (UEC), one of the early successful efforts to link environmental and social justice concerns.

A coalition of labor, environmental, and civil rights groups, the UEC tried "to help broaden the way the public defined environmental issues and to focus on the particular environmental problems of urban minorities" (Kazis & Grossman, 1991, p. 247). [4]

Despite these early attempts to bring environmental, labor, and civil rights leaders together to explore common interests, national environmental groups in the 1960s and 1970s largely failed to recognize and address the problems of urban residents or poor and minority communities.

Part of the difficulty lay in the discourse of environmentalism itself. Some community activists—particularly women of color—complained of obstacles when they tried to speak with traditional environmental groups. For example, in her account of efforts to stop the construction of a 1,600-ton-per-day solid waste incinerator in a south central Los Angeles neighborhood in the mid-1980s, Giovanna Di Chiro (1996) reported, "These issues were not deemed adequately 'environmental' by local environmental groups such as the Sierra Club or the Environmental Defense Fund" (p. 299). Di Chiro explained that, when residents of the predominantly African-American and low-income community approached these groups, "they were informed that the poisoning of an urban community by an incineration facility was a 'community health issue,' not an environmental one"[5] (p. 299). Activists in other parts of the country similarly complained that "the mainstream environmental community [was] reluctant to address issues of equity and social justice, within the context of the environment" (Alston, 1990, p.23).

By the early 1980s, residents and activists in some low-income neighborhoods and communities of color, faced with indifference on the part of the established groups, started to take matters into their own hands. In doing so, they worked to redefine the meaning of *environment* to include the places "where we live, where we work, where we play, and where we learn" (Cole & Foster, 2001, p. 16).

Toxic Waste and the Birth of a Movement

A key event, and new voices speaking for their environment, occurred in the protests against a PCB (polychlorinated biphenyl) toxic landfill by residents in rural Warren County, North Carolina, in 1982. Earlier, the state discovered that PCB chemicals had been illegally dumped along miles of highways. To dispose of the toxic-laced soil, officials decided to bury it in a landfill in the predominantly poor and African-American Warren County. Rather than accept this, local residents and supporters from national civil rights groups tried to halt the state's plan by placing their bodies in the middle of the roads leading to the landfill to block 6,000 trucks carrying the PCB-contaminated soil. More than 500 arrests occurred in what sociologists Robert Bullard and Beverly Hendrix Wright (1987) called "the first national attempt by Blacks to link environmental issues (hazardous waste and pollution) to the mainstream civil rights agenda" (p. 32). (For background on the Warren County protests as the symbolic birth of the environmental justice movement, see Pezzullo, 2001.)

Prompted by protests in Warren County and elsewhere, in the 1980s and 1990s federal agencies and scholars began to confirm patterns of disproportionate exposure to environmental hazards experienced by low-income populations and communities of color. For example, the U.S. General Accounting Office (1983) found that African-Americans constituted the majority of populations living near hazardous landfills. In a follow-up study, *Toxic Wastes and Race in the United States*, the United Church of Christ's Commission for Racial Justice discovered a similar pattern (Chavis & Lee, 1987). Among its key findings were these:

- Race proved to be the most significant among variables tested in association with the location of commercial waste facilities. . . . Although socioeconomic status appeared to play an important role in the location of [these] facilities, race still proved to be more significant. (p. xiii)
- Three out of every five Black and Hispanic Americans lived in communities with uncontrolled toxic waste sites. . . . (p. iv)
- Approximately half of all Asian/Pacific Islanders and American Indians lived in communities with uncontrolled toxic waste sites. (p. xiv)

A follow-up report, *Toxic Wastes and Race at Twenty, 1987–2007*, revealed that "racial disparities in the distribution of hazardous wastes are greater than previously reported" in the original 1987 study (Bullard, Mohai, Saha, & Wright, 2007, p. x).

Other research on the racial and income characteristics of communities near environmental hazards quickly followed. White (1998) reported that 87% of studies of the distribution of environmental hazards revealed racial disparities (p. 63). These studies concluded that minority and low-income populations not only are more likely to live near such hazards but also are "more severely exposed to potentially deadly and destructive levels of toxins from environmental hazards than others" (p. 63).

We Speak for Ourselves: Naming Environmental Racism

With the concentration of hazardous facilities in low income communities and communities of color, new voices and narratives of environmental harm began to arise. In many cases, such stories spoke of frustration in dealing with local officials and the search for words to express anger and suffering. Residents began to invent new words—or adapt old words—to explain their situations and to express these grievances. Many charged they were suffering from a form of environmental discrimination. This *critical rhetoric* (Chapter 8) spoke of communities there were being poisoned and targeted as *sacrifice zones*, which ignored people and welcomed polluting industries. Bullard (1993) coined the term **sacrifice zones** to describe characteristics shared by these communities: "(1) They already have more than their share of environmental problems and polluting industries, and (2) they are still attracting new polluters" (p. 12).

One powerful phrase seized upon by activists to describe their communities' plights was *environmental racism*. At a 1991 summit of activists from the environmental justice movement, Benjamin Chavis of the United Church of Christ's Commission for Racial Justice spoke of his attempt to describe what was going on in the persistent pattern of locating toxics in poor and minority neighborhoods. He said, "It came to me—*environmental racism.* That's when I coined the term"[6] (quoted in Bullard, 1994, p. 278). Chavis described **environmental racism** as

> racial discrimination in environmental policy-making and the enforcement of regulations and laws, the deliberate targeting of people of color communities for toxic waste facilities, the official sanctioning of the life-threatening presence of poisons and pollutants in our communities, and the history of excluding people of color from leadership in the environmental movement. (quoted in Di Chiro, 1996, p. 304)

While Chavis highlighted the "deliberate" targeting of people of color communities, others pointed out that discrimination also resulted from the *disparate impact* of environmental hazards on minority communities. The 1964 Civil Rights Act used the term **disparate impact** to recognize discrimination in the form of the disproportionate burdens that some groups experience, regardless of the conscious intention of others in their decisions or behaviors. In other words, racial (or environmental) discrimination results from the accumulated impacts of unfair treatment, which may include more than intentional discrimination or deliberate targeting.

Naming the problem as environmental racism was important. Residents in communities that suffered from environmental hazards often search for language to name their experiences. Rose Marie Augustine's experience in Tucson, Arizona, was typical. After trying unsuccessfully to get local officials to recognize the problems of polluted well water and illness in her neighborhood, Augustine attended a workshop for community activists in the Southwest. She said that, for the first time, "I heard words like 'economic blackmail,' 'environmental racism.' Somebody put words, names, on what our community was experiencing" (Augustine, 1993). In other cases, activists themselves began to call the conditions imposed on low-income communities a form of economic blackmail. For example, Bullard (1993) explained, "You can get a job, but only if you are willing to do work that will harm you, your families, and your neighbors" (p. 23).

As protests mounted against such patterns and the failure of the mainstream environmental movement to address the problems, activists began to insist that people in affected communities be able to "speak for ourselves" (Alston, 1990). Social justice activist Dana Alston (1990) argued, in her book *We Speak for Ourselves,* that environmental justice "calls for *a total redefinition of terms and language* to describe the conditions that people are facing" (quoted in Di Chiro, 1998, p. 105; emphasis added). Indeed, what some found distinctive about the critical rhetoric of the new movement was the way in which it transformed "the possibilities for fundamental social and environmental change through processes of redefinition, reinvention, and construction of innovative political and cultural discourses" (Di Chiro, 1996, p. 303). Environmental attorney Deehon Ferris put it more bluntly when she said, "We're shifting the terms of the debate" (Ferris, 1993).

Figure 9.1	Baltimore residents objected to a federally funded project that sprayed fertilizer made from human and industrial wastes on yards in poor, black neighborhoods in Baltimore to test whether it might protect children from lead poisoning in the soil. Families were assured the sludge was safe and were never told about any harmful ingredients.

AP Photo/Manuel Balce Ceneta

One important shift in the terms of debate occurred in 1990 when the SouthWest Organizing Project (SWOP) publicly criticized the nation's largest environmental groups, specifically those who belonged to the Group of Ten.[7] Called "the single most stirring challenge to traditional environmentalism" (Schwab, 1994, p. 388), the letter ultimately was signed by more than one hundred civil rights and community leaders. The letter accused the mainstream groups of racism in their hiring and policies. A particularly stinging passage stated the signers' grievance:

> For centuries, people of color in our region have been subjected to racist and geno-cidal practices including the theft of lands and water, the murder of innocent people, and the degradation of our environment. . . . Although environmental organizations calling themselves the "Group of Ten" often claim to represent our interests . . . your organizations play an equal role in the disruption of our communities. There is a clear lack of accountability by the Group of Ten environmental organizations towards Third World communities in the Southwest, in the United States as a whole, and internationally. (SouthWest Organizing Project, 1990, p. 1)

Coverage of the letter in the *New York Times* and other newspapers "initiated a media firestorm" and generated calls for "an emergency summit of environmental, civil rights, and community groups" (Cole & Foster, 2001, p. 31).

Building the Movement for Environmental Justice

The First National People of Color Environmental Leadership Summit

Such an emergency summit came when delegates from local communities and national leaders from social justice, religious, environmental,[8] and civil rights groups met in Washington, DC, for the **First National People of Color Environmental Leadership Summit** in October 1991. The summit is generally considered to be important for three reasons. First, it was a "watershed moment" in the history of the nascent environmental justice movement (Di Chiro, 1998, p. 113). For three days, activists from local communities shared stories of grievances and attempted to compose a collective critique of the narrow vision of the environment and the exclusion of people of color from decisions that affected their communities. Second, summit participants agreed upon the Principles of Environmental Justice that would powerfully shape the vision of the emerging movement. Finally, many viewed the meeting as a declaration of independence from the traditional environment movement. One participant declared, "I don't care to join the environmental movement, I belong to a movement already" (quoted in Cole & Foster, 2001, p. 31).

For the first time, different strands of an emerging movement for environmental justice joined together to challenge traditional definitions of environmentalism and compose a new discourse of environmental justice, borrowing from powerful rhetorics of both social justice and environmental protection. In doing so, the summit participants were able to insert their experiences of toxic poisoning into earlier narratives of the U.S. civil rights movement. Running a video on a monitor during the summit was a moving example of such critical rhetoric.

The video showed images of industrial pipes disgorging pollution into the air and water, along with scenes of African-American residents of Reveilletown, Louisiana, a community established by freed slaves after the Civil War. The community had become so badly polluted by wastes from a nearby chemical factory that it had to be abandoned in the 1980s. Janice Dickerson, an African-American activist working with similar communities, provided a running narration as the video showed documentary film images of the Ku Klux Klan burning crosses in the 1960s:

> From the perspective of the African American, it's a civil rights matter; it's interwoven. Civil rights and the environment movement are both interwoven. Because, again, we are the most victimized.... There's no difference in a petro-chemical industry locating two, three hundred feet from my house and killing me off than there is when the Klan was on the rampage, just running into black neighborhoods, hanging black people at will. (Greenpeace, 1990)

By drawing on the "morally charged terrain" of the civil rights movement, the summit participants dramatically shifted the terms of public debate about the environment (Harvey, 1996, p. 387). By placing concerns about toxic wastes and other environmental dangers into a civil rights frame, they were able to "characterize the distribution of environmental hazards as part of a broader pattern of social injustice, one that contradicts the fundamental beliefs of fairness and equity" (Sandweiss, 1998, p. 51). In so doing, they believed they could contest or redefine the meaning of *environment* itself.

Many of the speakers at the summit also urged participants to demand political representation and to speak forcefully to public officials, corporations, and the traditional environmental movement. At the summit, Chavis explained, *"This is our opportunity to define and redefine for ourselves. . . .* What is at issue here is our ability, our capacity to speak clearly to ourselves, to our peoples, and forthrightly to all those forces out there that have caused us to be in this situation" (*Proceedings,* 1991, p. 59). On the last day, participants did so in a dramatic way by adopting 17 **Principles of Environmental Justice,** an expansive vision for their communities and the right to participate directly in decisions about their environment.

The principles began with the deeply ethical statement, "Environmental justice affirms the sacredness of Mother Earth, ecological unity and the interdependence of all species, and the right to be free from ecological destruction" (*Proceedings,* 1991, p. viii). The principles developed an enlarged sense of the environment to include places where people lived, worked, and played and enumerated a series of rights, including "the fundamental right to political, economic, cultural, and environmental self-determination of all peoples" (p. viii).

The inclusion of the right of self-determination in the summit's Principles of Environmental Justice was especially important to the emerging movement. Many of the summit's participants had criticized the officially sanctioned decision making in their communities for failing to provide meaningful participation "for those most burdened by environmental decisions" (Cole & Foster, 2001, p. 16). In adopting the principles, they insisted that *environmental justice* not only referred to the right of all people to be free of environmental poisons but that at its core is the inclusion of all in the decisions that affect their health and the well-being of their communities. One delegate remarked that the Principles of Environmental Justice represented "how people of color define environmental issues for ourselves, as social and economic justice" (*Proceedings,* 1991, p. 54).

Following the summit, the Southern Organizing Conference for Social and Economic Justice applauded the "new definition of the term 'environment'"; the group invited community activists "to build a new movement" using the Principles of Environmental Justice adopted at the summit (personal letter, June 2, 1992). Indeed, many community activists and others from civil rights and social justice groups left the 1991 summit to continue building the communication tools and networks that would be required to change practices in their communities and in government agencies.

Opening the Floodgates

In the following decades, the environmental justice movement saw clear gains. Deehon Ferris (1993) of the Lawyers' Committee for Civil Rights in Washington, DC, observed that "as a result of on-the-ground struggles and hell-raising, 'environmental justice' [emerged as] a hot issue. . . . Floodgates [opened] in the media." Urban planning scholar Jim Schwab (1994) observed that "the new movement had won a place at the table. The Deep South, the nation, would never discuss environmental issues in the same way again" (p. 393). Ferris called the early 1990s "a watershed," and the *National Law Journal* reported that the movement—often led by women—had gained "critical mass" (Lavelle & Coyle, 1992, p. 5). A subsequent gathering—the Second National People of Color Environmental Leadership Summit—was held in Washington, DC, from October 23 to 26, 2002. Highlighting women's roles as leaders in the movement, the second event was even larger, attracting more than 1,400 participants.

The critical mass of the movement began to make an impression—media stories about the pollution of minority communities, new coalitions with environmental groups, training for grassroots and community groups, a presidential Executive Order on Environmental Justice, and the beginnings of awareness by state and federal agencies. Let's look at a few of these developments.

In 1993, the movement persuaded the Environmental Protection Agency (EPA) to set up a **National Environmental Justice Advisory Committee (NEJAC)** to ensure a voice in the EPA's policy making for environmental justice groups. The committee was chartered to provide advice from the environmental justice community and recommendations to the EPA administrator. For example, NEJAC produced advisory reports on the cleanup of brown fields (polluted urban areas), mercury contamination of fish, and new guidelines for ensuring participation of low-income and minority residents in decisions about permits for industries wanting to locate in their communities.

The movement also achieved an important political goal when President Clinton issued Executive Order 12898, Federal Actions to Address Environmental Justice in Minority Populations and Low-Income Populations, in 1994. The **Executive Order on Environmental Justice** instructed each federal agency "to make achieving environmental justice part of its mission by identifying and addressing . . . disproportionately high and adverse human health or environmental effects of its programs, policies, and activities on minority populations and low-income populations in the United States" (Clinton, 1994, p. 7629). (Although the Clinton administration began a plan to implement the Executive Order, the succeeding administration of President George W. Bush allowed it to lay dormant for eight years [Office of the Inspector General, 2004].)

Under the Obama administration, the Executive Order on Environmental Justice received new life. The EPA's new administrator, Lisa Jackson, hosted a White Forum on environmental justice and launched community meetings across the country. "Now, it's time to take it to the next level," Jackson said, adding that the Obama administration would focus on the creation of "green jobs" in disadvantaged communities (quoted in "Obama revives panel on environmental justice," 2010, p. 2A). (See later section in this chapter on "Green Jobs.")

Finally, the mainstream U.S. environmental movement itself underwent changes as a result of the critique of an environmentalism that stood apart from the places where people lived. Pezzullo and Sandler (2007), for example, observed that "much has changed within . . . and happened around" the mainstream and environmental justice movements (p. 12). Vigorous dialogue between leaders of the mainstream green groups and the environmental justice community led in some cases to collaborations between these groups with poor and minority communities. Greenpeace, Sierra Club, Earth Island Institute, and Earth Justice (a legal advocacy group) have been particularly active in their support of environmental justice concerns.

But, the movement for environmental justice also would confront new obstacles and a need to identify new ways to communicate to pursue the vision put forward in the Principles of Environmental Justice. The next section describes some of these challenges and one way—toxic tours—that some local communities are attempting to bring attention to their concerns.

Indecorous Voices and Toxic Tours

An important theme in the discourse of environmental justice is the right of individuals in at-risk communities to participate in decisions affecting their lives. In Chapter 5, I introduced Senecah's (2004) Trinity of Voices (TOV) model to describe some of the elements that must be present for citizens to be heard or participate effectively in such decision making. One element was a person's interpersonal standing—not in the legal sense as a plaintiff in court but "the civic legitimacy, the respect, the esteem, and the consideration that all stakeholders' perspectives should be given" (p. 24). In this section, I describe a barrier to such respect, esteem, or moral standing that arises when agency officials or experts view the residents of poor or minority communities as indecorous or inappropriate when they attempt to speak of their concerns in technical forums.[9]

Dismissing the "Indecorous" Voice

Let me begin by illustrating what I mean by the construction of an **indecorous voice.** By this, I mean the symbolic framing by some public officials of the voices of others as inappropriate or unqualified for speaking in official forums and their belief that ordinary people may be too emotional or ignorant to testify about chemical pollution or other environmental issues. Believing, for example, that a resident of a low-income community has violated such norms of knowledge or objectivity is one way of dismissing the public as unqualified to speak about technical matters. Rose Marie Augustine's story is typical of such dismissal by public officials.

Rose Marie Augustine's Story: "Hysterical, Hispanic Housewives"

On the south side of Tucson, Arizona, where Latin Americans and Native Americans are the main residents, chemicals from several industrial plants had seeped into the groundwater table. This contaminated the wells from which some 47,000 residents drew their drinking water. One of the residents, Rose Marie Augustine, described her own and her neighbors' fears: "We didn't know anything about what had happened to us. . . . We were never informed about what happens to people who become contaminated by drinking contaminated water. . . . We were suffering lots of cancers, and we thought, you know, my God, what's happening?" (Augustine, 1991). EPA officials later confirmed the severity of the toxic chemicals that had been leaching from nearby Tucson industrial plants into their well water and listed this site as one the nation's priority Superfund sites for cleanup (Augustine, 1993).

Prior to the area's listing as a Superfund site, residents from the south side had tried to get local officials to listen to their concerns. Augustine (1993) reported that, when residents met with officials, they refused to respond to questions about the health effects of drinking well water. She said that, when residents persisted, one county supervisor told them that "the people in the south side were obese, lazy, and had poor eating habits, that it was our lifestyle and not the TC [toxic chemicals] in the water that caused our health problems." Augustine said that one official "called us 'hysterical Hispanic housewives' when we appealed to him for help."

Dismissal by public officials of community residents' complaints about environmental illness has occurred in other cases. For example, Roberts and Toffolon-Weiss (2001) reported that local officials in Louisiana's Cancer Alley dismissed complaints about illness from pollution as due to lifestyle or to eating high-fat food (p. 117). Earlier, Hays (1987) found that, when community members offered bodily evidence of illness, they were often "belittled as the complaints of 'housewives'" (p. 200). As we saw in Chapter 1, such notions of the public sphere mistakenly assume a rational or technical mode of communication as the only permissible form of discourse in public forums.

Decorum and the Norms of Public Forums

The Tucson official's dismissal of Rose Marie Augustine's complaints suggests that Augustine had violated a norm or appropriateness in speaking with government officials. This may appear strange at first as it is the official's rudeness to her that surprises us. But, environmental justice advocates insist, poor and minority residents are often treated less seriously due to implicit norms for what counts as appropriate or reasonable in matters of environmental health and regulatory responsibilities. It is precisely this subtle barrier that some face as they work to build more inclusive and healthier communities.

In some ways, the unstated rules that operate in many forums addressing environmental problems reflect something similar to the ancient principle of *decorum*. **Decorum** was a virtue of style in the classical Greek and Latin handbooks on rhetoric and is usually translated as *propriety* or *that which is fitting* for the particular audience and occasion. The Roman rhetorician Cicero, for example, wrote that a wise speaker is one who is "able to speak in any way which the case requires" or in ways that are most "appropriate"; he proposed, "let us call [this quality] decorum or 'propriety'" (Cicero, 1962, XX.69).

Within the context of those in poor and minority communities who try to speak about technical matters, however, the idea of decorum has taken on a much more constraining, even demeaning, role. The norms for what is and is not appropriate in regulatory forums often construct the lay public's ways of speaking as indecorous because [ordinary citizens often] violate norms of speaking and the level of knowledge demanded by health and government agencies. Although the members of an environmentally harmed community may speak at public hearings, their standing, or the respect afforded them, may be constrained informally by the rules and expectations of agency procedures and norms for knowledge claims.

At this point, it might be useful to describe some of the norms and expectations that public officials may assume in public hearings or technical forums and the violations that encourage them to view members of low-income communities as indecorous.

"The Evidence Is in My Body!" Challenging Agency Norms

Agency Norms for Speaking

With exposure to chemical contamination and official denial or resistance, affected residents often become frustrated, disillusioned with authority, and angry. Ironically, such responses can be prompted by interaction with the very agencies whose official mandate is to help those who feel themselves to be at risk—for example, state health departments or the EPA. The individuals who become involved with these agencies often find themselves in a baffling environment of overlapping institutional jurisdictions, technical forums, and a language of risk assessment that speaks of parts per million of toxic substances. These are unfamiliar contexts for most of us, not simply for the residents of low-income communities. Environmental sociologist Michael Edelstein (1988) explained, "What is lost [for residents in these communities] is their ability to participate directly in understanding and determining courses of action important to their lives" (p. 118). They are, in a sense "captured by [the] agencies upon which they become dependent for clarification and assistance" (p. 118).

This *capture* is enabled by many agency officials' tendencies to frame the participation of the public within restricted parameters of agency procedures and norms. As we saw in Chapter 1, industry and government officials often try to move the grounding of environmental discussions from the public to the technical sphere, which privileges more "rational" forms of argument. This is also journalist William Greider's (1992) argument in his book *Who Will Tell the People?* In it, Greider wrote that technical forums often exclude the lay public by their assumptions about what constitutes legitimate evidence in debates about environment and community health.

The weight of past practices helps to explain why some agencies are reluctant to open technical hearings to the voices of aggrieved communities. Restricting the testimony of lay witnesses allows an agency to feel its decision making won't be hampered by "an aroused and possibly ignorant public" (Rosenbaum, 1983, quoted in

Lynn, 1987, p. 359). Under such norms of decorum, for some citizens to speak is therefore to confront a painful dilemma. On the one hand, to enter discussions about toxicology, epidemiology, or the technical aspects of water quality is tacitly to accept the discursive boundaries within which concerns for family health are seen as private or emotional matters. On the other hand, for worried parents to inject such private concerns into these conversations is to transgress powerful boundaries of technical knowledge, reason, and decorum and thus risk not being heard at all.

Charlotte Keys's Story: "The Evidence Is in My Body!"

Charlotte Keys transgressed such a boundary. Keys was a young, African-American woman in the small town of Columbia in southern Mississippi with whom I had worked in my role as president of the Sierra Club in the mid-1990s. Keys and her neighbors lived next to a chemical plant owned by Reichhold Chemical, which had exploded and burned years earlier. The explosion and fire spewed toxic fumes throughout the neighborhood. Residents also suspected some of the barrels of chemicals that had been abandoned by the company had leached into the yards of nearby homes and into tributaries of Columbia's drinking water sources.

Many of Keys's neighbors near the abandoned plant also complained of unusual skin rashes, headaches, and illnesses. Officials from EPA and Columbia's mayor initially dismissed the residents' complaints as unsubstantiated; no health assessment was ever conducted. Reichhold spokesperson Alec Van Ryan later acknowledged to local news media, "I think everyone from the EPA on down will admit the initial communications with the community were nonexistent" (in Pender, 1993, p. 1).

Ultimately, Charlotte Keys organized her neighbors to speak with local officials and at public meetings. One such meeting occurred with officials from the federal Agency for Toxic Substances and Disease Registry (ATSDR), who traveled to Columbia to propose a health study of the residents. However, the ATSDR officials proposed only to sample the neighbors' urine and hair and test these for recent, acute exposure to toxins. Keys and other residents objected. They explained their exposure had initially occurred much earlier, when the plant exploded, and had been ongoing since then. Having done their homework, they insisted that the appropriate test was one that sampled blood and fatty tissues for evidence of long-term, chronic exposure. Keys urged the ATSDR officials to adopt this approach because, she said, "The evidence is in my body!" (C. Keys, personal correspondence, September 12, 1995).

The ATSDR officials refused this request, citing budgetary constraints. In turn, the residents felt stymied in their efforts to introduce the important personal evidence of their long-term exposure to chemicals that they believed was evident in their bodies. The meeting degenerated into angry exchanges and ended with an indefinite deferral of the plans to conduct a health study.[10]

Unfortunately, the tension between the ATSDR and the residents of Columbia, Mississippi, is not unusual. Too often, agency officials dismiss the complaints and recommendations of those facing risk of chemical exposure in low-income communities, believing that such people are emotional, unreliable, and irrational. For example, in an early study of public comments on the EPA's environmental impact studies, political scientist Lynton Caldwell (1988) found that

> public input into the . . . document was not regarded by government officials as particularly useful. . . . The public was generally perceived to be poorly informed on the issues and unsophisticated in considering risks and trade-offs. . . . Public participation was accepted as inevitable, but sometimes with great reluctance. (p. 80)

I have also overheard agency officials complain, after hearing reports of family illness or community members' fears, "This is very emotional, but where's the evidence?" "I've already heard this story," or simply, "This is not helpful."

In short, viewing someone as indecorous—as emotional or ignorant—functions to dismiss the informal standing of ordinary people and their ability to question the claims of public agencies or industries. To be clear, I am not suggesting that the indecorous voice results in a person's rhetorical incompetence or a failure to find the "right words" to articulate a grievance. Instead, I'm suggesting that the arrangements and procedures of power may undermine the rhetorical standing—the respect accorded to such groups—by narrowly defining the acceptable rhetorical norms of environmental decision making.

The result is that citizens from poor and minority communities often face what environmental sociologist Michael Reich (1991) described as **toxic politics.** This is the dismissal of a community's moral and communicative standing or the right of residents to matter within the discursive boundaries in which decisions affecting their fates are deliberated. The phrase *toxic politics* refers not only to the politics of locating or cleaning up chemical facilities but to the poisonous nature of such politics on occasion.

In the face of such toxic politics, many at-risk communities are inventing new ways to communicate their grievances, bypassing official forums and experts and inviting witnesses to come into their homes and neighbors to see for themselves the hazards there.

Toxic Tours: Sights, Sounds, and Smells

One particularly striking form of communication used more and more by environmental justice groups to connect local communities and wider publics is what grassroots activists call **toxic tours.** Communication scholar Phaedra Pezzullo (2007), in her book *Toxic Tourism Rhetorics of Pollution, Travel, and Environmental Justice,* defines these as "non-commercial expeditions into areas that are polluted by toxins, spaces that Robert D. Bullard (1993) calls 'human sacrifice zones.' . . . More and more of these communities have begun to invite outsiders in, providing tours as a means of educating people about and, it is hoped, transforming their situation" (p. 5).

Often, these outsiders are reporters, environmental allies, religious groups, and other supporters who—in personally experiencing the conditions of a community under environmental stress—are likely to share their experiences more widely.

Unlike EPA or other agency inspections of toxic sites, toxic tours highlight "discourses of . . . contamination, of social justice and the need for cultural change" (Pezzullo, 2007, pp. 5–6). Although environmental advocates have taken reporters and others into natural areas such as Yosemite Valley and the Grand Canyon for the past century to build support for their protection, this use of toxic tours is more recent.

Seeing for Ourselves in the Maquiladoras

Some years ago, I had the opportunity to join Dr. Pezzullo and other environmental leaders on a toxic tour outside of Matamoros, Mexico, south of the U.S. border near Brownsville, Texas. This area, which is part of the *maquiladora* zone or manufacturing area, has large numbers of (largely unregulated) industrial plants. These plants relocated to this area from the U.S. as a result of the North American Free Trade Agreement (NAFTA). Living in nearby *colonias* (crowded, makeshift housing on unoccupied land), the *maquiladora* workers and their families are subject to severely contaminated air and water, abysmal sanitation, and unsafe drinking water; many suffer from a number of illnesses. (See Chapter 12 for a discussion of the high rate of anencephalic births in the *maquiladora* zone.)

| Figure 9.2 | The Conoco Philips refinery is a stop on the toxic tour of low-income neighborhoods in Los Angeles; the tour is sponsored by an environmental justice group. |

AP Photo/Ric Francis

The tour through the crowded *colonias* was organized by the Sierra Club and its Mexican allies to introduce leaders from environmental groups to the threats to human health from pollution and unhealthy living conditions for workers and their families. As we walked through the unpaved streets by the workers' homes, we felt overpowered by the sights, smells, and feel of an environment under assault. Strong chemical odors filled the air, small children played in visibly polluted streams by their homes, while others, barely older, scavenged in burning heaps of garbage for scraps of material they could sell for a few pesos.

Speaking of such experiences, Pezzullo (2004) later observed that being in a community harmed by such hazards opens visitors' senses of sight, sound, and smell and that this awareness builds support for the community's struggle: "Odorous fumes cause residents and their visitors' eyes to water and throats to tighten . . . a reminder of the physical risk toxics pose" (p. 248). She shared one toxic tour guide's observation that such tours give visitors "firsthand" evidence of "the environmental insult to residents [of having polluters so close to their homes], as well as the noxious odors that permeate the neighborhood" (p. 248). (For a description of a toxic tour in Louisiana's infamous Cancer Alley" see Pezzullo, 2003, 2007.)

While my experience with toxic tours was along the U.S.-Mexican border, toxic tours are used to introduce journalists, agency officials, and other outsiders to distressed areas across the United States. Activists with groups such as Communities for a Better Environment (cbecal.org), the Sierra Club's Delta Chapter in Louisiana (louisian.sierra club.org), and Texas Environmental Justice Advocacy Services (tejasbarriors.org) lead toxic tours in environmentally stressed areas in Los Angeles, New Orleans, Houston, Oakland, Denver, Detroit, Boston, and other cities. Toxic tours also are increasingly used by local organizing groups to bring state or federal officials into distressed areas to educate officials to conditions on the ground or to put a human face on environmental harms. (See: "FYI: Toxic Tour of Southern California's Coachella Valley.")

☞ FYI   Toxic Tour of Southern California's Coachella Valley

THERMAL, Calif.—Margarita Gamez stood in the baking heat Friday outside the trailer park where she lives with other farmworker families and begged visiting state lawmakers and environmental regulators to do something about the stench and dust from an abandoned dump across the street.

The trailer park was one of five stops on an "environmental justice" tour organized by community activists in Southern California's eastern Coachella Valley as they fight to clean up abandoned waste dumps, shoddy migrant housing and other hazards that are a fact of life in this poor, unincorporated region.

"We've been here for 12 years with this dump next to us and in the morning and in the afternoon we have to suffer through terrible stench," the 68-year-old Gamez said, speaking to about 30 visitors who clustered in the shade of a single tree after arriving by bus. "We're asking you to help us." . . .

(Continued)

(Continued)

The tour Friday made stops at two migrant encampments, the dump across from Gamez's home, [a] soil recycling facility and a mountain of decade-old composted human sewage that's on tribal land a quarter-mile from the local high school.

The so-called "toxic tour" preceded a state legislative committee hearing on environmental safety and toxins held at the same school. . . .

[One of the visiting state officials, Debbie Raphael, director of the state Department of Toxic Substances Control, commented:] "There's the human reaction of imagining myself raising my family in a mobile home where the water looks like it came out of a ditch," Raphael said, referencing arsenic-laced well water at one mobile home park the group visited. . . .

The eastern part of the valley is 98 percent Hispanic and the majority of residents are farmworkers, many of them migrants. They work in flat, sun-baked fields in this heavily irrigated region and come home to dangerously overcrowded trailer parks with limited septic systems and jerry-rigged electrical systems.

SOURCE: Gillian Flaccus, Associated Press, Jun 17, 2011. Used by permission.

As toxic tours show, the environmental justice movement continues to confront real-world, on-the-ground challenges for gaining voices for communities that are often excluded from official decision making. Indeed, the vision of environmental justice has always been more than removal of the disproportionate burden on low-income and minority communities. Beyond this, environmental justice activists insist the movement embodies "a new vision borne of a community-driven process whose essential core is a transformative public discourse over what are truly healthy, sustainable and vital communities" (National Environmental Justice Advisory Council Subcommittee on Waste and Facility Siting, 1996, p. 17).

Important to the nurture of such a transformative discourse is the democratic inclusion of people and communities in decisions affecting their lives. Yet, as we will see in the next section, threats from global climate change are raising new threats to communities and peoples throughout the world. And, with these threats come new challenges to ordinary peoples' ability to participant in meaningful ways in the geopolitical forums on such global concerns. As a result, a new movement for climate justice has arisen that has begun to articulate demands for environmental justice and human rights in a new context.

The Global Movement for Climate Justice

In recent years, the discourse of environment justice has been embraced by a vibrant and growing movement for climate justice. The largely dispersed, grassroots movement for **climate justice** views the environmental and human impacts of climate change from the frame of social justice, human rights, and concern for indigenous peoples. In ways similar to the criticism of mainstream environmentalism in the United States, climate justice advocates, indigenous peoples, and the poor in countries throughout Asia, South America, Africa, and the Pacific Island nations argue that climate change is not simply an environmental issue. Instead, the movement for climate justice asserts that global warming affects, disproportionately, the most vulnerable regions and peoples of the planet and that these peoples and nations often are excluded from participation in the forums addressing this problem.

In this section, I'll describe the construction of a new frame of climate justice as well as the efforts of peoples and communities affected by climate change to gain a voice in the international summits where representatives of world governments are negotiating new agreements on climate change.

Climate Justice: A New Frame

Climate scientists and advocates for climate justice generally agree that "the greatest brunt of climate change's effects will be felt (and are being felt) by the world's poorest people" (Roberts, 2007, p. 295). In its strongest statement to date, the Intergovernmental Panel on Climate Change (IPCC) forecast that "hundreds of millions of people in developing nations will face natural disasters, water shortages and hunger due to the effects of climate change" (Adam, Walker, & Benjamin, 2007, para. 5).

Already, extended droughts, crop failures, and conflict over scare resources are affecting many vulnerable peoples and nations. As I write in 2011, for example, the Environmental News Service (ENS) is reporting that the worst drought in 60 years is causing a severe food crisis in East Africa, particularly in Somalia and Kenya. In Kenya, the world's largest refugee camp is overwhelmed "as climate refugees from across the drought-stricken region arrive each week seeking water, food, and shelter" (Millions of African refugees desperate," 2011, para. 1; Knafo, 2011). More than 12 million people are facing famine and "are in desperate need of help" (Angley, 2011, para 1).

A Cruel Irony: Impacts of Climate Change

Human rights groups and environmental scholars also charge that the voices of those most affected by climate change are often not part of the conversation about solutions. Dale Jamieson (2007) notes that "seventy million farmers and their families in Bangladesh will lose their livelihoods when their rice paddies are inundated by seawater. Yet despite the vast number of people around the world who will suffer from climate change, most of them are not included when decisions are made" (p. 92). He adds, for this reason, "participatory justice is also important at the global level" (p. 92).

There is also a cruel irony in this exclusion: As former *New Yorker Times* reporter Andrew Revkin (2007) observed, "In almost every instance, the people most at risk from climate change live in countries that have contributed the least to the buildup of carbon dioxide and other greenhouse gases linked to the recent warming of the planet" (para. 2).

As the effects of climate change—particularly in vulnerable areas of Asia and Africa—began to be experienced by local communities and regions, nongovernmental organizations (NGOs) from these nations began to build alliances and coordinate with activists in Europe and the United States. One of the most consequential developments of this alliance would be the elaboration of climate justice as a new frame in their construction of messages about global warming and in the mobilizing of others.

Constructing a Climate Justice Frame

The phrase *climate justice* was apparently used first in academic literature by Edith Brown Weiss (1989) in her study *In Fairness to Future Generations: International Law, Common Patrimony, and Intergenerational Equity.* A more movement-oriented demand for climate justice, however, may have been voiced first in the mid-1990s, by Tom Goldtooth, the founder of the Indigenous Environmental Network; it was further developed in a 1999 CorpWatch report and was the basis for a resolution at the Second People of Color Environmental leadership Summit in 2002 (Tokar, 2010, pp. 45–46).

One of the first large-scale gatherings for Climate Justice supporters occurred in 2000 when thousands of grassroots organizations and climate activists met in The Hague, Netherlands, at the Climate Justice Summit. The summit was an alternative forum to a UN meeting on climate change and was intended as a discursive space "to raise the critical issues that are not being addressed by the world's governments" (Bullard, 2000, para. 5).

In the years following, NGOs, indigenous peoples' organizations, and other social justice activists came together to organize rallies, conferences, and protests alongside UN meetings on climate change. Two other early, important organizing efforts occurred when local activists and international NGOs met alongside official UN-sponsored sessions on climate change in Bali, Indonesia, in August 2002, and New Delhi, India, in October 2002.

In Bali, a coalition of international NGOs, including the National Alliance of People's Movements (India), CorpWatch (United States), Greenpeace International, Third World Network (Malaysia), Indigenous Environmental Network (North America), and groundWork (South Africa) crafted one of the first declarations redefining climate change from the perspective of environmental justice and human rights.

Meeting alongside the UN delegates preparing for the Bali session earlier, the coalition developed the **Bali Principles of Climate Justice.** The principles pledged to "build an international movement of all peoples for Climate Justice" (Bali Principles of Climate Justice, 2002, para. 19). The effort would be based on certain principles, echoing the 1991 Principles of Environmental Justice (earlier in this chapter). For example, the Bali Principles similarly began:

1. Affirming the sacredness of Mother Earth, ecological unity and the interdependence of all species,

2. Climate Justice insists that communities have the right to be free from climate change, its related impacts and other forms of ecological destruction.

3. Climate Justice affirms the need to reduce with an aim to eliminate the production of greenhouse gases and associated local pollutants.

4. Climate Justice affirms the rights of indigenous peoples and affected communities to represent and speak for themselves. (para. 20)

One consequence of the Bali Principles, as well as other declarations, was to shift "the discursive framework of climate change from a scientific-technical debate to one about ethics focused on human rights and justice" (Agyeman, Doppelt, & Lynn, 2007, p. 121). An important moment in this shift came on October 28, 2002, when more than 1,500 individuals—farmers, indigenous peoples, the poor, and youth—from more than 20 countries marched for climate justice in New Delhi, India (Roberts, 2007). The occasion was a meeting of a grassroots Climate Justice Summit to begin organizing for climate justice on an international scale. Representatives from affected communities gathered "to provide testimony to the fact that climate change is a reality whose effects are already being felt around the world" (Delhi Climate Justice Declaration, 2002, para. 1).

The culmination of the summit was the **Delhi Climate Justice Declaration.** The declaration concluded: "We, representatives of the poor and the marginalized of the world, representing fishworkers, farmers, Indigenous Peoples, Dalits, the poor, and the youth, resolve to actively build a movement . . . that will address the issue of climate change from a human-rights, social justice, and labour perspective" (para. 12). The declaration expressed the attendees' resolve to "build alliances across states and borders to oppose climate change inducing patterns and advocate for and practice sustainable development" (para. 12).

Other international gatherings and declarations have followed, including the Durban Declaration on Carbon Trading (2004), a critique of proposed market schemes for trading greenhouse gas emissions; the People's Declaration for Climate Justice (Sumberklampok Declaration) (2007), in Bali, Indonesia, an effort to influence the start of negotiations among the world's nations of a new post-Kyoto treaty; and the large, international mobilizations at the UN climate conferences in Copenhagen (2009) and Cancun (2010).

Mobilizing for Climate Justice

As a result of their exclusion from the official forums, climate justice activists have sought to create alternative structures for communication—outside of summits, as we saw earlier, with online networks that coordinate activities and update activists and groups across regions, and on the ground, as local activists organize around businesses or other sites linked to climate change.

Global Organizing

At the summits in New Delhi, Bali, and elsewhere, climate activists emphasized the need to create lines of communication across borders and within regions to build a movement for climate justice. In Bali in 2002, climate activists resolved "to begin to build an international movement of all peoples for Climate Justice" (para. 19). Similarly, in the Delhi Climate Justice Declaration (2002), the grassroots representatives resolved to "build alliances across states and borders" (para. 12). And, again, in the Durban Declaration on Carbon Trading in 2004, activists committed themselves "to help build a global grassroots movement for climate justice" (para. 9).

By the time of the 2007 Bali gathering, the movement had come to "the forefront of global civil society debates [about climate change] . . . and rose in prominence during the lead-up to the much-anticipated 2009 UN climate summit in Copenhagen" (Tokar, 2010, p. 44).

While the movement successfully turned out tens of thousands of supporters for it, the UN Climate Conference in Copenhagen in December 2009 also proved to be a turning point—and a disappointment—for the climate justice movement. In the months preceding the conference, climate justice groups from 21 countries had issued a Call to Action, as part of a mass-mobilization effort. By the time of the conference, thousands of activists had gathered in Copenhagen, holding rallies, mounting colorful displays, conducting workshops, and carrying out peaceful marches and demonstrations.

As the official conference continued, protests outside the Bella Center increased. Clashes with police began as activists felt angry at being left out of the official meetings. Although some NGO representatives and journalists were allowed inside, thousands of others were barred due to a lack of space. As a result, some activists attempted to force their way inside the Center for a "Peoples' Assembly." In blocking them, police fired tear gas and pepper spray at more than 1,000 activists; hundreds were arrested (Gray, 2009). Calling it "an affront to democracy," the executive director of Friends of the Earth complained to journalists that indigenous peoples and civil society groups were being "prevented from speaking up on behalf of communities around the globe within the talks themselves" (Gray, 2009, paras. 9, 10). Many felt that only by hearing directly from such groups could the UN delegates appreciate the urgency and human face of the effects of climate change.

Whether for this or other reasons, the delegates failed to reach a binding agreement at Copenhagen. Although informal agreement reached at the conference recognized the scientific case for keeping temperature rises to no more than 2°C, it "does not contain commitments to emissions reductions to achieve that" (Vidal, Stratton, & Goldenberg, 2009, para. 2). Nor would subsequent UN meetings in Cancun and elsewhere, as I write, come close to achieving a new, international treaty to replace the early Kyoto Accord.

The climate justice movement itself is sustained largely online through social networking sites and LISTSERVs that help to mobilize activists for actions at sites such as the Copenhagen conference. For example, the India Climate Justice Forum is hosted by the India Resource Center, a project of Global Resistance, whose goal is "to strengthen the movement against corporate globalization by supporting and linking local, grassroots struggles against globalization around the world" (indiaresource.org).

On the other hand, the climate justice movement has initiated (and continues to bring online) new social networking sites, blogs, and information sites of its own.

An important network is the London-based Rising Tide Coalition for Climate Justice (risingtide.org.uk), consisting of environmental and social justice groups from around the world, especially in Europe (Roberts, 2007). There is also a Rising Tide North American network (2008, risingtidenorthamerica.org). Rising Tide grew out of the efforts of groups who came together to organize events alongside a UN climate conference in The Hague in 2000.

Other prominent online networks include: Environmental Justice Climate Change Initiative (ejcc.org); It's Getting Hot in Here (itsgettinghotinhere.org,), a community media site involving student and youth activists against climate change; Climate Justice Now! (climatejustice.blogspot.com), an active blog with links to numerous climate justice sites; the Third World Network (twnside.org.sq); and 350.0rg, which has mobilized thousands of climate activists in coordinated, same-day protests around the world.

The number 350 in climate justice discourse refers to 350 parts per million of carbon dioxide as the level in the atmosphere that is safe for the global climate. Like many other online sites, 350.0rg provides daily updates, video uploads from local activists, and analyses of official proposals. The site also has played a prominent role in the past several years, mobilizing climate justice activists ahead of the UN climate conference in Copenhagen, Denmark, and annually since then, in same-day, international displays of concern. In addition, other climate justice groups formed the Mobilization for Climate Justice (actforclimatejustice.org) in 2009 "to link the climate struggle in the U.S. to the growing international climate justice movement" in an attempt to build support for actions at the Copenhagen conference (Tokar, 2010, pp. 48–49).

As a result of its online organizing, the climate justice movement brought together coalitions of students, antinuclear and social justice activists, indigenous peoples, academics, opponents of carbon trading, religious groups, and others.

Climate Change and Grassroots Energy

While the climate justice movement is largely made up of "a series of coalitions, which sometimes appear to exist mostly . . . on a website" (Roberts, 2007, p. 297), it clearly has other important strengths. These include, in addition to a " 'master frame' in which to claim injustice," substantial cross-border alliances, "some key resources in these networking groups, [and] grassroots energy" (p. 297). Much of this grassroots energy comes from the creative, direct actions of local groups as well as the initiatives of larger organizations.

Much of the local organizing initiative around climate justice comes from younger activists in the United States and Europe as well as from farmers, indigenous peoples, and human rights activists in Asia, Africa, and South America. "An emerging youth climate movement is carrying out creative direct actions, not only

Figure 9.3	Globally, a youth climate justice movement has been organizing to demand immediate action on climate change, at coal plants, corporate headquarters, and at international conferences.

at coal industry sites, but also at corporate headquarters [and] industry conferences" (Tokar, 2010, p. 48). One tactic has been the use of direct action events to publicize the links between global warming and banks that finance the mining of coal, a major source of greenhouse gases. For example, activists blockaded the Bank of America in Asheville, North Carolina, to draw attention to its lending of money for mountaintop mining of coal:

> Two activists locked down inside the main lobby and other activists blockaded the entrance to the downtown branch of the Bank of America. The protest included a large, lively group of concerned citizens dressed as canaries and polar bears. Activists carried signs and banners that read: "Bank of America Stop Funding Climate Change," "Bank of America Stop Mountaintop Removal,"... [and] "Bank of America Climate Criminal." (Climate Convergence, 2007, para. 2)

More recently, climate justice activists in the United States, Canada, Australia, the UK, and New Zealand used the April 20 anniversary of the BP *Deepwater Horizon* explosion and oil spill in the Gulf of Mexico to call for an international Day of Action Against Extraction. Activists staged "aggressive protests and acts of civil disobedience at the doorstep of fossil fuel extraction, including at corporate and government offices, mountaintop removal mine sites, power plants and gas stations (The Day of Action Against Extraction, 2011, paras. 4, 5).

Even as some activists continue to pursue largely symbolic protests—rallies at summits, civil disobedience at corporate offices, and so on—a debate has begun in the wider climate justice movement about the effectiveness of such tactics. On the one hand, many radical leaders insist that the climate catastrophe "will not be stopped in conference rooms or treaty negotiations"; what is required, they argue, is "mass action in the streets" (Rebick, 2010, pp. 7, 8).

Yet, others have questioned whether the reliance on mass action alone is equal to the scale and complexity of the global economic system that is responsible for climate change: "We really do need a longer term plan," acknowledged Patrick Bond, the director of the Center for Civil Society in South Africa, a plan that "will make the gains we've taken, on the streets and in the communities . . . actually real. How can they be turned into good public policy?" ("Only political activism," 2010, p. 186). Radical environmentalist Eirik Eiglad (2010) similarly asked, "How can we see beyond the current . . . focus on the major climate summits [like Copenhagen or Cancun], important as they may be?" (p. 10).

While environmental and climate justice groups failed to persuade the U.S. Congress to act on climate change, other environmental groups are pursuing more strategic campaigns outside of the political process to reduce greenhouse gases directly. Perhaps the most successful of these efforts has been the Sierra Club's Beyond Coal campaign against coal-burning power plants (described in Chapter 8). As a result of the targeting of state utility commissions, banks, and energy companies themselves, the campaign and its supporters have blocked or cancelled more than 150 proposed plants in the past five years. Yet, even as plants are cancelled in the United States, coal-fired power plants continue to be built as other nations pursue their own economic paths to development.

Others, therefore, acknowledge that slowing then reversing climate change will require a basic restructuring of the global economy. What is needed, they argue, are "broad and visionary alliances with people and movements around the world to begin the fundamental transformation of society" (Petermann & Langelle, 2010, p. 187). How to achieve this—and what strategic leverage is required to affect global economies—are challenging questions that are still being debated. (See "Act Locally! How Can You Make a Difference on Global Climate Change?")

Act Locally!

How Can You Make a Difference on Global Climate Change?

"Think globally, act locally" has been a saying in the environmental movement since Earth Day. Its advice is more relevant now than ever. But, how can an individual act locally on a problem like global climate change? Still, many students, families, and concerned individuals are finding ways to do this every day—reducing their individual carbon footprints, attending public hearings to oppose permits for coal-fired power plants, e-mailing public officials in support of renewable energy, and more.

(1) Investigate what your college or university is doing to reduce its energy consumption or operate in a more sustainable way. How can you add to these initiatives?

(Continued)

(Continued)

(2) Use an app or online carbon footprint tracker to calculate (and reduce) your own output of carbon dioxide. Check out the numerous trackers that are available, like Footprint Tracker at http://carbontracker.com, and iPhone, iPad, and Android all have carbon footprint apps for doing this. Better yet, initiate a crowd-sourcing contest to find the top three personal carbon footprint trackers for your campus or group.

(3) Call or go online to your local electric utility company for its energy savings guide or request an energy audit, identifying ways to save energy in your apartment or home.

(4) What opportunities do you have to speak at public hearings on renewable energy, such as a bill in your state legislature requiring a percentage of electricity in your state be produced from wind, solar, or another form of clean energy; or a town council's public comments on a proposal for a light rail or new bike lanes?

As I write, UN delegates meeting in Durban, South Africa, in December 2011, are attempting to find agreement on a post-Kyoto treaty to address climate change. Coming after their failures in Copenhagen (2009) and Cancun, Mexico (2010), they are struggling to find the political will among the major world economies, including the United States, Japan, the European Union, Brazil, and China, to reach a binding agreement. The decisions being made there and in the next two to three years will undoubtedly be consequential for future generations.

The Movement for Green Jobs

While climate justice advocates search for ways to influence upcoming UN negotiations, others in the United States have initiated a closely related movement for green jobs. The **green jobs movement** champions a new source of employment, particularly for depressed communities and unemployed workers, by funding labor-intensive, clean-energy projects such as weatherproofing buildings, installing solar panels, and building wind turbines, which at the same time, help to reduce U.S. emissions of greenhouse gases. Although the movement's goals are ambitious, it has already begun to shift the political conversation in the United States by its articulation or linking of jobs, clean energy, and climate change.

Shifting the Political Agenda

Within the last five years, the vision of green jobs, or a clean energy economy, has become commonplace in the media, political circles, and in new hiring by clean energy manufacturers and businesses. By the U.S. presidential campaign in 2008, for example, both Democratic and Republican candidates were promising their support for green jobs, with Barack Obama, for example, promising to spend

$150 billion over 10 years to create 5 million new green-collar jobs, while John McCain assured his campaign audiences that decarbonizing America's economy will produce "thousands, millions of new jobs in America" (Walsh, 2008, para. 1). Furthermore, the United Nations Environmental Program (2008) reported, for the first time at the global level, "green jobs are being generated in some sectors and economies" (p. vii).

Part of the reason for the apparent appeal of green jobs may be the elasticity of the phrase itself. As Conger (2010) noted, "Here isn't a broad agreement on what these highly touted jobs are in the first place" (para. 4). The United Nations Environment Program (2008), for example, defines a *green job*, also called a green-collar job, broadly "as work in agricultural, manufacturing, research and development (R&D), administrative, and service activities that contribute substantially to preserving or restoring environmental quality" (p. 3). Others insist green jobs must be linked explicitly to clean energy or work that contributes to a reduction of greenhouse gas emissions. The divergence in these definitions, as Michelle Melton, a research analyst at Georgetown University's Center on Education and the Workforce, explains, "is that the (green jobs) movement really didn't start with economists and statisticians. . . . It came from an advocacy movement" (quoted in Conger, 2010, para. 4).

For some movement policy centers, such as the Apollo Alliance—a coalition of labor and environmental groups—the rationale for green jobs originally grew from the need to address climate change. To curb greenhouse gas emissions, such groups argue, the United States will need to decarbonize the economy, that is, replace fossil-fuel sources of consumption (heating and cooling homes, driving, etc.) with cleaner energy sources. In turn, groups like the Apollo Alliance argue that this work will create millions of new jobs because someone will have to install the solar panels, build wind farms, and so on. Phil Angelides, chair of the Apollo Alliance, explained to a reporter:

> Between now and 2030, 75% of the buildings in the U.S. will either be new or substantially rehabilitated. Our inefficient, dangerously unstable electrical grid will need to be overhauled. The jobs that will go into that kind of work can be green-collar—provided that the government adopts the kind of policies that incentivize environmentally friendly choices." (quoted in Walsh, 2008, para. 6)

As the connections among climate change, decarbonizing the economy, and jobs became clear, others seized the phrase *green jobs* to frame this complex linkage and raise support for funding for these initiatives. Prime movers in this communicative work included, along with the Apollo Alliance, the Blue Green Alliance (bluegreen-alliance.org), a strategic partnership between labor unions and environmental groups, and leaders like Van Jones, founder of the Ella Baker Center for Human Rights (ellabakercenter.org), a nonprofit group committed to finding alternatives to violence and incarceration in urban neighborhoods. The center, under Jones, would also launch a green-collar jobs campaign that made explicit the linkage between a green economy and uplifting jobs.

Articulating Jobs and Clean Energy

Helping to account for the popularity of green jobs among the public and some political leaders has been a creative articulation or linking of several, basic frames in the American mind—the importance attached to jobs, energy security, and a clean environment. Although *green jobs* has referred at times to any employment in environmental services, such as waste management or recycling, the movement's original advocates conceived of green jobs as a solution to both unemployment and, specifically, climate change. Indeed, groups like the Blue Green Alliance, Green for All, and the Apollo Alliance sought to construct an inspiring vision of a new, prosperous economy that renewed communities and people while addressing the world's biggest challenge.

| Figure 9.4 | One of the prime movers of the green jobs movement is Van Jones, former Green Jobs Czar in the Obama administration and founder of Green for All in Oakland, California. |

© Lindsay Hebberd/Corbis

One of the prime movers of the green jobs movement is Van Jones, former Green Jobs Czar in the Obama administration and founder of Green for All in Oakland, California. In starting Green for All—whose logo is a sun rising over a crowded cityscape—Jones's goal has been to "broaden the appeal of the environmental movement and, at the same time, bring jobs to poor neighborhoods" (Kolbert, 2009, para. 5).

In his book, *The Green Collar Economy: How One Solution Can Fix Our Two Biggest Problems,* Jones (2008) makes clear the movement's linkage of jobs and climate change:

> [T]the best way to fight both global warming and urban poverty is by creating millions of "green jobs"—weatherizing buildings, installing solar panels, and constructing mass-transit systems. A percentage of these jobs—Jones is purposefully vague about how many—should go to the disadvantaged and the chronically unemployed. "The green economy should not be just about reclaiming thrown-away stuff," he writes. "It should be about reclaiming thrown-away communities." (Kolbert, 2009, para. 31).

Van Jones's emphasis upon renewal of communities as well as the environment illustrates one of the functions of what I described in Chapter 8 as *critical rhetoric,* or one form of advocacy. There, I defined critical rhetoric not only as the questioning or denunciation of a behavior, policy, or ideology but also the articulation of an alternate vision or ideology. For Jones, that vision sharply contrasts with the realities of many urban neighborhoods today. In a speech to the Center for American Progress, for example, Jones laid out this competing vision of America:

> You have construction workers who are idle, and they're going to be idle for twelve months, twenty-four months, thirty-six months. . . . We have people coming home from wars, coming home from prisons, coming out of high school with no job prospects whatsoever. Let us connect the people who most need work with the work that most needs to be done. (quoted in Kolbert, 2009, para. 40)

This vision is vividly displayed in Green for All's communication outreach and website, where videos of depressed neighborhoods, closed businesses, unemployed workers, and children suffering from pollution are contrasted with images of people weathering homes, installing solar panels, and rebuilding communities. The vision is one where millions of new, clean jobs are available for those who have been left out of the "old economy":

> Every day, about 135 million people go to work in the U.S. Imagine what would happen if millions of those jobs—plus new ones created for people who are currently unemployed—were in fields like renewable energy, sustainable agriculture, and green building. Our two crucial concerns about survival—the environment and making a living—would be combined. A person's commitment to their job would also be their commitment to the planet. (Greenforall.org/green-collar-jobs)

A similar articulation of jobs and clean energy is the theme of an annual summit of employers, labor unions, and environmental groups. This Good Jobs, Green Jobs National Conference is sponsored by the Blue Green Alliance and its allies from Fortune 500 companies, green industry trade associations, labor unions, environmental organizations, and educational institutions. The two-day conference hosts workshops, speeches, and panel displays for workers, business leaders, and public officials and showcases the frame of a clean energy economy—"an economy that creates green jobs, reduces global warming and preserves America's economic and environmental security" (from the 2011 conference website, www .greenjobsconference.org).

As I write in late 2011, the movement has gained popular support and some tangible victories. The demand for green jobs has begun a rallying cry for a broad coalition of environmental and antipoverty advocates, labor unions, clean technology businesses, and some political leaders. As early as 2007, the U.S. Congress had passed the Green Jobs Act, authorizing funds for low-income trainees; and more recently, the green jobs section of the 2010 stimulus bill passed by Congress included $5 billion for clean energy initiatives, green construction, and other sources of green employment.

SUMMARY

In this chapter, I've described some of the communication practices of the grassroots movements for environmental justice, climate justice, and green jobs, as well as their challenges to a discourse of the environment as a place apart from humans. As a consequence, these movements have created a new antagonism (Chapter 2), or a recognition of the limits of existing views or ideas; in turn, this has provided an opening that is allowing other voices and views to be heard.

- In section one, I described the emergence of a critical rhetoric of environmental justice as low-income neighborhoods and communities of color challenged mainstream environmental groups' discourse about the environment as a place apart from humans. This movement has:

  (1) demanded a halt to the inequitable burdens often imposed on poor and minority communities,

  (2) called for more opportunities for those who are most affected by environmental injustices to be heard in the decision making of corporations and public agencies, and

  (3) articulated a vision of environmentally healthy and economically sustainable communities.

- Section two introduced the concept of *indecorous voices,* a reference to the barriers often faced by residents in at-risk communities when they attempt to speak out against the hazards they face. We looked at two aspects of this:

  (1) communication practices that dismiss the voices of some as "inappropriate" or "emotional," and

  (2) the use of toxic tours by low-income neighborhoods and communities of color to call attention to the sights, sounds, and smells of environmental racism.

- In section three, I described the emergence of the global movement for climate justice and the ways in which it has reframed the threat of climate change as a matter of social justice, human rights, and concern for indigenous peoples as well as the environment.
- Finally, in section four, I described the growth of a green jobs movement in the United States.

Although its goals are ambitious, the green jobs movement has already begun to influence the political agenda in the United States by its linking of jobs, clean energy, and climate change. Indeed, the movements for environmental and climate change and a demand for green jobs may offer the best hope in the face of global environmental threats for creating a socially just and ecologically sustainable society.

SUGGESTED RESOURCES

- *Climate Refugees*, 2010, a documentary film about the human face of climate change at www.climaterefugees.com.
- Brian Tokar, *Toward Climate Justice: Perspectives on the Climate Crisis and Social Change*. Communalism Press, Porsgrunn, Norway, 2010.
- Phaedra C. Pezzullo, *Toxic Tours: Rhetorics of Pollution, Travel and Environmental Justice*. Tuscaloosa: University of Alabama Press, 2009.
- *Green for All*, a nationwide, nonprofit organization "working to build an inclusive green economy strong enough to lift people out of poverty," at www.greenforall.org.

KEY TERMS

DISCUSSION QUESTIONS

1. Should we be willing to accept some risks in order to enjoy the benefits of modern society? If so, who is most likely to receive the benefits? The risks?

2. Environmental historian Robert Gottlieb poses a challenging question: "Can mainstream and alternative groups find a common language, a shared history, a common conceptual and organizational home?" (in Warren, 2003, p. 254). What do you think? Are a common language and shared history needed for environmentalists and activists from poor and minority neighborhoods to work together?

3. Why have the United States and other nations been slow to act on global climate change? To what degree do you believe communication (news reports, blogs, cable TV) plays a role in the public's view of climate change and its likely causes?

4. What effect has the climate justice movement had to date in influencing action of climate change? How effective is mass action in the street or global, same-day protests like 350.0rg's October 24, 2009, International Day of Climate Action?

5. Do you believe a shift from a fossil-fuel economy (coal power plants, oil, etc.) to a renewable energy economy (wind turbines, solar panels, etc.) will create a net increase in jobs that are also green? Who is likely to get these jobs?

NOTES

1. I am indebted to Dr. Phaedra Pezzullo of Indiana University for permission to cite material from our unpublished paper, "Re-Articulating 'Environment': Rhetorical Invention, Subaltern Counterpublics, and the Movement for Environmental Justice."

2. In 1978, residents of Love Canal discovered "that Hooker Chemical Corporation . . . had dumped 200 tons of a toxic, dioxin-laden chemicals and 21,600 tons of various other chemicals into Love Canal. . . . In 1953, Hooker filled in the canal, smoothed out the land, and sold it to the town school board for $1.00 (Gibbs, 1995, p. xvii). For background on Love Canal, see Chapter 1.

3. Hays adapted this phrase from the title of Rachel Carson's first book, *The Sea Around Us* (New York: Oxford University Press, 1950, 1951).

4. Other attempts to forge diverse coalitions included the 1972 Conference on Environmental Quality and Social Justice at Woodstock, Illinois; the 1976 United Auto Worker's Black Lake Conference, Working for Environmental and Economic Justice and Jobs; and the 1979 City Care conference on the urban environment in Detroit, jointly convened by the National Urban League, the Sierra Club, and the Urban Environment Conference.

5. Di Chiro (1996) noted, "Eventually, environmental and social justice organizations such as Greenpeace, the National Health Law Program, the Center for Law in the Public Interest, and Citizens for a Better Environment would join [the] Concerned Citizens' campaign to stop [the proposed facility]" (p. 527, note 2).

6. Chavis's claim of having coined the term *environmental racism* has been disputed; some activists in Warren County insist that they used this phrase first.

7. The Group of Ten were the Environmental Defense Fund, Friends of the Earth, the Izaak Walton League, the National Audubon Society, the National Parks and Conservation Association, the National Wildlife Federation, the Natural Resources Defense Council, the Sierra Club, the Sierra Club Legal Defense Fund (now Earth Justice), and the Wilderness Society.

8. I was fortunate to have the opportunity to attend and participate in the sessions that included leaders of traditional environmental organizations.

9. Portions of this section are derived from a paper I presented at the Fifth Biennial Conference on Communication and the Environment (Cox, 2001).

10. Reichhold Chemical ultimately offered to assist community members by helping to fund a health study and a community advisory panel to assist in decisions about the polluted site.

REFERENCES

Adam, D., Walker, P., & Benjamin, A. (2007, September 18). Grim outlook for poor countries in climate report. Retrieved December 12, 2008, from http://www.guardian.co.uk/

Agyeman, J., Doppelt, B., & Lynn, K. (2007). The climate-justice link: Communicating risk with low-income and minority audiences. In S. C. Moser & L. Dilling (Eds.), *Communicating a climate for change: Communicating climate change and facilitating social change* (pp. 119–138). Cambridge, UK: Cambridge University Press.

Alston, D. (1990). *We speak for ourselves: Social justice, race, and environment.* Washington, DC: Panos Institute.

Angley, N. (2011, August 18). *Famine in East Africa.* Retrieved August 19, 2011, from www.cnn.com

Augustine, R. M. (Speaker). (1991). *Documentary highlights of the First National People of Color Environmental Leadership Conference* [Videotape]. Washington, DC: United Church of Christ Commission for Racial Justice.

Augustine, R. M. (Speaker). (1993, October 21–24). *Environmental justice: Continuing the dialogue* [Cassette recording]. Recorded at the Third Annual Meeting of the Society of Environmental Journalists, Durham, NC.

Bali Principles of Climate Justice. (2002). Retrieved December 11, 2008, from http://www.ejnet.org

Bullard, R. D. (1993). Introduction. In R. D. Bullard (Ed.), *Confronting environmental racism: Voices from the grassroots* (pp. 7–13). Boston: South End Press.

Bullard, R. D. (Ed.). (1994). *Unequal protection: Environmental justice and communities of color.* San Francisco: Sierra Club Books.

Bullard, Robert D. (2000, November 21). *Climate justice and people of color.* Retrieved May 25, 2009, from www.ejrc.cau.edu/climatechgpoc.html

Bullard, R. D., Mohai, P., Saha, R., & Wright, B. (2007, March). *Toxic wastes and race at twenty, 1987–2007.* Cleveland, OH: United Church of Christ. Retrieved December 14, 2008, from http://www.ejrc.cau.edu

Bullard, R. D., & Wright, B. H. (1987). Environmentalism and the politics of equity: Emergent trends in the black community. *Mid-American Review of Sociology, 12,* 21–37.

Caldwell, L. K. (1988). Environmental impact analysis (EIA): Origins, evolution, and future directions. *Policy Studies Review, 8,* 75–83.

Carson, R. (1962). *Silent spring.* Boston: Houghton Mifflin.

Chavis, B. F., & Lee, C. (1987). *Toxic wastes and race in the United States: A national report on the racial and socio-economic characteristics of communities with hazardous waste sites.* New York: Commission for Racial Justice, United Church of Christ.

Cicero, M. T. (1962). *Orator* (Rev. ed.). (H. M. Hubell & G. L. Hendrickson, Trans.). Cambridge, MA: Harvard University Press.

Climate Convergence. (2007, August 13). *Activists block Bank of America in downtown Asheville.* Retrieved December 10, 2008, from http://asheville.indymedia.org

Clinton, W. J. (1994, February 16). Federal actions to address environmental justice in minority populations and low-income populations. Executive Order 12898 of February 14, 1994. *Federal Register, 59,* 7629.

Cole, L. W., & Foster, S. R. (2001). *From the ground up: Environmental racism and the rise of the environmental justice movement.* New York: New York University Press.

Conger, C. (2010, November 24). What are green jobs? *Discovery News.* Retrieved July 5, 2011, from http://news.discovery.com/

Cox, J. R. (2001). Reclaiming the "indecorous" voice: Public participation by low-income communities in environmental decision making. In C. B. Short & D. Hardy-Short (Eds.), *Proceedings of the Fifth Biennial Conference on Communication and Environment* (pp. 21–31). Flagstaff: Northern Arizona University School of Communication.

The day of action against extraction is one week away! (2011, April 14). BeyondTalk.net. retrieved February 27, 2012, from www.beyondtalk.net/2011/04/the-day-of-action-against-extraction-is-one-week-away/

Delhi Climate Justice Declaration. (2002). India Climate Justice Forum. Delhi, India: India Resource Center. Retrieved December 11, 2008, from http://www.indiaresource.org

Di Chiro, G. (1996). Nature as community: The convergence of environment and social justice. In W. Cronon (Ed.), *Uncommon ground: Rethinking the human place in nature* (pp. 298–320). New York: Norton.

Di Chiro, G. (1998). Environmental justice from the grassroots: Reflections on history, gender, and expertise. In D. Faber (Ed.), *The struggle for ecological democracy: Environmental justice movements in the United States* (pp. 104–136). New York: Guilford Press.

Durban Declaration on Carbon Trading. (2004, October 10). Glenmore Centre, Durban, South Africa. Retrieved March 1, 2009, from http://www.carbontradewatch.org/

Edelstein, M. R. (1988). *Contaminated communities: The social and psychological impacts of residential toxic exposure.* Boulder, CO: Westview.

Eiglad, E. (2010). In B. Tokar, *Toward climate justice: Perspectives on the climate crisis and social change* (pp. 7–12). Porsgrunn, Norway: Communalism Press.

Flaccus, G. (2011, June 17). Sewage pile, illegal dump on Calif toxic tour list. Associated Press. Retrieved February 27, 2012, from http://abcnews.go.com/US/wireStory?id=13864711#.T0uXg9VNqcc

Ferris, D. (Speaker). (1993, October 21–24). *Environmental justice: Continuing the dialogue* [Cassette recording]. Recorded at the Third Annual Meeting of the Society of Environmental Journalists, Durham, NC.

Gibbs, L. M. (1995). *Dying from dioxin: A citizen's guide to reclaiming our health and rebuilding democracy.* Boston: South End Press.

Gottlieb, R. (1993). *Forcing the spring: The transformation of the American environmental movement.* Washington, DC: Island Press.

Gottlieb, R. (2002). *Environmentalism unbound: Exploring new pathways for change.* Cambridge, MA: MIT Press.

Gottlieb, R. (2003). Reconstructing environmentalism: Complex movements, diverse roots. In L. S. Warren (Ed.), *American environmental history* (pp. 245–256). Malden, MA: Blackwell.

Gray, L. (2009, December 17). Copenhagen climate conference: 260 arrested at protests. *The Telegraph* [UK]. Retrieved July 10, 2011, from www.telegraph.com

Greenpeace. (1990, April). *Ordinary people, doing extraordinary things.* [Videotape]. Public service announcement broadcast on VH-1 Channel.

Greider, W. (1992). *Who will tell the people? The betrayal of American democracy.* New York: Simon & Schuster.

Harvey, D. (1996). *Justice, nature, and the geography of difference.* Malden, MA: Blackwell.

Hays, S. P. (1987). *Beauty, health, and permanence: Environmental politics in the United States, 1955–1985.* Cambridge, UK: Cambridge University Press.

Jamieson, D. (2007). Justice: The heart of environmentalism. In P. C. Pezzullo & R. Sandler (Eds.), *Environmental justice and environmentalism: The social justice challenge to the environmental movement* (pp. 85–101). Cambridge, MA: MIT Press.

Jones, V. (2008). *The green collar economy: How one solution can fix our two biggest problems.* New York: HarperCollins.

Kazis, R., & Grossman, R. L. (1991). *Fear at work: Job blackmail, labor, and the environment.* Philadelphia: New Society.

Knafo, S. (2011, August 19). *Scientists link famine in Somalia to global warming.* Retrieved August 19, 2011, from www.huffingtonpost.com

Kolbert, E. (2009, January 12). Greening the ghetto: Can a remedy serve for both global warming and poverty? *The New Yorker.* Retrieved July 5, 2011, from www.newyorker.com

Lavelle, M., & Coyle, M. (1992, September 21). Unequal protection: The racial divide in environmental law. *National Law Journal,* S1, S2.

Lynn, F. M. (1987). Citizen involvement in hazardous waste sites: Two North Carolina access stories. *Environmental Impact Assessment and Review, 7,* 347–361.

Millions of African refugees desperate for food, water. (2011, July 6). *Environmental News Service.* Retrieved July 10, 2011, from ens-newswire.com

National Environmental Justice Advisory Council Subcommittee on Waste and Facility Siting. (1996). *Environmental justice, urban revitalization, and brownfields: The search for authentic signs of hope.* (Report Number EPA 500-R-96–002). Washington, DC: U.S. Environmental Protection Agency.

Obama revives panel on environmental justice. (2010, September 23). *USA Today,* p. 2A.

Office of the Inspector General. (2004, March 1). *EPA needs to consistently implement the intent of the executive order on environmental justice.* Washington, DC: Environmental Protection Agency. Retrieved March 1, 2009, from http://www.epa.gov/oig/reports

Only political activism and class struggle can save the planet. (2010). In I. Angus, (Ed.), *The global fight for climate justice: Anticapitalist responses to global warming and environmental destruction* (pp. 182–186). Black Point, Nova Scotia: Fernwood Publishing.

Pender, G. (1993, June 1). Residents still not satisfied: Plant cleanup fails to ease Columbia fears. *Hattiesburg American,* 1.

People's Declaration for Climate Justice (Sumberklampok Declaration). (2007, December 7). Bali, Indonesia. Retrieved March 1, 2009, from http://peoplesclimatemovement.net

Petermann, A., & Langelle, O. (2010). Crisis, challenge, and mass action. In I. Angus,

(Ed.), *The global fight for climate justice: Anticapitalist responses to global warming and environmental destruction* (pp. 186–195). Black Point, Nova Scotia: Fernwood Publishing.

Pezzullo, P. C. (2001). Performing critical interruptions: Rhetorical invention and narratives of the environmental justice movement. *Western Journal of Communication, 64,* 1–25.

Pezzullo, P. C. (2003). Touring "Cancer Alley," Louisiana: Performances of community and memory for environmental justice. *Text and Performance Quarterly, 23,* 226–252.

Pezzullo, P. C. (2004). Toxic tours: Communicating the "presence" of chemical contamination. In S. P. Depoe, J. W. Delicath, & M-F. A. Elsenbeer (Eds.), *Communication and public participation in environmental decision making* (pp. 235–254). Albany: State University of New York Press.

Pezzullo, P. C. (2007). *Toxic tours: Rhetorics of pollution, travel and environmental justice.* Tuscaloosa: University of Alabama Press.

Pezzullo, P. C., & Sandler, R. (Eds.). (2007). *Environmental justice and environmentalism: The social justice challenge to the environmental movement.* Cambridge, MA: MIT Press.

Proceedings: The First People of Color National Environmental Leadership Summit. (1991, October 24–27). Washington, DC: United Church of Christ Commission for Racial Justice.

Rebick, J. (2010). Foreword. In I. Angus (Ed.), *The global fight for climate justice: Anticapitalist responses to global warming and environmental destruction* (pp. 7–8). Black Point, Nova Scotia: Fernwood Publishing.

Reich, M. R. (1991). *Toxic politics: Responding to chemical disasters.* Ithaca, NY: Cornell University Press.

Revkin, A. C. (2007, April 3). The climate divide: reports from four fronts in the war on warming. *New York Times.* Retrieved July 10, 2011, from www.nytimes.com

Rising Tide North America. (2008, December 1). *Climate activists invade DC offices of environmental defense.* Retrieved December 14, 2008, from http://www.risingtide northamerica.org

Roberts, J. T. (2007). Globalizing environmental justice. In P. C. Pezzullo & R. Sandler (Eds.), *Environmental justice and environmentalism: The social justice challenge to the environmental movement* (pp. 285–307). Cambridge, MA: MIT Press.

Roberts, J. T., & Toffolon-Weiss, M. M. (2001). *Chronicles from the environmental justice frontline.* Cambridge, UK: Cambridge University Press.

Rosenbaum, W. (1983). The politics of public participation in hazardous waste management. In J. P. Lester & A. O. Bowman (Eds.), *The politics of hazardous waste management* (pp. 176–195). Durham, NC: Duke University Press.

Sandweiss, S. (1998). The social construction of environmental justice. In D. E. Camacho (Ed.), *Environmental injustices, political struggles* (pp. 31–58). Durham, NC: Duke University Press.

Schwab, J. (1994). *Deeper shades of green: The rise of blue-collar and minority environmentalism in America.* San Francisco: Sierra Club Books.

Senecah, S. L. (2004). The trinity of voice: The role of practical theory in planning and evaluating the effectiveness of environmental participatory processes. In S. P. DePoe, J. W. Delicath, & M-F. A. Elsenbeer (Eds.), *Communication and public participation in environmental decision making* (pp. 13–33). Albany: State University of New York Press.

SouthWest Organizing Project. (1990, March 16). Letter to the "Group of Ten" national environmental organizations. Albuquerque, NM. Retrieved March 1, 2009, from http://soa.utexas.edu

The Day of Action Against Extraction is one week away. (2011, April 14). Retrieved July 16, 2011, from www.beyond talk.net

Tokar, B. (2010). *Toward climate justice: Perspectives on the climate crisis and social change.* Porsgrunn, Norway: Communalism Press.

United Nations Environmental Program. (2008, September). *Green jobs: Toward decent work in a sustainable, low-carbon world.* Retrieved July 6, 2011, from http://www.unep.org

U.S. General Accounting Office. (1983). *Siting of hazardous waste landfills and their correlation with racial and economic status of surrounding communities.* Washington, DC: U.S. General Accounting Office.

Vidal, J., Stratton, A., & Goldenberg, S. (2009, December 19). Low targets, goals dropped: Copenhagen ends in failure. Guardian [UK]. Retrieved July 10, 2011, from www.guardian.co.uk

Walsh, C. (2008, May 26). What is a green-collar job, exactly? *TIME.* Retrieved July 5, 2011, from www.time.com/time/

Warren, L. S. (2003). *American environmental history.* Malden, MA, and Oxford, UK: Blackwell.

Weiss, E. B. (1989*). In fairness to future generations: International law, common patrimony, and intergenerational equity.* Ardsley, NY: Transnational.

White, H. L. (1998). Race, class, and environmental hazards. In D. E. Camacho (Ed.), *Environmental injustices, political struggle: Race, class, and the environment.* Durham, NC: Duke University Press.

As a result of a loose regulatory landscape, green product advertising may signal a wide range of meanings—from unsubstantiated claims to accurate information about the qualities of the product or the behavior of the corporation.

CHAPTER 10

Green Marketing and Corporate Campaigns

The deeper you go, the more good things you learn about oil and natural gas, an industry that supports 9.2 million American jobs. . . . From the energy in manufacturing plants to the fertilizer on farms to the building blocks of tomorrow's medicines, we're fueling all kinds of jobs.

—American Petroleum
Institute TV ad (2011)

The commercial appeared daily on my TV screen: A blond woman in a dark business suit calmly speaks to viewers as she descends in a glass elevator with an oil derrick and drilling shafts in the background. As she speaks of the "good things you learn about oil and natural gas," a large sign flashes on the screen: "9.2 million JOBS." The ad was sponsored by the American Petroleum Institute, a trade group that promotes the interests of energy producers like Exxon Mobil and more than 400 other producers, refiners, and ocean transport and services companies.

The TV advertisement for the oil and natural gas industry is one of many forms of environmental communication that corporations routinely use in the public sphere. These communications range from the advertising of "green" products and television and radio ads bolstering a corporation's image to lobbying campaigns aimed at influencing government agencies or the U.S. Congress.

Chapter Preview

- In the first section of this chapter, I will start by describing a free market discourse that underlies much of corporate environmental communication.
- In the second section, I'll examine corporate "green marketing" and its three major forms: (1) product advertising (sales), (2) image enhancement, and (3) corporate image repair.
- The third section explores two communication practices that take advantage of public support for environmental values:

  1. *greenwashing,* or the use of deceptive advertising to promote an environmentally responsible image, and
  2. a discourse of "green consumerism," doing "good" by buying green.

- In the fourth section, I explore the role of corporate advocacy campaigns in the public sphere to influence public opinion and environmental laws.
- Finally, I describe a third, less frequent communication practice, the use of Strategic Litigation Against Public Participation (SLAPP) suits, to discredit or intimidate individuals who criticize industry for harming the environment.

In general, corporate environmental communication may be one of three different types: (1) "green marketing," or the construction of an environmental identity for corporate products, images, and behaviors; (2) corporate advocacy campaigns that are aimed at affecting public opinion, environmental laws, or agency rules; and (3) more aggressive strategies used to discredit or intimidate environmental critics. In this chapter, I'll discuss examples of each type of these forms of communication. And, throughout this chapter, I will also describe a skillful and complex dance of identity in corporate communication—the effort by some (but not all) corporations to appear "green," often while actively opposing environmental protections.

Free Market Discourse and the Environment

Before looking more closely at the diverse forms of corporate communication, it's important to appreciate the ideological premises and sources of persuasion that underlie much of these appeals. Corporate advocacy regarding the environment does not occur in a vacuum. Instead, it often draws upon an ideological *discourse* (Chapter 3) that circulates a set of meanings about business and the proper role of government. This is a discourse about the nature of economic markets and the role of government and is particularly evident in the opposition of corporations to environmental standards.

Behind the discourse of much corporate environmental communication is the belief in a ***free market,*** a phrase that is usually meant to refer to the absence of governmental restriction of business and commercial activity. As a discourse, this sustains the idea that the private marketplace is self-regulating and ultimately promotes the social good. As a result, a discourse of free markets constructs a powerful *antagonism* (Chapter 2), that is, a questioning of environmental rules, taking such rhetorical forms as, "We need to get 'big government' off our backs," and "Companies will find the best solutions when left to themselves."

At the core of this rhetoric is the belief held by many business leaders that environmental protection can be secured by the operation of the marketplace through the unrestricted or unregulated buying and selling of products and services. Such faith in the market assumes that "the public interest is discovered in the ability of private markets to transform the individual pursuit of self-interest into an efficient social allocation of resources" (Williams & Matheny, 1995, p. 21).

The assumption that the market is the preferred means for addressing societal problems derives from the Scottish economist Adam Smith's theory of the **invisible hand** of the market first introduced in the 1700s. This metaphor is used to name an invisible or natural force of the private marketplace that determines what society values. In his classic 18th century book, *An Inquiry Into the Nature and Causes of the Wealth of Nations,* Smith (1910) argued that the sum of individuals' self-interested actions in the marketplace promotes the public's interest, or the common good. He explained that an individual "neither intends to promote the public interest nor knows how much he [*sic*] is promoting it. . . . He intends only his own gain. And he is in this . . . *led by an invisible hand to promote an end which was no part of his intention*" (p. 400, emphasis added). Libertarian interest groups such as the Cato Institute or the Heartland Institute implicitly evoke Adam Smith's premise when they argue that free and open competition in the market leads naturally to innovations that will ensure broader social goods such as cleaner air and safer products.

The discourse of the free market has been especially present during debates in the United States and Europe over so-called free trade agreements. Neoliberal economists and supporters of globalization, in particular, believe that, by opening global markets and encouraging investment abroad, poor nations not only will grow economically but will foster stronger environmental protections. For example, U.S. trade representative Robert Zoellick (2002) testified before the Congress that "free trade promotes free markets, economic growth, and higher incomes. And as countries grow wealthier, their citizens demand higher labor and environmental standards" (p. 1). And Samuel Aldrich and Jay Lehrwriting (2006), writing for the libertarian think tank the Heartland Institute argued that the "nations that have the best track records on environmental protection and improvement are those with the highest amount of free-market capitalism . . . [while] persons living in command-and-control economies, barely surviving on life's necessities of food, clothing, and shelter, use their natural resources to the absolute limit" (paras. 4, 6).

In the sections that follow, we'll see the use of free market discourse as a rhetorical and ideological rationale for some corporations' opposition to government-imposed standards for environmental performance. Indeed, this discourse underlies a wide range of corporate communication practices, including "green" marketing and a sophisticated program of corporate political influence.

Corporate Green Marketing

As popular support for the environment has increased in the past four decades, many industries have worked to improve their environmental performance. As a result, many corporations now have a twofold goal in their environmental communication programs: (1) Link corporate goals and behavior to popular environmental values, and (2) avoid if possible—and, if not, influence—additional environmental regulations that will affect their businesses.

In this section, I focus on the first goal: the use of corporate public relations and marketing to construct environmental identities for corporate products, images, and behaviors. U.S. corporations spend several billion dollars a year on such PR or what is sometimes called *green marketing*. **Green marketing** is a term used to refer to a corporation's attempt to associate its products, services, or identity with environmental values and images.

In this section, I use the term *green marketing* more specifically to refer to corporate communication that is used for three purposes: (1) product advertising (sales), (2) image enhancement, and (3) image repair. I'll also look at charges that these marketing efforts are a form of **greenwashing,** a pun on *whitewash*. The *Concise Oxford Dictionary* defines *greenwashing* as misleading information that is "disseminated by an organization so as to present an environmentally responsible public image" (quoted in Greenwash fact sheet, 2001, para.1).Whatever else green marketing may be, it is principally an attempt to influence the perceptions of consumers, media, politicians, and the public, and it is this function that invites much debate over corporations' behavior.

Green Product Advertising

The most familiar form of green marketing is the association of a company's products with popular images and slogans that suggest a concern for the environment. Such **green product advertising** is the attempt to market products as having a minimal impact on the environment and also to "project an image of high quality, including environmental sensitivity, relating both to a product's attributes and its manufacturer's track record for environmental compliance" (Ottman, 1993, p. 48; see also White, 2010, for the American Marketing Association's definition of green marketing of products).

Green Advertising and Eco Labels

The list of products that are marketed as "green" can be lengthy: Coffee, cars, water filters, clothing, hair sprays, SUVs, computers, allergy pills, breakfast cereals, lipstick, and children's toys are only a few examples. In one year alone, the U.S. Patent Office received more than 300,000 applications for environmentally related "brand names, logos, and tag lines" (Ottman, 2011).

Not surprisingly, the brands for these products are often accompanied by visual images of mountain peaks, forests, clear water, or blue skies. For example, Brita recently ran a TV ad showing an Eskimo drinking pure, cold Arctic water, when a lady suddenly runs across the ice, yelling "Yoo hoo!" She gives him a Brita filter bottle, saying, "This is from a drinking fountain in the mall." The Eskimo drinks from the Brita bottle and smiles. Viewed both as humorous and culturally insensitive, viewers, nevertheless, get the picture: Brita filters can purify water from anywhere.

What is being sold at the same time as a product, of course, is often a relationship with the natural environment: "An advertisement for an SUV shows the vehicle outdoors and . . . ads for allergy medications feature flowers and 'weeds.' In them, the environment per se is not for sale, but advertisers are depending on qualities and features of the nonhuman world to help in . . . selling [the] message" (Corbett, 2006, p. 150). In green advertising, the environment offers a seemingly limitless range of possibilities for such images or identifications. From Jeep ads encouraging urbanites to escape to mountain ridges to "all-natural" or "organic" breakfast foods, green ads rely on evocative appeals to nature as powerful rhetorical frames.

Examples of green product ads may be unlimited, but the underlying frames for such advertising draw on some common themes. What environmental communication scholar Steve Depoe (1991) first identified two decades ago still applies. There are three basic frames for green advertising: (1) nature as backdrop (Jeep ads using mountain terrain), (2) nature as product ("all-natural" raisins), and (3) nature as outcome (products do not harm and may even improve the environment). Communication scholar Julia Corbett (2006) observed that "using nature merely as a backdrop—whether in the form of wild animals, mountain vistas, or sparkling rivers—is the most common use of the natural world in advertisements" (p. 150).

A classic illustration of nature as backdrop was General Motors's full-page, color advertisement on the back cover of the nature magazine *Audubon*. The ad showed a new GM truck in a forest of "old-growth redwoods, with sunlight gently filtering through the trees to the ferns below" (Switzer, 1997, p. 130). The caption accompanying this image declared, "Our respect for nature goes beyond just giving you an excellent view of it," and stated that GM had made "a sizable contribution to The Nature Conservancy" (quoted in Switzer, p. 130).

In addition to the use of visual images, green product advertising also relies on the widespread practice of using environmentally friendly labels on products. These labels claim the product is *organic, nontoxic, phosphate free, biodegradable, all natural, free range,* and so forth. Products may also have the familiar symbol for recycled content. In fact, the use of green labels appears to be growing. The environmental marketing firm TerraChoice (2010a) found that the number of products marketed as *green* increased 73% in its survey of stores in 2010. The firm also found that false green labeling is also increasing. (I'll describe this practice of greenwashing below.)

Furthermore, a majority (84%) of U.S. consumers are buying green products—environmentally friendly clothing, foods, cleansers, personal-care products, and more (Ottman, 2011, p. 9). And, many are looking for eco-labels in stores. Not surprisingly,

Roper's Green Gauge poll has shown a related trend, "a growing tendency towards 'pro-cotting'—buying products from companies perceived as having good environmental track records" (quoted in Ottman, 2003, para. 4). The term **pro-cotting** is a play on *boycotting*, or the refusal to buy certain products. Roper's latest Green Gauge survey finds consumers from 25 countries "are still thirsty for greener options" in their stores (Green marketing insight, 2011, para. 2).

Finally, green product advertising is increasingly making use of the practice of environmental seals or **eco-label certification programs.** The presence of an eco-label on a product ostensibly signals an independent group's assurance to consumers that the product is environmentally friendly or produced in a manner that did not harm the environment. For example, the Environmental Protection Agency's (EPA's) *Energy Star* label on lightbulbs and appliances is meant to signal their energy savings. And, the Forest Stewardship Council's *FSC-certified* label on wood products indicates that the wood is from an ecologically managed forest.

The use of eco-labels or other certification seals has grown in recent years. Currently, there are now more than 400 green certification labeling systems. One problem has been that such labels may make broad, unqualified claims about a product. As a result, the proposed Federal Trade Commission (FTC) rules added a new section that addresses this problem. For example, companies must disclose if the eco-labels they use are certified by their own company or trade group or by a third party. And, the eco-labels themselves must be more specific; instead of a label certifying a product is "Green Smart," it would have to use a label like "Green Smart, Recyclable Certified" (Vega, 2010).

Guidelines for Green Marketing Claims

A word of caution about green advertising may be in order. This practice is largely unregulated. With the exception of *organic* (which is regulated by the U.S. Department of Agriculture), most environmentally friendly labels and green product claims in the United States are governed only by voluntary guidelines. The FTC does have regulatory oversight over green marketing claims and publishes its "Guidelines for Environmental Marketing Claims," or "Green Guides." In past years, however, these guidelines have been quite vague, and compliance has been voluntary for corporations.

The U.S. Department of Agriculture does set standards for organic products under its National Organic Program. (See www.ams.usda.gov/nop.) However, there is no uniform standard for other labels such as *free range* or *cage free*. In fact, "one company's free range label might mean that the animal went outside for 15 minutes a day, while another's might mean that the animal roamed a 10-acre field all its life" (Consumers beware, 2006, p. 23A; see also Foer, 2010).

As a result of a loose regulatory landscape, green product advertising may signal a wide range of meanings—from unsubstantiated claims to accurate information about the qualities of the product or the behavior of the corporation. In fact, the business blog *GreenBiz.com* (Marketing and communications, 2009) once trumpeted the opportunities being opened by "the lack of standards for determining what it means to be a green product—or a green company" (para. 1). It also noted that, with the number of consumers who want to buy green as well as the popularity of eco-labeling, an opportunity existed "for just about anything to be marketed as green, from simple packaging changes to products and services that radically reduce materials, energy, and waste" (para. 1).

In 2010, the FTC proposed revisions to its "Green Guides" to strengthen guidelines for marketing claims that are already addressed in the current regulations and provide new guidance for labels, such as "carbon offsets" that were not common when the guides were last reviewed in 1998 (Federal Trade Commission, 2010a). (See "Act Locally! Check for Deceptive Green Marketing Claims.")

Act Locally!

Check for Deceptive Green Marketing Claims

Have you ever wondered if the label on certain foods, personal care products, or clothing products were truly green or environmentally friendly? What does it mean to buy a product that is labeled as recycled, biodegradable, or nontoxic?

The Federal Trade Commission's (n.d.) "Guides for the Use of Environmental Marketing Claims" (Section 260.7) states:

"It is deceptive to misrepresent, directly or by implication, that a product, package or service offers a general environmental benefit." The FTC has the power to bring law enforcement actions against false or misleading environmental marketing claims under Section 5 of the FTC Act, which prohibits unfair or deceptive acts or practices.

How is the FTC using its power? Have the FTC guides given clearer definitions for green advertising claims? Has it taken actions against deceptive green ads? Check out the new "Guides" at http://www.ftc.gov. Then, answer the following questions:

- How accurate or helpful are the FTC guidelines for *recycled, biodegradable, compostable, renewable energy,* or *carbon offsets?*
- What enforcement actions against deceptive environmental ads or labels has the FTC taken recently? For specific corporations or products, you can check the FTC's Actions link, at www.ftc.gov/os/index.shtml. For example, a check of *bamboo* reveals the FTC has gone after several corporations that deceptively labeled certain products as being made from bamboo fiber, when they are actually made of rayon.
- Overall, how effective do you think the FTC's "Green Guides" are in discouraging false or misleading environmental labels or advertising?

The only enforcement power the FTC has is Section 5 of the Federal Trade Commission Act. This provision prohibits deceptive practices in advertising. Although its "Guidelines for Environmental Marketing Claims" are voluntary, the FTC can prosecute a corporation if it can be proved the corporation acted deceptively in its claims about a product. And, the FTC has brought several enforcement cases alleging false or unsubstantiated environmental claims. For example, in 2009, the commission brought charges against three companies for "making false and unsub-stantiated claims that their products were biodegradable" and charged four clothing and textile businesses with "deceptively labeling and advertising these items as made of bamboo fiber, manufactured using an environmentally friendly process, and/or biodegradable" (Federal Trade Commission, 2010b, pp. 19–20).

As a result of what some believe are unclear or weak enforcement of guidelines for green marketing claims, a number of independent groups have arisen to monitor or verify environmental advertising claims. The most prominent group is SourceWatch (sourcewatch.org), which monitors corporate funding and behavior generally. Other groups monitor specific claims, for example, that eggs are from *cage-free* chickens and that vegetables and meat are *natural, free range,* or *humanely raised.*

A few animal welfare groups issue their own labels that certify when products meet certain criteria. For example, the American Humane Society has the American Humane® Certified program (formerly known as the Free Farmed program); its cer-tified label assures consumers of third-party, independent verification that producers' care and handling of farm animals meet science-based animal welfare standards. And, Whole Foods has been developing an "animal-compassionate" program that will require that animals be raised "in a humane manner" (cage free, and so on) until they are slaughtered (Martin, 2006).

Finally, Canada has banned the use of eco-labels with "vague claims implying general environmental improvement" (Sustainable Life Media, 2008, para. 1). Instead, Canada's Competition Bureau released a set of guidelines that require companies to stick to "clear, specific, and accurate" claims that have been substanti-ated. Sheridan Scott, Commissioner of Competition, stated, "Businesses should not make environmental claims unless they can back them up" (Sustainable Life Media, 2008, para. 2).

Image Enhancement: Walmart and "Clean Coal"

Corporations navigate a constantly changing business environment. Doing so often requires an investment of resources to ensure that the public maintains a positive image of a corporation's identity and performance. This sometimes takes the form of an image advertising campaign. For example, when ExxonMobil proposed to extract oil from large deposits of tar sands in Canada—something environmentalists feared would cause huge greenhouse gas emissions—ExxonMobil (2011) sponsored a series of TV ads in promoting its concern for energy, jobs, and the environment. In one TV ad, a serious-looking engineer from ExxonMobil declared:

> America is facing some tough challenges right now. Two of the most important are energy security and economic growth. North America actually has one of the largest oil reserves in the world. A large part of that is oil sands. This reserve has the ability to create hundreds of thousands of jobs. At our Kearl plant in Canada, we'll be able to produce these oil sands with the same emissions as many other oils. And that's a huge breakthrough.

(For an analysis of some of the first corporate environmental image ads by Mobil and Exxon, see Crable & Vibbert, 1983, and Porter, 1992.)

Promoting a positive, environmental image for a corporation relies on the practice of **image enhancement.** This is the use of PR or advertising to improve the image of the corporation itself, reflecting its environmental concern and performance. As environmental values became increasingly popular in the United States and other countries, many corporations refined their communication with the public, bolstering their identities as environmentally responsible corporate citizens. This communication is particularly important when media, the government, or environmental groups question a corporation's behavior or intentions.

In this section, I'll illustrate the function of image enhancement in two green marketing campaigns: (1) the coal industry's touting of "clean coal" as a form of energy, and (2) Walmart's "sustainability" initiatives to eliminate waste and reduce its carbon footprint.

Redefining Coal as "Clean Coal"

One of the more visible image enhancements recently has been the coal industry's multimillion-dollar Clean Coal advertising campaign. High-quality-production ads appeared thousands of times on TV, radio, billboards, and online. Starting in 2002, the ads declared that "advancements in clean coal technologies are effectively making our environment cleaner," and assured listeners that "new coal-based power plants built beginning in about 2020 may well use technologies that are so advanced that they'll be virtually *pollution-free*" (emphasis added; quoted in SourceWatch, 2009, para. 4).

These ads are not trying to sell a product—a ton of coal or a new power plant. Instead, they are intended to reassure lawmakers and opinion leaders that the coal industry is vital to America's energy future and that, because coal is "clean"—that is, coal-burning power plants can produce electricity without causing pollution—the industry should not be regulated. Why? What is changing in the business environment that the U.S. coal industry feels it must navigate in order to survive?

Fundamentally, the business environment for coal is changing. The EPA has proposed tougher standards for pollutants like sulfur dioxide and mercury from coal-burning power plants and is currently proposing to regulate for the first time carbon dioxide (CO_2), a greenhouse gas and a major source of climate change. And, as we saw in Chapter 8, environmental groups have been blocking new coal plants, and major financial institutions have begun imposing stricter requirements on loans for the construction of such plants.

As a result, the coal industry invested heavily in a multimillion-dollar "clean coal" ad campaign in an attempt to forestall new regulations on coal-burning power plants. In 2008 alone, industry groups like the American Coalition for Clean Coal Electricity (ACCCE) spent $35 million to $45 million on image advertising, "most of it on television ads aired during the 2008 campaigns—pitching 'clean coal' as a new environmentally friendly fuel" (LoBianco, 2008, para. 2; Mufson, 2008). ACCCE, formerly called Americans for Balanced Energy Choices, is a public relations group for coal mining companies, coal transport (railroads), and coal-electricity producers (SourceWatch, 2009). Many of the TV and billboard ads directed viewers to more detailed information on ACCCE's sophisticated website, AmericasPower.org.

One of the ACCCE (2008) image enhancement TV ads was titled "Adios." It showed an elderly couple sitting on their porch, a young woman driving her convertible, two workers going into a factory, kids waving, and a family at the beach. A (male) voice declares:

> We wish we could say farewell to our dependence on foreign energy. And we'd like to say "adios" to rising energy costs. But first, we have to say "so long" to our outdated perceptions about coal. And we have to continue to advance new clean coal technologies to further reduce emissions, including the eventual capture and storage of CO_2. If we don't, we may have to say "goodbye" to the American way of life we all know and love. Clean coal. America's power. (America's Power, 2009)

The ad draws on the strategy of invoking social norms to suggest ordinary Americans—like "us"—are saying "so long" to "outdated perceptions about coal" and to suggest that coal can continue to power "the American way of life."

There is some evidence suggesting that the image campaign has had an impact on public attitudes as well as proposals to regulate coal plants. Attempts to enact legislation on climate change—and coal-burning plants—failed in the U.S. Congress in 2010. And, a public opinion poll on the eve of the 2008 U.S. presidential election found that "72 percent of opinion leaders nationwide support the use of coal to generate electricity, a significant increase over the past year and the highest level of support since the group began polling nearly 10 years ago" (*Business Wire*, 2008, para. 3). Finally, in 2011, the EPA delayed two of its planned regulations of coal-burning power plants.

Walmart's "Sustainability" Campaign

On October 24, 2005, the CEO of Walmart, Lee Scott, stood before a packed audience at Walmart's home office in Bentonville, Arkansas. Speaking to employees and via a live video feed to its 6,000 stores worldwide and 62,000 suppliers, Scott announced that Walmart was "going green in the biggest way imaginable, embracing sustainability" (Humes, 2011a, p. 100). Walmart was an unlikely corporation to appear to adopt environmental values. Known as the "Bully of Bentonville," the company had been a target for years, attracting "endless bad press, protests, political opposition, investigations, labor problems, health insurance problems, zoning problems, and more than ever, environmental problems" (p. 13). The initiative that Scott would announce on that day, however, would grow over the subsequent years to be one of the most ambitious, but often doubted, green corporate initiatives ever.

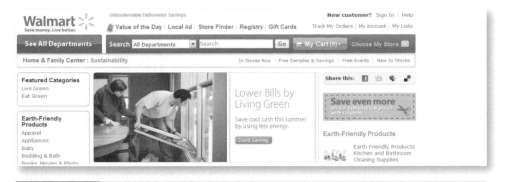

Figure 10.1	"It's getting harder to hate Wal-Mart." While its Sustainability Index "raises plenty of questions," if it succeeds, it "could literally change the face of retail forever" (a blogger at Treehugger.com).

In his Bentonville speech, Scott asked rhetorically, "What if we used our size and resources to make this country and this earth an even better place for all of us?" (quoted in Humes, 2011a, p. 102). He then went on to announce what would become Walmart's long-term environmental goals:

1. To be supplied 100% by renewable energy

2. To create zero waste

3. To sell products that sustain people and the environment. (Walmart, 2011, p. 1)

Scott's announcement created news headlines and puzzled the company's competitors. While a number of environmental groups expressed interest in Walmart's new, environmental goals, most of them reserved judgment, "waiting to see if the company's actions matched its lofty rhetoric" (Humes, 2011a, p. 104). Other reactions were harsher, ranging from to skepticism that such a large retailer could ever be sustainable to charges of greenwashing (Mitchell, 2007).

In the years following, however, Walmart would go on to announce and begin implementing a series of sustainability initiatives—lowering the carbon footprint of its stores, increasing the fuel efficiency of its transportation fleet, and seeking to curb wasteful packaging. In 2006, the company introduced "a green rating system designed to push their 60,000 worldwide manufacturing vendors to reduce the amount of packaging they use by 5%, to use more renewable materials, and to slash energy use" (Ottman, 2011, p. 172).

Then, in 2009, Walmart went further in announcing it would create a Sustainability Index. It would be a scorecard that measured the sustainability of Walmart's entire chain of suppliers. The index would measure a supplier's carbon footprint, use of natural resources, energy efficiency, water use, and so forth. Ultimately, Walmart hoped to translate the data on a supplier's performance into a score for each of its products, "a simple rating for consumers about the sustainability of products—the ultimate dream of green-minded shoppers" (Makower, 2010, para. 6). As a consequence, Walmart intended that the Sustainability Index would influence a wider circle of behaviors by its suppliers by determining which of their products qualified to get onto the store's shelves (Ottman, 2011, p. 168). (For more information about the Sustainability Index, see http://walmartstores.com.)

Public reactions were mainly positive. A *New York Times* editorial praised the index as "a sound idea" and added, "Given Wal-Mart's huge purchasing power, if it is done right it could promote both much-needed transparency and more environmentally sensitive practices" ("Can Wal-Mart be sustainable?, 2009, para. 2). Brian Merchant (2009), blogging at Treehugger.com, admitted, "It's getting harder to hate Wal-Mart." While the giant corporation's Sustainability Index "raises plenty of questions," if it succeeds, it "could literally change the face of retail forever" (para. 1). Two years later, Edward Humes (2011b), in a *Los Angeles Times* op-ed, was even more positive: "I'm no apologist for Wal-Mart. The giant retailer is still ripe for criticism on a number of fronts, from hiring and labor issues to its impact on local businesses and communities. But in this area of sustainability, Wal-Mart got it right" (para. 5).

There have also been doubts, and not a little criticism, from others. (See, for example, "Another Viewpoint: Wal-Mart a Long Way From Being Sustainable.") Some critics reminded Walmart that it cannot separate its sustainability goals from related concerns for the company's impacts on people and the environment. Writing in the *Penn Political Review,* Melissa Roberts (2011) argued that, while environmentalists had pushed for years for corporations to include sustainability in their bottom lines, "true environmentalism cannot separate environmental and social responsibility. If a company buys organic cotton but underpays farmers so that they have to use unsustainable farming practices [or] burn through the Amazon rainforest, there is no net gain for the environment" (para. 3).

Other criticism came from some who believed that Walmart and other big box retailers were fundamentally fueling an unsustainable economy. As they saw it, "no matter how genuine the effort and positive the result, sustainability only distracts the press and public from the fact that the real problem is the big-box economy itself" (Humes, p. 2011a, p. 227).

Whether Walmart's sustainability initiatives are genuine and ultimately succeed remain to be seen. Meanwhile, some environmental observers are optimistic in their assessments. Bridgette Meinhold (2009) editorialized at the website Inhabit, for example, that "Wal-Mart's sustainability index may be a game changer." But, she admitted, "It will take years of trials, tests, data collection and research to develop a fair, balanced and informative sustainability rating system.... At its current level of development, the Sustainability Index is yet an infant" (paras. 6, 7).

Another Viewpoint: "Wal-Mart a Long Way From Being Sustainable"

In October 2005, Wal-Mart announced a plan to enact wide-sweeping measures aimed at making the world's largest retailer a "good steward for the environment." Yet six years later, Wal-Mart has barely made a dent in cutting the massive amounts of carbon pollution it emits each year—equivalent to the 80th most polluting country in the world, never mind corporation.

The Sierra Club recently released "What Is Wal-Mart's True Environmental Footprint?" a new report that outlines the fundamental contradictions between Wal-Mart's business model and environmental sustainability.

The report shows that Wal-Mart's emissions, while inching down in recent years, aren't decreasing fast enough to hit the company's goals. The centerpiece of Wal-Mart's sustainability plan in the short-term is its pledge to cut carbon emissions at its stores, clubs and distribution centers by 20 percent by 2012 (as compared to 2005 emissions). Despite this goal, emissions from Wal-Mart's operations have remained relatively stable over the past several years in the U.S., dumping around 15 million metric tons of carbon pollution into the air each year. . . .

Wal-Mart's modest environmental initiatives have so far failed to make any significant cuts in the massive amounts of carbon pollution associated with its operations. Without major changes to their business model, Wal-Mart's major sustainability goals will remain out of reach.

SOURCE: Based on Margrete Strand Rangnes, "Report: Wal-Mart a Long Way From Being Sustainable." *Sierra Club Compass* [blog] (June 30, 2011). Posted at: http://sierraclub.typepad.com/compass. Reproduced from a Sierra Club website with permission of the Sierra Club.

Corporate Image Repairs: Apology or Evasion?

One form of corporate communication that is pivotal to a company's success in difficult times is the repair or recovery of its credibility. This practice of *image repair* is the use of PR to restore a company's credibility after an environmental harm or accident. Corporations that engage in wrongdoing often face a crisis of public trust and possible legal or economic repercussions. Corporate image repair, therefore, attempts to minimize the harm and any public perceptions that might "cause the organization irreparable damage" (Williams & Olaniran, 1994, p. 6). Image repair, also called *crisis management,* is vital to a company's continued operations, but the practice can be controversial, especially when a corporation's communication is viewed as insincere.

As I write in 2011, BP is still struggling to recover from the blow to its credibility from the 2010 rupture of its oil wellhead in the Gulf of Mexico. The Obama administration launched a criminal and civil investigation into the corporation in the weeks afterward, and civil lawsuits piled up. Still, BP initiated a number of efforts to try to restore its credibility. After the accident, the company began running TV ads and full-page ads in major newspapers like the *Wall Street Journal, USA Today,* and the *Washington Post,* as well as local ads in the Gulf States. One ad in the *New York Times* carried a photo of workers placing a boom to protect the shoreline from the oil slick. The tagline read, "BP has taken full responsibility for cleaning up the spill in the Gulf of Mexico. . . . We will make this right" (We will make this right, 2010, p. A11).

BP's crisis management during the oil spill, however, quickly became a case study of ineffective image repair. The corporation's credibility certainly was not helped by its CEO, Tony Hayward, in the immediate aftermath of the disaster. Hayward complained publicly about how much time he was spending on the disaster, saying, "I would like my life back," and he sought to play down the spill's ecological impacts. The Gulf is "a big ocean," he said; and "the environmental impact of this disaster is likely to be very, very modest" (MSNBC.com, 2010, para. 4).

| Figure 10.2 | BP CEO Tony Hayward, center, speaks at a news conference in Port Fourchon, Louisiana, during the worst offshore oil spill in U.S. history. |

AP Photo/Patrick Semansky

A much-studied and similar case of ineffectual image repair is the massive oil spill of the *Exxon Valdez* supertanker in Alaska's Prince William Sound in 1989. The tanker hit a reef, spilling nearly 11 million gallons of oil that "wreaked havoc on the immediate environment, despoiling almost eleven hundred miles of shoreline" (Hearit, 1995, p. 4). Called "the nation's worst oil spill" (Oil slick spreads, 1989, p. 1), the pollution killed thousands of seabirds, sea otters, and other wildlife and seriously harmed local fisheries.

Exxon faced a flurry of negative publicity as television, radio, newspapers, and magazines worldwide carried stories of oil-soaked birds and sea lions struggling to move or breathe. One story in the *New York Times* reported:

> On a small pebbled beach on Eleanor Island, what appeared to be a blackened rock turned out to be a seabird befouled with oil. As a helicopter descended, the frightened bird raised its wings to flee but was unable to lift itself into the air. Just off Seal Island, a large group of sea lions swam in a tight knot straining to keep their heads well above the oily surface. (Shabecoff, 1989; quoted in Benoit, 1995, pp. 119–120)

As a result of the tragic accident, Exxon offered to respond with remedial actions—help with the cleanup and cooperation with a federal investigation—and an extensive image repair campaign. In a full-court press, including publication of a full-page "Open Letter to the Public" from Exxon's chairman in major newspapers, the company launched a three-part strategy of image restoration. Communication scholar William Benoit (1995) noted that Exxon first sought to shift the blame for the accident to the captain of the *Exxon Valdez,* who was discovered to have been drinking before his ship hit the reef. The company also tried to lessen the offensiveness of the oil spill through what Benoit called "minimization" and "bolstering" (p. 123). That is, Exxon tried to minimize reports of damage to the environment itself, and it also tried to bolster the company's image by announcing that it had "moved swiftly and competently" to lessen the impact of the oil on the environment and wildlife (quoted in Benoit, 1995, p. 126).

Exxon's attempt at image repair, nevertheless, failed to alleviate public blame and a loss of credibility in the immediate aftermath of the *Exxon Valdez* disaster. Although the company sought to portray itself as repairing damage caused by the accident, its promises were vague and undermined by delays in the cleanup of the polluted coastlines. Benoit concluded that "Exxon's reputation suffered from the *Valdez* oil spill, and its attempts to restore it in the short term appear[ed] ineffective" (p. 128). Hearit (1995) reported that, as a result of Exxon's bureaucratic handling of the crisis and failure to reestablish legitimacy, the company's public communication did not end with its letter of apology but continued with "a long-term campaign designed to communicate continued concern for, and assessment of, the effects of the *Valdez* spill" (p. 12).

Greenwashing and the Discourse of Green Consumerism

Corporate practices of "green" advertising, image enhancement, and image repair have not been without their critics. In this section, I'll describe two criticisms in particular: (1) the charge that corporate green marketing is a form of greenwashing, and (2) a discourse of *green consumerism,* the belief that purchasing environmentally friendly products can help save the Earth.

Corporate Greenwashing

In an earlier study of corporate opposition to environmental regulations, Jacqueline Switzer (1997) noted that often corporate "public relations campaigns—called 'greenwashing' by environmental groups—[are] used by industry to soften the public's perceptions of its activities" (p. xv; see also Corbett, 2006). Earlier, I defined *greenwashing* as misleading information that is disseminated by an organization so as to present an environmentally responsible public image. And, the environmental marketing firm TerraChoice (2010b), a division of Underwriters Laboratories, describes the term this way: "the act of misleading consumers regarding the environmental practices of a company or the environmental benefits of a product or service" (para. 2).

Environmental groups routinely use the term *greenwash* to call attention to what they believe is deception by a corporation—an effort to mislead or divert attention from a corporation's poor environmental behavior or products. For example, Greenpeace (2008) gave the oil company BP its Emerald Paintbrush award in "recognition of the company's attempts to greenwash its brand over the course of 2008, in particular its multimillion dollar advertising campaign announcing its commitment to alternative energy sources . . . [and its use of] slogans such as 'from the earth to the sun, and everything in between'" (para. 4). Using internal BP documents, Greenpeace claimed that, in 2008, "the company allocated 93 per cent ($20bn) of its total investment fund for the development and extraction of oil, gas and other fossil fuels. In contrast, solar power (a technology which analysts say is on the brink of important technological breakthroughs) was allocated just 1.39 per cent, and wind a paltry 2.79 per cent" (para. 5). BP, on the other hand, insists that the company is committed to developing new, renewable energy sources (BP, 2009).

How, then, can someone tell if a corporate advertisement is greenwashing or the report of a legitimate environmental achievement? Most critics point to a basic standard of deception. Has the ad conveyed information or an impression that is countered by factual evidence? Many times, the truthfulness of a claim may be difficult for the ordinary consumer to determine. In other cases, there are groups such as SourceWatch (www.sourcewatch.org) that monitor the statements and behavior of corporations, provide information about their compliance with environmental regulations, and even evaluate specific marketing campaigns.

In a more general effort, the environmental marketing firm TerraChoice has identified six patterns, which it called the Six Sins of Greenwashing, commonly used by companies. For example, TerraChoice (2007) defines the *Sin of Irrelevance* as when a product ad makes "a statement that may be truthful but is unimportant and unhelpful for consumers seeking environmentally preferable products" (p. 4). A typical Sin of Irrelevance is the claim that a product, such as an oven cleaner, is "CFC free." CFCs (chlorofluorocarbons) are chemicals linked to depletion of the ozone layer; CFCs have been legally banned for more than 30 years. (See "FYI: The Six Sins of Greenwashing.")

☞ **FYI** **The Six Sins of Greenwashing**

The environmental marketing firm TerraChoice has identified six patterns, which it called the Six Sins of Greenwashing, used by companies in greenwashing. Here are the sins, along with brief excerpts from its 2007 report, including guidelines for marketers:

1. Sin of the Hidden Trade-Off: Suggesting a product is "green" based on a single environmental attribute (the recycled content of paper, for example) (p. 2)

2. Sin of No Proof: "Any environmental claim that cannot be substantiated by easily accessible supporting information, or by a reliable third-party certification" (p. 3)

3. Sin of Vagueness: A "claim that is so poorly defined that its real meaning is likely to be misunderstood by the intended consumer" (p. 3)

4. Sin of Irrelevance: "Making a statement that may be truthful but is unimportant and unhelpful for consumers seeking environmentally preferable products" (p. 4)

5. Sin of the Lesser of Two Evils: " 'Green' claims that may be true within the product category, but that risk distracting the consumer from the greater impacts of the category as a whole," such as "organic cigarettes" (p. 4)

6. Sin of Fibbing: "Making environmental claims that are simply false" (p. 4)

SOURCE: TerraChoice Environmental Marketing Inc. (2007).

The practice of greenwashing is actually quite high in the United States and Canada. In a recent survey, TerraChoice (2010b) discovered that "more than 95 per cent of consumer products claiming to be green are committing at least one of the 'sins' of greenwashing (para. 1). Furthermore, the firm found that the use of fake labels is increasing. Its 2010 survey reported that 32% of "green" products carried misleading information, compared to 26.8% in 2009 (TerraChoice, 2010a, p. 20). Interestingly, the survey also found that so-called big box retailer stores "stock more 'green' products and more products that provide legitimate environmental certifications than smaller 'green' boutique-style stores" (p. 13).

Finally, social media has also come to the aid of consumers who are trying to avoid businesses that engage in the greenwashing of their products. For example, University of California at Berkeley professor Dara O'Rourke has developed the GoodGuide app for the iPhone. You simply open the app in the store, scan or take a photo of the barcode on a product, and then see detailed environmental (as well as health and social responsibility) ratings for thousands of companies. The app has been "one of the biggest successes among green apps," with over 600,000 downloads (Graham, 2011, para. 3).

Discourse of Green Consumerism

Green marketing and discourses based on the free market raise another important question for students of environmental communication: Can consumers minimize damage to, or even improve, the environment by their purchase of certain products? That is, can we reduce air pollution, end the clear-cutting of national forests, or protect the ozone layer by buying recycled, biodegradable, nontoxic, and ozone-free products? Many people appear to think so. As we saw earlier, Roper's Green Gauge poll reported consumers' tendency toward *pro-cotting*, or buying products from companies that are perceived as having good environmental track records. Irvine (1989) was the first to refer to this "use of individual consumer preference to promote less environmentally damaging products and services" as **green consumerism** (p. 2). This is the belief that, by buying allegedly environmentally friendly products, consumers can do their part to protect the planet.

Whether green consumerism actually helps the environment is a matter of some debate. As we've seen, "green" labels are often vague, and federal standards for compliance with the content of such labels are largely unenforceable. And, as Canadian social theorist Toby Smith (1998) has pointed out, "Some ecologists insist that only a product that has passed a so-called cradle to grave environmental audit can be said to be authentically eco-friendly" (p. 89). For example, a product may be biodegradable but also toxic, and it can still claim to be environmentally friendly under some standards.

Why, then, is the idea of green consumerism popular? Most of us do not wish to harm the environment, and I suspect that most of us believe we can consciously choose to lessen our impact on the Earth through our actions. Helping to sustain this belief is a wider set of beliefs, buttressed by green advertising, that invite a specific identity. In her provocative book, *The Myth of Green Marketing: Tending Our Goats at the Edge of Apocalypse*, Toby Smith (1998) argues that green consumerism is not simply an act—the purchase of a certain product—but a discourse about the identity of individual consumers. (In Chapter 3, I described *discourse* as a recurring pattern of speaking or writing whose function is to circulate a coherent set of meanings about an important topic.) Smith explains that our purchasing does not occur in a vacuum but is "an act of faith"; that is, "it is based on a belief about the way the world works" (p. 89). Our actions have effects, and among these is the effect of our purchasing on producers of products. In other words, the discourse of green consumerism assures us that, when we buy green, our buying can affect the actions of large corporations, such as oil companies, and also can alter our relationship to, and impact on, the environment. In short, one takes on a particular identity as purchaser.

Smith argues that the idea of green consumerism resonates with us because the act of purchasing is cloaked in an aura of other, authoritative discourses that buttress our identities as purchasers. She explains that our belief that we can do well for the environment by green shopping is underwritten by certain discourses that encode our buying with significance. Two discourses in particular assign meaning to our purchasing decisions: the discourses of market forces and participatory democracy.

First, green advertising affirms the belief that the market can be an avenue for change; that is, that by doing our bit, we contribute to the free market's invisible hand, and as "all the little bits are counted, the consequence will be a net good" (Smith, 1998, p. 157). Second, the discourse of participatory democracy nurtures the belief that, in a liberal democracy, each of us is entitled to a voice in deciding about issues that matter to us. Thus, The Body Shop's founder, Anita Roddick, declared, "We can use our ultimate power, voting with our feet and wallets," while another retailer asserted, "Customers vote at the cash register" (quoted in Smith, p. 156). In each case, consumers are encouraged to believe that their purchases exercise a democratic influence: "Voting" at the cash register affects retailers directly in determining which products succeed and which are in disfavor, and it affirms the consumer's identity as someone who acts responsibly toward the Earth.

The discourse of green consumerism can be an attractive magnet, pulling one toward a persuasive identity as a purchaser. "Green consumerism makes sense," explains Smith (1998). "That is why people are attracted to it; they are not irrational, immoral, or uninformed. Quite the opposite: they are . . . moral in their desire to do their bit" (p. 152). Nevertheless, she believes that green consumerism also poses a danger by co-opting a more skeptical attitude toward the social and environmental impacts of excessive consumption. In a provocative charge, Smith claims that green consumerism serves to deflect serious questioning of a larger **productivist discourse** in our culture, one that supports "an expansionistic, growth-oriented ethic" (p. 10). Indeed, whether green consumerism can be a real force in the marketplace or a subtle diversion from the questioning of our consumer society is a question that invites serious debate in our classes and in research by environmental scholars.

In summary, the practice of green marketing is now widespread. It involves subtly and skillfully associating corporations' products, images, and behaviors with environmentally friendly values. As we saw, this effort to construct a green identity can serve any of three purposes: (1) product promotion (sales), (2) corporate image enhancement, and (3) image repair in the aftermath of negative publicity about a company. As we shall see in the following section, certain corporations may evoke a "green" image even as they oppose stronger environmental protections.

Corporate Advocacy Campaigns

As early as the 1960s, the fields of environmental chemistry and toxicology had begun to document the health risks from industrial and manufacturing processes. These health risks, in turn, led to new requirements for industry. As a result, the affected businesses challenged the environmental sciences "at every step, questioning both the methods and research designs that were used and the conclusions that were drawn" (Hays, 2000, p. 222). Regulated industries such as chemical manufacturing, oil and gas refineries, electric utilities, and older, extractive industries (mining and logging) put pressure on federal agencies like the EPA to justify the science behind the new regulations. Many corporations also mounted advocacy campaigns to weaken or defeat environmental laws and regulations for tougher clean air rules, car fuel standards, and safer disposal of toxic chemicals.

In this section, I'll describe two dimensions of corporate advocacy: campaigns to influence legislation and agency rule-making along with some of the message *frames* (e.g., jobs vs. the environment) that industry often uses in these campaigns. In the next section, I'll identify a more aggressive tactic: the use of the courts.

Corporate Campaigns

Not all corporations resist or try to weaken environmental standards that might affect their interests. As I described in the last section, some businesses, such Walmart, have initiated their own programs for sustainability. Other firms, such as Chrysler, DuPont, General Electric, and Duke Energy, have joined with moderate environmental groups to form the U.S. Climate Action Partnership (USCAP) "to call on the federal government to quickly enact strong national legislation to require significant reductions of greenhouse gas emissions" (www.us-cap.org).

Still, many corporations have invested considerable resources to forestall or defeat environmental restrictions in the U.S. Congress, in state legislatures, and in federal agencies that establish regulations. Journalist Mark Dowie (1995) once described the communication activities used in this process by corporations as the **three-bites-of-the-apple strategy:** "The first bite is to lobby against any legislation that restricts production; the second is to weaken any legislation that cannot be defeated; and the third, and most commonly applied tactic, is to end run or subvert the implementation of environmental regulations" (p. 86). In this section, I'll describe each of these bites of the apple.

| Figure 10.3 | The coal industry has used both a clean coal and a jobs frame to promote the continued mining and consumption of coal as a source of energy in the United States. |

Corporate Campaigns to Oppose or Weaken Legislation

Since the late 1990s, business groups have grown more influential in shaping environmental policies. Through their professional lobbyists, campaign contributions, trade associations, and well-funded PR groups like the American Coalition for Clean Coal Electricity, corporations exert a powerful influence on the writing of laws and regulations. Historians Gerald Markowitz and David Rosner (2002) describe some of the corporate communication practices that have been used to oppose environmental policies:

> Organizations such as the Business Roundtable, made up of the CEOs of two hundred of the largest corporations in the country, have intensified their lobbying efforts among government officials and established well-funded and large offices in Washington, D.C. Through political contributions, "message ads," support for pro-industry legislators, and direct contact with members of the executive branch—at the very highest levels—industry attempts to protect its interests. (p. 9)

These communication practices are routinely used in the three-bites-of-the-apple strategy. To understand this better, let's look at two examples of successful corporate advocacy: first, a campaign to block an environmental treaty on climate change and, in the following section, a successful effort to weaken a regulation against mountain-top coal mining.

One of the most effective corporate advocacy campaigns was launched by the Global Climate Coalition (GCC). Established in 1989, the GCC billed itself as "a leading voice for business and industry" (Global Climate Coalition, 2000, para. 1). Its early members included corporations and trade associations such as the U.S. Chamber of Commerce, Texaco, Shell Oil, General Motors, and the American Forest and Paper Association. The coalition stated that its role was to coordinate the participation of business in public debates about global warming: "The GCC represents the views of its members to legislative bodies and policymakers. And it . . . provides comments on proposed legislation and government programs" (para. 1). In fact, the GCC commanded a potent war chest that was used to wage aggressive PR campaigns to protect its members' interests.

Starting in 1997, the Global Climate Coalition launched a well-funded and extensive advocacy campaign to dispute the science behind the theory of global warming and to influence the terms of a new treaty that the United States and other nations had been negotiating in Kyoto, Japan. The Kyoto Protocol, signed in 1997, set international rules that required nations to reduce emissions of CO_2 and other gases that fuel climate change. The GCC's campaign included "aggressive lobbying at [the] international climate negotiation meetings, and raising concern about unemployment that it [claimed] would result from emissions regulations" (PR Watch, 2004, para. 6) as well as publication of reports suggesting uncertainty in the science of climate change. (I'll describe this trope of "uncertainty" in Chapter 11.)

Although the United States had signed the Kyoto Protocol in 1997, President Bill Clinton had to submit the treaty to the Senate for ratification under the U.S. Constitution. In response to this, the GCC conducted a separate advertising campaign objecting to the treaty's requirements in the United States. One of the GCC's major criticisms was that the United States would be required to meet stringent timelines for reducing greenhouse emissions, yet many developing countries, along with China, would be exempt.

As a result of the questions raised by the GCC and other critics, the Senate voted 97–0 against the ratification of the Kyoto Protocol in an advisory vote. As a result, President Clinton decided not to submit the treaty for ratification. As the GCC continued its efforts at the first bite of the apple, its campaign claimed victory when newly elected President George W. Bush formally withdrew the United States from the list of signatories to the Kyoto Protocol in 2001.

In 2002, the GCC disbanded. Its sponsors believed that the lobbying campaign had succeeded. The coalition's website announced, "The industry voice on climate change has served its purpose by contributing to a new national approach to global warming. . . . At this point, both Congress and the Administration agree that the U.S. should not accept the mandatory cuts in emissions required by the [Kyoto] protocol" (Global Climate Coalition, 2004).

Perhaps another reason the GCC closed shop may have been that many corporations no longer accepted one of its main premises, that climate change was not a serious threat. Major companies such as DuPont, Ford Motor Company, Daimler-Chrysler, Texaco, and General Motors all had left the GCC within three years of its creation, many announcing initiatives that promised to develop alternative, cleaner sources of energy.

Weakening Environmental Regulations

While lobbying to block or weaken a law is the most familiar mode of corporate advocacy, businesses also exert their influence inside the bureaucratic offices of federal and state agencies. In this third bite of the apple, the strategy is essentially an end run around the law itself to target the agency officials who write the regulations that implement that law. Switzer (1997) reported that the reason for this strategy is that "by removing an environmental issue from the legislative arenas to the *less visible and more difficult to track bureaucratic arena,* organized interests can better control the debate" (emphasis added; p. 154).

A dramatic example of the third-bite strategy has been the coal industry's campaign to weaken federal rules regulating mountaintop removal in the Appalachian region of the United States. As we've seen in earlier chapters, **mountaintop removal** is the removal of the tops of mountains to expose the seams of coal that are buried there. Environmentally, it is a particularly destructive form of mining. "Miners target a green peak, scrape it bare of trees and topsoil, and then blast away layer after layer of rock until the mountaintop is gone" (Warrick, 2004, p. A1). Adding to the damage, the operations dump tons of rocky debris from the blasts over the sides of the mountain into the valleys below, burying hundreds of miles of mountain streams.

Although the rules implementing the Clean Water Act expressly forbid the dumping of mine waste into streams, lax enforcement by the Army Corps of Engineers officials who administered the law had allowed the practice of mountaintop removal to continue for years. Environmental attorneys, however, had succeeded by 2000 in challenging this illegal practice, and the number of permits granted for mountaintop removal started to decrease. It was at that point that industry decided to take a third bite of the apple by quietly lobbying federal agencies to change the regulation defining waste, the dumping of which is forbidden by the Clean Water Act.

On April 6, 2001, lobbyists from the National Mining Association met with EPA officials in the Bush administration, arguing for "a small wording change" (Warrick, 2004, p. A1). They were referring to regulations that prohibited dumping of mountaintop soil and rocks into valley streams. As a result of the industry's lobbying, the agency "simply reclassified the [mining] debris from objectionable 'waste' to legally acceptable 'fill'" (p. A1). This substitution of "fill" (a legally-acceptable term) "explicitly allows the dumping of mining debris into streambeds" (p. A6). For its part, administration officials insisted that the rule change merely clarified existing policies.[1]

The revised mountaintop mining regulation illustrates the rationale for the third-bite strategy for opponents of environmental rules. *Washington Post* reporter Joby Warrick (2004) explained, "Rather than proposing broad changes or drafting new legislation, administration officials often have taken existing regulations and made subtle tweaks that carry large consequences" (p. A1).

A more recent example of a campaign targeting an agency's regulations occurred when industry and political interests opposed the Obama administration's tougher EPA rules enforcing the Clean Air Act. Facing "fierce resistance" from industry, the president withdrew, in 2011, proposed restrictions for ground-level ozone (called *smog*) that would have "compelled states and communities nationwide to reduce local air pollution or face federal penalties" (Eilperin, 2011, para. 1). Behind the scenes, affected businesses had launched "an all-out public relations blitz against the rules, saying that they should be delayed in light of the economic downturn" (paras. 1–2).

Framing the Message in Corporate Campaigns

Although the goal of a corporate campaign may be the defeat or weakening of a particular law or regulation, the battle may be fought initially in the media and in the court of public opinion. Media scholar Anders Hansen (2010) observed that, while much of industry's advocacy occurs through political channels and lobbying, "PR and public 'image management' more generally have increasingly become central and critical dimensions" in corporate campaigns (p. 68). Indeed, many of these campaigns in the past several decades have been fought "as discursive or rhetorical public contests/battles fought . . . in terms of 'image,' culturally resonant arguments, fear-tactics, 'spin,' style and 'slick' campaigning" (pp. 68–69).

Central to the "rhetorical public contests" of corporate campaigns is the framing of issues in a way that resonates with the values of the campaigns' audiences. (I described the *framing* of campaign messages in Chapter 8.) These campaigns seek to influence public debate about an environmental issue, particularly, by framing the issue in terms of economic growth, jobs, and so forth. In this section, I'll describe two of the most common frames in corporate messages that help to set the terms of debate about environment laws or regulations, the free-market frame and the so-called jobs-versus-the-environment frame.

The Free-Market Frame

Influencing the terms of public debate about the environment is often crucial to the success of a corporate advocacy campaign. As industries such as oil and chemical companies began to rally the public's opposition to environmental regulations in the 1970s and 1980s in the United States, many sought to frame the discussion in terms of popular values—economic growth, jobs, the free market, and so on. One of the earliest attempts to frame opposition to government regulations generally was by the Mobil Oil Corporation (now ExxonMobil). Mobil pioneered the use of issue ads in major newspapers to frame its concerns without the media's filters (Beder, 2002).

In an early issue ad, Mobil introduced the primary media frame that it would use in the future to oppose regulation of the marketplace. Evoking the values of national identity and patriotism, the frame conveyed the culturally resonant message: A free and unfettered business climate is the American way. One newspaper ad put it this way:

> Business, generally, is a good neighbor. . . . From time to time, out of political motivations or for reasons of radical chic, individuals try to chill the business climate. On such occasions we try to set the record straight. . . . And the American system, of which business is an integral part, usually adapts. . . . So when it comes to the business climate, we're glad that most people recognize there's little need to tinker with the American system. (Mobil Oil ad, quoted in Parenti, 1986, p. 67)

More commonly, the discourse of the free market is usually framed as a concern for economic growth or a robust economy. For example, efforts by environmental supporters to reduce acid rain, to raise the miles-per-gallon requirement for cars, and to impose strict safety rules for nuclear plants all have met criticism that such actions would cost jobs or damage the economy. Indeed, no more damaging charge has been brought against environmental progress over the years than the claim that such progress costs American jobs.

Jobs-Versus-the-Environment Frame

The charge that environmental regulations kill jobs has been a recurring and often successful frame used in corporate campaigns for years. One reason this frame has been so influential is that it is a conflict-oriented frame and, as such, fits well with typical newsworthiness standards in mainstream journalism (Chapter 6). It also taps a reservoir of concern about job security felt by many people.

A particularly powerful use of the jobs-versus-the-environment frame came in the controversy over the spotted owl in the Pacific Northwest in the early 1990s.

The region's old-growth forests are critical habitat for this endangered species. The timber industry, however, argued that restricting logging in these forests would cost jobs. Bumper stickers and signs reading "Save a Logger, Eat an Owl" and "This Family Supported by Timber Dollars" dotted pickup trucks and storefront windows in logging-dependent communities throughout Oregon and Washington State (Lange, 1993, p.251). Environmental communication scholar Jonathan Lange (1993) reported that the timber industry "succeeded in creating an 'owl versus people' scenario in the media" (p. 250) with stories about threatened job losses in *Time,* the *Wall Street Journal,* and other national media.

Although used often, the claim that environmental regulations will cost jobs has been questioned by many economists as being overly simplistic. Some point out that, though regulations may carry some costs—a factory may close rather than cleanup its pollution—the jobs frame ignores other factors. Short-term losses "are dwarfed by the gains in lengthened lives, reduced hospitalizations and other health benefits" (Rich & Broder 2011, p. B5). Economists also point out that, as other companies "develop new technologies to cope with regulatory requirements, some new jobs are created" (Rich & Broder 2011, p. B1). For example, when the EPA proposed to amend the Clean Air Act to reduce acid rain, caused by air emissions from coal-burning power plants,

> the electric utility industry warned they [the new regulations] would cost $7.5 billion and tens of thousands of jobs. But the cost of the program has been closer to $1 billion. . . . And the E.P.A., in a paper published [in 2011] cited studies showing that the law had been a modest *net creator of jobs* through industry spending on technology to comply with it" (emphasis added, p. B1).

In other cases, the basis for the core claim itself—that tougher environmental rules would kill jobs—proved to be exaggerated. For example, the jobs frame has been used prominently in campaigns, until very recently, to forestall attempts by the U.S. Congress to raise the fuel or miles-per-gallon standard for cars. In a study of these campaigns, communication scholar John Bliese (2002) reported one particularly suspect claim. U.S. automakers had charged that raising fuel standards to 40 miles per gallon "would devastate the industry, putting 300,000 auto workers out of their jobs" (p. 22). Claims such as this resonate with workers and families who, in turn, become influential constituencies in the debates before Congress. But, is this particular claim accurate? Where did the figure 300,000 come from?

In his study, Bliese (2000) discovered that the claim of 300,000 lost jobs was based on a faulty assumption. The auto industry's study, he said, "simply adds up all of their employees currently making cars that get less than forty miles per gallon and assumes that every single one of them would lose his or her job." In other words, the study assumed that "the industry would not even attempt to build a single new car that met the proposed gas mileage standard" (p. 22).

While the jobs-versus-the-environment frame may be overly simplified, or even false, it remains a potent appeal in many corporations' advocacy campaigns. The frame, for example, gained special salience during the recent downturn in the U.S. economy. As *Washington Post* reporter Juliet Eilperin (2011) observed that the campaign against EPA smog regulations featured charges that the new rules were "job-destroying" (para. 1). And, while the Obama administration has attempted to reframe the debate in terms of a green economy (investments in solar, wind, and other renewable energy sources) as a source for millions of new jobs (Dickerson, 2009), the jobs-versus-the-environment frame remains a potent appeal in the current economy.

SLAPP Lawsuits: Strategic Litigation Against Public Participation

While corporations and industry trade groups routinely engage in green marketing and advocacy campaigns, some have not been shy about responding aggressively to their critics in the environmental movement in other ways. In this final section, I'll describe a particularly chilling strategy used by some businesses to silence, discourage, or intimidate critics—a legal action known as the SLAPP lawsuit.

Consider the case of Colleen Enk: Enk had started to question a gravel mine proposed for the Salinas River near her neighborhood in San Luis Obispo County, California. Shortly afterward, she found herself the target of a lawsuit by the developers for libel and defamation, among other charges. The lawsuit also sought money damages. "It's pretty transparent why they did it," her attorney, Roy Ogden, said. "They wanted to shut her up" (Johnston, 2008, para. 12). Ultimately, Enk was forced to pay several thousand dollars in attorney fees and court costs.

The developers were proposing to dig and haul sand and gravel from the river over a 20-year period. After Enk and her neighbors questioned the plans, a process server appeared at her door one evening in May 2008. She was not at home. The next day, Enk voiced her opinion again at a meeting of the San Luis Obispo County Planning Commission. "My heart was pounding," she said (quoted in Johnston, 2008, para. 11). The next morning, the server caught her at home and served the summons to court. Her attorney said, "Colleen has been sued for exercising the right of free speech in America. She's been stomped."

More recently, a large cement corporation has proposed to build a coal-burning, cement-manufacturing plant near Wilmington, North Carolina. At a County Commissioners meeting, two local residents spoke against the plant. They cited the company's performance and the plant's potential health effects on children (Faulkner, 2011). In response, the corporation filed two lawsuits in federal court alleging the individuals slandered the company. One of the defendants, Kayne Darrell, reacted saying, "I'm kind of in shock right now. I'm just a mom and a housewife fighting a billion-dollar company trying to keep me from saying what I believe is right and true and from protecting my air and water" (quoted in Faulkner, 2011, para. 17). The Raleigh *News and Observer,* in an editorial, called the lawsuits "a blatant attempt at intimidation. If they're not outright SLAPP suits . . . they're a reasonable facsimile" (Bullying behavior, 2011, p. 9A). As I write in 2011, the case is in mediation.

Both Enk and Darrell found themselves faced with a strategy that "developers used against their opponents for years, a lawsuit known as a SLAPP" (Johnston, 2008, para. 3). Pring and Canan (1996) define a **SLAPP lawsuit** as one involving "communications made to influence a governmental action or outcome, which, secondarily, resulted in (a) a civil complaint [lawsuit] . . . (b) filed against nongovernmental individuals or organizations . . . on (c) a substantive issue of some public interest or social significance" such as the environment (pp. 8–9). Such lawsuits have become common. California's State Environmental Resource Center (2004) reported that, every year, thousands of people are hit with SLAPP suits.

In the end, most SLAPP lawsuits are dismissed because of First Amendment protections of citizens' rights to speak and petition government. But, the mere act of filing a lawsuit that alleges libel, slander, or interference with a business contract can be financially and emotionally crippling to defendants. Pring and Canan (1996) explain that corporations that file SLAPP suits "seldom win a legal victory—the normal litigation goal—yet often achieve their goals in the real world. . . . Many [of those who are sued] are devastated, drop their political involvement, and swear never again to take part in American political life" (p. 29). Even if the group or citizen wins, he or she most likely "has paid large sums of money to cover court costs and has been thrown into the public eye for months or even years. This unlawful intimidation pushes people into becoming less active and outspoken on issues that matter" (California State Environmental Resource Center, 2004, para. 7).

The purpose of a SLAPP is not necessarily to win the lawsuit but to cause the corporation's critics to spend time, energy, and money defending themselves and to discourage others from participating in public life. Yet, some have decided to fight back. In fact, many states are providing remedies for cases in which a court determines that a lawsuit against an individual is a SLAPP action. That is, some courts may agree quickly to dismiss a lawsuit if it appears to be motivated by the unconstitutional purpose of silencing speech and to require the plaintiffs to pay court costs.

Over the years, two principal sources of defense have arisen in response to SLAPP lawsuits—one based in constitutional guarantees of democratic rights and the other in personal injury law. Pring and Canan (1996) refer to these two sources of defense as the "one-two punch" that has characterized successful defense against SLAPP lawsuits.

The basic defense against a SLAPP lawsuit is derived from the rights granted to citizens in the First Amendment to the U.S. Constitution, particularly the right of freedom of speech and the right of the people to petition the government for redress of grievances. Often, a court will grant expedited hearings to dismiss a SLAPP if the citizen's criticism was part of a petition to the government. In such cases, the plaintiff (the party bringing the lawsuit) must show that the citizen's petition is a sham in order to proceed with the original lawsuit.

The second part of the defense involves what is known as a **SLAPP-back** suit against the corporation or governmental agency bringing the initial allegations against a citizen. Here, the defendant SLAPPs back by filing a countersuit alleging that the plaintiff infringed on the citizen's right to free speech or to petition the government. SLAPP-back lawsuits usually allow for recovery of attorneys' fees as well as punitive damages for violating constitutional rights and inflicting damage or injury on the defendant.

Environmentalists, labor, individual citizens, and others have won monetary awards in fighting SLAPP actions. Pring and Canan (1996) report that awards in SLAPP-backs occasionally have been large—jury verdicts of $5 million to a staggering $86 million were awarded against corporations that have brought SLAPP suits. Increasingly, developers, polluters, and others have had to weigh the chances of a SLAPP-back before bringing a SLAPP action. Pring and Canan observed, "Even though SLAPP-backs are not a panacea, this risk of having to defend against them may prove to be the most effective SLAPP deterrent of all" (p. 169).

SUMMARY

In this chapter, I described three major types of corporate communication about the environment—green marketing, including practices of greenwashing; corporate advocacy campaigns; and a communication strategy known as SLAPP lawsuits, used by some businesses to silence or intimidate their environmental critics.

- In the first section of this chapter, I described a free-market discourse underling much of corporate environmental communication.
- In the second section, I explored in more detail the practice of corporate "green marketing" and its three forms: (1) product advertising (sales), (2) image enhancement, and (3) corporate image repair.
- The third section explored two communication practices that take advantage of public support for environmental values:

  (1) greenwashing, or the use of deceptive advertising to promote an environmentally responsible image; and

  (2) a discourse of green consumerism that suggests consumers can help the environment by buying "green" products

- In the fourth section, I looked at the role of corporate advocacy campaigns and the three-bites-of-the-apple strategy—campaigns to block or weaken environmental laws and also weaken regulations.
- Finally, I described a third, more aggressive communication practice, the use of Strategic Litigation Against Public Participation, or SLAPP lawsuits, to discredit or intimidate individuals who criticize industry for harming the environment.

Despite such communication approaches, many U.S. corporations have come to appreciate the environmental values embraced by the general public, consumers, and the media. As a consequence, much of corporate communication illustrates a skillful dance of corporate identity—an attempt to associate its products and identity with green values while sometimes continuing to oppose environmental restrictions.

This intricate effort plays out in the midst of the public sphere—a crucible of diverse voices, each seeking to speak for nature or the nature of the relationship between society and the environment.

SUGGESTED RESOURCES

- Terry L. Anderson and Donald R. Leal, *Free Market Environmentalism* (Rev. ed.). New York: Palgrave Macmillan, 2011.
- Edward Humes, *Force of Nature: The Unlikely Story of Walmart's Green Revolution.* New York: HarperCollins, 2011.
- Jacquelyn A. Ottman, *The New Rules of Green Marketing.* San Francisco: Berrett-Koehler, 2011.
- Motoko Rich and John Broder, "A Debate Arises on Job Creation vs. Environmental Regulation." *New York Times,* September 5, 2011, pp. B1, B5.
- George W. Pring and Penelope Canan, *SLAPPs: Getting Sued for Speaking Out.* Philadelphia: Temple University Press, 1996.

KEY TERMS

Eco-label certification programs 288

Free market 284

Green consumerism 300

Green marketing 286

Green product advertising 286

Greenwashing 286

Image enhancement 291

Image repair 295

Invisible hand (of the market) 285

Mountaintop removal 304

Pro-cotting 288

Productivist discourse 301

SLAPP back 309

SLAPP lawsuits 309

Three-bites-of-the-apple strategy 302

DISCUSSION QUESTIONS

1. Do advertising labels on products, such as *organic, biodegradable,* or *recycled* affect your purchases? Are these labels always accurate?

2. How do you feel about government regulation of business to prevent harm to the environment? Or, do you side with Adam Smith's theory that there is an "invisible hand" in the marketplace that inexorably yields the public good?

3. Can green consumerism help to protect the environment? Can we have some effect—even if small—on air pollution, clear-cutting of our national forests, or global warming by buying products that are biodegradable, nontoxic, recyclable, and so forth?

4. Can Walmart or other big box stores ever be sustainable? How credible is Walmart's claim to be helping the environment while making a profit? Must a business need to have pure motives, wanting to protect the environment for its own sake, to be believable?

5. Are the corporations that file SLAPP lawsuits merely a few bad apples, or do corporations have a right to sue individuals that they believe defame or libel the company's activities?

NOTE

1. In 2011, the Obama administration's EPA released updated guidance on mountaintop coal mining. Referring to the Clean Water Act, the guidance states that no discharge of dredged or "fill" material may be permitted if the nation's waters would be "significantly degraded," if it causes or contributes to violations of a state's water quality standard, or "if a practicable alternative exists that is less damaging to the aquatic environment." The coal industry criticized the guidelines as killing jobs, while environmentalists felt the revised rule should have been even tougher (Cho, 2011, para.12).

REFERENCES

ACCCE. (2008, April 16). *I believe.* [TV ad]. Retrieved January 8, 2009, from http://www.youtube.com

Aldrich, S., & Lehrwriting, J. (2006). *Free enterprise protects the environment.* Retrieved January 8, 2009, from http://www.heartland.org

America's Power. (2009). *Ad archive.* Retrieved January 8, 2009, from http://www.americaspower.org

Beder, S. (2002). *Global spin: The corporate assault on environmentalism* (Rev. ed.). White River Junction, VT: Chelsea Green.

Benoit, W. L. (1995). *Accounts, excuses, and apologies: A theory of image restoration strategies.* Albany: State University of New York Press.

Bliese, J. R. E. (2002). *The greening of conservative America.* Boulder, CO: Westview Press.

BP. (2009). *Alternative energy.* Retrieved January 10, 2009, from http://www.bp.com

Bullying behavior. (2011, March 14). *Raleigh News and Observer*, p. 9A.

Business Wire. (2008, November 6). *New poll data reveals 70 percent public opinion approval for coal-fueled electricity.* Retrieved January 9, 2009, from http://biz.yahoo.com

California State Environmental Resource Center. (2004). *"Eco-SLAPPs" are a frequent occurrence.* Retrieved October 31, 2004, from http://www.serconline.org

Can Wal-Mart be sustainable? (2009, August 6). *New York Times.* Retrieved September 12, 2001, from http://www.nytimes.com.

Cho, R. (2011, August 11). Mountaintop removal: Laying waste to streams and forests. Retrieved September 9, 2011, from http://blogs.ei.columbia.edu

Consumers beware: What labels mean. (2006, November 19). *Raleigh News and Observer*, pp. 23A–24A.

Corbett, J. (2006). *Communicating nature: How we create and understand environmental messages.* Washington, DC: Island Press.

Crable, R. E., & Vibbert, S. L. (1983). Mobil's epideictic advocacy: "Observations" of

Prometheus-bound. *Communication Monographs, 50,* 380–394.

Depoe, S. P. (1991). Good food from the good earth: McDonald's and the commodification of the environment. In D. W. Parson (Ed.), *Argument in controversy: Proceedings from the 7th SCA/AFA Conference on Argumentation* (pp. 334–341). Annandale, VA: Speech Communication Association.

Dickerson, M. (2009, January 4). Why Obama's green jobs plan might work. *The Los Angeles Times.* Retrieved January 12, 2009, from http://www.latimes.com

Dowie, M. (1995). *Losing ground: American environmentalism at the close of the twentieth century.* Cambridge, MA: MIT Press.

Eilperin, J. (2011, September 2). Obama pulls back proposed smog standards in victory for business. *Washington Post.* Retrieved September 4, 2011, from www.washingtonpost.com.

ExxonMobil. (2011). "Oil sands" TV ad. Retrieved September 6, 2011, from http://exxonmobiloilcorp.net

Faulkner, W. (2010, March 4). Titan suing two residents for slander over comments made at commissioners meeting. *Star News Online.* Retrieved September 7, 2011, from www.starnewsonline.com

Federal Trade Commission. (n.d.). Guides for the use of environmental marketing claims. Section 260.7. *Environmental marketing claims.* Retrieved November 25, 2004, from http://www.ftc.gov

Federal Trade Commission. (2010a, October 6). Press release: Federal Trade Commission proposes revised "Green Guides." Retrieved September 5, 2011, from http://www.ftc.gov

Federal Trade Commission. (2010b, October). *Proposed revisions to the green guides.* Retrieved September 5, 2011, from http://www.ftc.gov

Foer, J. S. (2010). *Eating animals.* New York: Back Bay Books.

Global Climate Coalition. (2000). *About us.* Retrieved October 4, 2004, from http://www.globalclimate.org

Global Climate Coalition. (2004). [Statement]. Downloaded October 30, 2004, from http://www.globalclimate.org

Graham, J. (2011, May 13). GoodGuide app helps navigate green products. *USA Today.* Retrieved September 2, 2011, from www.usatoday.com

Green marketing insight from GFK Roper's Green Gauge® at green marketing conference. (2011, February 24). *PR Web.* Retrieved September 4, 2011, from www.prweb.com

Greenpeace. (2008, December 22). *BP wins coveted "emerald paintbrush" award for worst greenwash of 2008.* Retrieved January 10, 2009, from http://weblog.greenpeace.org

Greenwash fact sheet. (2001, March 22). Corpwatch. Retrieved September 4, 2011, from www.corpwatch.org

Hansen, A. (2010). *Environment, media, and communication.* London and New York: Routledge.

Hays, S. P. (2000). *A history of environmental politics since 1945.* Pittsburgh, PA: University of Pittsburgh Press.

Hearit, K. M. (1995). "Mistakes were made": Organizations, apologia, and crisis of social legitimacy. *Communication Studies, 46,* 1–17.

Humes, E. (2011a). *Force of nature: The unlikely story of Walmart's green revolution.* New York: HarperCollins.

Humes, E. (2011b, May 31). Wal-Mart's green hat. *Los Angeles Times.* Retrieved September 3, 2011, from http://articles.latimes.com

Irvine, S. (1989). *Beyond green consumerism.* London: Friends of the Earth.

Johnston, K. (2008, October 29). Shut down for speaking up: SLAPP suits continue to chill free speech, despite legislated remedies. *New Times, 23*(13). Retrieved January 12, 2009, from http://www.newtimesslo.com

Lange, J. I. (1993). The logic of competing information campaigns: Conflict over old growth and the spotted owl. *Communication Monographs, 60,* 239–257.

LoBianco, T. (2008). Groups spend millions in "clean coal" ad war. *The Washington Times.* Retrieved January 8, 2009, from http://www.washingtontimes.com

Makower, J. (2010, July 19). Walmart and the sustainability index: One year later. Retrieved September 12, 2011, from www.greenbiz.com/blog

Marketing and communications. (2009, January 8). *GreenBiz.com.* Retrieved January 8, 2009, from http://www.greenbiz.com

Markowitz, G., & Rosner, D. (2002). *Deceit and denial: The deadly politics of industrial pollution.* Berkeley: University of California Press.

Martin, A. (2006, October 24). Meat labels hope to lure the sensitive carnivore. *The New York Times.* Retrieved March 2, 2009, from http://www.nytimes.com

Meinhold, B. (2009, August 6). Is it green?: Wal-Mart's sustainability index. Retrieved September 12, 2011, from http://inhabitat.com.

Merchant, B. (2009, July 14). Walmart's sustainability index: The greenest thing ever to happen to retail? Retrieved September 3, 2011, from www.treehugger.com

Mitchell, S. (2007, March 28). The impossibility of a green Wal-Mart. Retrieved September 12, 2011, from www.grist.org

MSNBC.com. (2010, June 8). I would have fired BP chief by now, Obama says. Retrieved September 6, 2011, from www.msnbc.msn.com

Mufson, S. (2008, January 18). Coal industry plugs into the campaign. *The Washington Post,* p. D1. Retrieved October 4, 2008, from http://www.washingtonpost.com

Oil slick spreads toward coast: FBI begins probe. (1989, April 2). *The Los Angeles Times,* Sec. 1, p. 1.

Ottman, J. A. (1993). *Green marketing: Challenges and opportunities for the new marketing age.* Lincolnwood, IL: NTC Business.

Ottman, J. A. (2003). *Hey, corporate America, it's time to think about products.* Retrieved October 14, 2004, from http://www.greenmarketing.com

Ottman, J. A. (2011). *The New Rules of Green Marketing.* San Francisco: Berrett-Koehler

Parenti, M. (1986). *Inventing reality: The politics of the mass media.* New York: St. Martin's.

Porter, W. M. (1992). The environment of the oil company: A semiotic analysis of Chevron's "People Do" commercials. In E. L. Toth & R. L. Health (Eds.), *Rhetorical and critical approaches to public relations* (pp. 279–300). Hillsdale, NJ: Erlbaum.

PR Watch. (2004). Global Climate Coalition. Retrieved October 4, 2004, from http://www.prwatch.org

Pring, G. W., & Canan, P. (1996). *SLAPPs: Getting sued for speaking out.* Philadelphia: Temple University Press.

Rich, M., & Broder, J. (2011, September 5). A debate arises on job creation vs. environmental regulation. *New York Times,* pp. B1, B5.

Roberts, M. (2011, January 18). Wal-Mart environmentalism. Retrieved September 4, 2011, from http://pennpoliticalreview.org

Shabecoff, P. (1989, March 31). Captain of tanker had been drinking, blood tests show. *The New York Times,* pp. A1, A12.

Smith, A. (1910). *An inquiry into the nature and causes of the wealth of nations: Vol. 1.* London: J. M. Dent & Sons. (Original work published 1776)

Smith, T. M. (1998). *The myth of green marketing: Tending our goats at the edge of apocalypse.* Toronto: University of Toronto Press.

SourceWatch. (2009, January 5). *American Coalition for Clean Coal Electricity. (ACCCE).* Retrieved January 8, 2009, from http://www.sourcewatch.org.

Sustainable Life Media. (2008, June 26). Canada bans "green" and "eco-friendly" from product labels. Retrieved January 8, 2009, from http://www.sustainablelifemedia.com

Switzer, J. V. (1997). *Green backlash: The history and politics of environmental opposition in the U.S.* Boulder, CO: Lynne Rienner.

TerraChoice. (2007, November). *The six sins of greenwashing*. Retrieved January 8, 2009, from http://www.terrachoice.com

TerraChoice. (2010a). The sins of green-washing home and family edition 2010. Retrieved September 3, 2011, from www.terrachoice.com

TerraChoice. (2010b). TerraChoice 2010 sins of greenwashing study finds mis-leading green claims. Retrieved September 3, 2011, from www.terra choice.com

Vega, T. (2010, October 6). Agency seeks to tighten rules for "green" labeling. *New York Times*. Retrieved October 10, 2010, from www.nytimes.com

Walmart. (2011, August). Sustainability facts. Retrieved September 3, 2011, from http://walmrtstores.com

Warrick, J. (2004, August 17). Appalachia is paying the price for White House rule change. *The Washington Post*, pp. A1, 6–7.

We will make this right. (2010, June 1). [Advertisement]. *New York Times*, p. A11.

White, A. S. (2010, August 4). Defining green marketing. Retrieved September 4, 2011, from http://dstevenwhite.com

Williams, B. A., & Matheny, A. R. (1995). *Democracy, dialogue, and environmental disputes*. New Haven, CT: Yale University Press.

Williams, D. E., & Olaniran, B. A. (1994). Exxon's decision-making flaws: The hypervigilant response to the *Valdez* grounding. *Public Relations Review, 20*, 5–18.

Zoellick, R. B. (2002, February 6). *Statement of U.S. trade representative before the Committee on Finance of the U.S. Senate*. Washington, DC: Office of the U.S. Trade Representative.

PART V

Science and Risk Communication

In recent years, environmental scientists have played a more visible role in public debates over the loss of biodiversity, global climate change, air pollution, species extinction, and other problems.

CHAPTER 11

Science Communication and Environmental Controversies

To advocate or not advocate? That question is one of the most basic ethical dilemmas facing environmental scientists today.

—Vucetich and Nelson,
"The Moral Obligations of Scientists" (2010)

The public debate over climate change in the U.S. raises a number of questions about the role of scientists and science communication in moments of environmental controversies:

- What is the proper relationship of scientific research to public policy in a democratic society?
- Do scientists have an obligation to explain publicly the science behind important issues such as pollution, species extinction, or climate change?
- How can scientists communicate their findings publicly when science always has some uncertainty?

In this chapter, I explore the environmental sciences as a source of knowledge and also as a site of conflict over the proper role of scientists in a democratic society. Scientific claims become a site of conflict when the legitimacy of science itself is challenged by industry, climate skeptics, and others who seek to influence the public and government about the meaning and uses of science.

Chapter Preview

- The first section of this chapter describes how science became a source of symbolic legitimacy in a society beset with complexity and technical knowledge.

- In the second section, I describe the *precautionary principle* as a way to manage the problem of scientific uncertainty. Conversely, some critics, and those skeptical of climate science, play up claims of uncertainty as a ploy to delay actions that might be costly to industry.

- In the third section, I'll introduce the role of scientists as society's early warners, that is, the duty of scientists to inform, advise, or alert the public in moments of environmental danger.

- Section four looks at challenges to the credibility of environmental science, a form of *symbolic legitimacy conflict,* and I'll describe two cases of this challenge:

  (1) use of the rhetorical trope of uncertainty, and

  (2) the so-called scandal of Climategate, the controversy in which climate change skeptics accused scientists of falsifying their research and perpetuating a hoax of global warming.

- Finally, I'll describe recent initiatives by scientists, journalists, and media producers to improve communication about the science and impacts of climate change.

Upon finishing this chapter, I hope you will gain greater appreciation for the role of science and scientists in a democratic society as well as an interest in learning more about the science in the controversies over climate change and other environmental dangers.

Science and Symbolic Legitimacy

As I write in 2011, policy makers and environmentalists in my state (North Carolina) are arguing about how much the ocean along our coast will rise by the end of this century. A report in the journal *Proceedings of the National Academy of Sciences* has added new urgency to this debate. It reported that the rate of sea level rise along the U.S. Atlantic coast is the steepest increase in the last 2,000 years and is consistent with a rise in global surface temperatures (Kemp, Horton, Donnelly, Mann, Vermeeer, & Rahmstorf, 2011). How fast (and high) sea levels will rise as global temperatures increase has been the subject of uncertainty since the Intergovernmental Panel on Climate Change (2007) forecast a sea level rise of 1 to 2 feet by the year 2100 (mainly from thermal expansion of sea water).

Similar problems of complexity in scientific research appear in other, major environmental and human health issues: genetically modified organisms, the effect on human fertility of synthetic chemicals that mimic natural hormones, and the amount of critical habitat needed for endangered species. Such complexities in science are not new, nor are the difficulties of communicating to or involving the public in these issues. It may be useful, therefore, to look at an earlier era that confronted similar concerns as well as at the emerging role of science and science communication in guiding important decisions about the environment.

Complexity and the Problem of the Public

In the early 20th century, the philosopher John Dewey wrote about the complexity of modern life as the American public experienced problems with urban sanitation and industrial safety as well as revolutionary changes in communication technologies. In his book *The Public and Its Problems,* Dewey (1927) warned of an "eclipse of the public" that he felt would occur because citizens lacked the expertise to evaluate the increasingly complex issues before them. The decisions before the public are so large, he wrote, "the technical matters involved are so specialized . . . that the public cannot for any length of time identify and hold itself [together]" (p. 137). With the growing need for technical expertise in making decisions, Dewey feared the United States was moving from democracy to a form of government that he called **technocracy,** or rule by experts.

The solution favored by the Progressive movement of the 1920s and 1930s was grounded in the reformers' faith in science and technology as a source of legitimacy for state and federal regulation of the new industries. Williams and Matheny (1995) explain that, in regulatory policy, the Progressives wanted to rely on trained experts working within government organizations to discover an objective public interest (p. 12). Legitimacy for political decisions would come from these experts' use of "neutral, scientific criteria for judging public policy" (p. 12).

Although the **Progressive ideal** of neutral, science-based policy would be challenged later, the legitimacy or credibility accorded to science by the public grew steadily stronger. Indeed, during the 20th and into the early 21st century, popular culture would give "tremendous prestige and power to our official, publicly validated knowledge system, namely science" (Harman, 1998, p. 116). In doing so, the sciences acquired a kind of **symbolic legitimacy,** that is, a perceived authority or credibility as a source of knowledge. For example, when the Environmental Protection Agency (EPA) was criticized for taking too long in its study of the effects of hydraulic fracturing, or *fracking,* on drinking water (a final report not due until 2014), it replied that "sound science" was driving its research (Dlouhy, 2011, para. 13). (Fracking is a type of drilling used to extract natural gas from shale strata underground; see Chapter 4.)

The appeals to "sound science" reflect the ideal that policy should be free of bias and grounded in reliable and valid knowledge. As a result, government agencies have sought to incorporate the findings of environmental scientists not only in EPA policies but also in actions by the Department of the Interior and in agencies such as the U.S. Fish and Wildlife Service. Additionally, scientists from the National Research Council, universities, and various research centers routinely advise policy makers on the scientific implications of environmental proposals.

Still, the Progressive ideal of neutral, science-based policies often falls short of its promise. As we'll see later in this chapter, pressures from political or business interests, agency budget cuts, ideology, and other factors sometimes restrict the degree to which scientific research influences public policies, especially environmental policies. Let's look more closely at this problem and some of the reasons why environmental science is sometimes a site of conflict.

Challenging Science's Symbolic Legitimacy

Although the public generally views scientists as authoritative sources of knowledge—having symbolic legitimacy—the environmental sciences are also a site of conflict. This is particularly true as differing interests (industry, public health officials, and environmentalists) attempt to influence public perceptions or agencies' views about a problem or proposed action. For example, environmental historian Samuel Hays (2000) reports that, as the new environmental sciences began to document risks from industrial products in the 1960s and 1970s, affected businesses challenged the science "at every step, questioning both the methods and research designs that were used and the conclusions that were drawn" (p. 222). Industries such as electric utilities, oil and gas refineries, chemical manufacturing, and older extractive industries (mining and logging) will often put tremendous pressure on government agencies to justify the science behind new regulations.

As I write, for example, electric utilities are pressuring the EPA to delay its proposed rule that would reduce harmful pollution from coal-burning power plants. Based on research by EPA scientists, the American Lung Association, American Academy of Pediatrics, and other peer-reviewed studies, the EPA has concluded that power plants' air pollution—mercury and other metals such as arsenic, chromium, and nickel—is harmful to Americans' health, especially children (McGowan, 2011). On the other hand, environmental and public health groups are defending the EPA and the science behind its proposed rule.

In debates about environmental policies, one source of controversy is the question of whether there is "conclusive" or absolute proof, something that is often beyond the reach of science. John Fitzpatrick, director of the Cornell Laboratory of Ornithology, says this presents a dilemma: "A **paradox for conservation** is that knowledge is always incomplete, yet the scale of human influence on ecosystems demands action without delay" (quoted in Scully, 2005, p. B13). This paradox poses a serious challenge for the public's willingness to support steps to protect the environment. At the same time, it provides the opponents of stronger regulations with opportunities to contest the scientific claims, "to slow up application of scientific knowledge and establishes . . . caution on the part of decision makers in public agencies. Their watchword is 'insufficient proof' (Hays, 2000, p. 151)

The challenge for government agencies is especially acute when the science fails to tell officials how to choose between technical and political questions (for example, what is an "acceptable" risk?) or how to decide among competing values, such as the health benefits to be gained versus the costs to comply with a regulation. In the above example, the EPA's proposed regulation that coal-burning power plants are required to upgrade their antipollution equipment pits the cost of complying against the health benefits derived from reduced hospital visits, insurance costs, and so on.

Environmental sciences, then, must contend with some degree of uncertainty (as do all sciences) but also with a need to balance the benefits and costs from adopting an action. Because decisions about costs and benefits require value judgments, scientists are not the only voices involved. Two important questions, therefore, arise: What status or influence should scientists and science have in important decisions in a democratic society? And, do scientists have an obligation to explain publicly the science behind issues such as pollution, species extinction, or climate change? To ask these questions is also to ask about the symbolic legitimacy "boundaries" of science itself. (I'll describe some of the challenges to environmental science later in this chapter.)

To understand conflicts over science and the environment, therefore, we need to examine the ways in which the contending parties in society attempt to deal with scientific uncertainty as well as the communication used in resolving the trade-offs between the costs and benefits of acting, or not acting, on environmental and health issues. The fault line in such conflict occurs many times between supporters of a principle of caution and others whose interests are adversely affected by such caution and who seek, therefore, to contest the claims of science.

The Precautionary Principle

As we saw above, a paradox of environmental sciences is that knowledge about the effects of human behavior on the environment is always incomplete, yet the scale of our influence on the Earth demands that we take action. Stanford University biologists Paul Ehrlich and Anne Ehrlich (1996) once remarked that a great irony in the environmental sciences is that science itself can never provide "absolute certainty or the 'proof' that many who misunderstand science say [that] society needs" (p. 27). Although certainty evokes a powerful pull for social reformers, religious adherents, and popular radio commentators, "it is forever denied to scientists" (p. 27).

The absence of "absolute certainty" has spawned conflict and controversy in areas like chemical pollution, food safety, and such large-scale problems like climate change and the loss of biodiversity. The Ehrlichs (1996) note with some concern that, in the absence of more precise knowledge of complex environmental systems, "humanity is running a vast experiment on the biosphere and on itself" (p. 29).

The Problem of Uncertainty

The absence of scientific certainty also provides openings for some to call for delays before government takes action. For decades, the opponents of environmental regulation of industry have used the indeterminacy of science as a rationale for resisting new standards to regulate hazardous chemicals, such as lead, dichloro-diphenyl-trichloroethane (DDT), dioxin, and polychlorinated biphenyls (PCBs).

An infamous, classic case of industry's use of scientific uncertainty occurred in 1922 and involved the introduction of tetraethyl lead in gasoline for cars. Although public health officials thought lead posed a health risk and should be studied more carefully first, the industry argued that there was no scientific agreement on the danger and pushed ahead to market leaded gasoline for the next 50 years. Peter Montague (1999) of the Environmental Research Foundation writes, "The consequences of that . . . decision [to delay standards for leaded gasoline] are now a matter of record—tens of millions of Americans suffered brain damage, their IQs permanently diminished by exposure to lead dust" (para. 3).

Historically, the procedures for assessing risk have given the benefit of the doubt to new products, even though these may prove harmful later. (For a description of methods used in risk assessment, see Chapter 12.) For example, existing standards require only a tiny fraction of the 70,000 or more chemicals in commercial use in the United States today to be "fully tested for their ability to cause harm to health and the environment" (Shabecoff, 2000, p. 149). By the 1990s, however, a number of scientists, environmentalists, and public health advocates had begun to argue that the burden of proof should be shifted to require use of the precautionary principle.

As early as the 1960s, scientists such as René Dubos, Rachel Carson, and Barry Commoner had warned of possible ecological disaster and danger to human health from new chemicals appearing in water, air, soil, the food chain, and mothers' breast milk. Rachel Carson's (1962) *Silent Spring* became the most visible public warning about chemical agents such as DDT in agricultural spraying and pesticides. New stories of nuclear fallout from atmospheric tests on foods also fueled public anxieties. Others warned of dangers from the new organochlorines (such as PCBs) that can "reduce sperm counts, disrupt female reproductive cycles . . . cause birth defects, [and] impair the development and function of the brain" (Thornton, 2000, p. 6, in Markowitz & Rosner, 2002, p. 296).

The Precautionary Principle and Its Critics

Eventually, scientists and health officials urged that a new approach to environmental uncertainty be adopted, "one that takes science's uncertainty not as a sign that there is no danger but as a sign that serious danger might well exist" (Markowitz & Rosner, 2002, p. 298). This view emphasized an ethic of caution or prudence in evaluating products that, even with low levels of risk, could harm populations in the future. In 1991, the National Research Council offered a compelling rationale for the new precautionary approach: "Until better evidence is developed, prudent public policy demands that a margin of safety be provided regarding potential health risks. . . . We do no less in designing bridges and buildings. . . . We must surely do no less when the health and quality of life of Americans are at stake" (p. 270).

An important step came in 1998, in Racine, Wisconsin, when the Science and Environmental Health Network and foundations that funded scientific research convened the Wingspread Conference on the Precautionary Principle to define a new principle of prudence. The 32 participants—scientists, researchers, philosophers, environmentalists, and labor leaders from the United States, Europe, and Canada—shared the belief that "compelling evidence that damage to humans and the worldwide environment is of such magnitude and seriousness that new principles for conducting human activities are necessary" (Science and Environmental Health Network, 1998, para. 3).

At the end of the three-day meeting, the participants issued the "Wingspread Statement on the Precautionary Principle," which called for government, business, and scientists to take into account the new principle in making decisions about environmental and human health (Raffensperger, 1998). The statement provided this expanded definition of the **precautionary principle**: "*When an activity raises threats of harm to human health or the environment, precautionary measures should be taken even if some cause and effect relationships are not fully established scientifically. In this context the proponent of an activity, rather than the public, should bear the burden of proof*" (Science and Environmental Health Network, 1998, para. 5; emphasis added).

The new principle is to be applied when an activity poses a combination of potential harm and scientific uncertainty. It requires (a) an ethic of prudence (avoidance of risk) and (b) an affirmative obligation to act to prevent harm. The principle shifts the burden of proof to the proponents of an activity to show that "their activity will not cause undue harm to human health or the ecosystem;" furthermore, it requires agencies and corporations to take proactive measures to reduce or eliminate hazards, including "a duty to monitor, understand, investigate, inform, and act" when anything goes wrong (Montague, 1999, para. 13). (See "FYI: The Wingspread Statement on the Precautionary Principle.")

Not all parties rushed to embrace the precautionary principle. Some businesses, conservative policy centers, and politicians are concerned that the consequences of using the principle are at odds with assumptions in the dominant social paradigm (Chapter 3); that is, they object that the principle errs on the side of too much caution. Writing for the libertarian policy center, the Cato Institute, Ronald Bailey (2002) argued that "the precautionary principle is an anti-science regulatory concept that allows regulators to ban new products on the barest suspicion that they might pose some unknown threat" (p. 5).

Bailey (2002) cites the case of the European Union's (EU) ban on imports of genetically enhanced crops—what have been called genetically modified organisms (GMOs)—from the United States. Scientific panels have concluded that genetically modified foods are safe to eat, he argued, and that "the EU ban is not a safety precaution, but a barrier to trade" (p. 4). The dispute over the safety of genetically enhanced food is a continuing debate, one that has placed the precautionary principle squarely at the center of the controversy.

☞ **FYI** **The Wingspread Statement on the Precautionary Principle**

The release and use of toxic substances, the exploitation of resources, and physical alterations of the environment have had substantial unintended consequences affecting human health and the environment. Some of these concerns are high rates of learning deficiencies, asthma, cancer, birth defects and species extinctions; along with global climate change, stratopheric ozone depletion, and worldwide contamination with toxic substances and nuclear materials.

We believe existing environmental regulations and other decisions, particularly those based on risk assessment, have failed to protect adequately human health and the environment—the larger system of which humans are but a part.

(Continued)

(Continued)

   We believe there is compelling evidence that damage to humans and the worldwide environment is of such magnitude and seriousness that new principles for conducting human activities
are necessary.

   While we realize that human activities may involve hazards, people must proceed more
carefully than has been the case in recent history. Corporations, government entities, organizations, communities, scientists, and other individuals must adopt a precautionary approach to all
human endeavors.

   Therefore, it is necessary to implement the Precautionary Principle: When an activity raises
threats of harm to human health or the environment, precautionary measures should be taken
even if some cause and effect relationships are not fully established scientifically.

   In this context the proponent of an activity, rather than the public, should bear the burden
of proof.

   The process of applying the Precautionary Principle must be open, informed and democratic
and must include potentially affected parties. It must also involve an examination of the full
range of alternatives, including no action.

Debate over the precautionary principle mirrors a larger conflict over the role of
uncertainty in environmental policy. It is to this conflict, and attempts to challenge
the symbolic legitimacy of science itself, that we now turn.

Early Warners:
Environmental Scientists and the Public

In recent years, environmental scientists have played a more visible role in public
debates over the loss of biodiversity, global climate change, air pollution, species
extinction, and other problems. For some, scientists have a moral obligation to alert,
speak out, or warn the public and public officials in time to avert danger. Others fear
that such public warning or advocacy hurts scientists' credibility or is incompatible
with the ideal of science as an objective and neutral inquiry (Vucetich & Nelson, 2010).
Often hotly disputed, the role of scientists as early warners has gained greater urgency
than ever, as they warn of a *tipping point*, or a time when the catastrophic consequences of the warming of the planet will become irreversible.

   In this section, I'll review the debate over the public obligations of scientists as
early warners. I'll also look at several egregious cases of political interference in scientific research, including an effort to censor a well-known National Aeronautics and
Space Administration (NASA) scientist who was one of the earliest to speak out
publicly about climate change.

Dilemmas of Neutrality and Scientists' Credibility

In the debate over whether scientists have a moral duty to speak publicly, environmental scientists find themselves asked to choose between two very different and competing identities: Are they objective scientists whose duty is to remain neutral, limiting their communications to academic journals? Or are they environmental physicians of a sort, guided by a medical ethic—the impulse to go beyond the diagnosis of problem to a prescription for its cure? And, if not the duty of a physician, do they, at least, have an ethical duty to warn or speak out when the public remains unaware of hidden or looming dangers?

This dilemma over scientists' obligations was heightened by the new field of conservation biology, emerging in the late 1980s. One of its founders, biologist Michael Soulé (1985), insisted that conservation biology was a **crisis discipline**—its emergence was necessitated by a worsening ecological disturbance with irreversible effects on species and ecosystems (p. 727). He believed that scientists, therefore, could not remain silent in the face of a "biodiversity crisis that will reach a crescendo in the first half of the twenty-first century" (Soulé, 1987, p. 4). Indeed, scientists, he argued, have an ethical duty to offer recommendations to address this worsening situation, even with imperfect knowledge, because "the risks of non-action may be greater than the risks of inappropriate action" (Soulé, 1986, p. 6).

In 1996, the debate over the neutrality of scientists came to the forefront when the journal *Conservation Biology* published a special issue on the role of advocacy in the science of conservation biology. The gauntlet was thrown down in the first essay: "Conservation biology is inescapably normative. *Advocacy for the preservation of biodiversity is part of the scientific practice of conservation biology*" (Barry & Oelschlaeger, 1996, p. 905; emphasis added).

Other scientists took a differing view of the role of environmental scientists, reflecting the belief that advocacy taints a scientist's credibility. Traditionally, scientists have been viewed as neutral parties who use objective procedures, with the resulting empirical evidence laying the basis for any policy implications (Mason, 1962). Shabecoff (2000) summarized this view: "The scientist, free of preconceived values, seeks the truth and follows it wherever it leads. It is assumed that whatever the outcome of the search, it will benefit human welfare" (p. 140). As a result, some scientists fear that abandoning this identity, by publicly advocating responses to problems, would violate an ethic of objectivity and undermine the credibility of scientists (Slobodkin, 2000; Rykiel, 2001; Wiens, 1997).

Other scientists—especially ecologists and climate scientists—have begun to question the ethical appropriateness of scientists' silence outside their laboratories in the face of worsening environmental problems. For example, Rajendra Pachauri, the former director of the United Nations' Intergovernmental Panel on Climate Change, warned, "If there's no action [on climate change] before 2012, that's too late. What we do in the next two to three years will determine our future. This is the defining moment" (quoted in Rosenthal, 2007).

Yet, some scientists who have spoken publicly, particularly scientists working for the federal government, have faced repercussions and have seen their research criticized. The controversy over scientists' identities and their ethical duties in the face of ecological and human challenges has its roots in earlier controversies, and it may be useful to briefly review this history.

Environmental Scientists as Early Warners

Scientists' roles in the development of nuclear weapons in 1945 prompted one of the first major debates over the ethical responsibilities of scientists. Along with these scientists, molecular biologists also began to insist on a greater voice in informing the public and policy makers of the consequences of the new research emerging after World War II (Berg, Baltimore, Boyer, Cohen, & Davis, 1974; Morin, 1993). As a result, scientific associations such as the Federation of American Scientists, along with journals such as the *Bulletin of the Atomic Scientists,* arose to represent scientists in the public realm (Kendall, 2000).

> ### Act Locally!
>
> #### Should Scientists Be Society's Early Warners of Environmental Dangers?
>
> To gain an appreciation for the ethical and professional questions in the debate over scientists' responsibility to speak publicly about possible dangers, consider inviting a scientist from your campus to speak with your class.
>
> (1) What is her or his view of the role of science and scientists in a free society?
>
> (2) How does he or she balance a professional duty as a scientist to remain neutral and an ethical concern about warnings to the public of possible risks?
>
> (3) How far is he or she willing to go in speaking publicly: briefing reporters in a press conference, advising policy makers about the implications of his or her research, or advocating solutions? Where should one draw a line?
>
> Finally, where do you stand on the question of scientists' roles as early warners? How would you weigh the potential risks to your credibility as an objective, impartial scholar versus a duty to share your special knowledge or insights with the public in moments of environmental danger?

By 1969, the Union of Concerned Scientists (UCS) had formed to address survival problems in the late 20th century, foremost among these, the threat of nuclear war. Having since expanded its scope to problems of global warming and the potential dangers of genetic manipulation, the UCS now includes more than 250,000 scientists and citizens. The group defines its mission as combining "independent scientific research and citizen action to develop innovative, practical solutions and to secure responsible changes in government policy, corporate practices, and consumer choices" (Union of Concerned Scientists, 2011, para. 1).

Other scientists are also joining in public debates about environmental threats and the need for alerting the public. For example, Physicians for Social Responsibility, drawing on medical science, sees as its mission to alert the public to environmental and health problems that are caused by new technologies and industrial practices. And, British theoretical physicist Stephen Hawking, author of *A Brief History of Time*, has spoken sharply about the need for scientist to serve as early warners. In 2007, he told a gathering of scientists that they had a duty to speak out:

> As citizens of the world, we have a duty to alert the public to the unnecessary risks that we live with every day, and to the perils we foresee if governments and societies do not take action now. . . . As we stand at the brink of . . . a period of unprecedented climate change, scientists have a special responsibility. (quoted in Connor, 2007, paras. 5, 6)

More recently, the National Academy of Sciences (2011) is warning public officials in the United States that "climate change is occurring, is very likely caused primarily by human activities, and poses significant risks to humans and the environment." In the judgment of the academy, the report stated, "The environmental, economic, and humanitarian risks posed by climate change indicate a pressing need for substantial action" (para. 1).

The National Academy of Sciences, Michael Soulé, Stephen Hawkins, and other independent scientists are free to speak publicly if they choose. However, other scientists, particularly in government, have sometimes faced interference in their research and even censorship of reports and web postings intended for public release.

Censoring the Early Warnings of a National Aeronautics and Space Administration Scientist

On December 6, 2005, Dr. James E. Hansen, NASA's chief climate scientist, warned in a speech to the American Geophysical Union in San Francisco that "the Earth's climate is nearing, but has not passed, a tipping point, beyond which it will be impossible to avoid climate change with far-ranging undesirable consequences." Further warming of more than 1°C (or about 2°F), Hansen said, will leave "a different planet" (quoted in Bowen, 2008, p. 4). Hansen is director of the Goddard Institute for Space Studies, and it was he who first introduced global warming into the spotlight when he testified before the U.S. Senate nearly two decades earlier.

Hansen's warning in 2005 set off more than just scientific alarm bells. In the days following his speech, NASA officials ordered its public affairs staff to monitor Hansen's lectures, scientific papers, postings on the Goddard website, and journalists' requests for interviews (Revkin, 2006a). When the *Washington Post* reported the story, NASA staff tried to discourage the *Post*'s reporter from interviewing him. They agreed, finally, that Hansen "could speak on the record only if an agency spokeswoman listened in on the conversation" (Eilperin, 2006, p. A1). Other NASA scientists complained to the

| **Figure 11.1** | Hubbard Glacier in Alaska calving, further warming of more than 1°C will leave "a different planet" (Dr. James E. Hansen, Director of NASA's Goddard Institute for Space Studies). |

Kyle West/Flickr

New York Times about similar political pressures on them "to limit or flavor discussions of topics uncomfortable to the Bush administration, particularly global warming" (Revkin, 2006b, A11).

NASA later assured reporters that its scientists could speak freely to the media, but the clumsy handling of the Hansen incident had set off a storm of criticism in the mainstream media and blogosphere. Dr. Hansen himself defended his actions: "Communicating with the public seems to be essential . . . because public concern is probably the only thing capable of overcoming the special interests that have obfuscated the topic" of global warming (Revkin, 2006a, p. A1). Nevertheless, NASA officials warned Hansen that "there would be 'dire consequences' if such statements continued," according to public affairs officers at the agency (Revkin, 2006a, p. A1).

Similar reports of political interference in scientific reports appeared in news media, reports by monitoring groups, and the blogosphere during the eight years of the Bush administration, from 2001 to 2009 (Mooney, 2006; Revkin, 2005; Union of Concerned Scientists, 2004, 2008).

Political Interference in Scientists' Communication With the Public

One case occurred early in the Bush administration. On March 7, 2001, Ian Thomas, a 33-year-old government cartographer, posted a map of caribou calving areas in the Arctic National Wildlife Refuge (ANWR) on a U.S. Geological Survey website. At the time, Thomas had been working on maps for all of the national wildlife refuges and national parks using the new National Landcover Datasets (Thomas, 2001). Nevertheless, his timing in posting the new map of caribou calving areas landed him in the center of a national controversy. The U.S. Congress had begun to debate a proposal from President George W. Bush's administration to open parts of ANWR to oil and gas drilling, and the calving grounds appeared to be directly in the path.

On his first day at work after posting his map, Thomas was fired and his website removed. In an official statement, a public affairs officer for the U.S. Geological Survey stated that Thomas had been "operating outside the scope of [his] contract" and had not had his maps "scientifically reviewed or approved" before posting them on the website (Harlow, 2001). Thomas himself believed that his dismissal was "a high-level political decision to set an example to other federal scientists" who might not support the administration's campaign to open the refuge for oil and gas exploration. "I thought that I was helping further public and scientific understanding and debate of the issues at ANWR by making some clearer maps," Thomas (2001) wrote in an e-mail to colleagues.

More evidence of political interference in federal science communication soon appeared. In 2004, more than 60 prestigious scientists (including 20 Nobel Prize winners) issued a report sharply criticizing the misuse and suppression of science by federal agencies. The *Scientific Integrity in Policymaking* report, released by the UCS, charged that White House officials had engaged in "a well-established pattern of suppression and distortion of scientific findings" (p. 2). Among its findings, the report claimed that officials had "misrepresented scientific consensus on global warming, censored at least one report on climate change, manipulated scientific findings on the emissions of mercury from power plants, and suppressed information on condom use" (Glanz, 2004, p. A21).

In the following years, more evidence of political interference with science communication would emerge, for example, an especially egregious case, that of Philip A. Cooney, Chief of Staff for the White House Council on Environmental Policy. In 2005, the *New York Times* obtained documents showing that Cooney—a former lobbyist at the American Petroleum Institute—had personally edited reports intended for public release by the federal Climate Change Science Program in 2002 and 2003. In handwritten notes, Cooney "removed or adjusted descriptions of climate research that government scientists and their supervisors . . . had already approved" (Revkin, 2005, para. 2). *Times* reporter Andrew Revkin (2005) noted that the changes, "while sometimes as subtle as the insertion of the phrase 'significant and fundamental' before the word 'uncertainties,' *tend to produce an air of doubt about findings that most climate experts say are robust*" (para. 3; emphasis added). Nevertheless, it was this edited version of the federal report that the White House released to the public.

As I write in late 2011, there has been a lessening of ideological battles over science inside federal agencies themselves. Nevertheless, the environmental sciences have frequently been the target of questioning by special interest groups, dissident

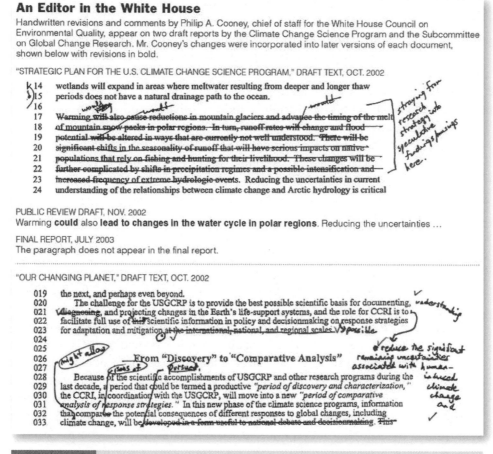

An Editor in the White House

Handwritten revisions and comments by Philip A. Cooney, chief of staff for the White House Council on Environmental Quality, appear on two draft reports by the Climate Change Science Program and the Subcommittee on Global Change Research. Mr. Cooney's changes were incorporated into later versions of each document, shown below with revisions in bold.

"STRATEGIC PLAN FOR THE U.S. CLIMATE CHANGE SCIENCE PROGRAM," DRAFT TEXT, OCT. 2002

14   wetlands will expand in areas where meltwater resulting from deeper and longer thaw
15   periods does not have a natural drainage path to the ocean.
16
17   Warming will also cause reductions in mountain glaciers and advance the timing of the melt
18   of mountain snow packs in polar regions. In turn, runoff rates will change and flood
19   potential will be altered in ways that are currently not well understood. There will be
20   significant shifts in the seasonality of runoff that will have serious impacts on native
21   populations that rely on fishing and hunting for their livelihood. These changes will be
22   further complicated by shifts in precipitation regimes and a possible intensification and
23   increased frequency of extreme hydrologic events. Reducing the uncertainties in current
24   understanding of the relationships between climate change and Arctic hydrology is critical

PUBLIC REVIEW DRAFT, NOV. 2002
Warming **could** also **lead to changes in the water cycle in polar regions**. Reducing the uncertainties ...

FINAL REPORT, JULY 2003
The paragraph does not appear in the final report.

"OUR CHANGING PLANET," DRAFT TEXT, OCT. 2002

019   the next, and perhaps even beyond.
020   The challenge for the USGCRP is to provide the best possible scientific basis for documenting,
021   diagnosing, and projecting changes in the Earth's life-support systems, and the role for CCRI is to
022   facilitate full use of this scientific information in policy and decisionmaking on response strategies
023   for adaptation and mitigation at the international, national, and regional scales.
024
025
026   From "Discovery" to "Comparative Analysis"
027
028   Because of the scientific accomplishments of USGCRP and other research programs during the
029   last decade, a period that could be termed a productive *"period of discovery and characterization,"*
030   the CCRI, in coordination with the USGCRP, will move into a new *"period of comparative
031   analysis of response strategies."* In this new phase of the climate science programs, information
032   that compares the potential consequences of different responses to global changes, including
033   climate change, will be developed in a form useful to national debate and decisionmaking. This

| Figure 11.2 | An excerpt from Philip A. Cooney's edit of a report on climate change during the Bush Administration. |

Philip A. Cooney, Chief of Staff for the White House Council on Environmental Quality (and former lobbyist at the American Petroleum Institute) personally edited reports intended for public release by the federal Climate Science Program in 2002 and 2003.

scientists, and corporations when environmental research has conflicted with their interests. More recently, personal attacks on climate scientists, including the Climategate controversy, have threatened to erode the symbolic legitimacy of science itself.

Science and Symbolic Legitimacy Conflict

Although science has produced "a cornucopia of material abundance for a substantial portion of the human race" (Shabecoff, 2000, p. 138), scientific knowledge about the environmental impacts of modern industry has been the site of controversy. Markowitz and Rosner (2002) observed that, during much of the 20th century, industry lobbyists argued there must be "convincing proof of danger before policymakers had the right to intrude on the private reserve of industry in America" (p. 287). Yet, even as proof emerged, some industries challenged the scientific consensus "at almost every step" when that knowledge might lead to new regulations (Hays, 2000, p. 138).

The reason for industry's feud with science is not hard to understand. The prospect that some products and industrial pollutants might be linked to cancers, endocrine disruptors, and other health problems, as well as to changes in the Earth's climate, raises not only issues of financial liability for these companies but tougher regulation of industry itself.

One result has been that the industries at risk of regulation by environmental science—especially petrochemicals energy, real estate development, and utilities—have "sought to turn science in their direction and [have] attracted scientists who could help with that objective" (Hays, 2000, p. 138). A look at several of these cases is instructive for understanding the communication used by industry and others to contest the legitimacy of scientific consensus.

Science and the Trope of Uncertainty

In the past two decades, some industries and climate change skeptics have used a range of communication to challenge the symbolic legitimacy of the environmental sciences. This includes the funding of friendly scientists, the production of books and media releases by **think tanks** that promote skepticism, and most important, the use of a rhetorical *trope of uncertainty.* (In Chapter 3, I described a *trope* as a turn or change in our perception that alters its meaning.) Let me describe this briefly and then illustrate the use of this trope and other communication that some have used to challenge the environmental sciences in recent years.

When opponents call for further research into the causes of global climate change or the effect of dams in the Pacific Northwest on runs of salmon, they are drawing on a familiar tool in industry's challenge to the legitimacy of science. This **trope of uncertainty** functions to nurture doubt in the public's perception of scientific claims and thereby to delay calls for action. In rhetorical terms, the trope of uncertainty turns, or alters, the public's understanding of what is at stake, suggesting there is a danger in acting prematurely or a risk of making the wrong decision. For this reason, Markowitz and Rosner (2002) have observed that "the call for more scientific evidence is often a stalling tactic" (p. 10).

A classic source for the strategy for nurturing doubt about the legitimacy of a group or issue is public relations expert Philip Lesly's (1992) article, "Coping With Opposition Groups." Lesly advises corporate clients to design their communication to create uncertainty in the minds of the public:

> The weight of impressions on the public must be balanced so people *will have doubts and lack motivation to take action.* Accordingly, means are needed to get balancing information into the stream from sources that the public will find credible. There is no need for a clear-cut "victory." ... Nurturing public doubts by demonstrating that this is not a clear-cut situation in support of the opponents usually is all that is necessary. (p. 331; emphasis added)

Feeling uncertain about an issue, the advice goes, the public will be less motivated to demand action, and the political will to solve a problem will weaken. For example, in their study of corporations' uses of PR strategies opposing government regulation, Sheldon Rampton and John Stauber (2002) observed, "Industry's PR strategy is not aimed at reversing the tide of public opinion, which may in any case be impossible. Its goal is simply to stop people from mobilizing to do anything about the problem, to create sufficient doubt in their minds about the seriousness of global warming that they will remain locked in debate and indecision" (p. 271).

Ironically, the trope of uncertainty is an attempt to reverse the precautionary principle. The principle stresses that, when an activity raises threats of harm to human health or the environment, precautionary measures should be taken even if some uncertainty remains. However, critics' calls for further research turn this "precaution" against the principle itself. A striking case of such deliberate introduction of uncertainty into debates over the politically sensitive matter of climate change occurred in the report of a prominent consultant to the Republican party.

Memo on Global Warming: Challenge the Science

Sometimes, the conflict over the legitimacy of scientific consensus may be fought on the terrain of language itself by engaging in what one political consultant called the "environmental communications battle" (Luntz Research Companies, 2001, p. 136). In a memo titled "The Environment: A Cleaner, Safer Healthier America," consultant Frank Luntz (2001) warned Republican party leaders that "the scientific debate is closing [against us] but not yet closed." Nevertheless, he advised, "There is still *a window of opportunity to challenge the science*" (p. 138; emphasis in original). The "window of opportunity" to which Luntz referred was the possibility that critics could raise enough doubts about the symbolic legitimacy of scientific claims about climate change that the public's uncertainty would delay governmental action in this area.

Luntz's memo offers a rare look into a behind-the-scenes debate over rhetorical strategy in high-level political circles. It is noteworthy especially for its frank assessment of the PR dilemma that faced many politicians. For example, Luntz had found that voters particularly distrusted the Republican party on the environment. His memo, therefore, is revealing for the rhetorical strategy that he believed Republicans needed in order to challenge the growing consensus—the symbolic legitimacy—for many environmental issues, such as safe drinking water, the protection of natural areas, and especially climate change.

In one section of the memo, Luntz asserts that voters currently believe there is no consensus about global warming in the scientific community. "Should the public come to believe that the scientific issues are settled," he writes, "their views about global warming will change accordingly." Advising party leaders, Luntz's memo states, "'Therefore, *you need to continue to make the lack of scientific certainty a primary issue in the debate*" (p. 137; emphasis in original). The purpose, he explained, is to weaken voters' desire to call for action. Instead, GOP officials should state,

"Until we learn more, we should not commit America to any international [climate] document that handcuffs us either now or in the future" (p. 137).

In challenging the science, Luntz advised, make use of sources that the public trusts. Be active especially "in recruiting experts who are sympathetic to your view, and much more active in making them part of your message." He explained, "People are willing to trust scientists, engineers, and other leading professionals" more than they trust politicians (p. 138).

Manufacturing Uncertainty: Industry and Conservative Think Tanks

Luntz's advice to "make the lack of scientific certainty a primary issue" appears as a major theme in other attempts by industry and other critics to challenge environmental science on issues ranging from chemical contamination to climate change. The objective of these efforts is to encourage the public's questioning of the legitimacy of scientific claims and scientific consensus about environmental problems. Let's look at some examples of this.

One of the earliest efforts by corporations to influence the public's views of environmental science was disclosed in a *New York Times* report in 1998. The *Times* reporter John Cushman (1998) had uncovered a plan by the American Petroleum Institute to spend millions of dollars to convince the public that the Kyoto treaty on global warming was based on "shaky science" (p. A1). The proposal included:

> a campaign to recruit a cadre of scientists who share the industry's views of climate science and to train them in public relations so they can help convince journalists, politicians and the public that the risk of global warming is too uncertain to justify controls on greenhouse gases like carbon dioxide that trap the sun's heat near Earth. (p. A1)

Other sources noted that the American Petroleum Institute's plan included a $5 million Global Climate Science Data Center to provide information to the media, government officials, and the public; grant money for "advocacy on climate science"; and funds for a Science Education Task Group to put industry information into school classrooms (National Environmental Trust, 1998).

The campaign by industry to influence public perceptions of climate science is not an isolated case. Independent monitoring groups and journalists have documented a range of communication practices used by industry to question the scientific consensus or legitimacy for other environmental concerns (Shabecoff, 2000).

Beyond these attempts, a more basic challenge has emerged in the past decade— the manufacturing of an attitude of "environmental skepticism" to shape public debates about environmental science and about climate change in particular. Among those engaging in this "skepticism" are conservative think tanks (CTTs) and tax-exempt organizations. *Conservative think tanks* are nonprofit, advocacy-based centers modeled on the image of neutral policy institutes (for example, the Heritage Foundation, the Cato Institute, and Heartland Institute). The message varies, but the strategy generally is to sow doubt about climate change, challenging the consensus of mainstream scientists: Is global warming really occurring? Is human activity truly to blame? And, are rising temperatures such a bad thing?

In their study of conservative think tanks, Jacques, Dunlap, and Freeman (2008) identified a systematic effort to nurture "environmental skepticism" about serious environmental problems—from loss of biodiversity to toxic chemicals, and especially, global warming (p. 349). They also found a key rhetorical strategy underlying this effort: the promotion in the think tanks' books, press releases, and policy papers of an attitude of **environmental skepticism** that disputes the seriousness of environmental problems and questions the credibility of environmental science itself (p. 351). In doing so, the authors of these books and press releases suggest that the environmental sciences have been "corrupted by political agendas that lead it to unintentionally or maliciously fabricate or grossly exaggerate these global problems" (Jacques, Dunlap, & Freeman, 2008, p. 353).

The think tanks study cites the example of Patrick Michaels, a climate skeptic and senior fellow at the Cato Institute. Michaels (2004) wrote in his book *Meltdown: The Predictable Distortion of Global Warming by Scientists, Politicians, and the Media* that, "global warming is an exaggerated issue, predictably blown out of proportion by the political and professional climate in which it evolved" (p. 5). Such skepticism, the study concluded, "is designed specifically to undermine the environmental movement's efforts to legitimize its claims via science" (p. 364).

The role of seemingly neutral policy think tanks is important in the strategy of manufacturing environmental skepticism. Many corporations learned that scientists directly funded by industry lacked the credibility of university scientists in debates on issues such as cigarette smoking, "so providing political insulation for industry has become an essential role for CTTs" (Austin, 2002; Jacques, Dunlap, & Freeman, 2008, p. 362). As a result, these think tanks relied upon the trope of uncertainty as a major strategy. Michaels and Monforton (2005) explain that, in doing this, "a *major tactic is to 'manufacture uncertainty,' raising questions about the scientific basis for environmental problems* and thereby undermining support for government regulations" (p. 362; emphasis added).

For a period, the efforts by dissident scientists, corporations, and CTTs succeeded in establishing themselves as a kind of counterintelligentsia on global warming, achieving an "equal legitimacy with mainstream science and academia" (Michaels & Monforton, 2005, p. 356). As a consequence, the news media in the United States have been "significantly more likely than media in other industrial nations to portray global warming as a controversial issue characterized by scientific uncertainty" (Jacques, Dunlap, & Freeman, 2008, p. 356). A particularly controversial case of injecting uncertainty into the public's mind occurred in the so-called Climategate scandal, leading up to the United Nations Copenhagen conference on climate change in late 2009.

Climategate: Contesting the Credibility of Scientists

Just weeks before the December, 2009, Copenhagen conference, hackers broke into computers at the University of East Anglia, a major climate research center, and downloaded more than 1,000 personal e-mails between well-known climate scientists. The e-mails discussed some of the challenges in doing research, and some also made impolite remarks about climate skeptics. The skeptics and allied bloggers quickly jumped on the story, fueling a narrative of skepticism and suspicion. Critics alleged that the e-mails exposed a "scandal," a "hoax," and a "conspiracy" by climate scientists to silence their critics.

Fanned by these bloggers and so-called online aggregators like *The Drudge Report,* the Climategate story quickly went viral, serving up headlines for cable TV news and newspapers across the United States and Europe. The hacked e-mails, the critics charged, were a "smoking gun," evidence that scientists had conspired to manipulate data to support their views that climate change was real or human influenced. A columnist for the British newspaper *The Telegraph* called Climategate, "the worst scientific scandal of our generation" (Booker, 2009, para. 1).

One week after a blogger coined the term, Google listed over nine million hits for Climategate. Ironically, newspaper coverage of climate change had been declining in the United States until the Climategate controversy broke. Then, framed as scandal, the coverage spiked. Typical was the allegation carried by one newspaper: "We have discovered that a good portion of the science used to justify 'climate change' was a hoax perpetrated by leftist ideologues with an agenda" (quoted in Israel, 2010, para. 3).

As a result of the media frame of scandal and misconduct, scientists began receiving hate mail; others were getting death deaths. Dr. Stephen Schneider, a prominent climatologist at Stanford University, whose name surfaced in the hacked e-mails, "says he has received 'hundreds' of violently abusive e-mails" (Hickman, 2010, para. 5). Another, Phil Jones, director of the Climatic Research Unit at East Anglia, told a reporter, "People said I should go and kill myself." The death threats, he said, "were coming from all over the world" (para. 4).

The real scandal, however, turned out to be the media's stumbling in the face of what were unproven allegations and a frame of scandal that was too juicy not to publish. Within months, six major, independent investigations in the U.K. and the United States had cleared the scientists of charges that they had falsified their research and exonerated the basic findings of climate science itself. The inquiries did find that some of the scientists used intemperate language or had ridiculed climate skeptics in their e-mail exchanges. The most serious finding was that some scientists had been overly cautious, refusing to share their data with their critics. None of the inquiries, however, found anything in the scientists' e-mails to question the basic science (Gulledge, 2011).

Despite these findings, "many people were left wondering whether climate change was really as much of a threat as it had been made out to be" (Rigg, 2011, para. 4). In the United States, for example, an opinion poll found that the public believed it was "very likely" (35%) or "somewhat likely" (24%) that scientists had falsified their research (Rasmussen Reports, 2009). Subsequent polls found that Americans were more likely to believe the seriousness of global warming had been "exaggerated" (Gallup, 2010, 2011). The reason for this is not hard to find.

While the Climategate stories have died down, similar narratives of scandal and charges of unethical behavior by climate scientists continue to percolate in climate skeptics' blogs and are stirred by aggregators like *The Drudge Report.* For example, after the National Oceanic and Atmospheric Administration (NOAA) announced in its annual State of the Climate report that 2010 tied with 2005 as the warmest year on record, *The Drudge Report* carried this "news" feed: "2010 tied for 'hottest' year?! Relax, it is 'purely a political statement.'"

Just weeks before the Climategate controversy, *New York Times* columnist Paul Krugman (2009) had reported on the frustration of many scientists in their attempts to educate the public about climate change. "Climate scientists have, en masse," he said, "become [like the Greek goddess] Cassandra—gifted with the ability to *prophesy* future disasters, but cursed with the *inability* to get anyone to believe them" (p. A21). How have scientists and others in the media responded to this grim outlook?

Communicating Climate Science

Stung by charges that they were "losing the PR wars" and were "lousy communicators" (Begley, 2010, p. 20), climate scientists have begun to reach out more proactively to the public. Dr. Gary W. Yohe of Wesleyan University, for example, noted, "A number of us, since 'Climategate' . . . have come to realize that the scientific community has an obligation to try to do better to communicate what it knows and what it doesn't know in an honest and clear way" to the public (quoted in Morello, 2011, para. 7).

There are, in fact, some encouraging initiatives underway by scientists, journalists, media producers, and communication scholars to engage the public with more news and information about climate change and energy policy. Notably, these initiatives go beyond traditional news platforms, using new media extensively. The UCS, for example, has launched one of the most comprehensive websites covering the basics of climate science and "big picture solutions" to the impacts from warming already underway (www.ucsusa.org/global_warming). Also, the American Geophysical Union—perhaps the premier organization of climate scientists—operates an interactive, online climate question-and-answer service, with more than 700 scientists taking shifts to answer reporters' questions or interact with the news media. And, in a similar initiative, more than 100 scientists have launched the Climate Science Rapid Response Team. The team makes climate scientists available on short notice to reporters, talk radio shows, or TV debates with climate skeptics.

In a related move, the UCS, in late 2010, arranged for climate scientists to meet with reporters from *60 Minutes,* Reuters and Bloomberg news services, *TIME, USA Today,* and other news organizations. The director of science and policy at the UCS, Peter Frumhoff, said that the reporters "were keenly interested in understanding how casting doubt about mainstream scientific findings that upset powerful financial interests . . . is a tactic that has been used time and again to delay or avoid regulation" (Samuelsohn, 2010, para. 11).

A growing number of scientific societies such as the American Association for the Advancement of Science and the American Geophysical Union are also sponsoring conferences and workshops on climate change for journalists, TV weather forecasters, talk radio hosts, and other news outlets. The American Geophysical Union, for example, "offered a veritable smorgasbord of communications-oriented workshops" on climate change for more than 19,000 registrants at a recent annual meeting (Yale Forum on Climate Change and the Media, 2011, para. 1). And, the American Meteorological Society, working with the National Communication Association, brought together climate researchers, communication practitioners, and meteorologists in 2011 to aid TV meteorologists' understanding and communication of climate science. If such meetings are any guide, the Yale Forum on Climate Change and the Media (2011) commented recently, "communications issues are increasingly moving up the ladder when it comes to the science community's priority interests" (para. 1).

Figure 11.3   Website for the Union of Concerned Scientists (www.ucsusa.org).

Finally, climate scientists are joining with journalists and media producers to develop new platforms and approaches to communicating climate change. One initiative that's received praise is the website ClimateCentral.com. Sponsored by a nonprofit journalism and research organization, the site is dedicated to "helping mainstream Americans understand how climate change connects to them."

Another Viewpoint: Are Scientists at Fault for Poor Communication?

Recently, science journalist Nicole Heller (2011) asked why the public appears to be confused about climate change or believe that scientists are divided over the question of whether the earth is warming or if humans are a cause of warming. She asks and then attempts to answer: Are scientists themselves confusing the public about climate change? Are scientists confusing the public about the science of global warming?

I think the most straightforward answer is no.

Putting the failure on the scientists, as the first two hypotheses do, assumes that there is a failure of understanding. It assumes that, if the American people had all the information at their fingertips, they would make a different choice. An equally likely scenario that emerges, particularly from insights found in humanities and social science research, is that people do understand, but the range of their other interests and values prohibits them from "believing" it's true, or making the sacrifices necessary to adjust behaviorally, or pushing more forcefully for action from political leaders.

Yale Professor Dan Kahan and colleagues' research on "cultural cognition" illustrates how the compatibility of empirical data with a person's cultural values influences his or her acceptance of that data. So, data that conforms to or reinforces an individual's preexisting values is more likely to be accepted, while data that is opposed to such values may be rejected. For instance, people who hold an individualistic worldview may be more reluctant to accept scientific evidence of man-made climate change because addressing the problem would require restrictions on commerce and industry....

In response to the communication disconnect, I would venture that it is not the scientists that are failing the public, rather the political and media environment is failing the scientist.... What's clear, and I think important ... is the complex nature of the problem and the shared responsibility for rectifying the disconnects between the public and the science community.

SOURCE: Nicole Heller, "Are Scientists Confusing the Public About Global Warming?" Climatecentral.com, 2011.

ClimateCentral.com features news, video, and interactive graphics that help to localize the impacts of climate change for visitors. ClimateCentral.com also works with other journalists to generate content for other news outlets as well. Recent topics on its site have included, for example, "the top five climate and weather-related events" of the year and, in its regular "How Do We Know" video, a color-graphic video explaining how NASA tracks CO_2 emissions from different regions using sophisticated satellites.

Other parties are also coming to the defense of climate scientists and to the assistance of the curious public. Numerous science and popular blogs, for example, now provide responses to the common misconceptions or arguments by climate change sceptics. (See, for example, www.grist.org/article/series/skeptics, www.skepticalscience.com/argument.php, and www.csicop.org/si/show/disinformation_about_global_warming.) The sites typically list global warming myths or arguments by skeptics and provide a summary or link to the relevant science in response. The Skeptical Science site also offers breaking news, videos, graphs, and articles examining climate skeptics' objections. Other sites, such as www.realclimate.org, operated by climate scientists themselves, offer analyses of skeptics' more technical claims questioning climate science.

There is also a popular iPhone app that gives responses to common arguments from skeptics about climate change. As a review at *Clean Technica* (cleantechnica .com) explains, the app user can search through three broad categories of objections to global warming—"It's not happening," "It's not us," and "It's not bad"—to find specific arguments and the scientific counterarguments; the Skeptical Science app also lets you view graphs and links to scientific papers (Shahan, 2010, para. 2).

Not surprisingly, climate skeptics have pushed back against the iPhone app. The Climate Realists website (climaterealists.com) warned, "There is an iPhone app trying to put down what we have to say. . . . We can only hope the general public can see through this as a cheap trick to prop up the FAILED SCIENCE OF MAN MADE CLIMATE CHANGE" (WARNING!, 2010, paras. 1, 3).

While better science communication may increase the public's understanding, other challenges remain. As climate communication scholar Susanne Moser (2010) reminds us, the actual phenomenon of global climate change does not always send adequate signals for the public to be convinced that it's real or to demand that public officials take steps to slow or protect against its harmful impacts. This challenge, therefore, raises a related issue: Is it possible also for scientists' communication or the news media to represent climate change as a serious problem, that is, as something the public should care about? A major opportunity will arrive when the Intergovernmental Panel on Climate Change (IPCC) releases its next assessments (in 2013 and 2014) of the rate and impacts of the global warming of the planet.

SUMMARY

In this chapter, we have considered several provocative questions about the discourse of science in public controversies over environmental policy. Who should control the uses of scientific research? How should society interpret the meaning of scientific claims when the research is characterized by uncertainty?

- The first section of this chapter described how science became a source of symbolic legitimacy in a society beset with complexity and technical knowledge.
- In the second section, I introduced the *precautionary principle* as a way to manage the problem of scientific uncertainty. The precautionary principle states that, when an activity threatens human health or the environment, even if some cause-and-effect relationships are not fully established scientifically, caution should be taken.

- In the third section, I described the debate over scientists' role as *early warners,* the duty of scientists to inform, advise, or alert the public in moments of environmental danger.
- Section four explored challenges to the symbolic legitimacy of the environmental sciences and described two aspects:

  (1) the use of the rhetorical trope of uncertainty to forestall action on global warming, and

  (2) the Climategate controversy in which climate change skeptics accused scientists of falsifying their research and perpetuating a "hoax" of global warming.

- Finally, I described recent initiatives by scientists, journalists, and media producers to improve communication about the science and impacts of climate change.

The challenges involved in environmental scientists' communication with the public about climate change or other environmental dangers can be serious, particularly when opposing parties mount campaigns to question or undermine the public's confidence in science. At stake are both the public's perception of the symbolic legitimacy of science and scientists' urgency about the loss of biodiversity and the dangers of climate disruption. Many feel that time is running out and "the risks of non-action may be greater than the risks of inappropriate action" (Soulé, 1986, p. 6). I'll explore this challenge in more detail in the final chapter, "Risk Communication: Environmental Dangers and the Public."

SUGGESTED RESOURCES

- *Climate Central:* "Sound science and vibrant media" (www.climatecentral.org): One of the best websites devoted to independent, multimedia journalism, and research, bringing "the immediacy and relevance" of climate change and its impacts, to visitors to its website.
- Fred Pierce, *The Climate Files: The Battle for the Truth About Global Warming.* London: Guardian Books, 2010 (an independent journalist's look into the infamous Climategate e-mail controversy).
- Stephen H. Schneider, *Science as a Contact Sport: Inside the Battle to Save Earth's Climate.* Washington, DC: National geographic, 2009 (cowinner of the 2007 Nobel Peace Prize, one of the world's leading climatologists provides an insider's account of the workings of, and debates over, climate science).
- *Planet Earth* (2006) and *Earth* (2009): Coproduced by the BBC and Disney, these nature documentaries provide high definition (HD) explorations of the diversity of species inhabiting our planet and the threats to their habitats.

Crisis discipline   327

Environmental
   skepticism   336

Paradox for conservation   322

Precautionary principle   325

Progressive ideal   321

Symbolic legitimacy   321

Technocracy   321

Think tanks   333

Trope of uncertainty   333

DISCUSSION QUESTIONS

1. Is the precautionary principle a clear guide to decision making, or does it leave too much discretion to bureaucrats or corporations to determine whether a product is unsafe or should be withdrawn from the market?

2. Should ecologists and other environmental scientists ever serve as advocates in the public sphere? Where do you draw the line—if at all—in how far scientists should go in entering the public sphere?

3. Bloggers and climate skeptics have charged that climatologists faked their data and that global warming is a "hoax." What do you believe? What sources of information do you use in forming a judgment?

4. Scientists, filmmakers, and others have warned of the catastrophic impacts of climate change—a sea level rise of 20 feet or more, prolonged drought, crop failures, and starvation. How effective do you think are such fear appeals in motivating the public to care about climate change? What approaches would be effective?

REFERENCES

Austin, A. (2002). Advancing accumulation and managing its discontents: The US anti-environmental movement. *Sociological spectrum, 22,* 71–105.

Bailey, R. (2002, August 14). *Starvation a by-product of looming trade war.* Cato Institute. Retrieved May 23, 2005, from http://www.cato.org

Barry, D., & Oelschlaeger, M. (1996). A science for survival: Values and conservation biology. *Conservation Biology, 10,* 905–911.

Begley, S. (2010, March 29). Their own worst enemies: Why scientists are losing the PR wars. *Newsweek,* p. 20.

Berg, P., Baltimore, D., Boyer, H. W., Cohen, S. N., & Davis, R. W. (1974). Potential biohazards of recombinant DNA molecules. *Science, 185,* 303.

Booker, C. (2009, November 28). Climate change: This is the worst scientific scandal of our generation. *The Telegraph.* Retrieved August 1, 2011, from http://www.telegraph.co.uk

Bowen, M. (2008). *Censoring science: Inside the political attack on Dr. James Hansen and the truth of global warming.* New York: Dutton.

Carson, R. (1962). *Silent spring.* Boston: Houghton Mifflin.

Connor, S. (2007, January 18). Hawking warns: We must recognise the catastrophic dangers of climate change. *The Independent.* Retrieved January 1, 2009, from http://www.independent.co.uk

Cushman, J. H. (1998, April 26). Industrial group plans to battle climate treaty. *The New York Times,* p. A1.

Dewey, J. (1927). *The public and its problems.* New York: Henry Holt.

Dlouhy, J. (2011, June 28). EPA officials: "Sound science" will guide hydraulic fracturing study. Retrieved July 22, 2011, from http://fuelfix.com/blog/2011

Ehrlich, P. R., & Ehrlich, A. H. (1996). *Betrayal of science and reason: How anti-environmental rhetoric threatens our future.* Washington, DC: Island Press/ Shearwater Books.

Eilperin, J. (2006, January 29). Debate on climate shifts to issue of irreparable change. *The Washington Post,* p. A1.

Gallup. (2010, March 11). Americans' global warming concerns continue to drop. Retrieved January 15, 2011, from www.gallup.com

Gallup. (2011, March 14). In U.S., concerns about global warming stable at lower levels. Retrieved, February 8, 2011, from www.gallup.com

Glanz, J. (2004, February 19). Scientist says administration distorts facts. *The New York Times,* p. A21.

Gulledge, J. (2011, March 1). Sixth independent investigation clears "Climategate" scientists. Pew Center on Global Climate Change. Retrieved March 13, 2011, from www.pewclimate.org

Harlow, T. (2001, March 16). [Message posted on Infoterra LISTSERV]. Retrieved June 17, 2003, from http://www.peer.org

Harman, W. (1998). *Global mind change: The promise of the twenty-first century.* San Francisco: Berrett-Koehler.

Hays, S. P. (2000). *A history of environmental politics since 1945.* Pittsburgh, PA: University of Pittsburgh Press.

Heller, N. (2011). Are scientists confusing the public about global warming? Retrieved February 27, 2012, from Climatecentral.com.

Hickman, L. (2010, July 5). US climate scientists receive hate mail barrage in wake of UEA scandal. *The Guardian.* Retrieved July 31, 2011, from www.guardian.co.uk

Intergovernmental Panel on Climate Change. (2007). *Climate change 2007: Synthesis report.* UN Environment Program. Retrieved November 2, 2008, from http://www.ipcc.ch/ipccreports

Israel, B. (2010, November 4). Global warming likely to get cool reception in Congress. *Live Science.* Retrieved March 12, 2011, from www.livescience.com

Jacques, P. J., Dunlap, R. E., & Freeman, M. (2008). The organisation of denial: Conservative think tanks and environmental skepticism. *Environmental Politics, 17*(3), 349–385.

Kemp, A. C., Horton, B. P., Donnelly, J. P., Mann, M. E., Vermeer, M., & Rahmstorf, S. (2011). Climate related sea-level variations over the past two millennia. *Proceedings of the National Academy of Sciences*

Kendall, H. W. (2000). *A distant light: Scientists and public policy.* New York: Springer-Verlag.

Krugman, P. (2009, September 27). Cassandras of climate. *The New York Times,* p. A21

Lesly, P. (1992). Coping with opposition groups. *Public Relations Review, 18*(4), 325–334.

Luntz Research Companies. (2001). The environment: A cleaner, safer, healthier America. In *Straight Talk* (pp. 131–146). Retrieved June 12, 2003, from http://www.ewg.org

Markowitz, G., & Rosner, D. (2002). *Deceit and denial: The deadly politics of industrial pollution.* Berkeley: University of California Press.

Mason, S. F. (1962). *A history of the sciences.* New York: Collier Books.

McGowan, E. (2011, June 17). New pressure on U.S. EPA to delay final mercury rule. Retrieved July 23, 2011, from www.reuters.com

Michaels, D., & Monforton, C. (2005). Manufacturing uncertainty: Contested science and the protection of the public's health and environment. *Public Health Matters, 95*(1), 39–48.

Michaels, P. (2004). *Meltdown: The predictable distortion of global warming by scientists, politicians, and the media.* Washington, DC: Cato Institute.

Montague, P. (1999, July 1). The uses of scientific uncertainty. *Rachel's Environment & Health News, 657.* Retrieved August, 25, 2002, from http://www.rachel.org

Mooney, C. (2006). *The Republican war on science.* New York: Basic Books.

Morello, L. (2011, February 2). Award-winning scientists ask Congress to take a "fresh look" at climate change. *Climatewire.* Retrieved July 19, 2011, from www.eenes.net/climatewire

Morin, A. J. (1993). *Science policy and politics.* Englewood Cliffs, NJ: Prentice Hall.

Moser, S. C. (2010). Communicating climate change: History, challenges, process and future directions.

National Academy of Sciences. (2011). *America's climate choices.* Retrieved July 24, 2011, from http://dels.nas.edu/

National Environmental Trust. (1998). *Monitor 404: Information missing from your daily news.* [Press release]. Retrieved September 2, 2005, from www.monitor.net

National Research Council Committee on Environmental Epidemiology. (1991). *Environmental epidemiology: Vol. 1. Public health and hazardous wastes.* Washington, DC: National Academy Press.

Raffensperger, C. (1998). Editor's note: The precautionary principle—a fact sheet. *The Networker, 3*(1), para. 1. Retrieved August 25, 2003, from http://www.sehn.org

Rampton, S., & Stauber, J. (2002). *Trust us, we're experts!* New York: Jeremy P. Tarcher/Putnam.

Rasmussen Reports. (2009, December 1–2). *National survey of 1,000 adults.* Retrieved July 30, 2011, from www.rasmussen-reports.com

Revkin, A. (2005, June 8). Bush aide softened greenhouse gas links to global warming. *The New York Times.* Retrieved January 6, 2009, from http://www.nytimes.com

Revkin, A. C. (2006a, January 29). Climate expert says NASA tried to silence him. *The New York Times,* p. A1.

Revkin, A. C. (2006b, February 8). A young Bush appointee resigns his post at NASA. *The New York Times,* p. A11.

Rigg, K. (2011, February 20). Skepticgate: revealing climate denialists for what they are. Retrieved, 2011, from www.huffingtonpost.com

Rosenthal, E. (2007, November 17). U.N. report describes risks of inaction on climate change. *The New York Times.* Retrieved November 3, 2008, from http://www.nytimes.com

Rykiel, E. J., Jr. (2001). Scientific objectivity, value systems, and policymaking. *BioScience, 51,* 433–436.

Samuelsohn, D. (2010, December 31). Climate PR efforts heats up. *Politico.* Retrieved July 31, 2011, from http://politico.com

Science and Environmental Health Network. (1998, January 26). *Wingspread conference on the precautionary principle.* Retrieved August 25, 2003, from http://www.sehn.org

Scully, M. G. (2005, October 3). Studying ecosystems: The messy intersection between science and politics. *Chronicle of Higher Education,* p. B13.

Shabecoff, P. (2000). *Earth rising: American environmentalism in the 21st century.* Washington, DC: Island Press.

Shahan, S. (2010, February 8). *iPhone app for telling a climate skeptic they're wrong.* Retrieved August 1, 2011, from http://cleantechnica.com

Slobodkin, L. B. (2000). Proclaiming a new ecological discipline. *Bulletin of the Ecological Society of America, 81,* 223–226.

Soulé, M. E. (Ed.). (1985). What is conservation biology? *BioScience, 35,* 727–734.

Soulé, M. E. (1986). *Conservation biology: The science of scarcity and diversity.* Sunderland, MA: Sinauer Associates.

Soulé, M. E. (1987). History of the Society for Conservation Biology: How and why we got here. *Conservation Biology, 1,* 4–5.

Thomas, I. (2001, March 16). Web censorship. [E-mail]. Retrieved June 16, 2003, from http://cartome.org

Thornton, J. (2000). *Pandora's poison: Chlorine, health, and a new environmental strategy.* Cambridge. MA: MIT Press.

Union of Concerned Scientists. (2004, February). *Scientific integrity in policymaking: An investigation into the Bush administration's misuse of science.* Cambridge, MA: Author.

Union of Concerned Scientists. (2008). *Freedom to speak? A report card on federal agency media policies.* Retrieved January 6, 2009, from http://www.ucsusa.org

Union of Concerned Scientists. (2011). *About us.* Retrieved July 24, 2011, from http:// www.ucsusa.org

Vucetich, J. A., & Nelson, M. P. (2010, August 1). The moral obligations of scientists. *The Chronicle of Higher Education.* Retrieved July 19, 2011, from http://chronicle.com

WARNING! New site set up as an iPhone app to put down "climate realists." (2010, February 14). Retrieved August 1, 2011, from http://climaterealists.com

Wiens, J. A. (1997). Scientific responsibility and responsible ecology. *Conservation Ecology, 1*(1), 16. Retrieved June 12, 2003, from http://www.consecol.org

Wiley Interdisciplinary Reviews—Climate Change 1(1): 31–53.

Williams, B. A., & Matheny, A. R. (1995). *Democracy, dialogue, and environmental disputes.* New Haven, CT: Yale University Press.

Yale Forum on Climate Change and the Media. (2011, February). Science societies' annual meeting agendas focusing increasingly on communications issues. Retrieved May 8, 2011, from www.yale climatemediaforum.org/

Fire crews battling the fire from the explosion on the offshore *Deepwater Horizon* oil rig in the Gulf of Mexico, April 21, 2010.

CHAPTER 12

Risk Communication: Environmental Dangers and the Public

Most, if not all, of the failures at [the BP oil well blowout in the Gulf of Mexico] can be traced back to underlying failures of management and communication. . . . Notwithstanding [the] inherent risks, the accident of April 20 was avoidable.

—National Commission on the
BP *Deepwater Horizon* Oil Spill and
Offshore Drilling (2011, pp. 122, 127)

Those who control the discourse on risk will most likely control the political battles as well.

—Plough & Krimsky (1987, p. 4)

H umans have always faced danger from natural events such as storms, earthquakes, famine, and crop failure. In modern society, however, we face ever-increasing dangers from human sources as well—toxins from industrial plants, chemical contamination of water and food, oil spills, and more. Spurred by public concern, governmental agencies have tried to evaluate and share information about the risk of environmental hazards with the public. This chapter explores some of the ways we understand risks and communicate environmental dangers to the public.

Chapter Preview

- This chapter begins by describing what German sociologist Ulrich Beck (1992) termed *risk society*—threats to human health and safety from modern society itself. I'll also describe two models for assessing risk and its meaning: (1) a technical model and (2) a cultural–experiential approach.

- The second section introduces the practice of *risk communication* of environmental dangers and two approaches:

    (1) a traditional model, influenced by technical meanings of risk, and

    (2) a cultural model of risk communication that involves the experiences of those who are affected by risk.

- The final section explores the ways media shape our perceptions of risks. I'll describe two dimensions of media reports:

    (1) debate over the accuracy of news reports of risk, and

    (2) different voices quoted in media reports of risk—first, society's *legitimizers*—e.g., public officials—and, second, the voices of the *side effects*—residents, parents of sick children, and others who are most affected by environmental dangers.

In sharing information about environmental risks, public health officials, news media, scientists, and the general public engage in an important and sometimes controversial communication practice called *risk communication*. For now, let's define **risk communication** in its simplest form as "any public or private communication that informs individuals about the existence, nature, form, severity, or acceptability of risks" (Plough & Krimsky, 1987, p. 6). While this includes the translation of technical information for the public, more recent approaches to risk communication are sensitive to the concerns of those who are affected by risk and about what constitutes an *acceptable risk* and to whom.

When you've finished the chapter, you should be able to recognize the difficulties in defining acceptable risk and to appreciate the different perspectives on risk that are held by agencies such as the Environmental Protection Agency (EPA), by news media, and by those impacted by risks themselves.

Dangerous Environments: Assessing Risk

The popular film *Erin Brockovich* (2000) dramatized the real-life experiences of residents in the small town of Hinkley, California, who discovered that toxic contamination of their drinking water from Pacific Gas and Electric Company (PG&E) may have caused Hodgkin's disease, breast cancer, and other diseases. The film portrayed residents' anger after they learned that PG&E's assurances that their water was safe were untrue. Ultimately, the company settled a multimillion-dollar lawsuit with 634 residents and pledged to clean up the contaminated groundwater. The film and the fears of the Hinkley families call our attention to the all-too-real dangers to human health and the environment in modern society. They also ask us to look closely at the communication about risk by technical experts, business leaders, health officials, and the media and at attempts to improve communication with those who may be affected by such dangers.

Risk Society

In his *Risk Society* and other writings, sociologist Ulrich Beck (1992, 2000, 2009) argued modern society has changed fundamentally in its ability to manage the consequences of its successful technical and economic development. Beck explained, "The gain in power from techno-economic 'progress' is being increasingly overshadowed by the production of risks" (1992, p. 13). Unlike risks from nature or 19th-century factories that affected individuals, today's **risk society** is defined by the large-scale nature of risks and the potential for irreversible threats to human life from modernization itself. These risks include such far-reaching and consequential hazards as nuclear power plant accidents, global climate change, chemical pollution, and the alteration of genetic strains from bioengineering.

In Beck's risk society, rapid scientific and technological changes may bring unintended consequences. What are most disturbing are what are called **black swan events.** The black swan theory was developed by the mathematical financier Nassim Nicholas Taleb (2010). According to Taleb, *black swan events* refer to unexpected, high-magnitude events that are beyond what modern society can usually predict. Recent examples are the unexpected and devastating impact of the earthquake and tsunami on the Fukushima nuclear power plants in Japan in 2011 and the BP oil spill in the Gulf of Mexico in 2010. Some argue climate change also poses a high risk of black swan events, such as massive releases of methane from thawing tundra, complete melting of Greenland's ice sheet, or the weakening or shutdown of the Gulf Stream (Pope, 2011).

In addition, exposure to risk in modern society is unevenly (and unfairly) distributed across the population. That is because the burden of coping with the hazards of new technologies and environmental pollutants often falls on the most vulnerable elements of the population—elderly people, children with respiratory problems, pregnant women, and as we saw in Chapter 9, residents of low-income neighborhoods with high concentrations of polluting facilities. As a result, serious conflicts occurred in the 1980s between the residents of at-risk communities and the technical experts who assured them that polluting factories or buried toxic wastes posed no harm. Lois Gibbs (1994), a former resident of Love Canal, New York, expressed the feelings of many: "Communities perceive many flaws in risk assessment. The first is who is being asked to take the risk and who is getting the benefit?" (pp. 328–329).

Because many voices struggle to define risk, it is important to distinguish its different meanings and what constitutes acceptable risk for different parties. Indeed, there is heated controversy about whether risk is a technical matter that is determined objectively or a social construction that emerges from communication among experts, affected parties, and public agencies. Therefore, we look at both technical and cultural meanings of *risk*, and in the next section, we examine the different approaches to risk communication that are invited by these meanings.

The Technical Model of Risk

By the 1980s, the public's fear of environmental hazards had led to pressure on the U.S. government to evaluate risk accurately and to do a better job in communicating with affected communities. In 1984, the EPA Administrator William Ruckelshaus proposed the term *risk assessment* "as a common language for justifying regulatory proposals across the agency" (Andrews, 2006, p. 266). From a technical perspective, **risk assessment** is defined as the evaluation of the degree of harm or danger from some condition such as exposure to a toxic chemical. In the years following, the EPA dramatically increased its technical analysis of risks from nuclear power, pollution of drinking water, pesticides, and other chemicals in order to justify new health and safety standards. Environmental policy expert Richard N. Andrews (2006) observed that, by the end of the 1980s, "the rhetoric of risk had become the agency's primary language for justifying its decisions" (p. 266).

In the United States, the EPA and the Food and Drug Administration (FDA) are two of the agencies responsible for evaluating health and environmental risks. For example, the FDA routinely evaluates the risks of food contamination and issues recalls of tainted products like peanut butter, eggs, or pet foods. Understanding the technical model of risk used by these agencies is important in its own right, but this also allows us to appreciate its limitations and why such an approach to risk communication has generated controversy among some affected publics.

Risk Assessment

In everyday terms, risk is simply a rough estimate of the chances of something negative happening to us, such an auto accident while texting and driving. However, for many agencies, risk is a highly quantitative concept. Such **technical risk** is the *expected annual mortality* (or other severity) that results from some condition. For example, the EPA defines risk as "the chance of harmful effects to human health or to ecological systems resulting from exposure to an environmental stressor" (United States Environmental Protection Agency, 2010b, para. 2). *Technical risk* is, then, a calculation of the likelihood that a certain number of people (or an ecological system) will suffer some harm over time (usually one year) from exposure to a hazard or environmental stressor; in other words, Risk = Severity × Likelihood.

How does an agency such as the EPA know the severity of a hazard and its likelihood of occurrence? In answering these questions, technical risk assessment uses the findings of research labs and experts such as toxicologists, epidemiologists, and other scientists. This process typically involves a **four-step procedure for risk assessment:** (1) identify the hazard, (2) define the pathways of human exposure to it, (3) determine humans' response to different levels of exposure, and (4) characterize the risk;

that is, is the risk safe or unacceptable? Let's take an example from Chapter 4—the use of fracking in drilling for natural gas—to see how this four-step procedure might work in an ongoing controversy.

In 2010, the EPA announced it would investigate the potential, adverse impacts of hydraulic fracturing (or fracking) in drilling for natural gas on human health and the environment. As we saw in Chapter 4, fracking involves injecting large volumes of water, sand, and chemicals into rock formations to create fissures, which release the trapped gas. As a result of public complaints, the EPA has begun to assess the human and environmental risks of this drilling method. What, then, would be involved in such a technical risk assessment?

The four-step procedure initially asks, what is the hazard or the potential source of danger? In our example, the EPA is identifying multiple, potential sources of danger, including "the chemicals and fluids used in the fracturing process, biogeochemical and physical-chemical reactions triggered by [hydraulic fracturing], leakage from gas-bearing formations," and runoff of chemicals from the drilling site (United States Environmental Protection Agency, 2010a, p. 6).

Second, a risk assessment asks, what are the pathways of human exposure to these sources? And, if humans are exposed, how much (what level) do these humans receive? In its study of fracking, the EPA is looking at activities that may "introduce contaminants into water, food, air, soils, and other materials over the [hydraulic fracturing] lifecycle"; specifically, the exposure pathways being explored by EPA include the "ingestion, inhalation, dermal exposure [of these contaminants] through water, air, food, and environmental exposures" (United States Environmental Protection Agency, 2010a, p. 8). Finally, the EPA will identify the different levels of exposure that populations may be receiving from the chemicals entering these pathways.

Third, the process seeks to model the effects of this exposure by asking, what is the relationship between the level or dosage that is received and any harmful responses or illnesses in the exposed population?

And, fourth, a technical risk assessment characterizes the risk; that is, it describes the overall implications of the dose responses for the health of the exposed population: In other words, is exposure to potential hazards of fracking an unacceptable or acceptable risk? Or, does such exposure to any one of the hazardous sources carry a likelihood of developing cancer or other illness? Initial results of the EPA's study of fracking are expected by the end of 2012.

More specifically, this fourth step draws on the prior three steps to estimate the mortality or other severities that can be expected from an exposure to the hazard (for example, an estimate of 0.22 cases of cancer over 10 years). Technical models of risk use such numerical values as the basis for judgments of **acceptable risk.** Acceptable or unacceptable risk, however, involves values other than just numerical estimates. Ultimately, an acceptable risk is a judgment of the harms or dangers that society or specific populations are willing to accept (or not). Such judgments may also involve a consideration of who is subject to the risk as well the costs that are required to reduce the risk.

Limitations of the Technical Model

Disagreements over what is safe or an acceptable risk are a major challenge to technical risk assessments. There are several reasons for this: There may be insufficient lab results; different studies may differ in their estimates of danger; or the studies may not be able to detect which of several sources may be causing a problem. And ultimately, our judgments about what is safe may be influenced by other voices in the public sphere. An example of such a controversy is the public debate over the chemical known as bisphenol A, or BPA.

BPA is used in thousands of products, including plastic bottles, baby food containers, and "the lining of nearly every soft drink and canned food product" (Parker-Pope, 2008, p. A21). We've been exposed to BPA so routinely that it has been detected in more than 90% of the U.S. population (Stein, 2010). Recent research, however, has raised concerns about the possible health effects from exposure to BPA products,

| Figure 12.1 | Disagreements over what is safe or an acceptable risk are a major challenge to technical risk assessments. |

including cancer (Grady, 2010), lowered sperm counts (Stein, 2010), and neural and behavioral effects in infants and babies from low-level, long-term exposures (Grady, 2010; Szabo, 2011). Nevertheless, the FDA had insisted in 2008 that BPA was safe. The director of the FDA's Office of Food Additive Safety told the *Washington Post,* "We have confidence in the data we've looked at to say that the margin of safety is adequate" (quoted in Layton, 2008, p. A3).

Despite its assurances, the FDA asked an independent scientific panel to review the research on which the agency, at that time, had based its characterization of the risk from BPA. At one point, the panel held a public hearing to receive testimony from the public, other scientists, and health groups. The public comments revealed sharp disagreements with the FDA's risk characterization. For example, a member of the Union of Concerned Scientists (UCS) complained to the panel that the FDA had based its characterization of BPA's risk largely on two studies funded by industry, "while downplaying the results of hundreds of other studies" (quoted in Layton, 2008, p. A3). In a "blistering report," the panel found that the FDA had "ignored important evidence in reassuring consumers about the safety" of BPA (Parker-Pope, 2008, p. A21).

Even today, the controversy continues, with "mountains of data" in technical risk studies showing "conflicting results as to whether BPA is dangerous" (Grady, 2010, p. D4). As a result of these limitations, new, federally financed research has been authorized, particularly for effects of BPA on infants. The results are expected in 2012 or later.

The Cultural–Experiential Model of Risk

The experience of communities such as the one in Mississippi illustrates another difficulty with the technical model of environmental risk. The complaint from individuals who are actually exposed to environmental dangers is that risk assessment is too often restricted to a technical sphere; it excludes those who are most affected. That is, technical models often ignore the judgments about the experience of those forced to live with imposed or involuntary risks. Yet, as Beck (1998) explained, "There is a big difference between those who take risks and *those who are victimized by risks others take*" (p. 10; emphasis added). As a result, most public agencies have begun to solicit the views of affected communities in their assessment of risks and their judgments about what is an acceptable risk. It is this **cultural–experiential model of risk** and the role of a wider public sphere that I now describe.

Environmental Hazards Versus Outrage

Our view of an environmental danger may sometimes differ from a technical risk assessment. While some who study risk perceptions remind us that most individuals are "irrational" in judging risks such as the odds of a shark attack or from dying in a plane crash (Ropeik, 2010; Slovic, 1987; Sunstein, 2004), others point to well-grounded reasons for our concerns. Political scientist Frank Fischer (2000) explains that the context in which an environmental risk is embedded raises questions that may affect one's judgment of whether a risk is acceptable or not: "Is the risk imposed by distant or unknown officials? Is it engaged in voluntarily? Is it reversible?" (p. 65).

Peter Sandman (1987, 2011), a well-known risk communication consultant, makes a similar point. Sandman proposed that risk be defined as a combination of technical risk and social factors that people often consider in judging risk. He suggested that what technical analysts call a *risk* instead be called a *hazard* and that other social and experiential concerns be called *outrage*. **Hazard** is what experts mean by risk (expected annual mortality), and **outrage** refers collectively to those factors that the public considers in assessing whether their exposure to a hazard is acceptable. According to Sandman (1987), "risk, then, is the sum of hazard and outrage" (p. 21).

Here are some of the main factors of outrage that Sandman believes people consider in judging an environmental risk:

1. *Voluntariness.* Do people assume a risk voluntarily, or is it coerced or imposed on them?

2. *Control.* Can individuals prevent or control the risk themselves?

3. *Fairness.* Are people asked to endure greater risks than their neighbors or others, especially without access to greater benefits?

4. *Diffusion in time and space.* Is the risk spread over a large population or concentrated in one's own community?

Sandman's model of Hazard + Outrage is particularly useful in calling our attention to the experiences of those left out of technical risk calculations. Sandman's definition is not without its critics, however. Some have suggested that this definition subtly characterizes scientific or technical assessments of hazards as rational and the emotional outrage of communities as irrational. They fear such characterizations can be used to trivialize community voices in debates about risk. Let's look at this cultural side of risk more closely.

Cultural Rationality and Risk

Judgments about social context or the experience of exposed communities to hazards raises the question of whether there exists a kind of cultural rationality about such dangers. Pioneering scholars in risk communication Alonzo Plough and Sheldon Krimsky (1987) define **cultural rationality** as a type of knowledge that includes personal, familiar, and social concerns in evaluating a real risk event. As distinct from technical analysis of risk, cultural rationality "is shaped by the circumstances under which the risk is identified and publicized, the standing or place of the individual in his or her community, and the social values of the community as a whole" (Fischer, 2000, pp. 132–133). Unlike technical rationality—the valorizing of scientific methods and expertise—cultural rationality includes folk wisdom, the insights of peer groups, an understanding of how risk impacts one's family and community, and sensitivity to particular events.

Harvard University professors Phil Brown and Edwin J. Mikkelsen (1990) provide a disturbing example of the differences between risk assessments made in a technical sphere and those made in a wider public sphere. In their classic study *No Safe Place: Toxic Waste, Leukemia, and Community Action,* they cite the experience of residents in Friendly Hills, a suburb of Denver, Colorado. In the early 1980s, mothers from the neighborhood wondered why so many of their children were sick or dying. After EPA and state health officials refused to study the problem, the women decided to canvass door to door to document the extent of the problem. They found that 15 children who lived in the neighborhood from 1976 to 1984 had died from cancer, severe birth defects, and other immunological diseases. The mothers suspected that the cause of these deaths was toxic waste discharge from a nearby industrial facility owned by the corporation Martin Marietta.

State health officials dismissed the mothers' findings and denied there was any environmental or other unusual cause of the children's deaths. They insisted that all the illnesses were within "expected limits," and although there were more childhood cancer cases than expected, the officials said that "they might be due to chance" (Brown & Mikkelsen, 1990, p. 143). One week after the officials declared the waste discharges safe, "the Air Force, which runs a test facility on the Martin Marietta site, admitted that the groundwater was contaminated by toxic chemicals" (p. 143). Brown and Mikkelsen describe what happened next: "Residents found that Martin Marietta had a record of toxic spills. . . . Several months later, EPA scientists found serious contamination . . . in a plume, or underground wave, stretching from the Martin Marietta site toward the water plant" (pp. 143–144). The Harvard professors concluded, "The belated discovery of what residents knew long before is eerie and infuriating—and, sadly, it is common to many toxic waste sites" (p. 144).

In cases such as Friendly Hills, a cultural–experiential model for evaluating risk challenged the credibility of technical agencies and their methods. That is, the questioning by mothers of the limited approaches of these agencies threatened the images of knowledge and authority that usually benefit such agencies.

At the same time, I want to stress that a reliance on cultural rationality does not reject technical assessments of risk. Technical risk assessments often help individuals, businesses, and governments alike to avoid unsafe practices. For example, the EPA's technical risk assessments of mercury—a highly dangerous neurotoxin found in fish—has led to health warnings for individuals eating fish from lakes polluted with mercury. And, our failures to heed technical risk warnings can lead to shocking consequences sometimes. (See "Another Viewpoint: Technical Risk Warnings About Deepwater Oil Drilling.") Nevertheless, an approach that draws upon cultural rationality expands the technical model of risk to include considerations of the contexts in which risks occur and the values of those who are asked to live with environmental dangers.

> **Another Viewpoint: Technical Risk Warnings About Deepwater Oil Drilling**
>
> In the weeks following the tragic BP oil spill in the Gulf of Mexico in 2010, reports surfaced that the federal agency responsible for regulating U.S. offshore oil drilling—the Minerals Management Service—had "repeatedly ignored warnings from government scientists about environmental risks" (Eilperin, 2010, para. 1).
>
> The risk warnings came from biologists and other scientists working for the National Oceanic and Atmospheric Administration and the Marine Mammal Commission (MMC). Meanwhile, risk assessments from the oil companies themselves routinely assured agency officials that drilling in deep water was safe and that any accident would cause only minimal damage. BP itself had assured regulators that the "unlikely event of an oil spill" would have "little risk of contact or impact to the coastline and associated environmental resources" (quoted in Wang, 2010, para. 14).
>
> Accepting the oil companies' assurances, officials at the MMC "discounted scientific data and advice—even from scientists elsewhere in the federal government—that would have impeded oil and gas companies drilling offshore" (Eilperin, 2010, para. 5). Investigations revealed that senior officials at the agency "frequently changed documents and bypassed legal requirements aimed at protecting the marine environment" (para. 2).
>
> Ignoring technical risk warnings meant allowing drilling methods that proved to be unsafe and that "dramatically weakened the scientific checks on offshore drilling," established under laws such as the Marine Mammal Protection Act and the National Environmental Policy Act (Eilperin, 2010, para. 3). The Gulf of Mexico oil spill is also a reminder that technical risk assessments, while they may reflect rigorous standards, may also occur within a wider political or economic context that affects their use by public officials or industry.

Finally, the differences between technical and cultural models of risk also raise important questions about how we convey information about risk to others. Such differences in risk communication matter in the public's understanding of risk and in larger society's response to environmental dangers. Let's look, therefore, at the different ways public agencies, as well as private interests, choose to communicate environmental risks to affected publics.

Communicating Environmental Risks to the Public

Although the study of risk communication barely existed before 1986, the field has grown dramatically in response to the environmental dangers of risk society as well as in response to complaints about the trustworthiness and accuracy of experts' risk reports. As we noted at the opening of this chapter, risk communication in its most general form is "any public or private communication that informs individuals about the existence, nature, form, severity, or acceptability of risk" (Plough & Krimsky, 1987, p. 6). However, as practiced by health and environmental agencies, risk communication has come to mean something more specific in its objectives and its assumptions about target audiences.

In this section, we look at two different models of risk communication, each reflecting one of the meanings of risk we described in the first section of this chapter. These are (a) the traditional or technical model of risk communication, which seeks to translate numerical assessments of risk for public audiences, and (b) the cultural model of risk communication, which draws upon the experiences and cultural rationality of affected communities as well as on laboratory models of risk assessment.

Technical Risk Communication

Early experiences with risk communication grew out of the need of federal managers of environmental projects (such as the cleanup of toxic waste sites) to gain the public's acceptance of risk estimates. Other experiences grew from health agencies' need to communicate about risk to target populations (for example, smokers or substance abusers). This early model was influenced heavily by the *technical* meaning of risk. This **technical risk communication** approach is defined as the translation of technical data about environmental or health risks for public consumption, with the goal of educating a target audience. Communication is usually one-way; that is, agency officials translate expert assessments of risk for a public or nonexpert audience, what one scholar has called an *elites-to-ignorant* model of risk communication (Rowan, 1991, p. 303). An example of this approach was the EPA's public announcement that, while small amounts of pollutants were created by the controlled burning of oil from the BP oil spill in the Gulf of Mexico, "the levels that workers and residents would have been exposed to were below EPA's levels of concern" (United States Environmental Protection Agency, 2010d, para. 1).

Inform, Change, and Assure

The goal of technical risk communication is to educate public audiences and others about numerical risk. As used by environmental and health agencies, this goal traditionally has three objectives: to inform, to change behavior, and (sometimes) to assure.

1. *To inform the public or local communities of an environmental or health hazard:* The U.S. EPA's (2007) guide for managers, *Risk Communication in Action,* defines risk communication explicitly this way: "The process of informing people about potential hazards to their person, property, or community" (Reckelhoff-Dangel & Petersen, 2007, p. 1). The agency explains that risk communication is a "science-based approach" whose purpose is to help affected communities understand risk assessment and management by forming "scientifically valid perceptions of the likely hazards" (p. 1).

Other agencies, including the FDA, use similar science-based and largely one-way communication, that is, from experts to a general public. A recent, dramatic example of such risk communication was the National Cancer Institute's warning of a link between our exposure to everyday chemicals—in drinking water, vehicle exhaust, canned foods, and more—and a risk of cancer and that such risks have been "grossly underestimated" (quoted in U.S. Cancer Institute Issues Stark Warning, 2010, para. 2).

The institute reported that there are nearly 80,000 "unregulated chemicals" in use, including "a variety of carcinogenic compounds that many people are regularly exposed to in their daily lives" (paras. 4, 5).

2. *To change risky behaviors:* Public agencies like the FDA and EPA have long had the goal of warning the public about unsafe food products, environmental dangers, and risky personal behaviors in order to avoid such dangers or behaviors. By changing one's behavior (for example, quitting smoking) or by avoiding certain products or exposures (such as eating or drinking from BPA containers), the risks are presumably reduced. For example, in the case just cited, the National Cancer Institute urged the U.S. government to "identify and eliminate [the] environmental carcinogens" that it had warned about, from workplaces, schools and homes" (U.S. Cancer Institute Issues Stark Warning, 2010, para. 4).

| **Figure 12.2** | At its core, technical risk communication is the process of informing the public or local communities of a potential environmental or health hazard. |

This focus on preventive education or action often targets the at-risk populations with national media campaigns and dedicated websites aimed at reducing health or environmental risks. These campaigns have aimed, for example, to end childhood obesity, reduce the consumption of fish with high levels of mercury poisoning, or decrease the incidents of distracted driving. For example, the Federal Communication Commission (FCC) has recently launched a website devoted to distributing information about the risks of texting while driving (http://www.fcc.gov/cgb/driving.html). The site is largely a compilation of links and information and mirrors the technical approach to risk communication.

3. *To assure those exposed to a hazard that a perceived risk is (sometimes) acceptable:* Those living near a potential, environmental danger are understandably concerned about the risks to their health or safety. Yet, not all hazards present serious health risks. For example, when the EPA discovered chemical contamination at Superfund waste sites, it issued a carefully nuanced statement to media, reassuring the public and, in particular, residents living near the waste sites. An Associated Press (2004) report handled the EPA statement this way:

> Almost one in 10 of the nation's 1,230 Superfund waste sites lack[s] adequate safety controls to ensure people and drinking water won't be contaminated, according to the Environmental Protection Agency. . . . [An EPA consultant said] the sites . . . "all have some contamination, but none . . . presents an imminent risk to human health" because of either emergency cleanup measures in place or the posting of fish advisories and other official warnings. (p. A3)

The EPA's careful qualification of risks reflects a shift in approach in communicating with at-risk communities. Earlier, agency officials had often sought to ease the public's fears or concerns about an environmental hazard by injecting even more expertise into their warnings, "so that *the affected public might more rationally evaluate the risks they face with hazardous wastes or at least respect more the expertise of professional decision makers*" (Williams & Matheny, 1995, p. 167, emphasis added). This belief that the public is irrational in assessing risks contributed to the dominance of the technical model of risk communication for many years. Fortunately, this view has begun to change.

Still, many communication scholars, as well as community activists, argue that the technical model, by itself, fails to acknowledge the concerns of those individuals who are most intimately affected by environmental dangers. One result has been that, in recent years, agencies like the EPA have turned to a more culturally sensitive model of risk communication.

Cultural Approaches to Risk Communication

In an early, influential essay "Technical and Democratic Values in Risk Analysis," former EPA advisor Daniel Fiorino (1989) argued that "the lay public are not fools" in judging environmental risks (p. 294). He identified three areas in which the public's intuitive and experiential judgments differed most from technical risk analysis:

1. *"Concern about low-probability but high-consequence events"*: For example, there may be a 1 percent chance that an accident will occur, but it will take a terrible death toll if it does occur.

2. A *"desire for consent and control in social management of risks"*: The public's feeling that they have a say in decisions about risk is the opposite of a coerced or involuntary imposition of risk.

3. *"The relationship of judgments about risk to judgments about social institutions"*: In other words, the acceptability of risk may depend on citizens' confidence in the institution that is conducting a study, managing a facility, or monitoring its safety. (p. 294)

Research since Fiorino's essay confirms that public input into risk assessment often increases the likelihood that decisions about risks will be seen as legitimate. In its recent study of decisions involving science—such as risk assessment—the National Research Council found that success depends on the ability of affected parties to participate in the risk decision process (Dietz & Stern, 2008). Let's look at what this more dialogic (two-way) communication about risk requires.

Citizen Participation in Risk Communication

One sign of a shift in risk communication has been the trend of some agencies to use an approach that draws upon the cultural rationality of communities. This **cultural model of risk communication** involves the affected public in assessing risk and designing risk communication campaigns. A major step forward was taken in 1996 when the National Research Council (1996) released its report, *Understanding Risk: Informing Decisions in a Democratic Society.* The report acknowledged that technical risk assessment was no longer sufficient to cope with the public's concerns about environmental dangers. It called for greater public participation and use of local knowledge in risk studies, and it pointedly noted that understanding risk requires "a broad understanding of the relevant losses, harms, or consequences to the interested and affected parties, including what the affected parties believe the risks to be in particular situations" (p. 2, emphasis added).

Some health and environmental risk agencies have taken this principle further to develop new practices in risk communication that recognize such cultural knowledge and experience of local communities. For example, the U.S. EPA (2007) has acknowledged that "an ideal risk communication tool would put a risk in context, make comparisons with other risks, and *encourage a dialogue between the sender and the receiver of the message*" (p. 3; emphasis added).

Similar concerns have begun to appear in the risk communication campaigns by agencies that work with vulnerable populations, such as children, expectant mothers, the elderly, or individuals suffering from asthma or other respiratory illnesses. In each case, agencies often interview affected groups or identify community partners to collaborate in designing communication campaigns that warn of specific risks. Examples of this cultural approach to risk are the efforts by the EPA, FDA, and Great Lakes states to warn pregnant and nursing women and others about the dangers of eating fish with high mercury levels.

Mercury Poisoning and Fish Advisories

Mercury Poisoning

Mercury is a highly dangerous *neurotoxin*—a chemical substance that can cause adverse effects in the brain and nervous system. It is present in everyday products such thermometers and compact fluorescent light bulbs (CFLs) and is dispersed widely in air pollution from coal-fired power plants. The EPA reports that people are most commonly exposed to mercury by eating fish or shellfish containing methyl mercury (CH_3Hg^+). (Methyl mercury accumulates in fatty tissues of certain kinds of fish as a result of mercury in air pollution, which is deposited in lakes or the ocean.) Although adults can be affected, young children and developing fetuses are most at risk. Numerous studies have found that, "for fetuses, infants, and children, the primary health effect of methyl mercury is impaired neurological development. Methyl mercury exposure in the womb . . . can adversely affect a baby's growing brain and nervous system" (United States Environmental Protection Agency, 2010c, para. 5).

Because mercury is a significant health risk, the EPA provides extensive, technical risk information on its website for mercury (http://www.epa.gov/hg) and in government publications and advisories. However, the challenge of risk communication in this case goes beyond such technical information. Health officials also hope to change the eating practices of at-risk populations who consume fish with high levels of mercury. (The Union of Concerned Scientists [2009] has estimated that, just 1/70th of a teaspoon in a 25-acre lake can make fish unsafe to eat.) As a result, the EPA and other agencies provide culturally sensitive risk communication materials online (www.epa.gov/waterscience/fish) and fund local health agencies to conduct public outreach to target populations.

Among the materials that the EPA and FDA make available is a brochure, "What You Need to Know About Mercury in Fish and Shellfish." It is a guide for pregnant or nursing women and young children on selecting and eating fish in order to reduce their exposure to mercury. The brochure poses a series of question (and concerns) from women who may be at risk and offers guidance to them. For example, "I'm a woman who could have children but I'm not pregnant—so why should I be concerned about methylmercury?" In response, the brochure advises:

> If you regularly eat types of fish that are high in methylmercury, it can accumulate in your bloodstream over time. Methylmercury is removed from the body naturally, but it may take over a year for the levels to drop significantly. Thus, it may be present in a woman even before she becomes pregnant. This is the reason why women who are trying to

become pregnant should also avoid eating certain types of fish. (United States Food and Drug Administration & United States Environmental Protection Agency, 2004, p. 3)

The brochure can be downloaded in English, Spanish, Chinese, Cambodian, Portuguese, Hmong, Korean, and Vietnamese—for different communities in the United States that rely heavily on fish in their diets. Similar guides and fish advisories are available as posters, illustrated brochures, key chain tags, and magnets for the kitchen.

At the local level, a successful (and culturally-appropriate) risk communication campaign about mercury and fish consumption has been unfolding in Wisconsin. In association with the National Institute of Environmental Health Sciences (NIEHS), the University of Wisconsin's Marine and Freshwater Biomedical Sciences Center has initiated a public education campaign with at-risk communities. One of the center's objectives was "to increase the knowledge and involvement of minority communities in environmental health issues, including awareness of the risks and benefits of fish consumption by the Hmong community in Milwaukee" (National Institute of Environmental Health Sciences, 2003, para. 1).

| Figure 12.3 | The challenge of risk communication goes beyond technical information. Health officials also hope to change the eating practices of at-risk populations who consume fish with high levels of mercury. |

Fish Advisories

The Hmong are immigrants from Southeast Asia. In Vietnam, they depended heavily upon fish for their diets. In fishing in local waters and in the Great Lakes, however, many have little understanding of pollution and contamination of waters and fish in Wisconsin. As a result, the Marine and Freshwater Biomedical Sciences Center departed from the technical model of risk communication and proposed, instead, to work in collaboration with the community to design its campaign. Collaboration between the center's scientists and the community included the Hmong American Friendship Association and the Sixteenth Street Community Health Center, the major health care provider for Hmong residents.

The communication plan that grew from this dialogic approach relied on the Hmong language and an awareness of Hmong cultural traditions. The main communication vehicle was a bilingual Hmong–English video titled *Nyob Paug Hauv Qab Thu* (*Beneath the Surface*). The video, which features local Hmong residents, "communicates in a simple, understandable, and culturally sensitive way the risks of eating contaminated fish and teaches methods of catching and preparing fish that can reduce these risks" (Thigpen & Petering, 2004, p. A738). And, because pregnant women and children were at higher risk, the center and its partners decided to develop approaches relating specifically to these populations. In addition, they relied upon Hmong focus groups to discuss the framing of the content of the communication campaign.

The center also relied upon volunteers in the Hmong community to distribute the video to households and to show it at Hmong festivals. Finally, the center and its partners worked with the local middle school to develop a module for its life science class that would educate inner-city students about eating contaminated fish. The risk communication project is ongoing among the Hmong community, largely as a result of the support and participation of local leaders, residents, and professionals in the community itself.

Both the EPA and University of Wisconsin's risk communication reflect many of the differences between technical and cultural approaches. Most importantly, the risk communication initiatives reflected the concerns and viewpoints of those were most affected by mercury poisoning, and these individuals were part of the decision-making about the risk materials. These are reflections of democratic values, and agencies increasingly are recognizing that they must be part of any communication among scientists, agency officials, and members of an at-risk community. (For a summary of these differences, see Table 12.1.)

Still, risk warnings do not occur in a vacuum. News reports of oil spills or the effects of eating contaminated fish also influence our perceptions of risk, prompting official actions and influencing the behavior of at-risk communities. I have explored some of the factors that influence media coverage of the environment in general in Chapter 6. Below, I describe some of the major concerns about media coverage of environmental risk.

| Table 12.1 | Models of Risk Communication |

	Technical Model	**Cultural Model**
Type of communication:	Usually one way (experts-to laypeople)	Collaborative (citizens, experts, agencies)
Source of knowledge of risk:	Science/technology	Science plus local, cultural knowledge and experience
Objectives:	1. To translate and inform	1. To inform by recognizing social contexts of meaning
	2. To change risky behavior	2. To change risky behavior when in the interests of affected groups
	3. To assure concerned groups	3. To involve affected groups in judgments of acceptable and unacceptable risks

SOURCE: Adapted from table located at: http://oehha.ca.gov/pdf/HRSguide2001.pdf page 5. Office of Environmental Health and Hazard Assessment.

Media and Environmental Risk

With a growing awareness of environmental hazards, many different groups have an interest in characterizing these risks—scientists, public health experts, industry, EPA officials, parents, and others may bring their concerns about risk into the public sphere. During the Gulf of Mexico oil spill in 2010, for example, government agencies, scientists, local businesses, and individuals all voiced their concerns through the media about food safety and other environmental dangers from the spill. With images of oil sheens and oil-soaked pelicans in the news daily, the U.S. FDA (2010) tried to assure Gulf Coast residents that, "there is no reason to believe that any contaminated product has made its way to the market" (para. 1). Others were not so sure. As the crisis played out, the Louisiana Seafood and Marketing Board launched an "ad campaign in major newspapers boasting that Louisiana's seafood is indeed safe to eat because most of the state's waterways remain untouched by oil" (Gray, 2010, para. 4).

Media now serve as an important public sphere within which differing voices warn, reassure, downplay, or define environmental risks. News reports, TV ads, marketing campaigns, and blogs provide public forums for discussing environmental and health risks ranging from contaminated fish to climate change. And, although media can be invaluable sources about risk, most mainstream media still labor under many of the same requirements for newsworthiness that I described Chapter 5, such as magnitude, conflict, and emotional impact. As a result, some risk stories may be exaggerated, while other stories struggle to translate technical risk assessments.

In this section, I describe some of the ways in which risk is represented and the factors that contribute to coverage of environmental dangers in mainstream media. And, I point to some of the challenges that at-risk groups—what Beck (1992) calls the "voices of the side effects"—have in gaining recognition in media reports.

Media Reports of Risk: Accurate Information or Sensational Stories?

Public awareness of risk as a problem is inextricably tied to media and other public forums in contemporary society. As environmental media scholar Libby Lester (2010) reminds us, knowledge of risks—"how we become aware of them, [and] assess their dangers"—relies upon "public claims made by a variety of actors, who compete to have the legitimacy of their claims recognized in the public sphere" (p. 102). This, in turn, is influenced by any number of challenges—how well reporters understand a technical risk report, whether dramatic visuals of an event overwhelm a more sober analysis, or whether the public views scientific claims themselves as sites of disagreement.

A common criticism from scientists is that journalists often give readers inaccurate information rather than substantive coverage of an environmental danger. A classic illustration of such misinformation occurred after the damage to the reactor core and release of radioactive materials at Pennsylvania's Three Mile Island nuclear plant on March 28, 1979. Rhetorical scholars Thomas Farrell and Thomas Goodnight (1981) described communication about the accident by news media, government spokespersons, and industry as a "conspicuous confusion and failure" (p. 283). In their study, they found that, "reporters were unable to judge the validity of technical statements. . . . Government sources, frequently at odds with one another, could not decide what information to release. . . . [And] some representatives of the nuclear power industry made misleading statements" (Farrell & Goodnight, 1981, p. 273). And, in 2010, media reports of the amount of oil spilled into the Gulf of Mexico by the blowout of the BP oil well reflected a similar confusion among scientists, the EPA, and oil company spokespersons.

News media also face other constraints in covering the environment, particularly the more complex news stories about biodiversity, climate change, or energy shortages. Thus, while attempting to provide information about serious hazards, reporters and editors also must negotiate a thicket of journalistic norms: Is the story newsworthy (Chapter 6)? Will it command the attention and interest of readers or viewers? Dr. John Graham, former director of the Harvard Center for Risk Analysis, has complained, for example, that, "what constitutes news is not necessarily what constitutes a significant health problem" and that reporters often stress "the bizarre, the mysterious," rather than more realistic risks (quoted in Murray, Schwartz, & Lichter, 2001, p. 116).

Media, for example, often overreport the risks generated by dramatic or sensational events, such as oil spills or tornados, while underreporting slower, less visible threats such as the loss of biodiversity (Allan, Adam, & Carter, 2000). A study of network TV found similar results. Airplane accidents received 29 times more coverage than the danger of asbestos, 41 times more likely to kill Americans (Greenberg, Sachsman, Sandman, & Salomone, 1989, p. 272).

Sociologist Ulrich Beck (2009) goes even further. Media, and especially television, Beck argues, play "a central role in maintaining both public knowledge and *public anxiety* about risk" (quoted in Lester, 2010, p. 54; emphasis added). One consequence of this is that it is sometimes "increasingly difficult to make a clear and binding distinction between hysteria and deliberate fear-mongering, on the one hand, and appropriate fear and precaution, on the other" (Beck, 2009, p. 12).

In fairness, journalists face difficult constraints in reporting risk issues. For one thing, scientific research itself may be ambiguous and hence difficult for reporters to interpret fairly or accurately for laypeople. And, risk stories—like everything else—compete with other breaking news. This is true even at the *New York Times*, "one of the last bastions of serious science journalism" (Brainard, 2008, para. 2). Speaking at a 2008 meeting of the American Association for the Advancement of Science, former *New York Times* science reporter Andrew Revkin said, despite interest in the environment, global warming remains a "fourth-tier" story in the press. Among the reasons, he explained, is "the 'tyranny of the news peg,' a dearth of print space, and different learning curves for complex stories like climate science . . . You don't get extra room in a newspaper just because the story's harder" (quoted in Brainard, 2008, para. 2).

☞ FYI Media Coverage of Environmental Risk

A survey of media coverage of risk by Lundgren and McMakin (2009) echoed many of the criticisms of news media by scientists and others. Their chief findings included:

1. "Scientific risk had little to do with the environmental coverage presented on the nightly news. Instead the coverage appeared driven by the traditional journalistic news values of timeliness, geographic proximity, prominence, consequence, and human interest, along with the television criterion of visual impact" (p. 210).

2. "Mass media disproportionately focus on hazards that are catastrophic and violent in nature, new, and associated with the United States. . . . Drama, symbolism, and identifiable victims, particularly children or celebrities, make risks more memorable" (p. 211).

3. "Concepts important to technical professionals, such as probabilities, uncertainties, risk ranges, acute versus chronic risks, and risk tradeoffs, do not translate well in many mass media formats" (p. 212).

4. "To humanize and personalize the risk story, news organizations often use the plight of an individual affected by a hazard, regardless of how representative the person's situation is" (p. 212).

Lundgren and McMakin (2009) stressed that these ways of simplifying or personalizing information about risk "may make information more accessible to the public, but may result in incomplete and sometimes unbalanced information for making personal risk decisions" (p. 212).

SOURCE: R. E. Lundgren and A. H. McMakin. (2009). *Risk Communication: A Handbook for Communicating Environmental, Safety, and Health Risks* (4th ed.). Hoboken, NJ: John Wiley.

Whose Voices Speak of Risk?

Our understanding of environmental dangers depends not simply on information but also on who speaks about or interprets the information about risk. One area of research in environmental communication is the nature of the sources used by media in reports about risks—government officials, scientists, at-risk publics, environmental groups, and so forth.

Legitimizers as Sources for Risk

Not surprisingly, news media echo some of the features of technical models of risk communication; that is, they rely upon **legitimizers,** or sources such as official spokespersons and experts to bring authority or credibility to news about risk. As a result, stories about environmental risk may quote an EPA spokesperson or a scientist to provide "content" for the coverage while using local residents or environmental groups for nontechnical aspects of the story such as "color, emotion, and human elements" (Pompper, 2004, p. 106).

In a study of this tendency, Pompper surveyed 15 years of environmental risk stories in three U.S. newspapers that target different social groups: the *New York Times, USA Today,* and the *National Enquirer.* Her conclusion was this: Mainstream media such as the *New York Times* and *USA Today* relied heavily upon government and industry sources, while the *National Enquirer* relied mostly on individuals, community members, and so forth. This is significant because experts and community members framed the risks quite differently. Government and industry were more likely to characterize risk in terms of official assessments and assurances of safety: Risk could be controlled; responsible agencies were providing oversight, and so on. On the other hand, community members spoke of personal concerns about dangers, such as cancer and industrial accidents.

Pompper's (2004) conclusion is stark: "Voices of common people who live with environmental risks every day and voices of groups organized to save the environment . . . are drowned out by elites cited most often in environmental risk stories. For non-elites . . . this study's major finding has grim implications, indeed. The news media essentially ignore them" (p. 128).

Classifying news sources as *elite* versus *nonelite* or *common people,* however, may be too simple. Sometimes, elite sources themselves differ about environmental or health risks: Is BPA in plastic bottles safe? Does air pollution from coal-burning power plants harm infants and young children? In cases of controversy among legitimizers, news media will often revert to conflict frames in covering the story. Earlier in this chapter, for example, we saw scientists challenging the FDA for relying on risk studies funded by industry (Parker-Pope, 2008). On the other hand, news media also quote industry sources themselves who challenge FDA or EPA authorities. Let's look briefly at a current example of this.

As I write in 2011, the FDA has been reviewing public comment on proposed guidelines that limit the use of antibiotics in farm animals. For years, large agribusinesses and small farmers alike have "routinely fed antibiotics to their cattle, pigs, and chickens to protect them from infectious diseases but also to spur growth and weight gain" ("Antibiotics and agriculture," 2010, p. A24). Medical experts, however, believe the overuse of antibiotics in these animals has led to "the emergence of antibiotic-resistant bacteria, including dangerous E-coli strains that account for millions of bladder infections each year, as well as resistant types of salmonella and other microbes" (Eckholm, 2010, p. A13).

News media coverage of the FDA's proposed guidelines featured conflicting assessments of the risk, quoting farmers and livestock producers as well as medical experts. For example, the *New York Times* framed a 2010 news story about antibiotics in farm animals as a conflict between industry and science. The story quotes the National Pork Producers Council, an industry source, who insisted the risks were remote: "There is no conclusive . . . evidence that antibiotics used in food animals have a significant impact on the effectiveness of antibiotics in people"; then the *Times* story stated, "But leading medical experts say the threat is real and growing" (Eckholm, 2010, A13).

As the antibiotics story illustrates, the coverage of risk in news media faces many of the same characteristics of news production, including the tension between norms of objectivity and balance that we reviewed in Chapter 6.

Voices of the "Side Effects"

The dominance of government, scientific, and industry sources in news media certainly affects the public's perceptions of risk. This dominance also raises an important question about the opportunities for cultural rationality in media outlets. Indeed, an important debate over media reporting of risk concerns what Ulrich Beck (1992) called the **voices of the "side effects"** (p. 61). Beck is referring to those individuals (and their children) who suffer the side effects of risk society, such as asthma and other illnesses from air pollutants, chemical contamination, and the like. Reflecting the tension between technical and cultural rationality that we discussed earlier, these voices of the "side effects" seek media recognition of a very different understanding of environmental dangers and the burdens of risk. Beck explains:

> What scientists call "latent side effects" and "unproven connections" are for them their "coughing children" who turn blue in foggy weather and gasp for air, with a rattle in their throat. On their side of the fence, "side effects" have voices, fears, eyes, and tears. And yet they must soon learn that their own statements and experiences are worth nothing so long as they collide with the established scientific [views]. . . . (p. 61)

As a result, voices of these "side effects" too often are not given the journalistic space to offer alternative, cultural rationality in news about environmental risks.

A rather extreme example of this occurred in a news story about the toll that the Gulf of Mexico oil spill in 2010 had on local citizens. Medical experts at the time observed that, "the impact of the disaster on human health and well-being has not even begun to be quantified" (Walsh, 2010, para. 1). The story on *TIME's Health & Science* blog included interviews with experts from various universities, the National Institute for Occupational Safety and Health, and the Children's Health Fund, commenting on the impacts of the oil spill on individuals. Typical was Dr. Irwin Redlener, director of the National Center for Disaster Preparedness at Columbia University: "These are people in a serious crisis," he said. "They're at ground zero of a catastrophe" (quoted in Walsh, 2010, para. 3).

Curiously, the news account never interviewed a single person who might have been affected by this catastrophe—unemployed workers, residents, or cleanup crews working under hazardous conditions—for insight into their well-being or health. The story did, however, open dramatically with this account:

> [A]n Alabama fisherman who reluctantly took an oil-spill cleanup job with BP, was found dead from a self-inflicted gunshot wound. He left no suicide note, and we'll likely never know why he took his own life, but friends told the media that he had been deeply troubled by the spill and the destruction it caused on the coast. In this instance, the voice of the "side effects," the Alabama fisherman, was literally silent, but used, nonetheless, for "emotion, and [a] human element" (Pompper, 2004, p. 106).

Yet, voices of "side effects" do manage to appear in news accounts on occasion. Earlier, in Chapter 10, you learned of the *indecorous voice,* that is, the struggles of individuals living in polluted communities to be heard against the established norms defining access to public forums. Like them, the voices of the "side effects" also turn to their own resources. Beck (1992) explains: Ordinary "people themselves become small, private alternative experts in risks.... Parents begin to collect data and arguments. The 'blank spots' of modernization risks, which remain 'unseen' and 'unproven' for the experts, very quickly take form under their ... approach" (p. 61). And sometimes, their voices appear in mainstream media accounts.

Media communication scholar Simon Cottle (2000) looked at this possibility in a study of environmental news on British television. Cottle found that, "ordinary voices" were more frequently (37%) cited in TV news than either government or scientific sources. However, he cautioned that ordinary voices and expressions of "lived experience" are used mainly to provide human interest or a "human face" for stories rather than for substantive analysis. The inclusion of such personal interviews is, of course, important for newsworthiness in stories. Nevertheless, these experiences are "sought out and positioned to play a symbolic role, not to elaborate a form of 'social rationality'" (Cottle, 2000, pp. 37–38). That is, they are used to provide color, variety, and human interest rather than to shed insight into a problem.

Act Locally!

How Do Local News Media Report Environmental Risks?

Recently, my local newspaper reported a reader's concern that bridges in our state may not be safe. The reporter interviewed the state department of transportation, which assured him the bridges were, indeed, safe for vehicles to cross. The tone of the article was calm, factual, and reassuring. Sources quoted in the news story were almost exclusively legitimizers, official spokespersons and safety experts. Only one citizen was quoted, who worried about the bridges. Could the voices of other, ordinary citizens—drivers and passengers—been useful in the article? Could they have had experiences that complemented or questioned the official voices of reassurance?

How do your local media cover possible environmental or health risks?

(1) Do the news stories provide enough information, background, or insight about the issue?

(2) Is the tone sensational, opinionated, or factual?

(3) What sources are included in the stories? Do they include the voices of the "side effects"?

(4) What function do these voices serve? Legitimizing official policies? Offering color or personal interest for readers or viewers?

An important caveat to the limitations of mainstream media, of course, is that online channels are now available for individuals (including the voices of the "side effects") to publicize their concerns. As risk communication scholar Sheldon Krimsky (2007) points out, "The Internet . . . has . . . expanded the breadth and channels of risk communication, while also providing new opportunities for stakeholders to influence the message" (p. 157). Numerous blogs, clearinghouses for different diseases, chat rooms, and advocacy groups' sites now populate social media and online sites and make possible discursive spaces for sharing of views about risks and other environmental dangers.

In summary, various media constitute a public sphere that is crisscrossed by competing claims about risk from a variety of sources—scientists, government agencies, industry, and (less often) the voices of the "side effects" who are directly affected by environmental dangers. Unlike many online platforms, reporters working in mainstream media must balance not only these differing voices but also journalistic norms for newsworthiness, particularly the need to gain readers or viewers. At times, such constraints sometimes push reporters to dramatize risk and underreport chronic and longer-term conditions and causes of environmental and health dangers.

SUMMARY

This chapter introduced the idea of *risk*, its different meanings and the challenge of communicating risk and other environmental dangers to the public.

- The first section described Ulrich Beck's (1992) idea of *risk society,* or the dangers from modern society itself. I also introduced two models for assessing risk and its meaning: (1) a technical model and (2) a cultural–experiential approach.

- The second section introduces the practice of *risk communication* and two approaches:

  (1) a traditional model, influenced by technical meanings of risk, and

  (2) a cultural model of risk communication that involves the experiences of those who are affected by risk.

- The final section explores the ways that news media shape our perceptions of risks and two dimensions of media reports:

  (1) debate over the accuracy of news reports of risk; that is, are they factual or sensational?

  (2) different voices who speak in media coverage of risk—society's legitimizers (e.g., public officials), and the voices of the "side effects": residents, parents of sick children, and others who are most affected by environmental dangers.

At the beginning of this chapter, you read that those who control the discourse on risk will most likely control the political battles as well. I hope, then, that this discussion of technical and cultural approaches to risk communication has helped you appreciate some of the reasons for conflict among technical experts, public officials, news media, and individuals who are exposed to environmental dangers. In the end, society's ability to reduce environmental hazards may depend less on the language of technical risk—parts per billion and dose exposures—than upon the ability of experts and affected communities to speak honestly to one another about what risks are acceptable and who benefits (and who suffers) from dangerous environments.

SUGGESTED RESOURCES

- *Gasland,* 2009, Filmmaker John Fox's journey across the United States to document the environmental and health risks from hydraulic fracturing, or fracking, used in drilling for natural gas; Sundance winner and Academy Award Nominee for best documentary.
- Ulrich Beck, *Risk Society: Toward a New Modernity.* London: Sage, 2002.
- Stuart Allan, Barbara Adam, and Cynthia Carter (Eds.), *Environmental Risks and the Media.* London and New York: Routledge, 2000.
- *Erin Brockovich,* 2000, film starring Julia Roberts, an unemployed mother who, as a paralegal, exposes a powerful corporation's toxic pollution of a rural California town.
- Sheldon Krimsky and Alonzo Plough, *Environmental Hazards: Communicating Risks as a Social Process.* Dover, MA: Auburn House, 1988.

DISCUSSION QUESTIONS

1. Do you trust government warnings about the health risks of smoking, texting while driving, tanning salons, or consuming alcohol while pregnant? Why or why not? Are these warnings effective? Do they affect your own behavior?

2. Is the public's outrage over environmental hazards rational? Although a toxic waste landfill may inconvenience those living near it, doesn't it have to go somewhere? Or does it? Does society manage fairly the risks associated with our chemical culture?

3. Recently, the Environmental Working Group (2010) found concentrations of hexavalent chromium, or chromium 6 (also featured in the movie *Erin Brockovich*), in the drinking water of 31 cities in the United States. If you lived in one of these cities, what would you want in a risk communication plan about your drinking water? What would persuade you that your water was safe or not? What would cause you to change your behavior, for example, to use bottled water instead?

4. Communicating the risks of climate change faces a challenge: Some do not accept that global warming is happening, while many do not feel any urgency to act, that is, by contacting a member of Congress. How can groups concerned about the risks from climate change design more effective risk communication? What would persuade you that such risks are real?

5. What do the voices of the "side effects" (such as parents of sick children) contribute to risk communication? Are these voices merely emotional, or do they have relevant insight into health or environmental dangers in their communities?

REFERENCES

Allan, S., Adam, B., & Carter, C. (Eds.). (2000). *Environmental risks and the media.* London & New York: Routledge.

Andrews, R. N. L. (2006). *Managing the environment, managing ourselves: A history of American environmental policy* (2nd ed.). New Haven, CT: Yale University Press.

Antibiotics and agriculture. (2010, June 30). *New York Times*, p. A24.

Associated Press. (2004, July 28). New Superfund concerns: Toxic exposure cited; in check at 80 percent of sites, officials say. *Richmond Times-Dispatch*, p. A3.

Beck, U. (1992). *Risk society: Towards a new modernity.* Newbury Park, CA: Sage.

Beck, U. (1998). Politics of risk society. In J. Franklin (Ed.), *The politics of risk society* (pp. 9–22). London: Polity.

Beck, U. (2000). Risk society revisited: Theory, politics, and research programs. In B. Adam, U. Beck, & J. V. Loon (Eds.), *The risk society and beyond: Critical issues for social theory* (pp. 211–229). London: Sage.

Beck, U. (2009). *World at risk.* Cambridge, UK: Polity.

Brainard, C. (2008, February 19). Dispatches from AAAS: A few thoughts on meeting's media-oriented panels. *Columbia Journalism Review* [Electronic version]. Retrieved December 9, 2008, from www.cjr.org

Brown, P., & Mikkelsen, E. J. (1990). *No safe place: Toxic waste, leukemia, and community action.* Berkeley: University of California Press.

Cottle, S. (2000). TV news, lay voices and the visualization of environmental risks. In S. Allan, B. Adam, & C. Carter (Eds.), *Environmental risks and the media* (pp. 29–44). London: Routledge.

Dietz, T., & Stern, P. C. (2008). *Public participation in environmental assessment and decision making.* National Research Council. Washington, DC: National Academies Press.

Eckholm, E. (2010, September 15). U.S. zeroes in on pork producers' antibiotics use. *New York Times*, pp. A13–19.

Eilperin, J. (2010, May 25). U.S. oil drilling regulator ignored experts' red flags on environmental risks. *Washington Post.* Retrieved December 29, 2010, from www.washingtonpost.com/

Environmental Working Group. (2010). Chromium-6 is widespread in US tap water. Retrieved January 11, 2011, from http://static.ewg.org/

Farrell, T. B., & Goodnight, G. T. (1981). Accidental rhetoric: The root metaphors of Three Mile Island. *Communication Monographs, 48,* 271–300.

Fiorino, D. J. (1989). Technical and democratic values in risk analysis. *Risk Analysis, 9,* 293–299.

Fischer, F. (2000). *Citizens, experts, and the environment: The politics of local knowledge.* Durham, NC: Duke University Press.

Gibbs, L. (1994). Risk assessments from a community perspective. *Environmental Impact Assessment Review, 14,* 327–335.

Grady, D. (2010, September 7). In feast of data on BPA plastic, no final answer. *The New York Times*, pp. D1, D4.

Gray, S. (2010, June 15). New Orleans' cuisine crisis. *Time.com.* Retrieved January 7, 2011, from www.time.com/

Greenberg, M., Sachsman, D. B., Sandman, P., & Salomone, K. L. (1989). Risk, drama and geography in coverage of environmental risk by network TV, *Journalism Quarterly, 66*(2), 267–276.

Krimsky, S. (2007). Risk communication in the internet age: The rise of disorganized skepticism. *Environmental Hazards, 7,* 157–164.

Krimsky, S., & Plough, A. (1988). *Environmental hazards: Communicating risks as a social process.* Dover, MA: Auburn House.

Layton, L. (2008, September 17). Study links chemical BPA to health problems. *Washington Post,* p. A3.

Lester, L. (2010). *Media and environment: Conflict, politics, and the news.* Cambridge, UK: Polity.

Lundgren, R. E., & McMakin, A. H. (2009). *Risk communication: A handbook for communicating environmental, safety, and health risks* (4th ed.). Hoboken, NJ: John Wiley.

Murray, D., Schwartz, J., & Lichter, S. (2001). *It ain't necessarily so, how media make and unmake the scientific picture of reality.* Lanham, MD: Rowman & Littlefield.

National Commission on the BP *Deepwater Horizon* Oil Spill and Offshore Drilling. (2011). *The White House.* Retrieved January 6, 2011, from http://www.oilspillcommission.gov/

National Institute of Environmental Health Sciences. (2003). *University of Wisconsin Milwaukee Community outreach and education program.* Retrieved July 27, 2004, from www-apps.niehs.gov

National Research Council. (1996). *Understanding risk: Informing decisions in a democratic society.* Washington, DC: National Academy Press.

Parker-Pope, T. (2008, October 30). Panel faults F.D.A. on stance that chemical in plastic is safe. *The New York Times,* p. A21.

Plough, A., & Krimsky, S. (1987). The emergence of risk communication studies: Social and political context. *Science, Technology, & Human Values, 12,* 4–10.

Pompper, D. (2004). At the 20th century's close: Framing the public policy issue of environmental risk. In S. L. Senecah (Ed.), *The environmental communication yearbook 1* (pp. 99–134). Mahwah, NJ: Erlbaum.

Pope, C. (2011, July/August). Bevies of black swans. *SIERRA,* p. 66.

Reckelhoff-Dangel, C., & Petersen, D. (2007, August). *Risk communication in action: The risk communication workbook.* Environmental Protection Agency. Cincinnati, OH: Office of Research and Development, National Risk Management Research Laboratory. Retrieved December 9, 2008, from http://www.epa.gov

Ropeik, D. (2010). *How risky is it, really?: Why our fears don't always match the facts.* Columbus, OH: McGraw-Hill.

Rowan, K. E. (1991). Goals, obstacles, and strategies in risk communication: A problem-solving approach to improving communication about risks. *Journal of Applied Communication Research, 19,* 300–329.

Sandman, P. (1987). Risk communication: Facing public outrage. *EPA Journal, 13*(9), 21–22.

Sandman, P. R. (2011). *Peter M. Sandman risk communication website.* Retrieved January 17, 2011, from http://www.psandman.com

Slovic, P. (1987). Perceptions of risk. *Science, 236,* 280–285.

Stein, R. (2010, October 28). Study: BPA has effect on sperm. *The Washington Post,* p. A16.

Sunstein, C. R. (2004). *Risk and reason: Safety, law, and the environment.* Cambridge, UK: Cambridge University Press.

Szabo, L. (2011, January 14). Pregnant women rife with chemicals. *USA Today,* p. 3A.

Taleb, N. N. (2010). *The black swan.* (2nd ed.). London: Penguin.

Thigpen, K. G., & Petering, D. (2004, September). Fish tales to ensure health. *Environmental Health Perspectives, 112*(13), p. A738.

Union of Concerned Scientists. (2009). Environmental impacts of coal power: Air pollution. Retrieved January 11, 2011, from www.ucsusa.org/

U.S. Cancer Institute issues stark warning on environmental cancer risk. (2010, May 17). *Ecologist.* Retrieved December 28, 2010, from www.theecologist.org/

United States Environmental Protection Agency. (2007, August). *Risk communication in action: The tools of message mapping.* Retrieved December 12, 2010, from http://www.epa.gov/

United States Environmental Protection Agency. (2010a, March). *Scoping materials for initial design of EPA research study on potential relationships between hydraulic fracturing and drinking water resources.* Retrieved December 14, 2010, from http://yosemite.epa.gov

United States Environmental Protection Agency. (2010b, August). *Risk assessment: Basic information.* Retrieved December 14, 2010, from http://epa.gov

United States Environmental Protection Agency. (2010c, October 1). Mercury: health effects. Retrieved January 4, 2011, from http://www.epa.gov

United States Environmental Protection Agency. (2010d, November 11). *EPA releases reports on dioxin emitted during Deepwater Horizon BP spill.* Retrieved December 27, 2010, from http://www.epa.gov/

United States Food and Drug Administration. (2010, August 6). *Gulf of Mexico oil spill: Questions and answers.* Retrieved January 7, 2011, from http://www.fda.gov/

United States Food and Drug Administration & United States Environmental Protection Agency. (2004). *What you need to know about mercury in fish and shellfish.* Retrieved January 5, 2011, from www.epa.gov/

Walsh, B. (2010, June 25). Assessing the health effects of the oil spill. *TIME.com.* Retrieved January 11, 2011, from http://www.time.com/

Wang, M. (2010, May 11). Despite previous equipment failure, BP says spill "seemed inconceivable." *ProPublica.* Retrieved December 29, 2010, from www.propublica.org/

Williams, B. A., & Matheny, A. R. (1995). *Democracy, dialogue, and environmental disputes: The contested languages of social regulation.* New Haven, CT: Yale University Press.

Glossary

Aarhus Convention: Adopted in 1998 in the Danish city of Aarhus, this is an environmental agreement of the United Nations Economic Commission for Europe (UNECE). It addresses three areas: access to information, public participation in decision making, and access to justice in environmental matters (similar to a right of standing).

Acceptable risk: From a technical perspective, a judgment based on the numerical estimate of deaths or injuries expected annually from exposure to a hazard. From a cultural perspective, a judgment of what dangers society is willing or unwilling to accept and who is subject to this risk; such a judgment inevitably involves values.

Access: The minimum resources that citizens need to exercise fully their opportunities to participate, including convenient times and places, readily available information, and technical assistance to help them understand the issues, and continuing opportunities for public involvement.

Administrative Procedure Act (APA): Enacted in 1946, this law laid out new standards for the operation of U.S. government agencies; it required that proposed actions be published in the *Federal Register* and that the public be given an opportunity to respond; it also broadened the right of judicial review for persons "suffering a legal wrong" resulting from "arbitrary and capricious" actions on the part of agencies.

Advocacy: Persuasion or argument in support of a cause, policy, idea, or set of values.

Advocacy campaign: A strategic course of action involving communication that is undertaken for a specific purpose.

Agency capture: The pressuring or influencing of officials by a regulated industry to ignore violations of a corporation's permit for environmental performance (for example, its air or water discharges).

Agenda setting: The ability of media to affect the public's perception of the salience or importance of issues; in other words, news reporting may not succeed in telling people what to think, but it succeeds in telling them what to think about.

Antagonism: Recognition of the limit of an idea, a widely shared viewpoint, or an ideology that allows an opposing idea or belief system to be voiced.

Anthropocentricism: The belief that nature exists solely for the benefit of humans.

Apocalyptic narrative: A literary style used by some environmental writers to warn of impending and severe ecological crises; evokes a sense of the end of the world as a result of the overweening desire to control nature.

App-centric: Mobile applications (on smartphones, iPads, etc.) will be our central portals for searching online.

Arbitration: The presentation of opposing views to a neutral, third-party individual or panel that, in turn, renders a judgment about the conflict; usually court ordered.

Attitude–behavior gap: Although individuals may have favorable attitudes or beliefs about environmental issues, they may not take any action; their behavior, therefore, is disconnected from their attitudes.

Bali Principles of Climate Justice: One of the first declarations redefining climate change from the perspective of environmental justice and human rights, crafted by a coalition of international nongovernmental organizations (NGOs) in Bali, Indonesia, in June 2002.

Base: A campaign's core supporters.

Black swan events: Unexpected, high-magnitude events that are beyond what modern society can usually predict.

Blog: An online site that is authored by an individual (usually) and that daily or occasionally posts information or commentary about specific topics.

Bottom-up sites: These provide online tools that enable users to start petitions on platforms like Facebook and Twitter.

Business as usual (BAU): The continued growth of carbon-based economies. *Carbon based* refers to the energy sources—primarily, fossil fuels or the burning of oil, coal, and natural gas—used to produce electricity, fuel transportation, and heating and power other dimensions of modern life.

Cases and controversies clause: The portion of Article III of the U.S. Constitution that ensures that lawsuits are heard by true adversaries in a dispute on the assumption that only true adversaries will represent to the courts the issues in a case; an important test of true adversary status is whether persons bringing the action are able to prove an injury in fact.

Citizen suits: Action brought by citizens in federal court asking that provisions of an environmental law be enforced; the right to bring such suits is a provision of major environmental laws.

Citizens' advisory committee: Also called a citizens' advisory panel or board, a group appointed by a government agency to solicit input from diverse interests in a community—for example, citizens, businesses, and environmentalists—about a project or problem.

Clicktivism: The taking of action simply by clicking on a response link online.

Climate justice: Views the environmental and human impacts of climate change from the frame of social justice, human rights, and concern for indigenous peoples. The movement for climate justice asserts that global warming not only impacts, disproportionately, the most vulnerable regions and peoples of the planet but that these peoples and nations often are excluded from participation in the forums addressing this problem.

Collaboration: "Constructive, open, civil communication, generally as dialogue; a focus on the future; an emphasis on learning; and some degree of power sharing and leveling of the playing field" (Walker, 2004, p. 123).

Communication tasks (of a campaign): (a) To create support or demand for the campaign's objectives, (b) to mobilize this support from relevant constituencies (audiences) to demand accountability, and (c) to develop a strategy to influence decision makers to deliver on their objectives.

Community-based collaboration: An approach to problem solving that involves individuals and representatives of affected groups, businesses, and other agencies in addressing a specific or short-term problem defined by the local community. Like natural resource partnerships, collaborative groups are usually voluntary associations without legal sanction or regulatory powers.

Compromise: An approach to problem solving in which participants work out a solution that satisfies each person's minimum criteria but may not fully satisfy all.

Condensation symbol: Graber (1976) defined a condensation symbol as a word or phrase that "stirs vivid impressions involving the listener's most basic values" (p. 289); political scientist Murray Edelman (1964) stressed the ability of such symbols to "condense into one symbolic event or sign" powerful emotions, memories, or anxieties (p. 6).

Confrontational rhetoric: The use of nonconventional forms of language and action, such as marches, demonstrations, obscenity, sit-ins, and other forms of civil disobedience (for example, the occupation of a campus building), to critique social norms or practices such as racism, war, or exploitation of the environment.

Consensus: The assumption that discussions will not end until everyone has had a chance to share differences and find common ground; often means that all participants agree with the final decision.

Conservation: The term used by early 20th-century forester Gifford Pinchot to mean the wise and efficient use of natural resources.

Constitutive: Communication about nature also helps us construct or compose representations of nature and of environmental problems as subjects for our understanding. Such communication invites a particular perspective, evokes certain values (and not others), and thus creates conscious referents for our attention and understanding.

Crisis discipline: Term used to characterize the new discipline of conservation biology; coined by biologist Michael Soulé (1985) to refer to the duty of scientists, in the face of a looming biodiversity crisis, to offer recommendations to address this worsening situation, even with imperfect knowledge.

Critical discourse: Modes of representation that challenge society's taken-for-granted assumptions and offer alternatives to prevailing discourses.

Critical rhetoric: The questioning or denunciation of a behavior, policy, societal value, or ideology; may also include the articulation of an alternative policy, vision, or ideology.

Cultivation analysis: Associated with the work of media scholar George Gerbner (1990), the theory that repeated exposure to a set of messages tends to produce, in an audience, agreement with the views contained in those messages.

Cultivation in reverse: The media's cultivation of an anti-environmental attitude through the persistent lack of environmental images or by directing the attention of viewers and readers to other, nonenvironmental stories.

Cultural model of risk communication: An approach that involves the affected public in assessing risk and in designing risk communication campaigns and that recognizes cultural knowledge and the experience of local communities.

Cultural rationality: In Plough and Krimsky's (1987) view, a basis for risk evaluation that includes personal, familiar, and social concerns; a source of judgment that arises when the social context and experience of those exposed to environmental dangers enter definitions of risk.

Decorum: One of the virtues of style in the classical Greek and Latin rhetorical handbooks; usually translated as *propriety* or *that which is fitting* for the particular audience and occasion.

Delhi Climate Justice Declaration: Final declaration of Climate Justice Summit, New Delhi, 2002, which declared, "Climate change is a human-rights issue"; also resolved "to actively build a movement from the communities" to address climate change from a social justice perspective.

Direct action: Physical acts of protest such as road blockades, sit-ins, and tree spiking.

Discourse: A pattern of speaking, writing, or other symbolic action that results from multiple sources. Discourse functions to circulate a coherent set of meanings about an important topic.

Disparate impact: Term used to denote the discrimination resulting from environmental hazards in minority communities; adopted from the 1964 Civil Rights Act, which used it to recognize forms of discrimination that result from the disproportionate burdens experienced by some groups regardless of the conscious intention of others in their decisions or behaviors.

Dissensus: Term coined by communication scholar Thomas Goodnight (1991), meaning a questioning of, refusal of, or disagreement with a claim or a premise of a speaker's argument.

Dominant discourse: A discourse that has gained broad or taken-for-granted status in a culture; for example, the belief that growth is good for the economy; its meanings help to legitimize certain policies or practices.

Dominant Social Paradigm (DSP): A dominant discursive tradition of several centuries that has sustained attitudes of human dominance over nature. The DSP affirms society's belief in economic growth and its faith in technology, limited government, and private property.

Earth Day (1970): Twenty million people took part in protests, teach-ins, and festivals throughout the country, in one of the largest demonstrations in American history.

Eco-label certification programs: Certified products reflect an independent group's assurance to consumers that the product is environmentally friendly or produced in a manner that did not harm the environment.

Ecotage: Acts such as vandalism and arson that are undertaken for the purpose of protecting nature; while clearly illegal, these acts are specifically intended not to harm humans.

Electronic Freedom of Information Amendments: Amendments to the Freedom of Information Act (FOIA) that require federal agencies to provide public access to information in electronic form. This is done typically by posting a guide for making a freedom of information request on the agency's website.

Emergency Planning and Community Right to Know Act (Right to Know Act): Enacted in 1986, this act requires industries to report to local and state emergency planners the use and location of specified chemicals at their facilities.

Environmental advocacy: Discourse (legal, educational, expository, artistic, public, and interpersonal communication) aimed at supporting conservation and the preservation of finite resources; aims also include support for

both natural and human environments and the well-being of the life such environments sustain.

Environmental communication: The pragmatic and constitutive vehicle for our understanding of the environment as well as our relationships to the natural world; the symbolic medium that we use in constructing environmental problems and in negotiating society's different responses to them.

Environmental impact statement (EIS): Required by the National Environmental Policy Act (NEPA) for proposed federal legislation or actions significantly affecting the quality of the environment; an EIS must describe (a) the environmental impact of the proposed action, (b) any adverse environmental effects that could not be avoided should the proposal be implemented, and (c) alternatives to the proposed action.

Environmental justice: As used by community activists and scholars studying the environmental justice movement, the term refers to (a) calls to recognize and halt the disproportionate burdens imposed on poor and minority communities by environmentally harmful conditions, (b) more inclusive opportunities for those who are most affected to be heard in the decisions made by public agencies and the wider environmental movement, and (c) a vision of environmentally healthy, economically sustainable communities.

Environmental melodrama: A genre used to clarify issues of power and the ways advocates "moralize" an environmental conflict. As a genre, melodrama "generates stark, polarizing distinctions between social actors and infuses those distinctions with moral gravity and pathos," and is therefore "a powerful resource for rhetorical invention" (Schwarze, 2006, p. 239).

Environmental news services (ENSs): Online platforms offering access to both working journalists and readers looking for more in-depth environmental news and timely information.

Environmental racism (and more broadly, **environmental injustice**): Refers not only to threats to communities' health from hazardous waste landfills, incinerators, agricultural pesticides, sweatshops, and polluting factories but also the disproportionate burden that these practices placed on people of color and the workers and residents of low-income communities. See also **disparate impact.**

Environmental skepticism: An attitude that disputes the seriousness of environmental problems and questions the credibility of environmental science.

Environmental tort: A legal claim for injury or a lawsuit related to an environmental harm.

Exceptionalism: The view that, because a region has unique or distinctive features, it is exempt from the general rule. Some critics are concerned that place-based decisions reached at the local level in one area can become a precedent for exempting other geographical areas and thus compromise more uniform, national standards for environmental policy.

Executive Order on Environmental Justice: Issued by President Clinton in 1994, Executive Order 12898, titled "Federal Actions to Address Environmental Justice in Minority Populations and Low-Income Populations," instructed each federal agency "to make achieving environmental justice part of its mission by identifying and addressing ... disproportionately high and adverse human health or environmental effects of its programs, policies, and activities on minority populations and low-income populations in the United States" (Clinton, 1994, p. 7629).

First National People of Color Environmental Leadership Summit: A key moment in the new movement for environmental justice, when delegates from local communities and national leaders from social justice, religious, environmental, and civil rights groups met in Washington, DC, in October 1991.

Four-step procedure for risk assessment: Procedure used by agencies to evaluate risk in a technical sense; the four steps are (1) hazard identification, (2) assessment of human exposure, (3) modeling of the dose responses, and (4) a characterization of the overall risk. See **risk (technical).**

Frame: First defined by Erving Goffman (1974) to refer to the cognitive maps or patterns of interpretation that people use to organize their understanding of reality. See also **media frames.**

Free market: Usually, the absence of governmental restriction on business or commercial activity; the belief that the private marketplace is self-regulating and ultimately promotes social good.

Freedom of Information Act (FOIA): Enacted in 1966, this act provides that any person has the right to see documents and records of any federal agency (except the judiciary or Congress).

Friends of the Earth, Inc., v. Laidlaw Environmental Services, Inc.: A 2000 case in which the Supreme Court reversed its strict Lujan doctrine, ruling that plaintiffs did not need to prove an actual (particular) harm; rather, the knowledge of a possible threat to a legally recognized interest (clean water) was enough to establish a sufficient stake in enforcing the law.

Gamification: A term originating in digital media and defined as "the use of game design elements in nongame contexts by applying the elements of a game—competition, fun, and social engagement with others."

Gatekeeping: The role of editors and media managers in deciding to cover or not cover certain news stories; a metaphor used to suggest that individuals in newsrooms decide what gets in and what stays out.

Goal (of a campaign): Describes a long-term vision or value, such as protection of old-growth forests, reduction of arsenic in drinking water, or making economic globalization more democratic.

Green consumerism: Marketing that encourages the belief that, by buying allegedly environmentally friendly products, consumers can do their part to protect the planet.

Green jobs movement: Champions a new source of employment, particularly for depressed communities and unemployed workers, by funding labor-intensive, clean-energy projects such as weatherproofing buildings, installing solar panels, and building wind turbines, which at the same time, help to reduce U.S. emissions of greenhouse gases.

Green marketing: A corporation's attempt to associate its products, services, or identity with environmental values and images; generally used for (a) product promotion (sales), (b) image enhancement, or (c) image repair. Recently defined to include communication about environmentally beneficial product modifications.

Green product advertising: The marketing of products as having minimal impact on the environment and to "project an image of high quality, including environmental sensitivity, relating both to a product's attributes and its manufacturer's track record for environmental compliance" (Ottman, 1993, p. 48).

Greenwashing: "Disinformation disseminated by an organization so as to present an environmentally responsible public image. . . . origin from *green* on the pattern of *whitewash*" (Pearsall, 1999, p. 624).

Groupthink: Term coined by psychologist Irving Janis (1977) referring to an excessive cohesion in groups that impedes critical or independent thinking, often resulting in uninformed consensus.

Hazard: In Sandman's (1987) model of risk, or what experts mean by risk (that is, expected annual mortality). See **outrage.**

Hydraulic fracturing or **fracking:** A method used in drilling for natural gas that involves injecting large volumes of water and chemicals under high pressure into rock or shale strata to create fissures, which release the trapped gas.

Image enhancement: The use of public relations or advertising to improve the image of a corporation itself, reflecting its environmental concern and performance.

Image events: Actions by environmentalists that take advantage of television's hunger for pictures; such events often succeed by reducing a complex set of issues to (visual) symbols that break people's comfortable equilibrium, inviting them to ask if there is a better way to do things.

Image repair: The use of public relations (PR) to restore a company's credibility after an environmental harm or accident.

Indecorous voice: The symbolic framing by some public officials of the voices of others as inappropriate or unqualified for speaking in official forums, in other words, their belief that ordinary people may be too emotional or ignorant to testify about chemical pollution or other environmental issues; believing, for example, that a resident of a low-income community has violated such norms of knowledge or objectivity is one way of dismissing the public as unqualified to speak about technical matters.

Influence: In Senecah's Trinity of Voices (TOV) model, a term referring to participants' opportunities to be part of a "transparent process that considers all alternatives, opportunities to meaningfully scope alternatives, opportunities to inform the decision criteria, and thoughtful response to stakeholder concerns and ideas" (Senecah, 2004, p. 25).

Injury in fact: Under common law, this normally meant a concrete, particular injury that an individual had suffered due to the actions of another party. Currently, it is one of three tests used by U.S. courts to determine a plaintiff's standing or right to seek redress in court for a harm to a legally protected right; criteria for defining injury in fact have varied from the denial of enjoyment or use of the environment to a concrete, tangible harm to the plaintiff.

Invisible hand (of the market): Scottish economist Adam Smith's theory of the working of the market; a metaphor for an invisible or natural force of the private marketplace that determines what society values. In his classic book, *An Inquiry Into the Nature and Causes of the Wealth of Nations,* Smith (1776) argued that the sum of individuals' self-interested actions in the marketplace promotes the public's interest or the common good.

Irreparable: A forewarning or opportunity to act before it is too late to preserve what is unique or rare before it is lost forever. Cox (1982, 2001) identified the four characteristics of an appeal to the irreparable nature of a decision or its consequences: A speaker establishes that (a) the decision threatens something unique or rare and thus of great value, (b) the existence of what is threatened is precarious and uncertain, (c) its loss or destruction cannot be reversed, and (d) action to protect it is therefore timely or urgent.

Jeremiad: Originally named for the lamentations of the Hebrew prophet Jeremiah, the jeremiad refers to speech or writing that laments or denounces the behavior of a people or society and warns of future consequences if society does not change its ways.

Legitimizers: Sources such as official spokespersons and experts who, presumably, bring authority or credibility to news about risk.

Lujan v. Defenders of Wildlife: A 1992 case in which the Supreme Court rejected a claim of standing by the group Defenders of Wildlife under the citizen suit provision of the Endangered Species Act (ESA), ruling that the Defenders had failed to satisfy constitutional requirements for injury in fact because plaintiffs had not suffered a tangible and particular harm. It overturned the more liberal standard established in *Sierra Club v. Morton.*

Mainstreaming: An alleged effect in consistent viewers of media whereby differences are narrowed toward cultural norms represented in media programs.

Media effects: The influence of different media content, frequency, and forms of communication on audiences' attitudes, perceptions, and behaviors.

Media frames: The central organizing themes that connect different semantic elements of a news story (headlines, quotes, leads, visual representations, and narrative structure) into a coherent whole to suggest what is at issue. See also **frame.**

Media political economy: The influence on news content of ownership and economic interests of the owners of news stations and television networks.

Mediation: A facilitated effort, entered into voluntarily or at the suggestion of a court, counselors, or other institution, that involves an active mediator who helps the disputing parties find common ground and a solution upon which they can agree.

Message: A phrase or sentence that concisely expresses a campaign's objective and the values at stake in the decision of the primary audience. Although campaigns develop considerable information and arguments, the message itself is usually short, compelling, and memorable and accompanies all of a campaign's communication materials.

Metaphor: One of the major tropes; *Mother Nature, Spaceship Earth, population bomb,* and the *web of life* are just a few examples. A metaphor's function is to invite a comparison by talking about one thing in terms of another.

Microvolunteering: Sites that allow people to do small, bite-sized tasks via mobile apps, which sponsors believe will have meaningful impacts for different environmental groups or charitable causes.

Mind bomb: Term coined by Greenpeace cofounder Robert Hunter referring to a simple image, such as Zodiac boats interposing themselves between whales and their harpooners, that "explodes in people's minds" to create a new awareness (quoted in Weyler, 2004, p. 73).

Mountaintop removal: The removal of the tops of mountains in the Appalachians to expose seams of coal buried in the mountain; a particularly destructive form of mining environmentally.

Naming: The mode by which we socially represent objects or people and know the world, including the natural world.

Narrative framing: Media's organization of phenomena through stories to aid audiences' understanding.

National Environmental Justice Advisory Council (NEJAC): A federal advisory committee in the Environmental Protection Agency (EPA) that is intended to provide the EPA administrator with independent advice, consultation, and recommendations related to environmental justice.

National Environmental Policy Act (NEPA): Requires every federal agency to prepare an environmental impact statement and invite public comment on any project that would affect the environment. Signed into law by President Richard M. Nixon on January 1, 1970, NEPA is the cornerstone of modern environmental law.

Natural resource partnerships: Informal working groups organized around regions with natural resource concerns such as the uses of rangelands and forests as well as protection of wildlife and watersheds. Partnerships operate collaboratively to integrate their differing values and approaches to the management of natural resource issues.

Networked: The multiple, intersecting flows of communication, "using online tools and platforms to find, rank, tag, create, distribute, mock, and recommend content" (Clark & Slyke, 2011, p. 239).

News hole: The amount of space that is available for a news story relative to other demands for the same space.

Newsworthiness: The ability of news stories to attract readers or viewers; often defined by such criteria for selecting and reporting environmental news as prominence, timeliness, proximity, impact, magnitude, conflict, oddity, and emotional impact.

Notice of Intent (NOI): A statement of the agency's intent to prepare an EIS for a proposed action. The NOI is published in the *Federal Register* and provides a brief description of the proposed action and possible alternatives.

Objective (of a campaign): A specific action or decision that moves a group closer to a broader goal; a concrete and time-limited decision or action.

Objectivity and balance: Norms of journalism for almost a century, the commitment to which is made by news media to provide information that is accurate and without reporter bias and, where there is uncertainty or controversy, to balance news stories with statements from all sides of the issue.

Outrage: In Sandman's (1987) model, a term for factors the public considers in assessing the acceptability of their exposure to a hazard. See **hazard.**

Paradox for conservation: Awareness that "knowledge is always incomplete, yet the scale of human influence on ecosystems demands action without delay" (quoted in Scully, 2005, p. B13).

Persuadables: Members of the public who are undecided but potentially sympathetic to a campaign's objectives; they often become primary targets in mobilizing support.

Pollutant Release and Transfer Register (PRTR): Like the U.S. Toxic Release Inventory (TRI), international PRTR programs require mandatory reporting of specific chemical releases into the air, water, or land and public access to these data.

Pragmatic: Instrumental; a characteristic of environmental communication whereby it educates, alerts, persuades, mobilizes, and helps to solve environmental problems.

Precautionary principle: As defined by the 1998 Wingspread conference, "When an activity raises threats of harm to human health or the environment, precautionary measures should be taken even if some cause and effect relationships are not fully established scientifically. In this context the proponent of an activity, rather than the public, should bear the burden of proof" (Science and Environmental Health Network, 1998, para. 5).

Preservationism: The movement to ban commercial use of wilderness areas and to preserve wild forests and other natural areas for appreciation, study, and outdoor recreation.

Primary audience: Decision makers who have the authority to act or implement the objectives of a campaign.

Principles of Environmental Justice: Principles adopted by delegates at the First National People of Color Environmental Leadership Summit in 1991 that enumerated a series of rights, including "the fundamental right to political, economic, cultural, and environmental self-determination of all peoples."

Pro-cotting: Buying products from companies perceived to have good environmental track records; the opposite of *boycotting.*

Productivist discourse: Discourse supporting "an expansionistic, growth-oriented ethic" (Smith, 1998).

Progressive ideal: Put forth by the 1920s and 1930s Progressive movement, the concept of a neutral, science-based policy as the best approach to government regulation of industry.

Public comment: Required of federal agencies under the NEPA, public input must be solicited by a federal agency on any proposal significantly affecting the environment; usually takes place at public hearings and in written reports, letters, e-mails, or faxes to the agency.

Public demand: Active demonstration of support for a campaign's objective by key constituency groups, such as families with small children, voters in key swing districts, elderly persons suffering from respiratory problems, hunters, anglers, or urban commuters.

Public hearing: The common mode of participation by ordinary citizens in environmental decision making at both the federal and state levels; a forum for public comment to an agency before the agency takes any action that might significantly impact the environment.

Public participation: The ability of individual citizens and groups to influence environmental decisions through (a) the right to know or access to relevant information, (b) public comments to the agency that is responsible for a decision, and (c) the right, through the courts, to hold public agencies and businesses accountable for their environmental decisions and behaviors.

Public sphere: The sphere of influence created when different individuals engage each other in communication—through conversation, argument, debate, questions, and nonverbal acts—about subjects of shared concern or topics that affect a wider community.

Quincy Library Group (QLG): A high-profile effort by a local community to develop a consensus approach for managing national forest lands in northern California. The effort ended by moving in a different, more adversarial direction, a move that appears to have undercut its initial goals.

Rhetoric: The faculty (power) of discovering the available means of persuasion in the particular case.

Rhetorical genres: Distinct forms or types of speech that share characteristics distinguishing them from other types of speech.

Rhetorical perspective: A focus on purposeful and consequential efforts to influence society's attitudes and ways of behaving through communication, which includes public debate, protests, news stories, advertising, and other modes of symbolic action.

Right to know: The public's right of access to information about environmental conditions or actions of government that potentially affect the environment.

Risk (cultural–experiential): The effort by some public agencies to solicit the experience and views of affected communities in risk assessment.

Risk (technical): The expected annual mortality (or other severity) that results from some condition, such as exposure to a chemical substance; a calculation of the likelihood that a certain number of people (or an ecological system) will suffer some harm over time (usually one year) from exposure to a hazard or environmental stressor; risk may include illness and injuries as well as death.

Risk assessment: The evaluation of the degree of harm or danger from some condition such as exposure to a toxic chemical.

Risk communication (general): Any public or private communication that informs individuals about the existence, nature, form, severity, or acceptability of risks; also includes the translation of technical information to the public, and in more recent approaches, it involves sensitivity to the concerns of those who are affected by risk and their concerns about what constitutes an acceptable risk.

Risk communication (technical): The translation of technical data about environmental or health risks for public consumption, with the goal of educating a target audience.

Risk society: Term coined by German sociologist Ulrich Beck (1992) to characterize today's society according to the large-scale nature of risks and the threat of irreversible effects on human life from modernization.

Roadless Rule: Adopted by the U.S. Forest Service in 2001, the rule prohibits road building and restricts commercial logging on nearly 60 million acres of national forest lands in 39 states.

Sacrifice zones: Term coined by sociologist Robert Bullard (1993) to denote communities that share two characteristics: "(1) They already have more than their share of environmental problems and polluting industries, and (2) they are still attracting new polluters" (p. 12).

Sagebrush Rebellion: An effort in the late 1970s and 1980s by traditional land users to take control of federal land and natural resources in the West.

Scoping: A preliminary stage in an agency's development of a proposed rule or action, including any meetings and how the public can get involved; it involves canvassing interested members of the public to determine what the concerns of the affected parties might be.

Secondary audience: Segments of the public, coalition partners, opinion leaders, and the media whose support is useful in holding decision makers accountable for the campaign's objectives; also called *public audiences.*

Self-organizing: The ability of individuals, through what are often called *bottom-up websites,* to initiate actions via social media that actively engage others.

Shannon–Weaver model of communication: A linear model that defines human communication as the transmission of information from a source to a receiver.

Shock and shame response: If community members found out that a local factory was emitting high levels of pollution, their shock could push the community into action. In some cases, the polluting facility itself may feel shame from disclosure of its poor performance.

Sierra Club v. Morton: A 1972 case that established the first guidance for determining standing under the Constitution's cases and controversies clause in an environmental case; the Supreme Court held that the Sierra Club need only allege an injury to its members' interests—for example, that its members could not enjoy an unspoiled wilderness or their normal recreational pursuits.

SLAPP lawsuits: Strategic Litigation Against Public Participation—as defined by Pring and Canan (1996), a SLAPP is a lawsuit involving "communications made to influence a governmental action or outcome, which secondarily, resulted in (a) a civil complaint [lawsuit] . . . (b) filed against nongovernmental individuals or organizations . . . on (c) a substantive issue of some public interest or social significance" such as the environment (pp. 8–9).

SLAPP-back: A lawsuit against the corporation bringing an initial SLAPP suit against a citizen. Defendants SLAPP-back by filing a countersuit alleging that plaintiffs infringed on a citizen's right to free speech or to petition government; a SLAPP-back suit allows for recovery of attorneys' fees as well as punitive damages for violating constitutional rights and inflicting damage or injury on the defendant (malicious prosecution).

Social media: The use of web-based technologies and mobile applications for personal interactions, including use of Web 2.0 platforms that allow for creating and sharing of user-generated content.

Social networking: Websites or communities that allow users to interact with each other, post content, and receive updates and information relevant to their interests.

Social–symbolic perspective: Describes the social and discursive constructions that influence our understanding of nature; it focuses on the sources that help to constitute or shape our perceptions of what we consider to be natural or an environmental problem.

Stakeholders: Those parties to a dispute who have a real or discernible interest (a stake) in the outcome.

Standing: The legal status accorded a citizen who has a sufficient interest in a matter and who may speak in court to protect that interest. Also, a term in Senecah's TOV model that refers to *civic legitimacy*—the respect, esteem, and consideration that all stakeholders' perspectives should be given. In this second context, the term does not refer to legal standing in a court of law.

Strategy: A critical source of influence or leverage to bring about a desired change.

Sublime: An aesthetic category that associates God's influence with the feelings of awe and exultation that some experience in the presence of wilderness.

Sublime response: Term used to denote (a) the immediate awareness of a sublime object (such as Yosemite Valley), (b) a sense of overwhelming personal insignificance and awe in its presence, and (c) ultimately, a feeling of spiritual exaltation.

Sunshine laws: Laws intended to shine the light of public scrutiny on the workings of government, requiring open meetings of most governmental bodies.

Superfund: Legislation enacted in 1980 authorizing the EPA to clean up toxic sites and hold the responsible parties accountable for the costs.

Superfund sites: Abandoned chemical waste sites that have qualified for federal funds for their cleanup under the Comprehensive Environmental Response Compensation and Liability Act (commonly called the Superfund law).

Sustainability: A movement that encompasses three basic goals or aspirations—environmental protection, economic health, and equity or social justice, often called the *Three Es.*

Symbolic action: The property of language and other acts to do something as well as literally to say something; to create meaning and orient us consciously to the world.

Symbolic annihilation: Media's erasure of the importance of a theme by the indirect or passive deemphasizing of that theme.

Symbolic legitimacy: The perceived authority or credibility of a source of knowledge, such as scientists.

Tactics: Specific actions—alerts, meetings, protests, and so forth—that implement a broader strategy.

Technical Assistance Grant (TAG) Program: A program initiated in 1986 to help communities at Superfund sites by providing funds for citizen groups to hire consultants who can help them understand and comment on information provided by the EPA and the industries responsible for cleaning these sites.

Technocracy: John Dewey's term denoting a government ruled by experts.

Terministic screens: The means whereby language orients us to see certain things—some aspects of the world and not others. Defined by literary theorist Kenneth Burke (1966) to mean "if any given terminology is a *reflection* of reality; by its very nature as a terminology it must be a *selection* of reality; and to this extent it must function also as a *deflection* of reality" (p. 45).

Think tanks: Nonprofit, advocacy-based groups modeled on the image of neutral policy centers.

Three-bites-of-the-apple strategy: Phrase used by journalist Mark Dowie (1995) to describe the communication activities used by many corporations to shape environmental law: "The first bite is to lobby against any legislation that restricts production; the second is to weaken any legislation that cannot be defeated; and the third, and most commonly applied tactic, is to end run or subvert the implementation of environmental regulations" (p. 86).

Toxic politics: Term introduced by sociologist Michael Reich (1991) that refers to the dismissal of a community's moral and communicative standing in deliberations about chemical pollution.

Toxic Release Inventory (TRI): An information-reporting tool established under the Emergency Planning and Community Right to

Know Act (1986) that enables the EPA to collect data annually on any releases of toxic materials into the air and water by designated industries and to make this information easily available to the public.

Toxic tours: "Non-commercial expeditions organized and facilitated by people who reside in areas that are polluted by toxics, places that Bullard (1993) has named 'human sacrifice zones'... Residents of these areas guide outsiders, or tourists, through where they [residents] live, work, and play in order to witness their struggle" (Pezzullo, 2004, p. 236). (See **sacrifice zones.**)

Traditional news media: Newspapers, news magazines, network television, and radio news programs, as opposed to online and social media.

Transcendentalism: Belief that a correspondence exists between a higher realm of spiritual truth and a lower one of material objects, including nature.

Transparency: Openness in government; citizens' right to know information that is important to their lives. In regard to the environment, the United Nations has declared that the principle of transparency "requires the recognition of the rights of participation and access to information and the right to be informed.... Everyone has the right of access to information on the environment with no obligation to prove a particular interest" (Declaration of Bizkaia on the Right to the Environment, 1999).

Tree spiking: The practice of driving metal or plastic spikes or nails into trees in an area that is scheduled to be logged to discourage the cutting of the trees.

Trinity of Voices (TOV): Senecah's (2004) model for assessing the quality of public participation processes; the model poses three elements—access, standing, and influence—that empower

stakeholders and are shared by most effective participatory processes.

Trope of uncertainty: An appeal that functions to nurture doubt in the public's perception of scientific claims and thereby to delay calls for action; in rhetorical terms, the trope of uncertainty turns, or alters, the public's understanding of what is at stake, suggesting there is a danger in acting prematurely, a risk of making the wrong decision.

Tropes: The uses of words that turn a meaning from its original sense in a new direction.

Tweet: A short text message, up to 140 characters, sent through the online Twitter service.

Unbundling: Freeing of content from a single portal for information, such as a website, that is, ensuring that it is available at other places online, where people are going.

Utilitarianism: Theory that the aim of action should be the greatest good for the greatest number.

Visual rhetoric: The capacity of visual images and representations to influence public attitudes toward objects such as the environment.

Voices of the "side effects": Term used by Beck (1992) to refer to those individuals (or their children) who suffer the side effects of the risk society, such as asthma and other illnesses from air pollutants, chemical contamination, and so forth.

Widget: A short programming code that enables something interesting to appear on your blog, wiki, or smartphone.

Wise Use groups: Groups that organize individuals who oppose restrictions on the use of their own (private) property for purposes such as protection of wetlands or habitat for endangered species; also called *property rights groups.*

Index

About the Author

Robert Cox (PhD, University of Pittsburgh) is Professor Emeritus at the University of North Carolina at Chapel Hill. His principal research areas are environmental communication, climate change communication, and strategic studies of social movements. One of the nation's leading scholars in environmental communication, he has been President of the Sierra Club three times (2007–2008, 2000–2001, and 1994–1996) and has served for 20 years on the Sierra Club's Board of Directors. His published work includes critical studies on the discourse of the civil rights, peace, labor, and environmental movements. Cox is also on the Board of Directors for Earth Echo International, dedicated to oceans and marine ecology. He currently advises the Sierra Club on its communication outreach in the United States and serves on editorial boards of journals such as *Environmental Communication: A Journal of Nature and Culture.* Cox advises U.S. environmental groups on their communication programs. He regularly participates in environmental initiatives and has campaigned with former Vice President Al Gore and singer Melissa Etheridge.

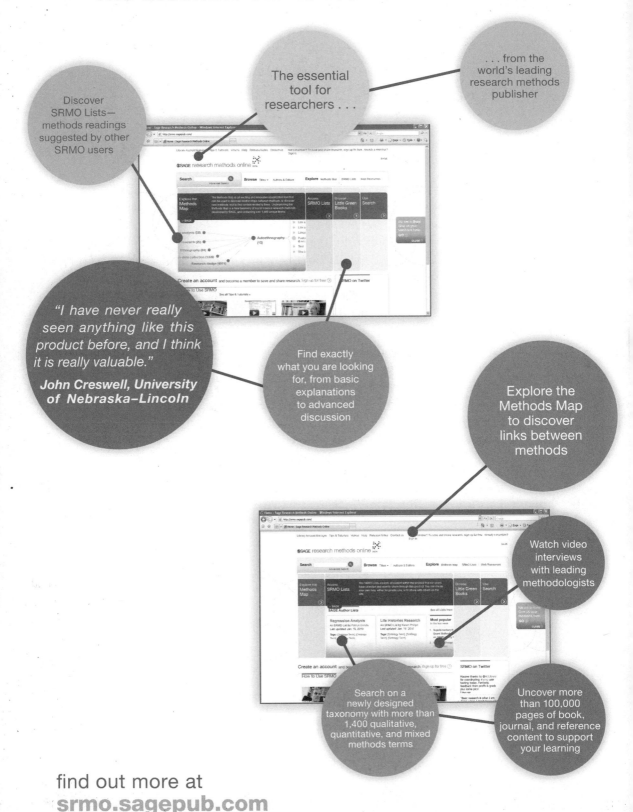

SAGE researchmethods
The Essential Online Tool for Researchers

The essential tool for researchers . . .

. . . from the world's leading research methods publisher

Discover SRMO Lists—methods readings suggested by other SRMO users

"I have never really seen anything like this product before, and I think it is really valuable."

John Creswell, University of Nebraska–Lincoln

Find exactly what you are looking for, from basic explanations to advanced discussion

Explore the Methods Map to discover links between methods

Watch video interviews with leading methodologists

Search on a newly designed taxonomy with more than 1,400 qualitative, quantitative, and mixed methods terms

Uncover more than 100,000 pages of book, journal, and reference content to support your learning

find out more at
srmo.sagepub.com